Alan Ellman's

Complete Encyclopedia for Covered Call Writing

A low-risk, wealth-building strategy for average investors which utilizes stocks and options to create monthly cash flow

By Alan Ellman: The Blue Collar Investor

Flow charts by Barry Bergman

The Blue Collar Investor presents **Alan Ellman's Complete Encyclopedia for Covered Call Writing**

Copyright © 2011 Alan Ellman.

All rights reserved. No part of this book may be reproduced or retransmitted in any form or by any means without the written permission of the publisher.

Paperback ISBN: 978-1-937183-19-6
Hardcover ISBN: 978-1-937183-96-7
E-Book ISBN: 978-1-937183-15-8

Second Edition - 2019

1. Finance, Personal. 2. Investments. 3. Investment analysis. 4. Stock options. I. Blue Collar Investor (Firm) II. Title. III. Title: Exit strategies for covered call writ-ing : making the most money when selling stock options

Printed in the United States of America

Published by Digital Publishing of Florida, Inc.
www.digitaldata-corp.com

On Average Retail Investors Becoming Financially Independent:

"Reject the old-school brainwash that we can't and won't and embrace our mission statement that we can and will."

>Alan Ellman, on behalf of
>Blue Collar Investors all over the world

Table of Contents

Acknowledgments..vii
Introduction...viii

1. An Introduction and Preview Examples of Covered Call Writing.............................1

2. Option Basics..5

3. Fundamental Analysis..23

4. Technical Analysis..37

5. Portfolio Management.......................................87

6. Calculations...101

7. Factors that Impact the Value of the Option Premiums...155

8. Common Sense Factors......................................203

9. Executing Covered Call Trades.............................217

10. Exit Strategies...247

11. Dollar Cost Averaging and Exchange-Traded Funds.........305

12. Stock Splits..325

13. Tax Treatment of Covered Call Writing....................335

14. Portfolio Overwriting.....................................345

15. Covered Calls and LEAPS...................................351

16. Margin Accounts...359

17. Naked and Cash-Secured Puts
    and Covered Call Writing.......................................367

18. Time Value of Money and Compounding
    the eighth wonder of the world............................373

19. Other Factors that Influence Stock Performance.......379

    - Company news (aside from earnings reports)
    - Market psychology
    - Key economic indicators
    - Globalization
    - Interest rates
    - Yield curves
    - Triple and quadruple witching Friday
    - Using leading economic indicators
    - Using our understanding of economics in
      covered callwriting

20. Related Topics of Interest.......................................397

    - Commingling of Asset Classes
    - Dividend Capture Strategy
    - Using Covered Calls to Increase Stock Value
    - Flash Trading
    - Pump and Dump Scams
    - S&P Futures and Fair Value
    - Money Market Accounts and Funds
    - Derivatives
    - Classification of Stock
    - Common Stock versus Preferred Stock
    - Dark Pools
    - CBOE Volatility Index- VIX
    - After Hours Trading
    - How our Trade Orders are Executed
    - Pinning the Strike
    - Using Covered Calls to Increase Dividend Yield
    - Inverse Exchange-Traded Funds
      and Covered Call Writing

Appendix..457

    I.   Master List of Charts and Graphs

    II. My First Book, Cashing in on Covered Calls

    III. My second Book, Exit Strategies for Covered Call Writing

    IV. Resource Center

    V.   Quick Start Form

    VI. Profit and Loss Form

    VII. Securities with Weekly Expirations

    VIII. Securities with Quarterly Expirations

    IX. Paper Trading and Monitoring Positions

    X.   Technical Analysis Chart and Terms

    XI. Flow Chart I- Fundamental Analysis

    XII. Flow Chart II- Technical Analysis

    XIII. Flow Chart III- Exit Strategies before expiration Friday

    XIV. Flow Chart IV- Exit Strategies on or near expiration Friday

    XV. Mean Analyst Rating (MAR)

    XVI. On Balance Volume (OBV)

Glossary..489

About the Author...514

Index..515

Acknowledgments

First and foremost I must acknowledge my family:

My wife Linda;

My son and daughter-in-law Jared and Aubrey;

My son Craig;

My stepson David; and

My mom Minnie

It is the pride and support that we share with each other that energizes me to achieve goals I never expected to realize.

I would also like to recognize Barry Bergman, who provided a critical second set of eyes in reviewing all the information disseminated in this book.

In addition, a salute to Owen Sargent for his assistance in the development of the Ellman Calculator.

To my son Craig: Thanks for watching over Dad's shoulder ensuring that his grammar and sentence structure will not embarrass the family name.

This book was a team effort.

Introduction

My third book all started with a day at the casino!

This will be my third book in four years! Why am I writing yet another book on the subject of covered call writing? What does this have to do with a casino? The unusual aspect to this situation is that none of the books were planned; they just happened. Here's how it all started:

In 1972 I graduated from NYU Dental School and embarked in my professional career as a general dentist. I soon came to the realization that it would be prudent to invest some of my income to help make a better life for my family. To that end, I endeavored to educate myself on the intricacies of real estate investing and the stock market. Several years later I owned multiple properties, both commercial and residential, in four different states. A local real estate club on Long Island heard about some of the deals I had executed in Austin, Texas and asked me to speak before 250 club members about these transactions. During the course of my presentation, I mentioned that I purchased my first property with the profits I generated from selling stock options called covered call writing. Much to my surprise, I was inundated with requests to explain covered call writing and how I was able to use this strategy to turn handsome profits. Finally, I decided to hold a seminar to address the questions posed by these inquisitive investors, which, in another pleasant surprise, was a complete sellout! I continued to write more advanced seminars, which only increased the interest of these prospective covered call writers. One day I turned to my wife Linda and said, "I have a book here!" That moment of enlightenment led to the penning of *Cashing in on Covered Calls*. I owe a sincere debt of gratitude to you, my fellow blue collar investors, for making my first book such a success.

I was extremely fortunate to have received valuable feedback from blue collar investors across the country and around the world after *Cashing in on Covered Calls* was published. Many of the inquiries I received related specifically to exit strategies, or the management of stock and options positions in the face of unfavorable market conditions. Although this topic was addressed in *Cashing in on Covered Calls*, it became readily apparent to me that the thirst for more information on this particular aspect of covered call writing was more than sufficient to warrant publication of my second book, *Exit Strategies for Covered Call Writing*. Thank you all for making *Exit Strategies for Covered Call Writing* equally as successful as my first book.

In between writing my first two books, I was also composing weekly journal articles, the majority of which were either responsive to specific questions posed by fellow blue collar investors, or discussed topics that Blue Collar Investor ("BCI") members suggested I write about. As a result, these articles covered not only the "meat and potatoes" of covered call writing, but also some of the more esoteric, peripherally related topics. Many hours were dedicated each week to researching and writing these articles, which, in addition to other related matters, are posted on the blog to my website, www.thebluecollarinvestor.com. One day, a member of our BCI community wrote to me suggesting that I write a third book incorporating much of the information detailed in the journal articles with the information disseminated in my first two books. "This would be the most complete book on covered call writing ever written," the BCI member enthusiastically wrote. This concept was subsequently presented to me several more times by other BCI members. As you can see, I finally decided to oblige!

So what does this have to do with a casino? My mother, Minnie, and my beautiful wife Linda, both love to play the slot machines. Periodically, Linda and I will pick up Mom and we will all head to the local casino for a family outing of gambling and dinner. Admittedly I am a full participant in the dinner portion of our day, however given my preference to make-not lose-money; I prefer to refrain from gambling and battling odds which are stacked against me.

So it was a Saturday early in 2010 that Linda and I were preparing to pick up my Mom and head to the local casino for a day of gambling. Linda searched for cash to deposit in the casino machines, while I packed my first two books along with a list of all the journal articles I have written over the past three years. Once we arrived at the casino, Linda and my mother gambled while I outlined. Four hours later, my outline was complete and they were out of cash! A mixed day of success and failure, wouldn't you say? Actually, it was a success because I felt that I had written a pretty good outline and my mother and wife had a fun day out.

My reference to casinos, however, has a more significant relevance. As noted above, I choose not to gamble because I know that the odds are stacked against me; I want to be the casino, not the gambler. In this regard, I truly believe that as a covered call writer, you can effectively become the casino, rendering the person or entity who buys your call options the gambler. Like the casino, you will have to pay up every now and again; however, I believe that if you do your homework and implement the correct strategy, you will win more times than you lose! It is my hope that this book will provide you the knowledge, or at the least, the confidence, to use covered call writing to stack the trading odds in YOUR favor so that, more often than not, profitable periodic streams of income are generated in your brokerage account on a monthly basis.

Chapter 1

An Introduction and Preview Examples of Covered Call Writing

Chapter outline

1- Real estate example

2- Stock example

For those new to covered call writing, or for those investors who haven't utilized this strategy in the recent past, review of a few preview examples will serve as a useful foundation prior to learning the more intricate details of this strategy. Generally speaking, the concept of selling options works as follows: you purchase an asset such as a house or a stock, and then sell some unknown person (trading is done online) the right, but not the obligation to purchase that asset from you at a specific price (that YOU determine), by a specific date (that YOU determine). In return for undertaking this obligation, you are paid a premium (that the MARKET determines). The cash is generated into your account instantly and available for immediate investment or whatever you chose to do with it. A simple real estate example provides useful guidance as to how covered call writing generally works.

Real estate example

You do your due-diligence and purchase a property for $100k. You feel comfortable that the property will increase in value and would have no problem owning the property for the long term. However, if you were offered $120k for this property at any time over the next six months, you would accept it for a quick $20k profit. Now, along comes investor OB (the option buyer). He loves your property and feels that it could appreciate in value up to $150k during the next six months. However, Mr. OB has many other investments and doesn't want to risk the full $120k at this time, but he sure would like to control this property. He offers you $10k for the right, but not the obligation, to purchase your property for $120k at any time over the next six months. This 10k option premium is yours to keep whether OB exercises the option and buys your property or not (in many real estate deals the premium IS applied to the purchase price; however this is NOT the case in the stock market. For this particular example, you keep the premium under all circumstances). After the six month period, there are two possible outcomes:

Scenario I:

The option is not exercised and you keep both the premium and the property. This would occur if the value of the property never surpasses the agreed-upon $120k sales price during the six month lifespan of the option. After all, why would OB buy your property for $120 when he could buy a similar property for less money? In this case, you garner a $10k profit on an investment of $100k which is a 10%, 6-month return or 20% annualized. You are now free to sell another option on the same property.

Scenario II:

The option is exercised and the property is sold for $120k as per your obligation. Let's say that OB was correct and the value of the property appreciated to $150k. He can buy the property from you at $120k and sell it at market for $150k, making a nice profit. We, however, are the option sellers, so let's see how we made out in this second possible outcome. We have the $10k option premium PLUS an additional $20k profit on the sale of the property, yielding a total profit of $30k. On an investment of $100k, that represents a six month profit of 30% or 60% annualized.

From the description of the two possible outcomes, it almost looks like you can't lose. Unfortunately and realistically, that's not the case. If the value of the property declines in value by more than the option premium received, you start to lose money. The cost of the asset minus the option premium received is known as the breakeven. In this example, if the property value depreciates under $90K, you will be in a losing situation. However, you will have lost less money than the investor who purchased a similar property and didn't sell an option. The risk is in the underlying asset, not in the sale of the option.

Stock market example

In this example, the underlying asset is stock instead of property. You purchase 100 shares of company XYZ @ $48 per share. Your investment or cost basis is therefore $4800. Once again, you now sell (i.e. "write") the option. You are selling the right, but not the obligation, for some unknown person (Mr. OB) to buy your shares for (in this hypothetical) $50 per share (called the strike price) at any time over the next (in this hypothetical) one month. A fair premium for this would be $1.50 per share or $150 for the 100 shares. This cash is generated into your account immediately and yours to keep whether the option is exercised or not. Let's examine the two possible outcomes.

Scenario I:

The stock value does not surpass the $50 agreed- upon sales price and the shares are not sold. You have profited $150 on a $4800 investment or a 3.1%, 1-month return, 38% annualized. You are now eligible to sell another option on those same shares.

Scenario II:

The stock value does surpass the $50 agreed-upon sales price and the option is exercised, triggering your stock to be sold for $50 per share. You have now generated $150 from the option sale plus $200 profit from the sale of the stock for a total of $350. This represents a 7.3%, 1-month return, or 87% annualized.

Once again, bear in mind that there is some risk in this strategy. The risk is in the stock. If the stock depreciates in value by more than the $1.50 per share generated from the option sale, you will start to lose money. Your loss, however, will be less than an investor who bought the stock and didn't sell the corresponding option. With this general concept in mind, let's move on to the basics of options and covered call options in particular.

Test your knowledge of key points

1- When we sell a covered option, we are selling the *right*, but not the obligation to *purchase* an asset at a certain *price* by a certain *date*.

2- An option will NOT be exercised if the price of the asset does NOT surpass the *strike price*

3- The risk is in the *stock*, not in the *option*.

Answers:

1- Right, buy, price, date

2- Strike (sale) price

3- Stock, sale of the option

Chapter 2

Option Basics

Chapter outline

1- Why sell options

2- Why there so few investors who sell covered call options

3- Three golden rules for covered call writing

4- Definitions

5- Components of an options contract

6- Risk-reward profile for covered call writing

Why sell options

I don't expect you to sell options because I said so, or because a so-called "expert" on TV touted covered call writing as the only strategy for you. The only reason you should embark on utilizing covered call writing is because you have made the decision that it is right strategy for you. This can be accomplished by educating yourself and practicing (paper trading) the system. Only then can you come to the determination that you should be a covered call writer. Personally, covered call writing is my strategy of choice primarily for the following ten reasons:

1- Of all the low-risk strategies I have utilized during my twenty year tenure as a stock market investor, I have generated the highest returns writing covered calls. This, in essence, is one of the mission statements of the Blue Collar System: *maximizing profits while minimizing risk.*

2- Covered call writing works efficiently in most market conditions: moderately bullish (slightly uptrending), moderately bearish (slightly downtrending) and neutral. In markets appreciating exponentially, it is best to own the stocks and not sell the options. In markets plummeting precipitously, it is best to move into another asset class like bonds or real estate. Here is a diagram (Figure 1) that explains these market conditions:

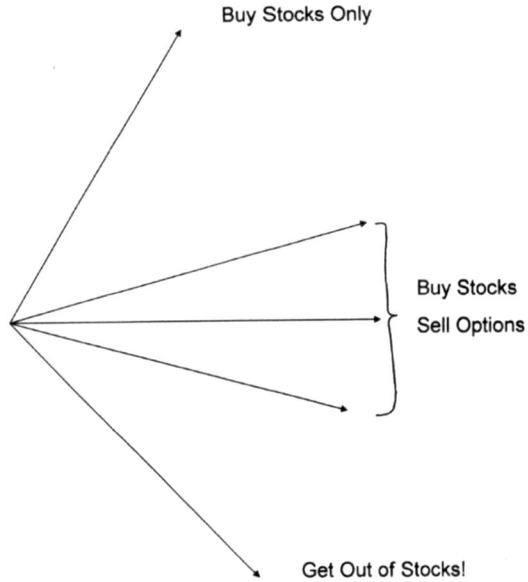

Figure 1- Market conditions

3- You can generate income from the comfort of your home. All you need is a computer, the proper education, and motivation to succeed.

4- You can compound your profits instantaneously. The cash generated from the option sale is immediately deposited into your brokerage account and available for use either at that moment (T+0) or the next trading day (called T + 1), depending on the terms of your brokerage account agreement.

5- You can control profits and losses through the use of exit strategies. There is an incredible amount of control an investor has with when writing covered calls, and you must take advantage of all these opportunities to maximize your bottom line.

6- You can create downside protection on your investments. In the preview stock example above, you sold the option for $1.50 after purchasing the stock for $48. This made your breakeven point $46.50. The breakeven point is different from the downside protection of the the option premium, as will be discussed throughout this book.

7- You can develop a trading skill that you can pass on to your children, or use to benefit the older generation. I have been trading covered call options in my mothers account for years, thereby enhancing the quality of her life. Recently, I have been teaching this strategy to my children.

8- You, as the option seller, capture all corporate dividends, not the option buyer (Mr. OB). This is because the option seller owns the stock.

9- Actively managed mutual funds historically underperform the market. Writing covered calls gives you an opportunity to beat the market. John Boggle, the founder of the Vanguard Family of Mutual Funds, states his case against actively managed mutual funds in Figure 2 below:

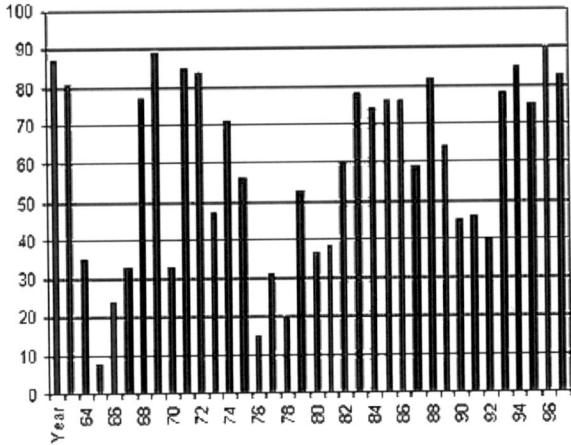

Source: John Bogle, Common Sense on Mutual Funds : New Imperatives for the Intelligent Investor, p. 119.

Figure 2

10- The government considers covered call writing so safe, it actually allows you to employ this strategy in your self-directed IRA accounts.

So there you have it - my top 10 list of why I sell covered call options. It's not as funny as Letterman's top 10, but I hope it serves as useful guidance in assisting your decision as to whether this strategy is the right one for you.

Why there so few investors who sell covered call options

If this strategy offers so much opportunity, why isn't everybody using it? I get this question at all of my seminars. Here are my thoughts on this topic:

1- We didn't learn about this in school. Our education system failed us.

2- It is in nobody's best interest to teach it to us.

3- Financial advisors are either not fully familiar with the strategy or realize that it is not time or cost efficient to monitor our positions.

4- Average retail investors get nervous when they hear the term "stock" and literally scared to death when it is associated with the word "option."

5- Our society has convinced us that we are not capable of investing on our own. This is simply not true.

6- Many fear the learning curve and time commitment.

Although there is no one strategy that is right for every investor, educating yourself about covered call writing will allow you to make an intelligent decision whether it is right for you and your family.

The three golden rules

Over the years I have noticed certain characteristics that were common to successful covered call writers. I'm not referring to obvious qualities such as motivation, education or diligence. Those attributes apply to all forms of investing, and arguably, to all facets of life if you're seeking success. I am talking about the three "golden rules" that must apply to you if you are to maximize your success when selling covered calls. Specifically, the following three "golden rules," in my opinion, are necessary components shared by successful covered call writers:

1- *You must be able to tolerate some risk.* Remember this is a low-risk strategy, not a no-risk strategy. In the short run, the market experiences whipsaws, known as volatility, which is the propensity of the underlying security's market price to fluctuate either up or down. It is this volatility that gives value to our options, It is crucial to understand that volatility is a natural component of the stock market, and that in order to become successful investors, we must learn to react in a non-emotional, intelligent manner in the face of volatility, particularly when your stocks decline in value. In Figure 3, which depicts a 6-month chart of the S&P 500 (an index widely used to gauge the trend of the overall stock market), volatility can be seen by the red arrows, which depict up trends, and the blue arrows, which demonstrate down trends:

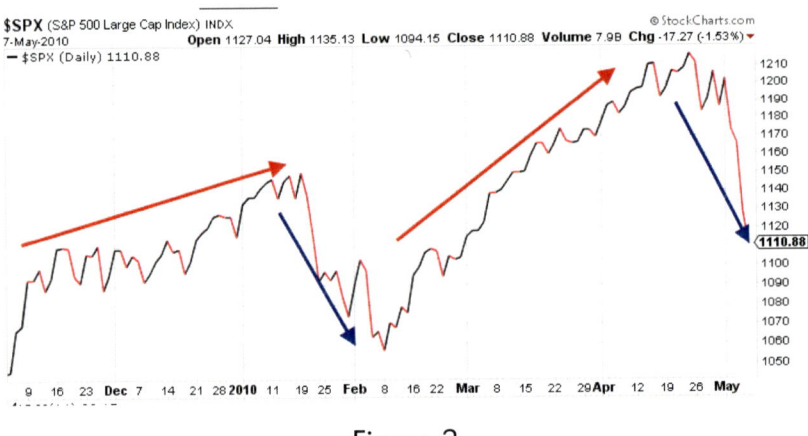

Figure 3

Figure 4 below also tracks the S&P 500, but over an 82 year period. Note that in the long run, the market is much less volatile and generally trends in one direction-upward:

Figure 4

You must be able to understand, tolerate and react, if necessary, to these normal whipsaws in market movement to succeed in covered call writing. It is also important for the quality of your life.

2- *You must only sell options on stock that you would otherwise want to own.* This means that you should not purchase a stock simply because its corresponding option returns a high premium. Buying a stock solely based on a high option premium is usually a mistake because high premium equities are extremely volatile and will enhance the degree of risk in our portfolios (personally, I avoid stocks that offer huge 1-month option returns). The best approach is to select only the greatest performing stocks, from both a fundamental and technical standpoint, that are also located within the greatest performing industry groups or segments. In my system, a stock is chosen before you even glance at the option premium the security will return. The bottom line: *don't get greedy*. Selling covered calls is a conservative strategy that can be immensely rewarding, but without question requires a dedicated degree of patience coupled with an intelligent, rational approach.

3- *You must have a plan with multiple exit strategies.* Stocks will not always perform in the manner we expect. Even if we purchase what should be the greatest performing stocks from both a fundamental and technical standpoint, inevitably some will misbehave! On the flip side, other stocks may outperform our expectations. We must be prepared to react in either scenario; in other words, we must have plans in place to control losses or enhance gains. With the proper preparation, you will oftentimes be able to create multiple streams of income from the same stock in the same option month. In my seminars, I describe two types of option sellers. First, there are the investors who are prepared to implement multiple exit strategy plans if and when needed. These investors make non-emotional decisions based on sound fundamental and technical principles, in addition to common sense. Then there are what I like to call the religious investors. These folks buy the stock, sell the option, clasp their hands, get down on their knees and pray for a happy outcome. I'm in no way knocking religion, but it has no place in covered call writing!

Definitions

It is essential to understand all the terminology related to covered call writing in order to be successful. In other words, we must be able to "talk the talk." New investors should read through these terms now and refer back to them as needed until they become second nature.

Option- the right, but not the obligation, to buy or sell 100 shares of stock at a fixed price (called the strike price) by a specified date (called the expiration date). It is the right to execute a stock transaction.

Call option- the right, but not the obligation of the option holder (buyer), to BUY 100 shares of stock at a fixed price by a specified date.

Put option- the right, but not the obligation of the option holder, to SELL 100 shares of stock at a fixed price by a specified date.

Covered call writing- Implicit in the term covered call writing is the fact that we are selling call options. They are covered because we first own the underlying equity prior to selling the option. Thus, in covered call writing, we are purchasing stock and selling the corresponding option(s) on a share-for-share basis. One option contract = 100 shares; 5 contracts = 500 shares and so on.

Delta: This is the amount an option value will change for every $1 change in the price of a stock. The greater the chance of the strike ending up in-the-money, the higher the delta. Delta values for calls run from 0 to 1.

Option Strike price as it relates to the Stock Price

At-the-money (A-T-M) - the strike price of the option is identical to the value of the underlying stock. For example, if you sell a $50 call option (i.e. an option with a strike price of $50, which is the price you agreeing to sell your stock if the option is exercised) on a stock currently trading at $50, the call option you sold is considered at-the-money. Closely related to A-T-M strikes are near-the-money strikes where the stock value is close to, but not exactly the same as, the market value of the stock. For example, if the stock for a $50 call option is trading at $50.10, the $50 call option is said to be near-the-money. These strikes generate the greatest initial option returns.

In-the-money (I-T-M) - the strike price of the option is lower than the value of the stock. For, example if you sell a $50 call option on a stock trading at $52, the call option that you sold is considered in-the-money. These strikes offer the most protection and have deltas near 1, allowing us to buy back the option at a cheaper price if the stock value declines. It is the most conservative covered call position.

Out-of-the-money (O-T-M) - the strike price of the option is higher than the value of the stock. For example, if you sell a $50 call option on a stock trading at $48 per share, the call option that you sold is considered out-of-the-money. These strikes offer the greatest final potential returns and have the lowest deltas. They are the most bullish of covered call positions.

Option Value as it relates to Strike Price

Intrinsic value – Intrinsic value is the dollar amount that the option premium is in-the-money. Only in-the-money strikes have intrinsic value as a component of the option premium.

Time value – The option premium above any intrinsic value. Here is an example of these last two definitions:

Purchase a stock for $56 per share

Sell the $50 call option for $8

The option strike price is $6 in-the-money ($56 - $50). This is the intrinsic value. The remaining premium value is therefore time value of $2 ($8 - $6 = $2). The critical equation to remember is:

Option Premium = Intrinsic Value + Time Value

Time value is a decaying asset. We are the sellers of this asset. The option holders, not the sellers, are incurring the option risk as they are betting that the strike will end up in-the-money by expiration Friday. Either way, we collect the option premium playing the role of "casino" and not "gambler".

The Option Contract - The option sets the terms of a contract about a possible future transaction involving the underlying stock. Since the option value is directly related to or derived from that security, options are said to be derivatives. When the holder of the option makes use of the right granted by the option, the contract is said to be exercised. It is important to remember that until that option is exercised (it may never be exercised) the option writer (that's us) retains all rights conferred by stock ownership. For example, if a dividend is distributed prior to the security changing hands, the option seller (e.g. the covered call writer) will enjoy those profits.

Opening and Closing a position - When we sell (write) a call option, it is referred to as *opening a position*. Since we sold the contract we are said to be opening a short position. The holder (i.e. buyer of the option) has opened a long position with respect to the option. We, as the option seller, can close our short options position by buying back the same contract. This will cancel the original sale and we will then only own the stock long (simply stock ownership). Buying back options contracts is the basis for our exit strategies. More than 80% of option contracts go unexercised. Option holders can either sell the option they bought or exercise it and buy the shares. The former is more common than the latter. As covered call writers we must be aware of the stock price as it relates to the option strike price because our shares will be sold if the strike ends up in-the-money by expiration Friday. Later in this book, we will discuss how to avoid this (starts with buying back the option) or why we may "allow" it.

Components of an options contract

In February of 2010, the options symbology changed. The previous option ticker symbols consisted of the root symbol of the underlying security (QAA below), then a letter that signified both the expiration date and whether we were dealing with a call or put option ("E" below), followed by another letter that described the strike price ("D" below):

The Former ticker symbol looked like this:

QAA-ED

The New or Current Symbols now look like this (Figure 5):

Figure 5

- AAPL is the ticker symbol of the stock
- 05/22/2010 is the expiration date, the third Friday of April
- "20.00" is the strike price
- "C" represents a call option

Risk-reward profile of covered call writing

A risk reward profile is a chart of the theoretical maximum profit or loss a particular investment can have in your portfolios. For example, let's look at the risk-reward profile of stock ownership (Figure 6):

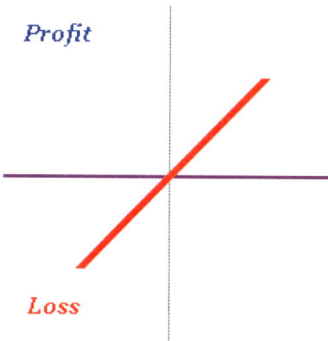

Figure 6- Risk-reward profile of stock ownership

This graph demonstrates that, in theory, the potential profit for a long stock position is unlimited; it can go to the moon! However, the potential loss for the same position is also unlimited; theoretically, you can lose your entire investment. For savvy investors, will either of these events ever occur? No. Even, the most solid of companies will hit bumps in the road and give us reason to sell some or all of our shares. Furthermore, which educated, prepared investor will sit idle while his or her stock price drops to zero?

Theoretical Risk-Reward Profile for Covered Calls:

Let's analyze this graph (Figure 7):

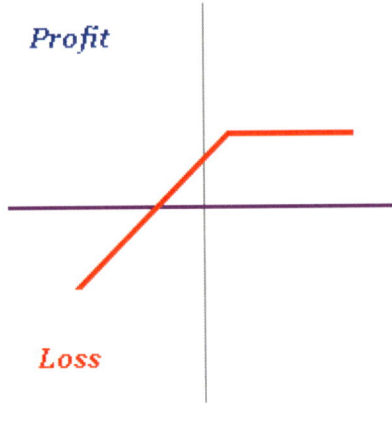

Figure 7

Risk-Reward for an Unmonitored Covered Call

When selling a covered call option, we are placing a ceiling on the share appreciation; our profit is limited to the option premium plus any stock appreciation up to the strike price, assuming an out-of-the-money strike was sold. The downside appears to be dramatic, as we can theoretically lose all of our equity value and retain only the cash from the sale of the option. If we were to base our decision regarding the efficacy of covered call writing solely on this profile, we would reject it immediately. It appears that the odds are against our success. Fortunately, there is a major difference between theoretical and practical applications of risk-reward profiles. Enter the wonderful world of exit strategies.

Practical Risk-Reward Profile for Covered Calls:

Let's now analyze an enhanced graph (Figure 8) that has application in the world of the informed and prepared investor:

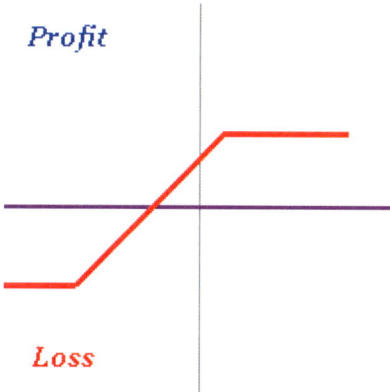

Figure 8 - Risk-Reward Profile
for a Monitored Covered Call Position

The actual profit potential can actually be elevated in some instances by instituting one of our exit strategies, and the potential losses, without question, can be minimized by properly utilizing the same. Some investors buy puts to limit losses. This is called a collar strategy and will be discussed later in this book. The key point, however, which is all too often missed by the uneducated investors, is as follows: This horizontal line that represents potential loss can be elevated closer to the zero line by instituting appropriate exit strategies, selecting the best strike prices, factoring in market tone and equity technicals. These are the marks of true Blue Collar Investors and are what set us apart from all the others. When evaluating information to make an intelligent investment decision, we must know the limitations of that tool, in this case the risk-reward profile, so we can apply it in the proper manner. Comparing the graphs depicted in Figures 7 and 8 demonstrates that viewing the theoretical risk-reward profile for covered call writing can be misleading because it ignores the use of exit strategies.

Test your knowledge of key points

1- The best market conditions to sell covered calls are _slightly ap_ _slightly down_ and _side ways_

2- Corporate dividends are captured by the _stock owner_.

3- True or False? You can use covered call writing in your self-directed IRA accounts? _True_.

4- True or False? It is important to use stocks that generate the highest option premiums? _False_.

5- If a stock declines in value, we must be prepared to implement an _exit_ _strategy_

6- Implicit in covered call writing is that we must first _buy the stock_ before selling the associated option.

7- The two components of an option premium are _time_ and _intrinsic value_

8- Components of an options contract include _strike price_ _call or put_ and _ending date_

9- The theoretical risk-reward profile for covered call writing shows that we can lose our entire investment except for _premium_. This ignores the use of _exit strategies_

10- If we bought a stock for $53 and sold the $50 call for $5, _$2_ would be time value of the premium and _$3_ would be the intrinsic value of the premium.
This is _in the money_.

11- If we bought a stock for $53 and sold the $55 call for $2, __$2__ would be time value and __$0__ would be intrinsic value.

Answers:

1- Moderately bullish, moderately bearish and neutral.

2- Option seller or covered call writer

3- True

4- False (may be too volatile and therefore too risky)

5- Exit strategy

6- Own the stock (this makes it a "covered" position)

7- Intrinsic value and time value

8- Stock ticker symbol, expiration date, strike price and call or put option.

9- The option premium collected, exit strategies

10- $2, $3

11- $2, $0.00 (at-the-money and out-of-the-money strikes have no intrinsic value)

Chapter 3

Fundamental Analysis

Creating a Watchlist of the Greatest-Performing Stocks

Chapter outline

1- What is fundamental analysis?

2- Common ratios used

3- Free websites used to locate fundamental ratios

4- BCI system screens for fundamental analysis

5- Fundamental ratios incorporated in the BCI screens

What is fundamental analysis?

Fundamental analysis is a method of analyzing the prospects of a security by observing the accepted accounting measures such as earnings, sales, and assets and so on. Ratios are calculated from the financial data and compared to those of other corporations. Institutional investors like banks, mutual funds, hedge funds and insurance companies tend to favor stocks that are financially sound. These companies have stellar earnings and revenues and locating these "greatest performing corporations" is step #1 for covered call writers in our BCI system. We want to own stocks that are on the radar screen of these "big boys".

Commonly used fundamental ratios

Here are some of the more common fundamental ratios used by institutional and retail investors when evaluating corporations fundamentally (don't worry; <u>you're NOT going to have to look these stats up or memorize them!</u>):

1- PE ratio- P/E Ratio or Price-Earnings Ratio is a valuation ratio that compares the price of a stock to it's per share annual earnings.

2- PEG Ratio- PEG = PE Ratio/Annual Earnings per Share Growth

3- Earnings Per Share Growth- Analyzed on both a quarterly and annual basis. Earnings are a basic measurement of a company's ability to make a net profit and grow.

4- Sales growth- A company's annual and quarterly rate of increase in revenues (sales). A measure of growth and success as long as it is accompanied by an equally strong rate of increase in earnings per share. You want to see both in a potential investment.

5- Return on Equity- The amount of net income returned as a percentage of shareholders equity. Return on equity measures a corporation's profitability by revealing how much profit a company generates with the money shareholders have invested. ROE is expressed as a percentage and calculated as:

Return on Equity = Net Income/ Shareholder's Equity

6- Pretax margin- The difference between a product's (or service's) selling price and the cost of production before taxes.

7- Net profit margin- A ratio of profitability calculated as net income divided by revenues, or net profits divided by sales. It measures how much out of every dollar of sales a company actually keeps in earnings.

Fundamental Analysis | 25

8- Operating margin- A ratio used to measure a company's pricing strategy and operating efficiency.

9- Debt/Equity Ratio- A measure of a company's financial leverage calculated by dividing its total liabilities by stockholders' equity. It indicates what proportion of equity and debt the company is using to finance its assets.

10- Dividend yield- A financial ratio that shows how much a company pays out in dividends each year relative to its share price. In the absence of any capital gains, the dividend yield is the return on investment for a stock.

11- Book value- The net asset value of a company, calculated by total assets minus intangible assets (patents, goodwill) and liabilities.

12-Price-to-book ratio- A ratio used to compare a stock's market value to its book value. It is calculated by dividing the current closing price of the stock by the latest quarter's book value per share.
Also known as the "price-equity ratio".

13- Free cash flow- A measure of financial performance calculated as operating cash flow minus capital expenditures. Free cash flow (FCF) represents the cash that a company is able to generate after laying out the money required to maintain or expand its asset base. Free cash flow is important because it allows a company to pursue opportunities that enhance shareholder value.

14- Sponsorship- Refers to the shares of a company owned by an institution. The largest sources of demand for stocks are mutual funds, hedge funds, banks and insurance companies.

Additional information on PE and PEG ratios

Years ago, investors, stock brokers and financial advisors wanted to know the "P/E" of the equity before making a buy-decision. To this day I get questions about it at each and every one of my seminars so I decided to include an additional section on this topic. A low P/E meant that the stock was cheap and market forces would lead to price appreciation. The opposite theory also was considered Wall Street fact: A high P/E represents an over-valued stock and one that would devalue in the future. If you mentioned a stock, the next question was: "What's its P/E?" Before we go further, let's define once again:

P/E Ratio or Price-Earnings Ratio- A valuation ratio that compares the price of a stock to it's per share earnings:

$$P/E\ Ratio = Price\ per\ Share / Earnings\ per\ Share\ (EPS)$$

If the previous 4 quarters of earnings are used, it is referred to as *trailing P/E*. If the expected next 4 quarters are used, it is called *forward P/E*.

The problem I noticed right from the get go was that many of the companies with high P/Es back in the early 1990s were the ones that performed the best. These were the growth companies. Institutional investors were willing to pay more for these companies, driving the prices up due to the expectations that earnings should be increasing. Peter Lynch, in his book, *One up on Wall Street,* addressed this issue by stating that "The P/E ratio of any company that's fairly priced will equal its *growth rate.*" He added that "every stock price carries with it a built-in growth assumption." So, if the P/E = Growth, the stock is fairly priced no matter what the P/E is. Enter the *PEG ratio*.

PEG Ratio:

$$PEG = PE\ Ratio / Annual\ EPS\ Growth$$

Once again, the PE can be trailing or projected, and the EPS Growth can be expected growth for the next one year or five years. Yahoo Finance uses a 5-year expected growth rate and an averaged PE when calculating PEG (information on how to access these stats referenced below). In general, the lower the PEG the better; e.g. a PEG of "1" is considered to represent a fairly valued equity. Since the institutional investors are willing to pay more for high growth companies (thereby creating high PE ratios) factoring in EPS growth levels the playing field for these corporations.

Disadvantages of the PEG Ratio

- Larger corporations offer higher dividends and less growth opportunities
- Does not relate corporate growth to overall growth of the economy
- Inflation is not factored in
- Growth projections may not be accurate

Despite these limitations, in the eyes of this investor, the PEG is of much greater application (than the PE ratio) to us as we write calls predominantly on high growth companies. In addition, we can more accurately compare companies in different industries. If a stock has a high PE in a high growth industry, PEG will level the playing field with a low-PE stock in a slower growth group. Please note that if a company offers dividends, the PEG Ratio does NOT take this into account and therefore renders the PEG less applicable for these companies. So how do we account for companies that provide dividend income? Enter the PEGY Ratio:

PEGY Ratio:

PEGY = PE Ratio/ Expected Earnings Growth + Dividend Yield

Where to access this information

Go to http://finance.yahoo.com/
Type in stock ticker and "get quote"

In left column, under "Company" click on "key statistics" Below (figure 9) is an example of the page with these stats:

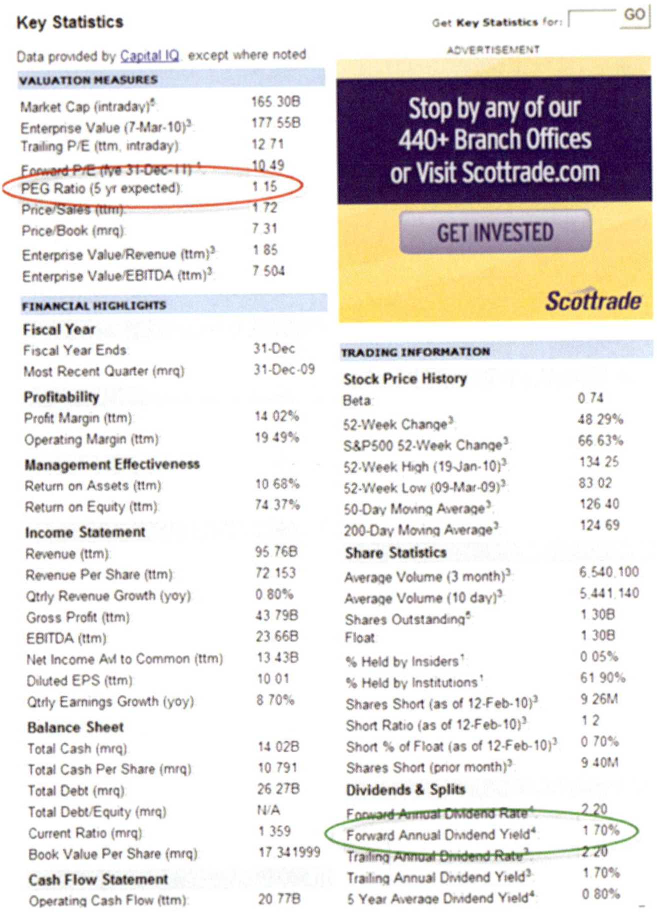

Key Statistics

Get Key Statistics for: GO

Data provided by Capital IQ, except where noted

VALUATION MEASURES	
Market Cap (intraday)⁵	165.30B
Enterprise Value (7-Mar-10)³	177.55B
Trailing P/E (ttm, intraday)	12.71
Forward P/E (fye 31-Dec-11)¹	10.49
PEG Ratio (5 yr expected)	1.15
Price/Sales (ttm)	1.72
Price/Book (mrq)	7.31
Enterprise Value/Revenue (ttm)³	1.85
Enterprise Value/EBITDA (ttm)³	7.504

FINANCIAL HIGHLIGHTS	
Fiscal Year	
Fiscal Year Ends	31-Dec
Most Recent Quarter (mrq)	31-Dec-09
Profitability	
Profit Margin (ttm)	14.02%
Operating Margin (ttm)	19.49%
Management Effectiveness	
Return on Assets (ttm)	10.68%
Return on Equity (ttm)	74.37%
Income Statement	
Revenue (ttm)	95.76B
Revenue Per Share (ttm)	72.153
Qtrly Revenue Growth (yoy)	0.80%
Gross Profit (ttm)	43.79B
EBITDA (ttm)	23.66B
Net Income Avl to Common (ttm)	13.43B
Diluted EPS (ttm)	10.01
Qtrly Earnings Growth (yoy)	8.70%
Balance Sheet	
Total Cash (mrq)	14.02B
Total Cash Per Share (mrq)	10.791
Total Debt (mrq)	26.27B
Total Debt/Equity (mrq)	N/A
Current Ratio (mrq)	1.359
Book Value Per Share (mrq)	17.341999
Cash Flow Statement	
Operating Cash Flow (ttm)	20.77B

TRADING INFORMATION	
Stock Price History	
Beta	0.74
52-Week Change³	48.29%
S&P500 52-Week Change³	66.63%
52-Week High (19-Jan-10)³	134.25
52-Week Low (09-Mar-09)³	83.02
50-Day Moving Average³	126.40
200-Day Moving Average³	124.69
Share Statistics	
Average Volume (3 month)³	6,540,100
Average Volume (10 day)³	5,441,140
Shares Outstanding⁵	1.30B
Float	1.30B
% Held by Insiders¹	0.05%
% Held by Institutions¹	61.90%
Shares Short (as of 12-Feb-10)³	9.26M
Short Ratio (as of 12-Feb-10)³	1.2
Short % of Float (as of 12-Feb-10)³	0.70%
Shares Short (prior month)³	9.40M
Dividends & Splits	
Forward Annual Dividend Rate⁴	2.20
Forward Annual Dividend Yield⁴	1.70%
Trailing Annual Dividend Rate³	2.20
Trailing Annual Dividend Yield³	1.70%
5 Year Average Dividend Yield⁴	0.80%

Figure 9 - PEG and PEGY Ratios

Circled in red is the PEG based on a 5-year expected growth rate and circled in green is the projected dividend yield for calculating PEGY ratio.

Free websites to locate fundamental ratios

www.finance.yahoo.com
www.msn.com/en-us/money/stockscreener/
www.screener.reuters.wallst.com/Stock/US/Index?quickscreen=gaarp

Before you get a headache picturing looking up and calculating all this data I have some great news. You don't have to do all the legwork yourself. There are a myriad of fundamental screens, some free, that will do the heavy lifting for you.

The BCI System for fundamental analysis

- IBD® 50 Index
- IBD SmartSelect® Ratings
- Mean Analyst Rating
- On Balance Volume
- CAN SLIM® (auxiliary screen, not required)

There are a myriad of screening programs available to the Blue Collar Investor, and over the years I have evaluated many of them. The computer age has simplified and expedited the process of fundamental evaluation of our securities. The process that I am about to describe is the one that works best for me and is based on over twenty years of meticulous testing and real life investing. Whether you use the same methodology that I use or another equally effective one, our goal is to locate the greatest performing stocks, both fundamentally and technically, that have options associated with them (i.e. are "optionable"). I have found that a watchlist of 40-60 of these equities is both adequate and manageable for most covered call writers. Since there are more than 7,000 equities available, a computerized screening process is essential.

Before discussing the specifics of screening for the most fundamentally sound stocks, a brief note on *Investors Business Daily* is necessary. Those of you who are familiar with my system are aware of how invaluable a tool I view *Investors Business Daily* to be. For those of you who are new to the Blue Collar Investor ("BCI") system, it should briefly be noted that two of the screening tools used to perform fundamental analysis during the stock selection process in this system are obtained via *Investors Business Daily,* which is a financial publication similar to *The*

Wall Street Journal, but more mathematically and statistically oriented. The cost of a subscription to *Investors Business Daily* for the Monday edition and access to the website is $210 per year. This will allow full access to the IBD® website (www.investors.com), where both of the *Investors Business Daily*-related screens used in the BCI system (i.e. the IBD® 50 Index and the IBD SmartSelect® Ratings) are located. Auxiliary screens such as CAN SLIM®) can also be immediately accessed. Although neither I nor the bluecollarinvestor.com have any affiliation (of any kind) with Investors Business Daily, I am a big proponent of this newspaper and the various research tools it offers, and truly believe a subscription is money well spent! Subscription-related information to Investors Business Daily can be found at the following link:

www.investors.com

Step 1- IBD® 50 Index (formerly the IBD 100®):

My stock selection process starts by creating a list, of all optionable securities on the IBD® 50 Index (the "IBD® 50"). The IBD® 50 is a computer-generated ranking of 50 leading companies trading in the U.S., and is available via one of several subscriptions offered by *Investor's Business Daily*. Most of the criteria that Investors Business Daily factors into selecting the securities on the IBD® 50 are fundamental in nature, and include parameters such as earnings, sales, return on equity, pre-tax margin, and management ownership. Since its inception in 2003, the IBD® 100 has outperformed the S&P 500 by 5-to-1 (at the time this book was written). The charts adjacent to the IBD® 50 show share prices in the upper right hand corners. Some of these prices display an "o" in front of the price. This "o" means that the stock is optionable, and thus, available for further screening. If there is no "o" in front of the price, the stock is no longer considered a viable choice for my system. For most weeks, the IBD® 50 will have a list with between 35-45 optionable stocks, which I then consider candidates for stock selection and circle for the additional screening I use in my system.

Step 2- IBD SmartSelect® Ratings:

The IBD SmartSelect® Ratings ("SmartSelect® Ratings") is another great IBD® proprietary ratings system which measures a company's key characteristics, including earnings growth, profit margins, price performance, and relative price strength of the stock's industry, among others. In other words, these ratings are a compilation of both fundamental and technical rankings. To access this screen, type in a ticker symbol on the homepage (www.investors.com) and then click on "get quote." On the quote page, scroll down under the chart, and on the left side you will find the six SmartSelect® Ratings for the particular security you are researching. Each of the six ratings correspond to a column titled "Ratings" (which ranks the stock via a number or a letter), in addition to a column titled "Checklist" (which references either a red, yellow or green circle, with green being the highest rank). To simplify the BCI system and expedite the stock selection process, you need only focus on the column titled "Checklist." Specifically, if all six of the SmartSelect® Ratings are green, the stock passes this test and is still a viable candidate for covered call writing.

Step 3- MAR and OBV

Update to The Weekly Stock Screen and Watch List

The Blue Collar Investor Team has upgraded the Weekly Stock Screen And Watch List by adding 2 new *institutional screens* and removing the original risk/reward screen.

After months of research, we have made the decision to incorporate the *Mean Analyst Rating or MAR* and *On Balance Volume or OBV* to enhance the quality of our screening process and our Premium Member Stock Reports. We feel the MAR and OBV institutional components will strengthen the screening process for several reasons:

MAR

- The metric is non-proprietary and is the mean rating from multiple analysts…that is, not from a single perspective or model but from several independent viewpoints.

- It is available at no cost from multiple well-known financial websites such as Yahoo Finance, Finviz, and others.
  www.finviz.com
  www.finance.yahoo.com

- We will be able to update the MAR every week vs. every two weeks as we currently do with risk/reward, so the data will be more current.

- The MAR comes from the views of institutional analysts who follow the specific stock in question. As we always mention, the market is driven by the "big boys", that is, the institutions. So, we are taking advantage of this body of knowledge.

- The MAR is a more intuitive metric than the risk/reward metric, and as such, we believe that it will assist us in our personal stock selection. There won't be any interpretation necessary.

OBV

For years, the BCI methodology has stressed the significance of the institutional investors (the "big boys") in impacting stock performance. This explains why we require a minimum average stock trading volume and option open interest before entering our option-selling trades. By incorporating OBV, we are factoring in the trend of institutional interest or lack thereof in each security and adding another dimension to our stock screening process.

The absolute value of the OBV indicator is less important than the direction of the OBV. The relative direction (▲, ▶, ▼) of the indicator is what we are looking for…are the institutions accumulating shares and supporting the stock (▲ & ▶) or are they exiting from the stock (▼).

Fundamental Analysis | 33

The OBV indicator is non-proprietary and is available in virtually every charting platform, including the following free platforms:

www.stockcharts.com

www.freestockcharts.com

www.barchart.com

www.tradingview.com

OBV is typically available in the charting packages provided by your broker as well.

As always, we're there to answer any questions that you might have with our improved screen.

***Detailed explanations of these 2 metrics can be found in the appendix section of this book.

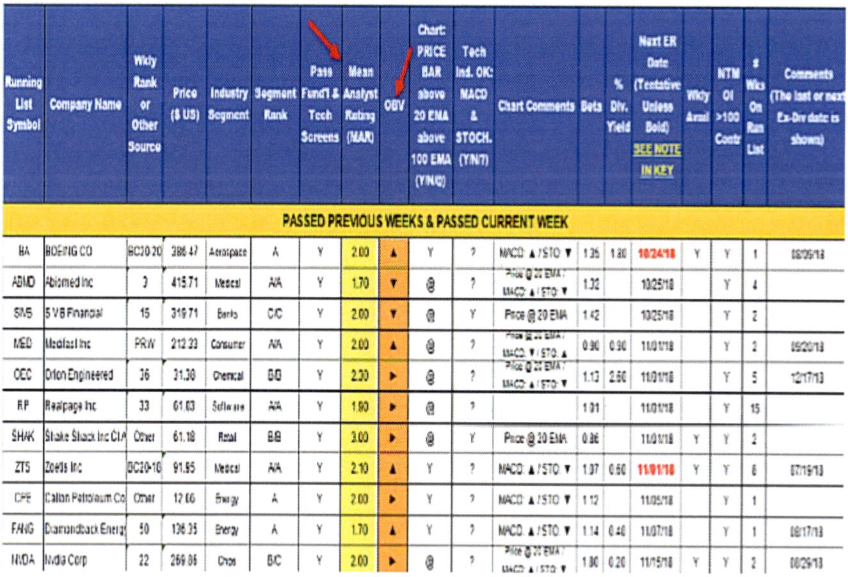

Figure 9a - Location of MAR and OBV in Stock reports Beginning November 2018

Auxiliary screen to locate even more stock candidates

CANSLIM®- another IBD® Screen:

==The IBD® 50 is my main source for locating the greatest performing stocks.== It is not, however, the only source. CAN SLIM®, a screening system created by William O'Neil, the founder of Investors Business Daily is another great resource and an additional screen that can be used in the BCI system. CAN SLIM® tracks market-leading stocks that show strong earnings growth, positive institutional sponsorship (i.e. the "big boys" are buying this equity), excellent industry strength, solid sales growth, profit margins, and return on equity. CAN SLIM® also screens stocks for minimum price and volume levels. I will periodically check the CAN SLIM® list, eliminate those equities on this list which overlap with stocks already on my initial watchlist, and run the remainder of the CAN SLIM® stocks through the additional screens used in the BCI system, which are discussed in further detail below. Assuming authorization, the CAN SLIM® can also be found on the *Investors Business Daily* website, Specifically, on the left side of the home page/default screen (www.investors.com), click on the link titled "Stock Research," followed by the "Screen Center" link, and finally, the "CAN SLIM Select" link.

What Fundamentals are utilized by the BCI System?

It considers plenty, although it doesn't take us all that long to calculate. First, let's look at the *IBD 50 stocks* and the fundamentals evaluated:

- Return on Equity
- Earnings per Share rating
- Annual EPS % change
- Last Quarter EPS % change
- Next Quarter EPS % change
- Last Quarter Sales % change

Fundamental Analysis | 35

In addition, we run the stocks through the *SmartSelect (Green Alert) ratings*. The "EPS Rating" compares a company's earnings per share growth on both a current and annual basis with other publicly traded companies. It compares the company's most recent two quarters of EPS growth with its 3-5 year annual growth rate.

Test your knowledge of key points

1- The key financial data found in most fundamental ratios are _Earnings_ and _Sales_

2- A watchlist of _50_ stocks is adequate for most covered call writers.

3- The BCI system uses the following three predominantly fundamental screens: _IBD-50_, _IBD Smart Select_ & ?

4- To pass the IBD SmartSelect® screen a stock must show _6 green circles_

5- To pass the BCI risk-reward screen a stock must have a Scouter rating of _6_.

6- An auxiliary screen used to locate additional stocks is called the _CAN SLIM_.

Answers:

1- Earnings and sales

2- 40 to 60

3- IBD 50®, IBD SmartSelect® and the Scouter rating.

4- 6 green circles

5- 5 or higher (up to 10)

6- IBD CANSLIM®

Now that we have all fundamental bases covered, and even some technical ones, it's time to unleash the power of the charts…it's time for technical analysis.

Chapter 4
Technical Analysis
The Power of the Charts

Chapter outline

1- What is technical analysis?

2- Types of price charts
- Line
- Bar
- Candlestick

3- The four technical indicators
- Moving averages
- MACD and MACD histogram
- Stochastic oscillator
- Volume

4- Constructing a technical chart

5- Sample charts
- Positive technicals
- Mixed technicals

6- The Premium Report and technical analysis

7- Technical market theories

What is technical analysis?

Technical analysis is the method of predicting future stock price movements based on observation of historical stock price movements. It is an essential tool in the armamentarium of covered call writers, and critical in achieving maximum success.

We use technical analysis in our stock selection process, buy/sell decisions, strike price selections and exit strategy determinations.

There are a myriad of technical indicators, and the ones you choose may differ from those that I have incorporated into my system. In this chapter, I will discuss the four technical indicators that are part of the BCI system (Moving Averages, MACD Histogram, Stochastics and Volume) and how I use these parameters to screen for the greatest stocks in our stock universe. Before we get into a detailed explanation of the four parameters, let's look at how we will graph the price of the stock over time which is what a price chart is all about:

Line Charts, Bar Charts and Candlestick Charts

Before you screen your stocks using technical analysis, you must first determine which chart type you are most comfortable working with. The three most commonly used charts are line charts, bar charts and candlestick charts.

Line Chart

The Line Chart is a very basic chart created by connecting a line across a series of closing prices for a particular security.

Figure 10 is an example of a line chart:

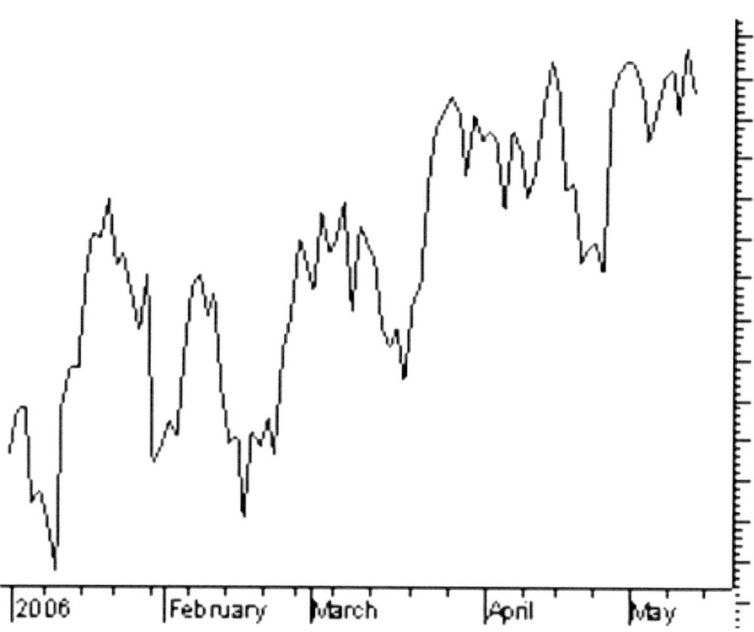

Figure 10- Line Chart of Closing Prices

Candlestick Chart

The candlestick chart is created by displaying the high, low, open and closing prices for a security each day over a certain time frame. Figure 11):

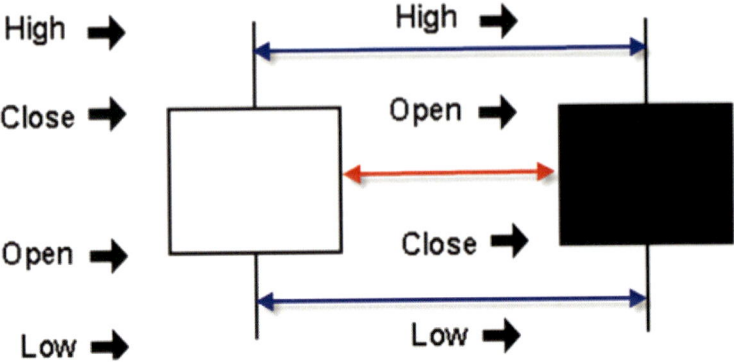

Figure 11 - Candlestick Lines

The following information is derived from these two candlesticks (Figure 11)

- The left candlestick closed HIGHER than it opened and therefore appears in white (or green); the right candlestick closed LOWER than it opened and therefore appears in black (or red)
- The middle portion (red arrows in Figure 11) is called the body and represents the opening and closing prices that day
- If the body is in black or red, the stock closed at a lower price than it opened
- If the body is white or green, the stock closed at a higher price than it opened
- The lines above and below the body are called shadows (upper and lower) and represent the session's high and low prices (blue double-sided arrows in figure 11)
- Note: A *weekly* candlestick is based on Monday's open, the weekly high-low range and Friday's close

- The candlestick to your left in figure 11 (white) closed higher than the open

- The candlestick to your right in figure 11 (black) closed lower than the open.

- So....white or green is bullish and black or red is bearish (simple but accurate!)

Let's take a broader look at a candlestick chart (Figure 12):

Figure 12- Candlestick Chart

Red candlesticks closed lower than it opened and white candlesticks closed higher than it opened. Black candlesticks in this chart represent an expanded version of candlestick charting where the stock price closed lower than it opened (bearish) but still higher than the previous day's close (bullish).

Bar Chart (my favorite):

Like the candlestick chart, this price chart consists of session high and lows as well as the opening and closing prices. It is also referred to as the *O-H-L-C bar* (open-high-low-close).

Figure 13 is an example of a single bar of the many bars typically plotted on a bar chart:

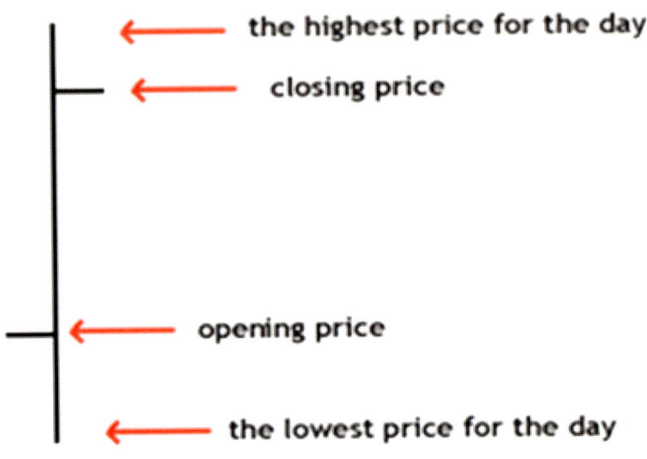

Figure 13- Bar or O-H-L-C Bar

As you can see, the information that can be gleaned from a bar chart is similar to that of the candlestick lines. To establish the relationship between the opening and closing prices on the bar chart, we look at the horizontal lines that emanate to the right and left from the vertical line. By contrast, in candlestick charts, we look for the differences in color in the body of the candlestick. Most financial websites will also color code the OHLC bars red or black:

- Red: Depicts a lower closing price than the previous day's closing price

- Black: Depicts a higher closing price than the previous day's closing price

Common Features of Bar and Candlestick Charts:

- Display high, low, open and close prices

- Neither chart reflects the sequence of events between the open and close

- Provide much more information than the line chart

Major Differences between Bar and Candlestick Charts:

- In candlestick charts, the relationship between open and close is depicted by the color of the body, whereas with bar charts that relationship is shown by horizontal lines projecting from the vertical.

- The bar chart places greater emphasis on the closing price of the stock in relation to the PRIOR periods close. The candlestick version places the highest importance of the close as it relates to the open of the SAME day. This is the main reason I prefer the bar chart but the difference is negligible.

Chart Comparison:

Nearly every financial chart imaginable, including the bar and candlestick charts discussed above can be constructed by using the free website Stockcharts.com, which is by far the most popular charting resource among BCIs. Figures 14 and 15 were both formed using Stockcharts.com, and represent a candlestick chart and bar chart, respectively. In figure 15, I highlighted all four technical parameters for future reference:

Figure 14- ANR- Candlestick

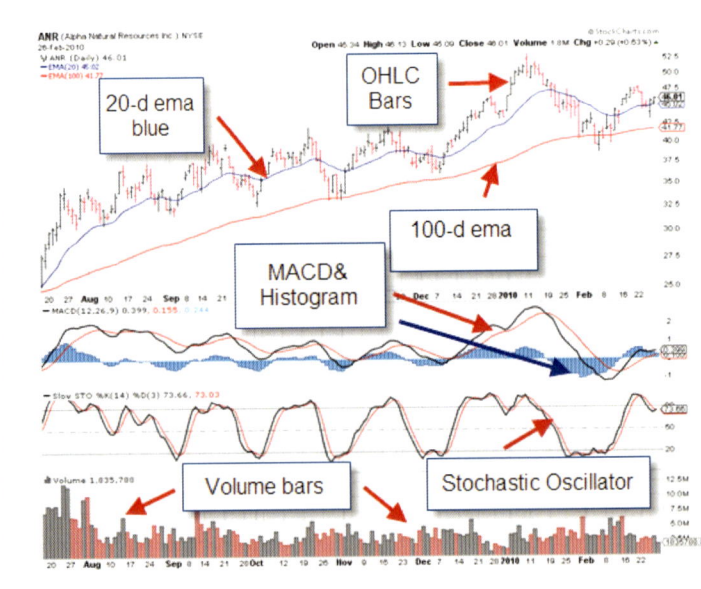

Figure 15- ANR- Bar Chart (note the OHLC bars)

Conclusion:

Both the candlestick and bar charts offer much more information than the line charts. Some chartists prefer the color feature of the candlestick bodies, while others prefer the emphasis on closing price comparison with the previous period offered by the bar charts. You can't go wrong with either one. My advice is to select the chart you like and use it consistently so reading a technical chart will take only a few seconds. For the remainder of this book, most price charts will be shown in price bar format.

The four technical indicators

The four technical indicators used in the BCI system include moving averages, MACD or moving average convergence divergence, the stochastic oscillator and volume. Before we get into a detailed discussion of each I will give a brief definition of each parameter and ask you to refer to figure 15 above to get an initial glance as to how these parameters appear on a bar chart:

- Moving averages (20-d ema and 100-d ema) - An indicator frequently used in technical analysis showing the average value of a security's price over a set period. Moving averages are generally used to identify trends and define areas of possible support and resistance.

- MACD - A trend-following momentum indicator that shows the relationship between two moving averages of prices. The MACD is calculated by subtracting the 26-day *exponential moving average* (EMA) from the 12-day EMA. A 9-day EMA of the MACD (red line), called the *signal line*, is then plotted on top of the MACD, functioning as a trigger for buy and sell signals.

- MACD Histogram (blue arrow above) - A common technical indicator that illustrates the difference between the MACD and the trigger line. This difference is then plotted on a chart in the form of a histogram (bar chart) to make it easy for a trader to determine a specific asset's momentum.

- Stochastic Oscillator - A momentum indicator that measures the price of a security relative to the high/low range over a set period of time. The indicator oscillates between 0 and 100. Readings below 20 are considered oversold. Readings above 80 are considered overbought.

- Volume - The number of trades in a security over a period of time. On a chart, volume is usually represented as a histogram (vertical bars) below the price chart.

MOVING AVERAGES

For me the moving average is king of these technical parameters, with the others playing confirming roles. Each indicator by itself will not suffice, but as a whole, they paint a very important picture relating to our buy-sell decisions. First, some key terminology.

Definitions:

- *Moving Average (MA)* - the average value of a security's price over a set period of time. It is used to locate trends and define areas of possible support and resistance.

- *Simple Moving Average (SMA)* - a moving average that gives equal weight to each day's price data.

- *Exponential Moving Average (EMA)* - similar to a SMA except more weight is given to the most recent data.

- *Support* - the price level at which a stock has had difficulty falling below. It is a price point where a lot of buyers tend to purchase stock.

- *Resistance* - the price level at which a stock has had difficulty rising above. It is a price point where sellers tend to outnumber buyers.

- *Uptrend* - the price movement of a stock is in an upward direction. The stock price forms a series of higher highs and higher lows.

- *Downtrend* - the price movement of a stock is in a downward direction. The security forms a series of lower highs and lower lows.

- *Consolidation (sideways pattern)* - the horizontal price movement of an equity where the forces of supply and demand are equal. The stock simply cannot establish an uptrend or a downtrend. *The moving average parameter is less reliable in a sideways pattern.*

- *Trendline* - A line that is drawn over price highs or under price lows to show the prevailing direction of price. Trendlines give a visual representation of support and resistance in a given time frame.

Simple vs. Exponential Moving Averages

When selling 1-month options, I prefer the EMA to the SMA because the EMA responds more quickly to a recent change in the stock price. The EMA also avoids false positives (signal to buy or sell when a price moves above or below the moving average), where a stock may jump above the SMA but not above the EMA. In Figure 16 below, which charts Apple Inc (AAPL), the red line represents the EMA and the blue line depicts the SMA. Note in Figure 16 how the EMA (which is more sensitive to price changes) starts moving up faster than the SMA as the stock price appreciates (in January where the red line moves above the blue line), and that the EMA would have avoided the false positive in February, at which time the price momentarily broke through the SMA (blue) but not above the EMA (red), and dropped precipitously shortly thereafter (blue arrow):

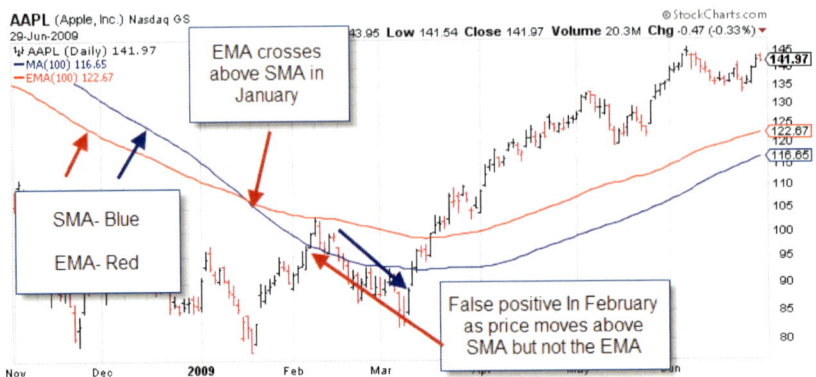

Figure 16- Simple vs. Exponential Moving Averages

The parameters I prefer to use (for 1-month covered call writing) are the 20-day (20-d) and 100-day (100-d) EMAs. The 20-d approximates the number of trading days in the 1-month contract. The 100-d represents 20 weeks (5 trading days/week) or five months, and gives us a longer-term perspective to use as a basis of comparison with the shorter-term 20-d EMA. When viewing the moving average indicator, we like to see the 20-d EMA above the 100-d EMA and the price bars at or above the 20-d EMA. This shows a positive upward momentum and favors (but does not guarantee) continued price appreciation. Moving averages are considered *lagging indicators*, which means they trail the price action of a stock. Thus moving averages confirm trends but do not predict them. However, once a trend is identified, we want to be part of that wild ride to cash profits! Figure 17 below depicts the same chart of AAPL (as in Figure 16), inclusive of the 20-d and 100-d EMAs:

Figure 17- Short-Term (blue) vs. Long-term (red) EMAs

Notice, at the red arrow, that at the end of March, after the short-term EMA (20-d in blue) moved above the longer-term EMA (100-d in red) the stock went to the moon (blue arrow), which coincided with its price bars remaining at or above the 20-d EMA.

When to use moving averages- practical application:

Moving averages have little value when the stock price is in a period of consolidation (moving sideways and not establishing a definitive trend). In these instances, we turn to our confirming indicators or exclude the stock from consideration. When the stock is downtrending, we opt for another equity. If a security is trending upwards while it's short-term (20-d EMA) is above its longer-term (100-d EMA), and its price bars remain at or above the 20-d EMA, we have a strong buy signal. The signal is even stronger if confirmed by MACD, stochastics and volume (discussed below). Most winning stocks never make a serious breach of the 20-d EMA, which, in a bullish situation, serves as support (discussed in further detail directly below) for the share price. Such support is indicative of institutional interest in that equity. On the other hand, when a stock drops sharply below support (the 20-d EMA) on high volume, the major players (e.g. mutual funds, banks, insurance companies, pension funds etc.) are starting to move out of the stock, and so should we.

Support and resistance:

You now know that the first step we take in conducting the technical analysis portion of our stock screening system involves spotting uptrending price patterns by utilizing moving averages to confirm these trends. As discussed above, in an ideal situation, the price bars (OHLC) bounce off and above the short-term EMA (20-d), which serves as *support* for the price of the stock. In the inverse situation, where the price is trading below, and bouncing off and under, the 20-d EMA, the 20-d EMA serves as resistance for the equity price. Let's take a closer look at support, *resistance* and uptrending scenarios so that we know exactly how to spot these technical signals when screening our stocks:

Support:

A price level at which there is sufficient demand for a stock to cause a halt in a downward trend and turn the trend up. Support levels indicate the price at which most investors feel that the prices will move higher. Figure 18 depicts a chart where there is support at $51.25, at which point the stock price turns up at the arrows:

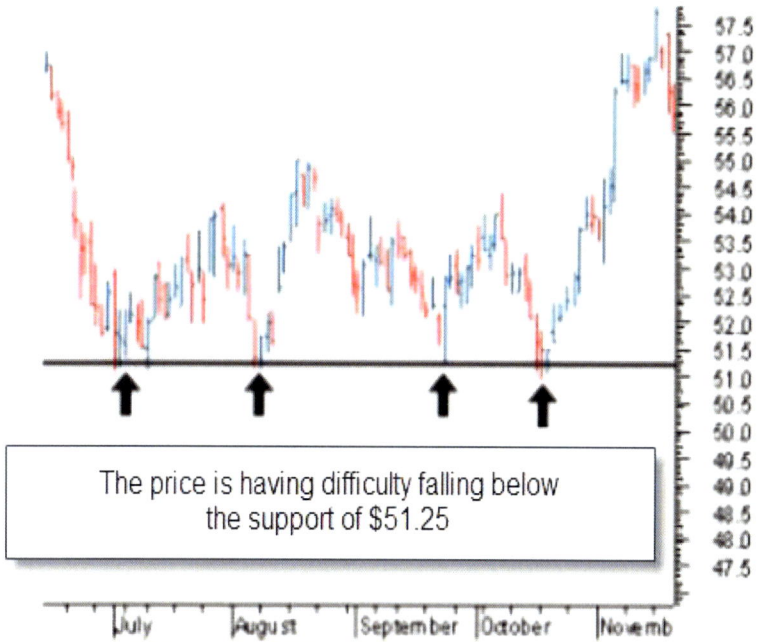

Figure 18- SUPPORT

Resistance:

The price level at which there is a large enough supply of stock available to cause a halt in the upward trend and turn the trend down. Resistance levels indicate the price at which most investors feel that the prices will move lower. Figure 19 on the next page depicts a stock that encounters resistance at $50.50, the point at which the price of the stock is turned down:

Figure 19- Resistance

In our system of locating the greatest performing stocks in the greatest performing industries, we search for price patterns in an uptrend. *An uptrend is established when a security forms a series of higher highs and higher lows.* Figure 20 depicts a stock exhibiting an uptrending price pattern:

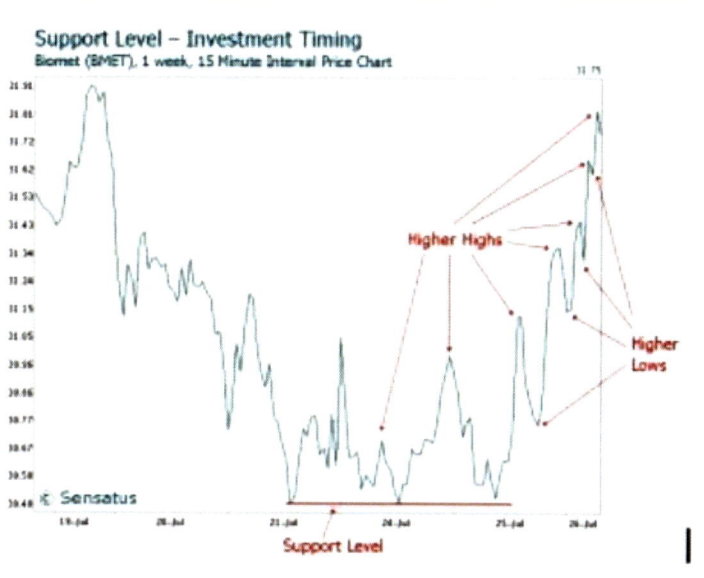

Figure 20- Uptrending Price Pattern

When uptrends are identified in normal market conditions, they present ideal situations to sell out-of-the-money call options (i.e. the strike price of the call option is higher than prevailing market price of the underlying stock). In such a situation, the option premium (the premium we receive for selling the call option) + share appreciation (the increase in the price of the uptrending underlying equity we buy/own) will bring our monthly returns into the 3-4% range, and in many cases, higher returns. This, of course, assumes our other system criteria are met. As they say on Wall Street, "The trend is your friend".

Figure 21 (a line chart) provides an example of an ideal situation (from a moving average perspective) in which we would want to sell out-of-the-money covered calls on STEC, Inc. (STEC). Here, all the moving average technical criteria we have discussed are met: (1) STEC's 20-d EMA (blue line) is above its 100-d EMA (red line); and (2) STEC's. 20-d EMA is uptrending and serving as support for its "higher lows" price points (green circles):

Figure 21 - STEC- Uptrending MA + Support

As indicated in Figure 21, the green circles demonstrate areas of support (20-d ema or blue line is serving as support).

(For future reference)

Note that in early August (purple double-side arrow) the chart shows that the price of STEC had a large drop on high volume (tall price bar at the bottom of the purple arrow). The price temporarily dropped below the 20-d EMA. This was the result of an earnings report and exemplifies why we avoid equities that are reporting earnings in a particular contract period, a subject which will be discussed in detail later in this book. For now, simply take note that STEC reported earnings on August 4th, and as can be seen in Figure 21 (purple arrow), the market reacted negatively. Those who follow my system would not have owned this stock at that particular time, and thus would not have suffered any short-term losses. However, prior to August 4th, the technicals indicate that STEC was ripe for the sale of out-of-the-money covered calls.

Moving Average Summary:

ONE aspect of technical analysis is trend identification. The tool we use for this purpose is the moving average which can represent either support or resistance. The chart below (Figure 22) demonstrates how moving averages can represent both support and resistance or can simply trade sideways in a trading range:

Figure 22- Support and Resistance

#1- Price breaks below support (20-d ema); blue line is now serving as resistance

#2- Price breaks above resistance and is now in an uptrend (blue arrow); 20-d ema is now serving as support

#3- Yellow highlighted areas show a sideways trading pattern with no definite up or downtrend

#4- Price breaks below support and a downtrend is beginning as the 20-d ema serves as resistance

Here are some of the ways this information can put CASH in our pockets:

- Sell O-T-M strikes when we have identified an uptrending moving average in normal market conditions (blue arrow in figure 22).
- Avoid equities in a downtrend (#s 1 and 4 in figure 22).

- Avoid the stock or sell I-T-M strikes when stocks are trading sideways (consolidating) or not in any particular trend (neither up nor down as in #3 in figure 22).

- If a stock breaks through support (moves down) on high volume, be prepared to execute an exit strategy (#s 1 and 4 in figure 22; examples will be given in the chapter on exit strategies)

- If a stock breaks through resistance (moves up) on high volume, consider this a major technical positive. See #2 in figure 22.

Conclusions:

Moving averages are effective tools for identifying and confirming trends as well as support and resistance. I use moving averages as the first step of my technical analysis. In an ideal world, I would like an uptrending price pattern with the 20-d ema above the 100-d ema and the price bars at or above the 20-d ema. This facilitates our trading system as it assists in making our buy-sell decisions. Since it is a lagging indicator, it is not predictive of change, unlike the Moving Average Convergence Divergence (MACD), the second of our technical screens discussed directly below. But as they say on Wall Street, "the trend is your friend" and we want as many friends as possible when investing our hard-earned money. As with all technical tools, moving averages should not be used alone, but rather in conjunction with our other technical indicators.

MOVING AVERAGE CONVERGENCE DIVERGENCE (MACD):

Technical analysis is as much an art as it is a science. No one parameter, by itself, will allow us to make our buy/sell decisions. However, when all the indicators are used together, they paint a picture that is critical to maximizing our covered call success.

One of the most simple and reliable of these parameters is the *Moving Average Convergence Divergence, or MACD.*

Definition:

MACD is one of the most basic and effective "momentum" indicators that also serves as a trend-following indicator. So let's call the MACD *a trend-following momentum indicator.* Momentum is defined as the rate of acceleration of a stock's price and trend in an upward or downward direction. The MACD is formed by subtracting a longer-term EMA from a shorter-term EMA (which are trend following indicators). The resulting plot forms a line that oscillates above and below zero without any upper or lower limits. So what does the MACD tell us? In short, MACD gives us prior notice before two EMAs cross. This notice can be used to discern bullish (buy) and bearish (sell) signals, as described in detail below.

MACD Formula (common example):

The stock's 26-d EMA is subtracted from its 12-d EMA. The resulting line created by these price points is called the MACD. A 9-d EMA of the MACD itself is also plotted and acts as a *"trigger line."* A 9-day EMA is used so we can get a quick reading on the potential changing momentum of an equity's price. The subtraction of the trigger line from the MACD itself is the basis for the *MACD Histogram,* an even quicker indicator than the MACD. Let's look at a chart (Figure 23) which depicts these parameters:

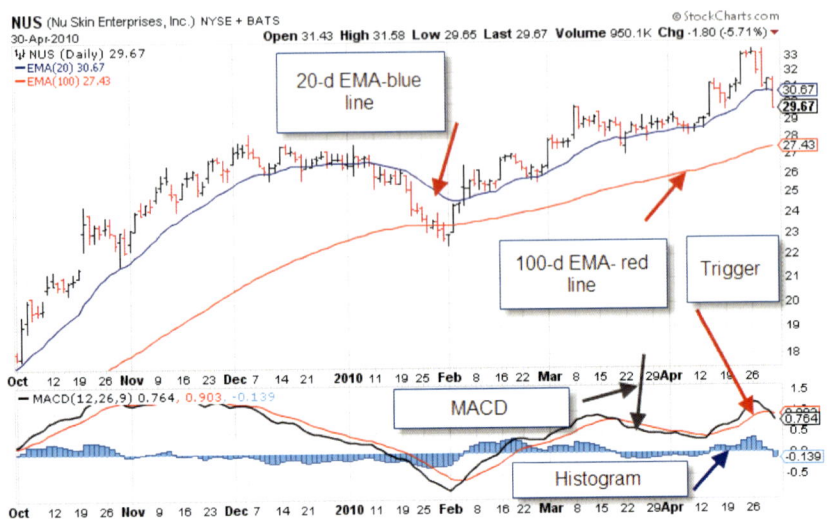

Figure 23- MACD - Basic Chart (<u>bottom quarter of this chart</u>)

The black arrow shows the MACD itself (black line); the red arrow shows the trigger line (red line); and the blue arrow points to the MACD Histogram (light blue bars). Note how the MACD oscillates above and below the zero line, which is also known as the "centerline."

MACD- Bullish Signals

There are three types of bullish signals that can be detected from the MACD: (1) positive divergence; (2) bullish moving average crossover; and (3) bullish centerline crossover.

1- *Positive Divergence*- the MACD begins to advance while the security itself remains in a downtrend (Figure 24):

Technical Analysis - The Power of the Charts | 59

Figure 24- MACD- Positive Divergence

Note how the green MACD trend lines are positive (below the green arrow on left), while the actual price of the security is in a downtrend , as evidenced by the downward sloping (negative) red trend lines, which corresponds with a downward sloping 20-d EMA (blue line) . The green arrow also indicates a positive MACD histogram (blue bars are above zero).

2- *Bullish moving average crossover (Figure 25)* - the actual MACD moves above its 9-d EMA (the trigger line).

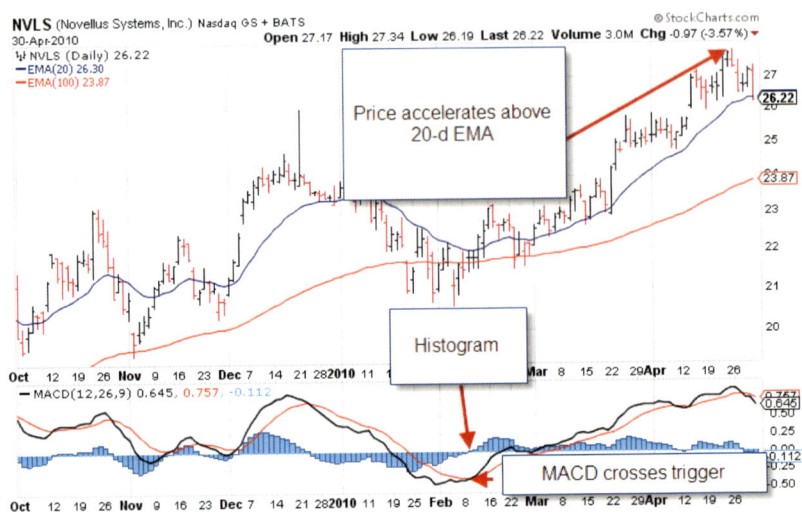

Figure 25- MACD- Bullish Moving Average Crossover

Note how the red arrows depict the MACD (black line) crossing above the trigger line (red line), with the histogram (light blue bars) turning positive. The price of the stock then skyrockets (long red arrow). Whenever the MACD itself crosses the trigger (9-d EMA) the histogram will be positive (discussed below).

3- *Bullish Centerline Crossover (Figure 26)* - the MACD moves above the zero line (centerline) and into positive territory. This can be used as a confirmation of the positive divergence and bullish moving average crossover rather than choosing any one of the three.

Figure 26- MACD- Positive Centerline Crossover

As the MACD (black line) moves above the zero line (red arrows), the stock heads north (blue arrows). Using a combination of these bullish signals can produce a more meaningful signal than using just one. I favor the MACD Histogram by itself as it is an earlier indicator of a price change and easily viewed on a chart. The three just described can serve as confirmation when evaluating stocks in more detail.

MACD- Bearish Signals

- Negative Divergence- MACD declines as security moves sideways or up.
- Bearish Moving Average Crossover- MACD declines below its 9-d EMA.
- Bearish Centerline Crossover- MACD moves below zero into negative territory.

Utilizing a combination of the three bearish signals above will provide a more reliable indicator of a negative price change in the equity. Once again, when it comes to MACD I generally view the histogram which I will discuss later in this chapter.

Advantages of MACD (black line):

- It is a reliable indicator that should be used in conjunction with other indicators (moving averages, the stochastic oscillator and volume).
- Incorporates both trend and momentum into one indicator
- Using exponential moving averages eliminates some of the lag found in simple MAs.
- Foreshadows moves in the underlying security.

MACD Histogram

This represents the difference between the MACD and its trigger, the 9-d EMA. It is plotted in the form of a histogram (bar graph) rendering divergences and centerline crossover easily identified.

Bullish histogram signals:

- A centerline crossover (i.e. the histogram bars move above the centerline) into positive territory. This is equivalent to the MACD moving average crossover signal, in which the MACD moves above (for a bullish signal) or below (for a bearish signal) its trigger line.
- Increases in the positive histogram show strengthening momentum.
- Positive divergence of the histogram will usually precede a positive move of the MACD itself.

Bearish Histogram Signals

- A centerline crossover (i.e. the histogram bars move below the centerline) into negative territory. This is equivalent to the MACD moving average crossover signal, in which the MACD moves below (for a bearish signal) its trigger line.

- Increases in the negative histogram show strengthening momentum in a negative direction.

- Negative divergence of the histogram will usually precede a negative move of the MACD itself thereby giving us an earlier warning signal of a potential price decline.

Figure 27 below depicts both bullish and bearish MACD Histogram signals:

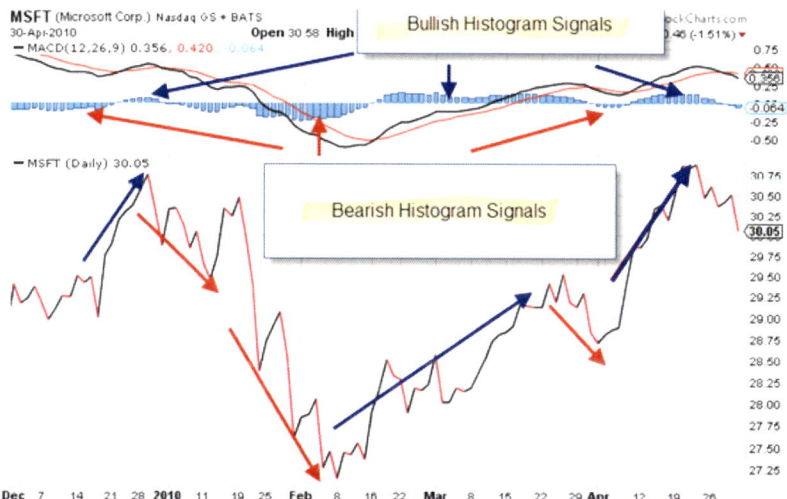

Figure 27 - MACD vs. MACD Histogram

Bullish signals are highlighted by the blue arrows where the graph moves above zero and the price of the stock then rises. Bearish signals are noted by the red arrows where the bars drop below zero and the price of the equity then declines. It is important to note that these histogram signals occur before the MACD itself (black line) moves above or below zero. This is why I prefer the histogram…it is a quicker indicator of change.

How to use the MACD Histogram:

A widening gap between the MACD and its trigger line (also known as the histogram which is the difference between the MACD and its trigger) shows strengthening momentum, while a shrinking gap will demonstrate weakening momentum. A bullish signal occurs when there is positive divergence or a widening gap between the two and a bullish centerline crossover. A bearish signal exists when there is negative divergence (closing gap between the two) and a bearish centerline crossover. Notice in Figure 27 above how the histogram provides a bearish signal *before* the MACD (January, 2010 for example)) and a bullish signal prior to the MACD (March, 2010 for example). Specifically, *the histogram crosses the zero line before the MACD itself. Therefore it can be said that the MACD and the MACD Histogram are independent of each other.*

Advantages of the MACD Histogram:

- Divergences are apparent before MACD moving average crossovers.
- Can be used to signal impending reversals.
- Easy to read and quick to interpret.

Conclusion:

MACD and the MACD Histogram are two of the more reliable technical analysis tools available to us. They incorporate both trend-following and momentum identifying qualities and are predictive in nature. As with other technical tools, they should be used in conjunction with other indicators to assist in painting a picture for potential buy/sell decisions.

STOCHASTIC OSCILLATOR

The stochastic oscillator is a momentum indicator that shows the location of the current closing price relative to the high-low range over a set number of periods, usually 14 trading days. Closing levels that are near the top of the range indicate *accumulation* or buying pressure, while those near the bottom of the range indicate *distribution* or selling pressure. Another way to view this indicator is this that it graphically depicts the prevailing victor in the battle of the bulls versus the bears over a specified period of time. The indicator oscillates between 0 and 100. Readings below 20 are considered oversold while readings above 80 are considered *overbought.* The idea behind this indicator is that *prices tend to close near the extremes of the recent range before turning points.*

Assume that during the past 14 trading days, stock XYZ has seen a low of $30 and a high of $40 and that today it closed at $38. Today's $38 closing price signifies that the stock is up $8 or is "at the 80%" for the 14-day, $10 trading range. Had XYZ closed today at $32, it would be "at the 20%." This point within the range (0% to 100%) is known as "%K" in stochastic lingo. Buy-sell signals occur when %K crosses its 3-day simple moving average, which is known as "%D" or the trigger line. Let's look at another chart (Figure 28) that shows the stochastic oscillator (shown near the bottom of the chart):

Figure 28- Stochastic Oscillator

Note the following:

- Stochastic oscillator = thick black line highlighted by the black arrow = %K

- Trigger line = red line highlighted by red arrow = %D (3-d sma)

- Overbought (80%) and oversold (20%) levels are highlighted by the green circles.

Some chartists use crossovers of %K and %D as buy/sell signals. However, these signals occur quite frequently and can result in whipsaws, or a myriad of short-term signals. A more reliable transaction signal (in my view and that of many other chartists) occurs when the oscillator moves from overbought (above 80%) to below 80%, or from below the oversold threshold (20%) to above 20%. *A strong stochastic signal* occurs when the positive divergence (from below 20% or oversold) above 20% or a negative divergence (from above 80% or overbought) below 80% takes place for a second time or a double dip. The following guidelines illustrate bullish and bearish signals that can be gauged from the stochastic oscillator:

Buy signal: %K crosses above the 20% for the second time

Sell signal: %K moves below the 80% for the second time

There is no need to worry about the trigger line for this indicator.

In Figure 29 on the next page (CTSH charted from November of 2009 to May of 2010)), the green circle highlights the area where %K crossed the 20% for the second time, which, according to the guidelines referenced directly above, is a strong bullish signal to buy. Note that immediately after %K crossed the 20% for the second time, the price of CTSH accelerated, as highlighted by the green arrow on the top of the chart. There is also a definitive sell signal wherein %K crossed below the 80% for the second time (red circle) which was followed with a decline in the price of CTSH (red arrow).

68 | Complete Encyclopedia for Covered Call Writing

Figure 29- Stochastic Oscillator- buy-sell signals

The Slow Stochastic Oscillator:

One of the problems with %K in relation to %D is the high number of false breaks, whipsaws and crossovers as discussed earlier. To mitigate this issue, the Slow Stochastic Oscillator was developed. This is derived by applying a 3-day simple moving average (SMA) to %K, which smoothes the data and forms a slower version of %K. In short, this means that the slow stochastic oscillator is equal to the 3-d SMA of the fast stochastic oscillator, as summarized in the equation below:

Slow Stochastic Oscillator = %K (slow) = %D (Fast)

To form a trigger line for this slower version, a 3-d SMA is created and applied to the new %K (slow). So the 3-d SMA of slow stochastics is the 3-d SMA of the 3-d SMA of the fast stochastics (get the Tylenol!).

When building a chart, there is usually a choice of selecting slow or fast stochastics. *I prefer to use the slow stochastic oscillator,* as it is easier to read and interpret, and eliminates many of the false triggers inherent in the fast oscillator.

Full Stochastic Oscillator:

There is actually a third stochastic oscillator called the Full Stochastic Oscillator. Rather than using the 3-d SMA of the %K (as the Slow Stochastic Oscillator does), traders who desired more flexibility created a third variable, called the smoothing variable, which alters the amount of days used in the smoothing of %K. One can also recreate the fast and slow stochastics by the full stochastic. To mimic the fast stochastic, use a 1-day SMA (smoothing number). To mimic the slow stochastic, use a 3-day SMA (smoothing number).

Conclusion:

For purposes of 1-month covered call writing, I have found the Slow Stochastic Oscillator the most useful and time efficient of all the stochastic oscillators discussed above. The Slow Stochastic Oscillator is a widely used momentum indicator that measures who is winning the daily battle between the bulls and the bears. We look to see movements above and below the 20% and 80% areas. An ascending stochastic oscillator is also a bullish signal. As always, it is prudent to use this oscillator in conjunction with our other technical indicators.

VOLUME

Volume is the number of shares or contracts that trade over a specific period of time, usually one day. On a chart, volume is represented as a histogram (vertical bars) overlaid on or below the price chart. This indicator is an essential part of every technical formation, as a price pattern will typically have a volume pattern attached to it. In other words, we use volume to confirm trends and chart patterns. *If a stock is truly in an uptrend, then the uptrend should correspond with high volume*, which is indicative that the uptrend will continue. Any price movement up or down with relatively high volume is seen as stronger and more reliable than a similar movement in price on weak volume. These same guidelines apply for changes in the MACD and stochastic oscillators. If we see positive or negative signals in these indicators, they are more significant on high volume and less significant on low volume. Volume tends to precede price so if a stock is trending up or down and volume begins to weaken we may be in for a trend reversal.

Some chartists will draw a trendline on volume and compare it to the trends of the price of the security in addition to other technical indicators. If they are not moving in the same direction, we have a *negative volume divergence*. For example, if price is rising and volume is declining, there could be a trend reversal on the horizon. On the other hand, if price is declining and volume is accelerating, this negative trend is confirmed and a sell signal is more meaningful. Such an example can be found in Figure 30:

Figure 30
Volume confirmation of all negative technical signals

- The red arrows highlight strengthening volume
- The blue arrows show a declining price trend
- Volume is also confirming a negative MACD divergence (green circles). In other words, the green encircled area depicts a bearish moving average crossover (MACD line drops below trigger line) which is occurring on high volume (red arrows)
- Volume is also confirming a negative stochastic oscillator divergence (red circles). In other words, the red encircled area depicts a stochastic sell signal (%K moves below the 80% in these two instances) which is occurring on high volume (red arrows).

Figure 31 depicts an example of a negative volume divergence (volume is trending in the *opposite* direction of price and other technical indicators) which, as noted, is indicative of a potential trend reversal:

Figure 31- Trend reversal- volume and price

- Red arrows highlight volume confirmation of price acceleration
- Blue lines show weakening volume and price consolidation (sideways pattern) indicating a possible trend reversal
- The green arrow shows a severe price reversal with volume confirmation (green circle) as the volume bars are much higher than during consolidation

As previously stated *volume oftentimes precedes price*. If volume is weakening during an uptrend, it is oftentimes a signal that the trend is about to reverse. Note the price trend reversal as volume weakens in April in figure 31 above.

Conclusion:

Volume is an essential technical analysis tool that will verify the significance of a price pattern or technical analysis indicator confirmation or divergence. It can also be predictive of upcoming changes in chart patterns. We use volume to corroborate buy/sell signals. A positive or negative signal on high volume is much more significant than one on low volume. Volume surges (1.5 x normal volume) are especially significant. Next let's put all this information to use in our Blue Collar System of selling 1-month covered call options.

Constructing a technical chart @ www.stockcharts.com

I- Create a chart now:

      A- Style- Sharp Chart

      B- Enter ticker symbol

      C- Hit "Go"

*****see Figure 32 for II, III and IV:

II- Chart Attributes:

      A- Periods- Daily

      B- Range- 1 year

      C- Type OHLC Bars

D- Size- 700 or landscape

E- Volume- Off

III- Overlays

A- Exp Moving Average- 20

B- Exp Moving Average- 100

IV- Indicators

A- MACD- 12, 26, 9- Below

B- Slow Stochastics- 14, 3- Below

C- Volume- Below

Once information is entered, click on "update".

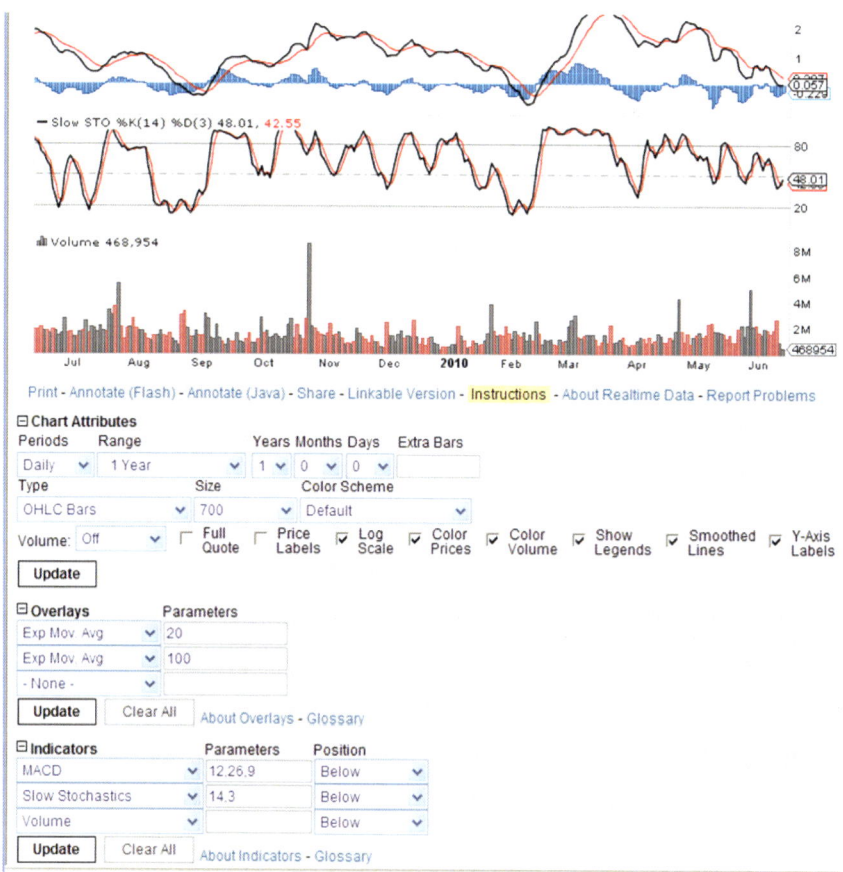

Figure 32- Setting up a technical chart

Technical Analysis, the Premium Report and Covered Call Writing

As we have learned, one of the most powerful tools covered call writers have in their arsenal is technical analysis. We use this investigative tool to predict future stock price movements based on observation of historical stock price movements. As detailed above, the four indicators used in our BCI system are:

- Moving Averages
- MACD (Histogram)
- Stochastic Oscillator
- Volume

These tools allow us to make important decisions in our investment strategy. The decisions that are impacted by technical analysis are:

- Stock Selection
- Strike Selection
- Exit Strategy Determination

It is important to understand that technical analysis does not stand alone in our decision-making process. We also factor in market tone, equity fundamentals, and earnings reports and many other parameters but this section will hone in on the technical analytical aspect of our determinations.

Sample charts

So let's first view a chart (Figure 33) with predominantly positive technicals:

Technical Analysis - The Power of the Charts | 77

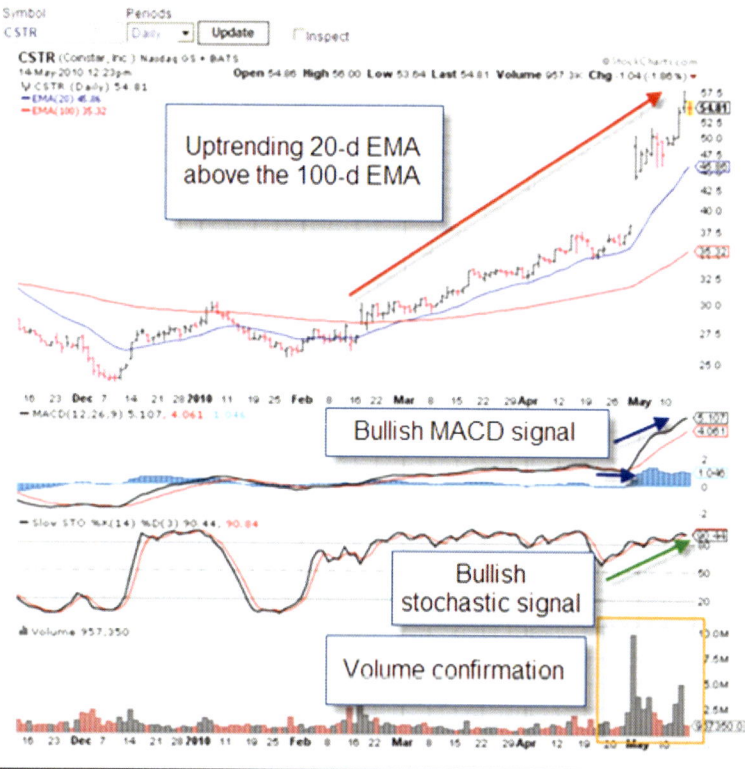

Figure 33- Positive Technicals

The following positive technical indicators are depicted on Figure 33:

- Moving averages (red arrow) are uptrending as the 20-d EMA is above the 100-d EMA, and both trending are higher as the price bars remain at or above the 20-d EMA.

- MACD and its Histogram (blue arrows) are positive.

- The Stochastic Oscillator (green arrow) has been trending up and is now above the 80% (overbought), however many equities have stayed in this territory for months. On the BCI Premium Report, we consider this (above 80%) a "neutral" indication.

- All of these positive indicators have occurred on relatively high volume (orange square).

A Positive Technical Chart and our Covered Call Decisions:

- We are more likely to select a stock to buy with a positive chart pattern (Figure 33) than one with a mixed technical picture. (Figure 34 below depicts a mixed technical chart).

- We are more likely to sell at-the-money call options (strike price of the call option is equal to the current stock price) or out-of-the-money (strike price of the call option is higher than the price of the underlying security) calls options with positive technicals.

- We are more likely to attempt to "hit a double" rather than roll down or unwind when using mid-contract exit strategies. (These are more bullish exit strategies which will be discussed in the chapter on exit strategies).

- We are more likely to roll out and up (rather than just rolling out) with positive chart technicals when utilizing exit strategies on or near expiration Friday. (also discussed in the chapter about exit strategies)

Next let's view a chart (Figure 34) with mixed technicals:

Technical Analysis - The Power of the Charts | 79

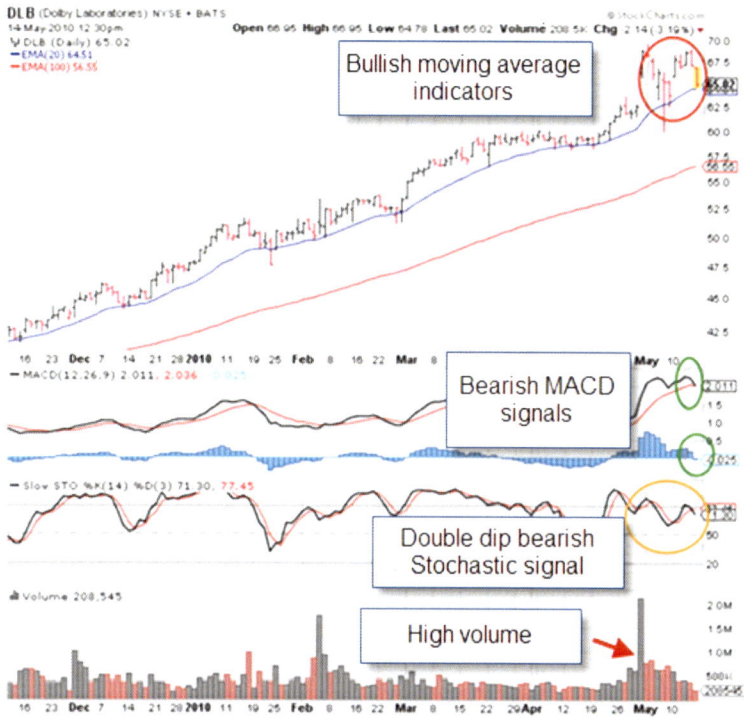

Figure 34- Mixed technicals

Note the following technical indicators depicted on Figure 34:

- Moving averages (red circle) are still positive and holding.

- MACD is showing a bearish crossover with the trigger line causing the histogram to move into negative territory (green circles).

- The stochastic oscillator (orange circle) has just completed a "double dip" below the 80%, a bearish signal.

- These mixed signals have taken place on average to higher than average volume.

A Mixed Technical Chart and our Covered Call Decisions:

- We are less likely to select buy a stock with this chart pattern than one with a stronger technical picture.

- We are more likely to sell in-the-money (strike price of call option is lower than the price of the underlying security) call options with mixed technicals.

- We are more likely to roll down or unwind when using mid-contract exit strategies. (This is discussed in the chapter about exit strategies).

- We are more likely to roll out as opposed to out and up with mixed chart technicals when utilizing exit strategies on or near expiration Friday. (Also discussed in exit strategy chapter).

Technical Analysis and the Premium Report

The Weekly Stock Screen and Watch List is a report produced by The Blue Collar Investor Corp. (BCI) each week. It includes a weekly re-screening of technicals of each stock under consideration, and is broken down into two categories:

- The chart pattern
- Technical indicators with commentary

Here is a sample of the BCI Premium Report (Figure 35) that relates to technical analysis:

Technical Analysis - The Power of the Charts | 81

WEEKLY STOCK SCREEN AND WATCH LIST
WEEKLY STOCK SCREENING...AS OF CLOSE ON 05/13/11

- Weekly Rank or Other Source...Indicates Weekly Top 50 Rank Or Other Database As Source Of Stock
- (?) Indicates Chart or Technical Indicators Mixed...OK To Keep On Watch List
- ER Dates Are Based On Currently Available Information...Check Actual ER Date Prior to Establishing Your Position

Symbol	Company Name	Weekly Rank or Other Source	Price	Opts Avail (Y/N)	Report Same Store Sales (Y/N)	Pass Fund'l And Tech'l Screens (Y/N)	Avg. Vol.: >250K Sh/Day (Y/N)	Pass Risk vs. Reward (Y/N)	Chart: ▲Price ▲20EMA ▲100EMA (Y/N/?)	Tech Ind. OK: MACD Stoch. (Y/N/?)	Earn. Report In This Option Month (Y/N)	Comments
\multicolumn{13}{c}{**Passed All Screens**}											
ATHN	Athenahealth Inc	Other	46.28	Y	N	Y	Y	Y	Y	Y	N	
BCR	Bard C R Inc	Other	109.56	Y	N	Y	Y	Y	Y	Y	N	
BMC	B M C Software Inc	Other	54.47	Y	N	Y	Y	Y	Y	Y	N	
CMG	Chipotle Mexican	17	280.40	Y	N	Y	Y	Y	Y	Y	N	
ENDP	Endo	29	42.39	Y	N	Y	Y	Y	Y	Y	N	
FOSL	Fossil Inc	4	105.37	Y	N	Y	Y	Y	Y	Y	N	
NFLX	Netflix Inc	6	246.52	Y	N	Y	Y	Y	Y	Y	N	
RL	Polo Ralph Lauren Co	Other	133.31	Y	N	Y	Y	Y	Y	Y	N	
RVBD	Riverbed	8	37.42	Y	N	Y	Y	Y	Y	Y	N	
SLH	Solera Holdings Inc	Other	57.74	Y	N	Y	Y	Y	Y	Y	N	
SRCL	Stericycle Inc	Other	93.02	Y	N	Y	Y	Y	Y	Y	N	
\multicolumn{13}{c}{**Passed Screens, Have Earnings Report In Current Month, OK For Watch List**}											
\multicolumn{13}{c}{**Mixed Data In Risk/Rwrd, Chart, And Technical Indicators, OK For Watch List**}											
DHX	Dice Holdings Inc	Other	16.84	Y	N	Y	Y	Y	?	?	N	Price @20 EMA / MACD - ▼ / STO - ▲
VIV	Vivo Participacoes A	Other	40.62	Y	N	Y	Y	n/a	?	?	N	Price @ 20 EMA / MACD - ▼ / STO - ▲
A	Agilent Technologies	Other	52.58	Y	N	Y	Y	Y	?	?	N	MACD - ▼ / STO - ▲
AMMD	American Med Systm	Other	29.89	Y	N	Y	Y	Y	?	?	N	MACD - ▼ / STO - ▲
AVGO	Avago Technologies	Other	34.89	Y	N	Y	Y	n/a	Y	?	N	MACD - ▲ / STO - ▼
CERN	Cerner Corp	Other	119.28	Y	N	Y	Y	Y	Y	?	N	MACD - ▲ / STO - ▼
CHSI	Catalyst Health	18	64.18	Y	N	Y	Y	Y	Y	?	N	MACD - ▲ / STO - ▼
COH	Coach Inc	Other	59.99	Y	N	Y	Y	Y	Y	?	N	MACD - ▲ / STO - ▼
CROX	Crocs Inc	Other	22.20	Y	N	Y	Y	Y	Y	?	N	MACD - ▲ / STO - ▼
EL	Estee Lauder Cos Cl A	Other	100.17	Y	N	Y	Y	Y	Y	?	N	MACD - ▲ / STO - ▼
FEIC	F E I Co	Other	39.50	Y	N	Y	Y	Y	Y	?	N	MACD - ▲ / STO - ▼
HLF	Herbalife Ltd	11	106.75	Y	N	Y	Y	n/a	Y	?	N	MACD - ▲ / STO - ▼
HS	Healthspring Inc	14	43.44	Y	N	Y	Y	Y	Y	?	N	MACD - ▲ / STO - ▼
HUM	Humana Inc	41	78.33	Y	N	Y	Y	Y	Y	?	N	MACD - ▲ / STO - ▼
ICON	Iconix Brand Group I	Other	24.52	Y	N	Y	Y	Y	Y	?	N	MACD - ▲ / STO - ▼
ILMN	Illumina Inc	24	76.26	Y	N	Y	Y	Y	Y	?	N	MACD - ▲ / STO - ▼

Figure 35- BCI Premium Report-The Weekly Stock Screen and Watch List

The chart information is found in the red rectangle and the commentary in the blue rectangle. We will be discussing this report in more detail in the next chapter and throughout the book.

Conclusion:

Technical analysis is a critical tool covered call writers utilize in our investment determinations. It paints a picture as to what the institutional investors are doing regarding a particular security. It should be used in conjunction with each other in addition to other factors such as fundamental analysis, market tone, earnings report dates and other screens, as described earlier in this book (and in my first book, *Cashing in on Covered Calls*).

Related Information

Technical Market Theories:
More Tools for the Technical Analyst

Another set of tools available to the technical analyst are the numerous theories regarding market activity. They, too, reference historical patterns in the market that may signal a bullish or bearish sentiment. The purpose of this section is to present an overview of some of these theories and the rationale behind them.

The Short Interest Theory:

This theory states that a larger short interest is the predecessor of an increase in the price of a stock. A *short sale* is the sale of a stock not owned by the seller. An investor who sells a security short borrows that security from a broker and then sells the borrowed security without having ever actually owned the same. The short-seller must eventually buy the security back, or "close" the open short position. In a short sale, the seller anticipates a decline in equity value and realizes a profit by covering (buying back) the short sale, assuming the price of the security declines after the stock is sold short. To the contrary, the short-seller loses money if the price of the security has risen at the time he closes his position.

Short interest is the number of shares sold short that have yet to be covered. As noted, shares ultimately will need to be purchased after they are sold short to cover the short position. Some short sellers who fear a rise in the price of a short security may cover their positions sooner than anticipated or suddenly as bullish news regarding the underlying security is perceived. This is called a *short squeeze*. A rising short interest is considered a bullish indicator.

Odd Lot Theory:

This is the ultimate insult to Blue Collar Investors all over the world! This theory is based on the assumption that the small (retail) investors are always wrong (bring it on!). Since these investors usually buy and sell in odd-lot amounts (less than 100 shares) and have low risk-tolerance (the theory continues), they tend to buy high and sell low. A bullish signal is when odd-lot sell orders increase relative to odd-lot buy orders.

The Advance-Decline Theory:

Also called the *Breadth of Market Theory*, this theory states that the market direction can be determined by the number of stocks that have increased in price compared to those that have decreased in value. It is considered bullish if more shares are advancing than declining.

The Dow Theory:

This theory states that the market is in an upward trend if one of the averages (industrial or transportation) advances above a previous significant high, and is accompanied by a similar advance in the other. A major trend is identified only when BOTH the Dow Industrial and Dow Transportation Averages reach a new high or a new low. Without this confirmation, the market will return to its previous trading pattern.

Free sites to locate information:

1- Advance Decline:

www.marketinout.com/chart/market.php?breadth=advance-decline-line

2- Short Interest:

www.finance.yahoo.com/
Type in ticker and "get quote". On right side of page, click on "more key statistics"

3- Dow Industrial Average:

https://money.cnn.com/data/markets/dow

4- Dow Transportation Average:

https://money.cnn.com/data/markets/dowtrans

***See Appendix XI for an overview chart of technical analysis

Test your knowledge of key points

1- The simplest chart form which connects a series of closing prices is called a _____.

2- Candlestick charts with a body in white or green signifies that the price_____.

3- Bar charts give the following four pieces of information: _____. _____.

4- Technical indicators that identify but do not predict trends are called _____.

5- Moving averages can serve both as support and _____.

6- An ideal price chart as it relates to moving averages in the BCI system has the following three features: _____.

7- The technical indicator that subtracts a long term from a short term moving average is called the _____.

8- The subtraction of the trigger (9-d EMA) from the MACD will result in the   .

9- The stochastic oscillator is considered overbought if it moves above the _____ and oversold if it dips below the _____.

10- All technical indicators are more significant if they occur on _____ volume.

11- Weakening volume may signify a _____ reversal.

12- A chart showing ALL positive technical indicators would favor the sale of a _____ strike if all other system criteria are met.

Answers:

1- Line chart

2- Closed higher than it opened

3- OHLC- open, high, low, and close

4- Moving averages

5- Resistance

6- Uptrending moving averages; the 20-d EMA above the 100-d EMA; price bars at or above the 20-d EMA

7- MACD or moving average convergence divergence

8- MACD histogram

9- 80%; 20%

10- High

11- Price or trend

12- Out-of-the-money

Chapter 5

Portfolio Management

Chapter outline

1- What is portfolio management?

2- Forming watchlists of stocks and options

3- Profit and loss spreadsheet and the Schedule D of the "Elite Calculator" (see chapter 6)

4 The BCI Premium Report

5- Modern Portfolio Theory

I am a big believer in setting yourself up for success. This is accomplished through education, motivation, commitment and *organization.* Investors reading this book and others are definitely seeking education, and are both motivated and committed. However, without organization the process will become difficult and perhaps unmanageable. As we create a watchlist of the greatest performing stocks in the greatest performing industries and then buy certain equities and sell their associated options, it becomes essential to set up organized lists of accurate information. Enter *portfolio management.*

What is portfolio management?

Portfolio Management is the art and science of making decisions about investment mix and rules, as we coordinate investments to our goals, asset allocation and balancing risk versus returns. The lists required include:

- Stocks on our watchlist
- Stocks selected and purchased for our portfolio that month
- Options sold in a given contract cycle
- Spreadsheet of options sold showing profits (losses)

Having these organized lists will allow us to do the following in a time efficient and accurate manner:

- Select the most appropriate covered call candidates
- Prepare for potential exit strategy executions
- Monitor our stock and option positions
- Calculate and monitor the success of our investments

Forming watchlists of stocks and options

Watchlists of the greatest stocks and stocks purchased

We have learned to pick the greatest performing stocks in the stock universe by using the core fundamental and technical screens discussed in Chapters 3 and 4. As noted above, it is imperative that we keep an organized list of these securities, as well as the corresponding call options we sell, so that our positions can be properly managed.

Figure 36 demonstrates an organized list of stocks and their current prices, both highlighted in yellow. You can also enter the original transaction price if these were also the actual list of stocks purchased for a particular contract cycle. These lists are created by entering the ticker symbols of all selected stocks and options when creating a portfolio.

Portfolio Management | 89

SYMBOL	TRANS TYPE	CURRENT SHARES	TRANS PRICE	INITIAL VALUE*	CURRENT PRICE	CURRENT VALUE	TODAY'S CHANGE	TODAY% CHANGE
ANR	Long	0.00	0.00	0.00	35.63	0.00	-0.20	-0.56%
ARST	Long	0.00	0.00	0.00	21.56	0.00	-0.08	-0.37%
ATHR	Long	0.00	0.00	0.00	33.86	0.00	+0.28	+0.83%
BCSI	Long	0.00	0.00	0.00	27.62	0.00	+0.24	+0.88%
BUCY	Long	0.00	0.00	0.00	48.64	0.00	-1.42	-2.84%
CMG	Long	0.00	0.00	0.00	138.83	0.00	+3.06	+2.25%
CTSH	Long	0.00	0.00	0.00	48.80	0.00	-0.69	-1.39%
CTXS	Long	0.00	0.00	0.00	44.53	0.00	-0.14	-0.31%
DECK	Long	0.00	0.00	0.00	134.28	0.00	+0.58	+0.43%
DLB	Long	0.00	0.00	0.00	62.25	0.00	+0.29	+0.47%
EL	Long	0.00	0.00	0.00	58.78	0.00	-0.12	-0.20%
EZPW	Long	0.00	0.00	0.00	18.05	0.00	+0.01	+0.06%
FFIV	Long	0.00	0.00	0.00	68.00	0.00	+1.10	+1.64%
GIL	Long	0.00	0.00	0.00	28.05	0.00	-0.05	-0.18%
GMCR	Long	0.00	0.00	0.00	23.62	0.00	+0.30	+1.29%
HAS	Long	0.00	0.00	0.00	39.60	0.00	+0.07	+0.18%

Figure 36- Watchlist of stocks or stocks purchased

We now have a list of stocks to choose from (watchlist) or stocks actually purchased and have written covered calls for.

Watchlist of the options sold in a particular contract cycle:

SYMBOL	TRANS TYPE	CURRENT SHARES	TRANS PRICE	INITIAL VALUE*	CURRENT PRICE	CURRENT VALUE	TODAY'S CHANGE	TODAY% CHANGE
APKT_06	Long	0.00	0.00	0.00	2.83	0.00	+0.82	+41.25%
CSTR_06	Long	0.00	0.00	0.00	3.50	0.00	+0.85	+32.08%
CVLT_06	Long	0.00	0.00	0.00	0.45	0.00	-0.02	-5.26%
LOPE_06	Long	0.00	0.00	0.00	1.93	0.00	+0.05	+2.67%
UHS_06	Long	0.00	0.00	0.00	3.00	0.00	-0.02	-0.83%
UHS_06	Long	0.00	0.00	0.00	0.72	0.00	-0.15	-17.14%
			0.00		0.00	0.00	+0.00*	+0.00%*

Figure 37- Watchlist of options sold

The option symbols and current market values are highlighted in yellow. Transaction prices can also be included. When option values drop, we may want to initiate an exit strategy to generate additional income or reduce losses. This will be addressed later in the book. By simply clicking on this watchlist of options we can readily view option values and decide whether an exit strategy should be considered.

Spreadsheet of options sold with profits (losses)

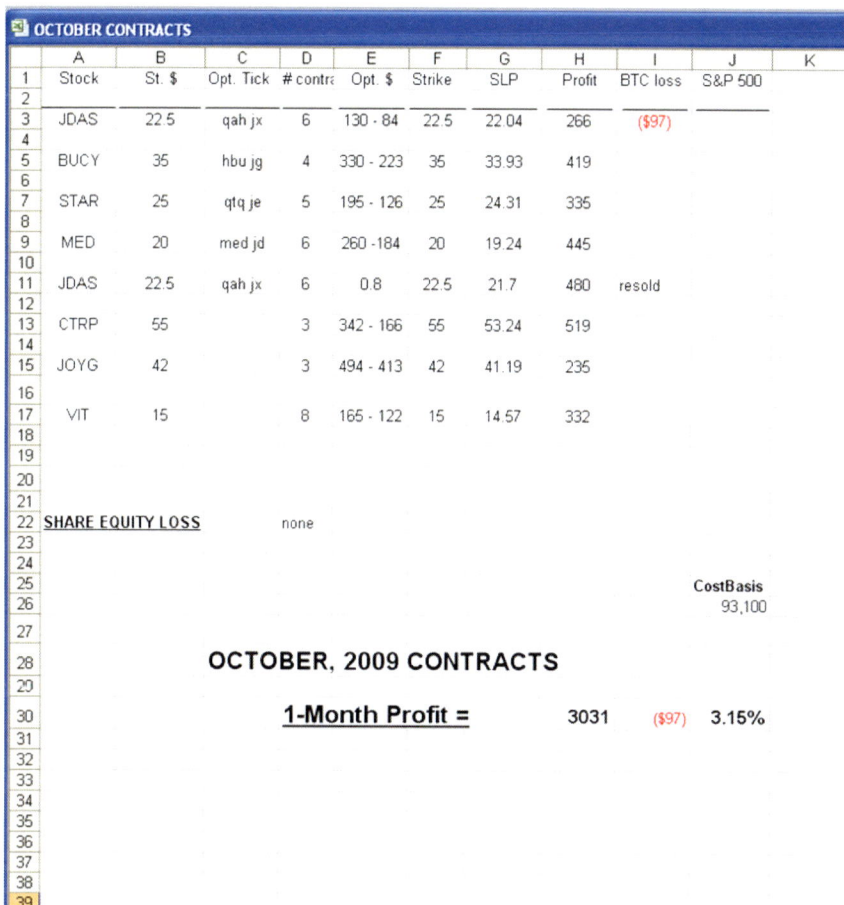

Figure 38- Spreadsheet of options sold with profits (losses)

A- Stock ticker
B- Purchase price of stock (includes intrinsic value of option which is deducted from the stock price for in-the-money strikes)
C- Option ticker (original format is shown)
D- # contracts sold
E- Premium per contract minus intrinsic value of option
F- Strike price of option sold
G- Breakeven
H- Profit generated by original option sale
I- Buy-to-close (B-T-C) cost for exit strategies

The information on the spreadsheet in figure 38 is entered and calculated manually or you can use the Schedule D of the Elite Calculator discussed in the next chapter.

Schedule D of the Elite Calculator:

The six tabs of the Schedule D found in the elite version of the Ellman Calculator can be used to calculate your final returns. This spreadsheet contains the mathematical formulas that will calculate final returns in all possible scenarios. See chapter six for detailed information.

The BCI Premium Report

Premium members of the Blue Collar Investor Corp receive a report each week where my team screens a database of thousands of stocks and exchange-traded funds looking for the best one-month covered call write candidates. Stocks are screened both fundamentally and technically (using all the screens detailed in chapters 3 and 4) and a watchlist, called the *running list*, is generated. This will reduce the time and effort required for our members although all final decisions and management of positions is still required. Figure 39 will show you the first page of the screening process. The "Weekly Stock Screen" portion of the report faithfully follows the Blue Collar Investor stock selection process. Note the thick blue area towards the top categorizes the screens discussed earlier in this book:

Portfolio Management | 93

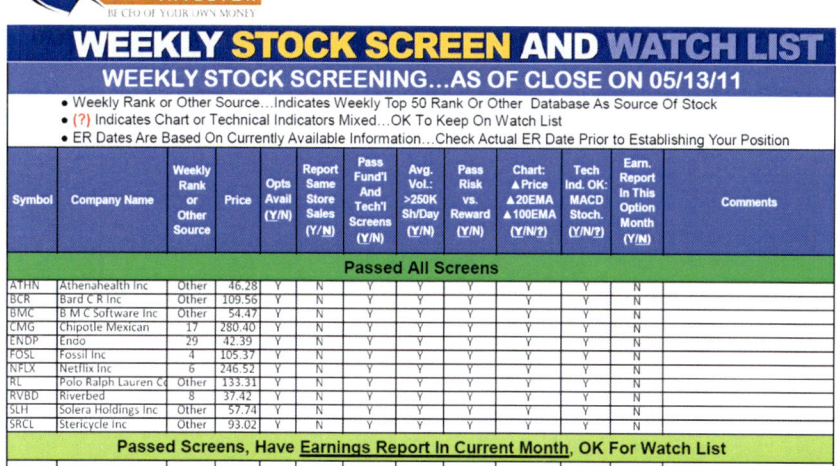

Figure 39 - Premium report- stock screen

The end of the report generates your watchlist of the greatest performing stocks in the greatest performing industries. We call it the "running list" because it is constantly being re-screened and updated to provide the most recent information. Figure 40 is one such running list:

► For Diversification, Experts Say Portfolio Should Have Stocks That Are From A Minimum Of Five Different Industry Segments
► ▇ Indicates Stock that has been on "Running List" in the past but failed screening in current week

Prev. Expiry Month 06/18/10	Current Month				Running List	Next ER Date	Industry Segment	Segment Rank	Beta	Comments
	Week 1 06/25/10	Week 2 07/02/10	Week 3 07/09/10	Week 4 07/16/10	Week 5					
ABV	ABV	CVLT	ABV		ALTR (2)	07/14/10	Chips	A/A	1.19	
AKAM	**ABX**	CYD	AKAM		XLNX (1)	07/15/10	Chips	A	1.10	
APKT	AKAM	EPB	ALTR		TPX (1)	07/16/10	Consumer	C/C	1.69	
BVN	ALTR	HSP	APKT		HAS (7)	07/20/10	Consumer	A/A	0.76	
CLR	APKT	ROVI	AZO		VLTR (5)	07/20/10	Chips	A/A	1.50	
CMG	AZO	SLH	BVN		SY (3)	07/21/10	Comp Sftwr	A/A	0.70	
CRM	BVN		CRM		CMG (13)	07/22/10	Retail	A/A	0.98	
CXO	CLR		**CTSH**		CRUS	07/22/10	Chips	A/A	1.57	
DECK	CMG		CVLT		FFIV (16)	07/22/10	Internet	A/A	1.36	
DGIT	CXO		EGO		SWKS (6)	07/22/10	Semicondtr	C/C	1.49	
DISCA	CYD		EPB		TSCO (2)	07/22/10	Retail	B/B	0.98	
FFIV	DLB		**FFIV**		VMW (5)	07/22/10	Software	A/A	1.40	
GIL	EGO		HAS		WIT (1)	07/22/10	Busn Svcs	B/C	1.35	
HAS	EPB		**HLF**		DECK (4)	07/23/10	Apparel	A/A	1.39	
IAG	FFIV		HSP		LTM (6)	07/23/10	Leisure	B/B	1.92	
LULU	**GOLD**		LZ		NEM (3)	07/23/10	Mining	B/A	0.88	
LZ	HAS		NEM		NFLX (14)	07/23/10	Retail	A/A	1.09	
NEM	IAG		**NETL**		GOLD (1)	07/28/10	Miniong	A/A	1.03	
NETL	LSTZA		NFLX		SRCL (2)	07/28/10	Machine	B/B	0.63	
NFLX	**NEM**		NTAP		UA (5)	07/28/10	Apparel	C/C	1.64	
NTAP	NFLX		NVO		AKAM (5)	07/29/10	Internet	A/A	1.40	
PII	NVO		OPEN		HSP (2)	07/29/10	Medical	A/A	0.70	
PVH	PAY		PAY		NETL (3)	07/29/10	Chips	A/A	1.44	
SLW	PRGO		ROVI		WRLD (2)	07/29/10	Finance	B/C	1.30	
SWKS	ROVI		SRCL		ABX (1)	07/30/10	Mining	B/A	0.83	
TPX	SIRO		SWKS		APKT (11)	07/30/10	Telecom	B/B	1.22	
TSCO	**SLW**		VLTR		DLB (11)	07/30/10	Consumer	C/C	0.82	
UA	**SRCL**		VMW		EGO (4)	07/30/10	Mining	B/A	1.15	
VLTR	SWKS		**WPZ**		LZ (4)	07/30/10	Chemical	B/B	1.27	
VMW	UA		WRLD		SLW (5)	07/30/10	Mining	B/A	1.61	
WPZ	**VRX**		XEC		BVN (3)	07/31/10	Mining	B/A	1.13	
XEC	WPZ		XLNX		SIRO (1)	07/31/10	Medical	B/B	0.98	
	WRLD				CXO (2)	08/03/10	Energy	B/A	1.65	
					HLF (1)	08/03/10	Consumer	C	1.19	
					CTSH (1)	08/04/10	Busn Svcs	B	1.25	

Figure 40- Premium report – running list

Conclusion:

Organizing our lists of stocks, options, and creating a spreadsheet of options sold, will allow us to become both time efficient and increase our opportunities of achieving the very highest of returns. We are setting ourselves up for success. These lists will facilitate stocks selection, prepare us for potential exit strategy opportunities and help us track our returns.

<u>Related Information</u>

We have been discussing how to set up portfolios for covered call writing and creating lists that will allow us to access information to make the best possible decisions. We will conclude this chapter with a discussion of how many financial advisors determine the overall mix of your ENTIRE investment portfolio. I want to emphasize that this topic is only peripherally related to covered call writing but a subject that interests and benefits many Blue Collar Investors.

Modern Portfolio Theory (MPT)

You (and your spouse) nervously enter the office of your investment advisor representative with a boatload of papers and a myriad of questions. One of those questions may be, "What questions should I ask?" You sit down and then you are offered a cup of bitter coffee. Your mouth is feeling fine but somehow you feel like you're about to have a root canal! After pleasantries are exchanged, you fill out numerous forms and surveys. Questions are asked and answered, some of which seem more psychological than financial in nature. An appointment is made for a follow-up consultation.

You return a week later and a folder is handed to you with a roadmap as to how you should handle your financial future. All the information from the previous week was fed into a computer and these are the results. Well, how did that happen and why? Were names of investment securities picked out of a hat, or was there sound rationale behind this process? Enter the *Modern Portfolio Theory*.

In simplistic terms, this theory assumes that investors want the highest returns for the least amount of risk. As opposed to the older *Prudent Man Rule*, which stated that a properly constructed portfolio should have no risk (hello T-bills), the MPT assumes that risk cannot be totally avoided, but rather, can be appropriately managed. In the MPT, the portfolio in its entirety (not the individual securities within the portfolio) is evaluated. More specifically, the MPT states that holding options in an account is acceptable as long as the risk is counterbalanced by other entities within that portfolio. A risk-free portfolio will be overcome by inflation.

Three Basic Concepts of the MPT

Expected Return:

Expected return is the possible return from a portfolio under different market conditions (bullish, bearish and neutral), weighted by the likelihood that the return will occur. For example, if Portfolios A and B both have expected returns of 6%, but Portfolio A has a range of expected returns from (-)10% to +25% in different market conditions, while B has a range between 1% and 15%, wouldn't you sleep better at night with plan B? B would be considered a more optimal plan because you are getting the same return for less risk.

Standard Deviation:

This is a statistical measurement that sheds light on historical volatility. For example, a volatile stock will have a high standard deviation while the deviation of a stable blue chip stock will be lower. MPT prefers stocks and portfolios with low standard deviations. Standard deviation is a measure of the dispersion of a set of data from its mean. The more spread apart the data, the higher the deviation. Standard deviation is calculated as the square root of variance.

- Around 68% of data are within one standard deviation of the mean
- Around 95% of data are within two standard deviations of the mean
- Around 99% of data are within three standard deviations of the mean

Correlation:

This measures the degree to which investments within a portfolio are related. Assets showing a low degree of correlation produce the best long-term results. This has everything to do with proper diversification. Correlation is quantified as follows:

- 1.0 = Perfect correlation. Returns move in the same direction at the same time.

- 0 = Uncorrelated. No correlation between the returns of two securities

- -1.0 = Perfect negative correlation. Returns move in opposite directions at the same time.

Most investment advisors prefer a portfolio with a slightly negative correlation.

Constructing Optimal Portfolios:

According to the MPT, there is a series of possible portfolio mixes that are optimal, that is, they have the greatest returns for a given amount of risk. These portfolios are diversified into several asset classes including stocks, bonds and cash equivalents. When fed into the computer a graph of these optimal portfolios is produced and referred to as the *Efficient Frontier.* This is an asset pricing model that describes the relationship between expected risk and expected return for a portfolio. Let's look at such a graph below (figure 41):

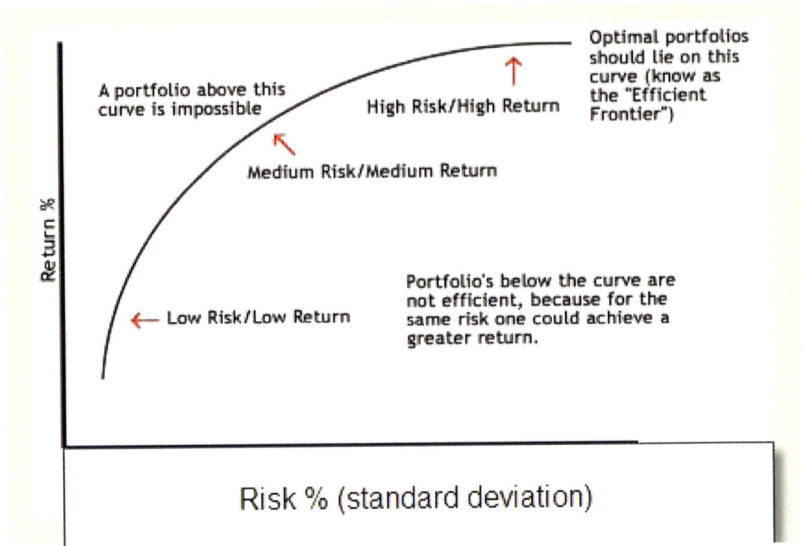

Figure 41 - Efficient frontier

As you can see, the lower the volatility (risk or the horizontal line), the lower the returns (vertical line). Based on the information you gave to your investment advisor, an appropriate portfolio can be selected for you that falls on the efficient frontier (curved line). If a portfolio falls to the right or under the EF, it is not an optimal portfolio because it would have the same expected return with a higher anticipated volatility or risk.

The mathematics is not important. However, the concept behind this MPT is. Finding a portfolio that is right for you involves locating the proper mix of securities that will give you the best chance to achieve the highest returns for the risk tolerance that meets your comfort level. There you have it....just like most root canals....painless!

Thus far, we have selected the greatest performing stocks in the greatest performing industries and placed them in organized, easily accessible lists. In essence, we have formed the foundation to launch our conservative strategy of selling covered call options. The next step in the process is to compute our potential returns, since cash generation on a monthly basis is what this is all about...it's time for calculations

Test your knowledge of key points

1- The art and science of making decisions about investment mix and rules, as we coordinate investments to our goals, asset allocation and balancing risk versus returns is called _____.

2- . The lists required for proper portfolio management include these four: _____.

3- Having these lists will facilitate the following three objectives: _____.

4- The Schedule D of the Elite Calculator can also be used as a _____ spreadsheet.

5- A portfolio optimization methodology that utilizes the mean variance of investment returns and uses the standard deviation of all returns as a measure of risk is called the _____ _____.

Answers:

1- Portfolio management

2-
- Stocks on our watchlist
- Stocks selected and purchased for our portfolio that month
- Options sold in a given contract cycle
- Spreadsheet of options sold showing profits (losses)

3-
- Selecting the most appropriate covered call candidates
- Preparing for potential exit strategy executions
- Monitoring our stock and option positions

4- Profit and loss

5- Modern Portfolio Theory

Chapter 6

Calculations

Chapter outline

1- Formulas

    Return on option (ROO)

    Downside protection of ROO

    Breakeven of total position

2- How to read an options chain

3- Strike price selection

4- The role of delta in strike selection

5- The Basic Ellman Calculator (formerly ESOC)

6- The Elite Calculator

As you begin reading this chapter, you may have noticed that although we are discussing a strategy of generating cash, not a word of calculations has yet been mentioned outside the preview example. This has to do with golden rule #2, discussed in chapter 2. To review:

You must only sell options on stocks that you would otherwise want to own. This means that you should not purchase a stock simply because it returns a high option premium. This is usually a mistake because high premium equities are extremely volatile and can enhance the degree of risk in our portfolios. The best approach is to select only the greatest performing stocks both fundamentally and technically that are also located within the greatest performing industry groups or segments. In my system, stock selection comes first before you even glance at the option premium that security will return. Bottom line: *don't get greedy*. This is a conservative strategy that can be immensely rewarding if approached properly.

Now that we have mastered the selection process, it's time to make some money! This process involves accessing information found in the option chains, selecting the most appropriate strike prices, calculating our returns and selecting the number of shares to purchase for our covered call positions. I want you to know that a lot of care and consideration went into the penning of this chapter as mathematics is a subject that incites fear and concern in many Blue Collar Investors. My goal is for you to have a thorough understanding of the rationale behind these calculations, however, the actual computations themselves will be done by a calculator that I have developed and will provide to you for FREE. So sit back and relax as you will not have to take off your shoes and start counting toes! You will simply access the information, feed it into the calculator, print out the results and make your decisions. This process will become second nature to you as you go through the steps several times. I always recommend paper (practice) trading for several months before you start actually trading your hard earned money.

Formulas

Let's start with the basic formulas we use to calculate our option returns. Keep in mind that premium returns (returns generated from selling the option) are quoted (in the option chain) in per share amounts, so we multiply a quoted option premium by 100 for the total premium of one option contract. (Remember that you also purchased 100 shares of the underlying equity prior to selling the option so that you are fully "covered"). To simplify the following discussion, we will exclude brokerage commissions from our calculations. Here are the basic equations you need to know:

Return on Option (ROO)

ROO is the percentage of profit realized from the sale of a covered call option based on the cost basis (purchase price) of the underlying stock. We use two similar, but different equations to calculate ROO, depending on whether we are selling out-of-the-money, in-the-money, or at-the-money call options.

1- % Return on option (ROO) for Out-of-the-Money and At-the-Money Call Options = (option premium x 100) / (price per share x 100)

In the preview example referenced in Chapter 1 we bought 100 shares of stock XYZ @ $48, and sold a $50 call option (i.e. the call option had a strike price of $50) for $1.50. Note that this $50 call option is out-of-the-money because the $50 strike price of the option is higher than the $48 market price of XYZ. When we sell an out-of-the-money call option, the entire option premium is time value, and thus, is considered the total profit from selling the option. Bearing in mind that we are selling an out-of-the-money call option in this example, the calculation for ROO would be as follows:

ROO = $150/$4800 = 3.1%

The formula for *in-the-money call options* is slightly different:

2- ROO for In-the-Money Call Options = time value of option premium x 100 / (price per share – intrinsic value of premium) x 100

Now don't worry, I'm going to explain this and you *will* understand the logic behind it. Let's say we buy stock XYZ for

$56, and sell a $50 call option for $8. We have sold an in-the-money call option because the strike price of the option ($50) is lower than current market value of XYZ ($56). In this scenario, we cannot justify claiming the entire $8 as profit because we will lose $6 on the sale of the stock if the option is exercised. Remember, we bought XYZ for $56, but have sold someone else the option or right to buy it from us for $50. The $8 premium consists of $6 of intrinsic value and $2 of time value. Only the $2 of time value is considered profit. So what happens to the other $6? We use this $6 to "buy down" the cost of the stock. In other words, this $6 is considered "downside protection" which protects our ROO; on paper, this $6 is used to reduce the cost basis (initial purchase price) of XYZ to $50 ($56-$6). The remaining $2, as noted, is considered the profit from the sale of the option. That $2 profit is protected as long as our shares do not depreciate by more than $6 during the one-month lifespan of the option (we sold a one month option). Let's calculate the ROO for the in-the-money option referenced at the beginning of this paragraph:

ROO = $2 x 100/ [($56 - $6) x 100] = 4%

Note: The same percentages can be achieved without multiplying by 100 but I included it in the formula to stress the fact that option contracts *almost* always consist of 100 shares of the underlying security.

A key philosophical approach to the BCI system when selling in-the-money call options is to view the intrinsic value of the option premium as downside protection for our ROO. As discussed above, we only view the time value portion of our option premium as profit. However, the intrinsic value portion of an in-the-money-option protects this profit. The following formulas summarize this philosophical point:

3- Cost basis for calculating ROO for In-the-Money Call Options

= price per share - intrinsic value of option premium

In the preceding example, the cost basis for our ROO calculation would be $56-$6=$50. This means that our one-month profit of $2 (or 4% ROO) is protected as long as the price of the underlying security does not decline under $50 during the life of the option.

Downside Protection of ROO (%) = intrinsic value of option premium / price per share

In percentage terms, our *downside protection* of ROO (%) for this same example is $6 / $56 (or $600/$5600) = 10.7%. This figure represents % of downside protection <u>for the premium profit</u> or ROO. In other words, our 4%, one-month profit is protected as long as our shares do not depreciate by more than 10.7% in the next month (or during the life of the option contract). If the stock does not decline in value by more than 10.7%, we still receive the full $2 one-month profit from the call option that was sold.

It is important to realize that our downside protection is different from the breakeven point, which is the price you paid for the stock minus the <u>total</u> option premium:

4- Breakeven Point=Purchase Price of Stock – Total Option Premium

More specifically, the breakeven point is the point where you will not lose money on your *total investment*, but also will not capture the time value profit from selling the option. Thus, using the same in-the-money example cited above, the breakeven point is $56 - $8 = $48. In other words, in order for you to breakeven (or better) for the transaction at issue (purchased 100 shares of XYZ for $56/share and sold the in-the-money $50 call for $8) the price of XYZ must remain at or above $48 by contract expiration. As noted, distinguishing downside protection of ROO from breakeven is a philosophical approach that forms the basis for the BCI system, which is predicated upon cash generation and the protection of those profits.

Downside protection in connection with the sale of in-the-money call options will be discussed in further detail later in this chapter. Furthermore, additional formulas will be provided when we discuss exit strategies in Chapter 10. For now, simply familiarize yourself with the above-referenced formulas, bearing in mind that these are the basic calculations you will be utilizing when choosing your three strike price choices (i.e. in-the-money; out-of-the-money; and at-the-money). Of course, the Ellman Calculator will do all the mathematics for you!

How to read an option chain

So how much cash can we generate selling options on the stocks that have passed our fundamental and technical screens? The answer lies in the *option chain*. This is a list that quotes option prices for a given security. For each underlying security, the option chain lists the various strike prices, option premiums, expiration dates and whether it is a call or put option. These lists can be found through your online discount brokerage or through various free websites such as:

www.finance.yahoo.com
www.cnbc.com

The first time I looked at an option chain it reminded me of the first examination I took in Organic Chemistry.....I thought I was prepared for it but boy was I wrong! However, like most challenges (except perhaps organic chemistry) these hurdles can be overcome by simply doing your due-diligence and via repetition. For many experienced cover call writers, the knowledge gleaned from the option chain has become second nature and a source of information for our lucrative returns. Knowing how to read an option chain is an essential

Calculations | 107

prerequisite to writing covered calls or any form of options trading.

Definition of an option chain:

An option chain is a method of quoting option prices through a list of all options for a given underlying security. The option chain reveals the various strike prices, expiration dates and identifies them as calls or puts.

Figure 42 shows what a typical option chain looks like for June 2010 expiration call options only for Mercadolibre, Inc. (NASDAQ: MELI)

View By Expiration: **Jun 10** | Jul 10 | Sep 10 | Dec 10 | Jan 11 | Jan 12

CALL OPTIONS — Expire at close Friday, June 18, 2010

Strike	Symbol	Last	Chg	Bid	Ask	Vol	Open Int
22.50	MELI100619C00022500	24.80	0.00	22.90	25.30	0	1
30.00	MELI100619C00030000	18.60	0.00	15.60	17.90	0	216
35.00	MELI100619C00035000	15.22	0.00	10.80	13.10	0	189
40.00	MELI100619C00040000	7.74	0.00	6.40	8.50	0	132
42.50	MELI100619C00042500	5.50	↓ 1.70	5.10	6.40	12	290
45.00	MELI100619C00045000	3.70	↓ 0.60	4.20	4.50	2	355
47.50	MELI100619C00047500	2.00	↓ 0.73	2.70	2.95	10	332
50.00	MELI100619C00050000	1.60	↑ 0.10	1.50	1.75	358	1,636
52.50	MELI100619C00052500	0.70	↓ 0.40	0.80	1.00	1	429
55.00	MELI100619C00055000	0.38	↓ 0.02	0.35	0.45	215	863
57.50	MELI100619C00057500	0.36	0.00	0.15	0.30	0	119
60.00	MELI100619C00060000	0.05	↓ 0.20	0.05	0.15	252	531
65.00	MELI100619C00065000	0.21	0.00	N/A	0.10	0	330
70.00	MELI100619C00070000	0.15	0.00	N/A	0.10	0	158
75.00	MELI100619C00075000	0.05	0.00	N/A	0.05	0	215
80.00	MELI100619C00080000	0.10	0.00	N/A	0.05	0	114

Figure 42- The Option Chain

The components of the option chain (columns from left to right):

1- **Strike price**- Also called the exercise price. For call options, this is the price at which the option holder (buyer) can purchase the underlying security. The strike price usually trades in increments of $2.50 when under $25, in $5 increments when above $25, and in $10 increments for strike prices above $200. Some stocks and exchange-traded funds trade in $1 increments and others in $2.50 increments (above $25) as a result of a stock split (as is the case in Figure 42). Additional exceptions are discussed later in this book

2- **Symbol**- These are the ticker symbols for options. They identify the underlying equity, the strike price, the expiration date and identify it as a call or put option. The option ticker symbol will always contain the ticker of the underlying security (in the above chart "MELI").

3- **Last**- This is the price at which the last trade of that particular option was executed. For example, in Figure 42, the last trade for $50 strike was executed @ $1.60.

4- **Change**- This column indicates how much the price of the option has risen or fallen from yesterday's closing price. In Figure 42, the $50 strike had increased $0.10 from the prior day's closing price at the time the information in the chart was obtained.

5- **Bid**- The price at which the market makers are willing to buy your option, or in other words, the price you will receive when you sell an option (sell at the *bid,* the lower price).

6- **Ask**- The price at which market makers are willing to sell the option, or in other words, the price you will pay when you buy an option (buy at the *ask*, the higher price).

7- **Volume (Vol)** - The number of contracts traded for that option *during that trading day*. The higher this daily volume, the more "liquid" this option contract becomes vis a vis options with a lower daily volume. However, because each trading day brings a new daily volume, volume is not the most accurate measure of option liquidity. Furthermore, obtaining historical daily volume information for options is much more difficult than obtaining historical daily volume information for stocks.

8- **Open interest**- The open interest of an option contract is the number of outstanding options of that particular option which currently have not been closed out or exercised. For example, if the open interest for a particular call option is 1,000, this means that there are currently 1,000 active options that have either not been exercised or sold. Because an option is simply a contract, more contracts can be created every day, however the current open interest figure allows investors to gauge the extent of interest that investors have in a particular option contract. It is a cumulative figure, not a daily statistic as with volume. The higher the open interest, the more liquid the option contract is considered.

Example of using option chain to calculate ROO

Now that we are familiar with primary components of an option chain, let's view an example of how we can use the option chain to calculate ROO or time value, using the option chain in Figure 42 for our example.

- Assume we buy 100 shares of MELI @ $50. Our cost basis for the purchase of the underlying equity is thus $50/share for a $5,000 total investment.

- Since we now own 100 shares of MELI, we can sell 1 call option (which equals 100 shares) of MELI in order to be "covered" (i.e. we own 100 shares of MELI, and sell someone else the right to buy 100 shares of MELI from us). For this example, assume we sell one $50 strike (one MELI call option with a strike price of $50) for $1.50. Remember, we always sell at the bid, not at the ask.

- We are selling an at-the-money option because current price of MELI is equal to the strike price of the option. Accordingly, the $1.50 option premium we receive consists only of time value (it does not have any intrinsic value), and as such, the entire $1.50 option premium is considered profit.

- Our initial 1- month option return (ROO) is 150/5000 = 3% = 36% annualized

Strike price selection

A few years ago I read an article authored by an options broker working for one of the larger brokerage houses. He did a study of the returns gleaned from covered call writing versus those from stock index funds. An *index fund* is a mutual fund that mirrors a particular segment of the market. For example, the Vanguard "0040" fund mirrors the S&P 500. In his investigation, he sold only out-of-the-money (O-T-M) strikes on the S&P 500 index over a 1-year period. He compared these results to the returns garnered from investing an equal amount of money in an S&P 500 index fund. At the end of the 1-year period, the ROI (returns on investment) were nearly the same. His conclusion was: why sell covered call options when you can get the same returns by investing in a stock index fund.

I remember smiling to myself but also being shocked that an expert would write about and execute such an obviously flawed study. Here are some of the major concepts ignored in his research (or lack thereof):

- There was no stock selection process; poorly performing stocks were allowed to be part of his study....why?
- There were no exit strategies employed. This is a key element to all investment strategies....why not?
- Options were sold through earnings reports. Way too risky (as we will soon learn). Why take the chance?
- Only O-T-M strikes were sold, a common *rookie mistake* in selling covered call options. A discussion of strike selection is pertinent to successful covered call writing.

Out-Of-The-Money (O-T-M) Strike Prices

There is a reason why these are popular strikes for many investors. When an option is sold, we generate an option premium that is ours to keep no matter what happens to the stock or whether that option is ultimately exercised or not (remember, the risk is in the stock, not the option). In the case of an O-T-M strike, we have an opportunity to make additional profit on stock appreciation; however, we have no downside protection of the premium. For example, assume we buy 100 shares of XYZ @ $28 and sell a $30 call option. Because the option holder has the right to buy our 100 shares of XYZ at $30 per share, he or she will not exercise the call option until the price of XYX increases to $30 or more. If and when the option is exercised, we would then be obligated to sell 100 shares XYZ at $30 per share. Thus, if exercised, we can generate an additional $2 per share or $200 per contract on the sale of the stock (bought at $28, sold at $30). When we sell at-the-money or in-the-money strikes, there is NO CHANCE of such additional profits (additional capital can be made via exit strategies, which is a point more fully addressed in chapter 10). So from a profit potential perspective, O-T-M strikes are more attractive. Selling O-T-M strikes is the most bullish approach when selling covered call options. That said, it should also be noted that while Blue Collar Investors love profit, we also understand that profit is only a part of a bigger picture. Specifically, we must ensure we never ignore risk and focus solely on profits. Indeed, the failure to account for risk in selecting which call options to sell is a major error that many covered call writers are guilty of, and in my view, is a key fact that separates the men (women) from the boys (girls).

In-The-Money (I-T-M) Strike Prices

If we buy 100 shares of XYZ for $32 and sell a $30 call, we have sold an I-T-M call option because the strike price of the call option ($30) is lower than current price of XYZ ($32). The sale of this call option obligates us to sell 100 shares of XYZ for $30/share (or $3,000 in total) if the option is exercised. Should XYZ increase in price from $32 to $40, we make no additional income due to our obligation to sell our shares @ $30. The option premium we receive from the sale of this option has $2 of intrinsic value ($32 − $30). The remainder of the option premium is solely time value, which represents our true profit (ROO). Thus, if we received $3.50 in total option premium from the sale of the $30 call option, the $3.50 premium we receive consists of $2 of intrinsic value and $1.50 ($3.50-$2) of time value. Because our true profit is represented by time value only, in this example we generated an option profit of $1.50/share or $150 per contract, which represents a 5% ROO (the $2 intrinsic value "buys down" our cost basis to $30) per share).

As we previously discussed, although the $2 additional premium of intrinsic value we received from the I-T-M strike in the example above is not considered profit, it does provide downside protection for our profit or ROO. Referring to the example in the preceding paragraph, we use the $2 of intrinsic value to "buy down" or lower the initial purchase price (cost basis) of the XYZ shares. Thus, we have $2 per share, or $200 per contract, of downside protection for our ROO. This $200 per contract represents 6.3% of downside protection ($2/$32). In other words, we are guaranteed a 5% one-month return as long as the price of XYZ does not decline by more than 6.3%. In terms of a specific price point (ROO protection price point), it can alternatively be stated that our 5% profit is fully protected as long as our shares do not decline below $30.

Our breakeven point (which we know is *not* the same as the downside protection for our ROO) is $28.50 ($32-$3.50). In other words, if XYZ declines to, but not below, $28.50, we will not lose money on our total investment of $32 per share, or $3200 per contract. However, at this price point, we also will not capture the time value profit from selling the option premium. If the stock declines below $30 but remains above $28.50 a profit will be generated, but a smaller one than the initial $1.50 or 5%. In the BCI system, our primary focus is on the ROO protection price point, not the breakeven point. In other words, we choose to view our strategy as one focused on protecting the profits from our investment, not on ensuring a breakeven on our initial investment!

Factors that determine which strike to sell

1- *Your risk tolerance:* If you can't sleep at night when your portfolio value declines, opt for the I-T-M strikes that offer more downside protection. However, you need to accept the possibility that the shares may appreciate.

2- *Market Tone*: In an uptrending and stable market environment, O-T-M strikes make sense in order to take advantage of share appreciation. In volatile or bearish markets, I-T-M strikes make more sense.

3- *Technical Analysis*: The more bullish the chart pattern of a stock, the more likely I am to sell an O-T-M strike. This would involve an uptrending moving average with all confirming indicators (bullish MACD and stochastic signals along with strong volume confirmation).

Laddering of Strike Prices

Laddering is an investment technique whereby investors purchase multiple financial products with different maturity dates. For example, when I purchase bonds (boring!!!!), I may buy 1,2,3,4 and 5 year maturations. This will protect me from interest rate risk. I have borrowed the term laddering and applied it to strike price selection in connection with covered call writing. Each month, I will try to have a mix of I-T-M, A-T-M and O-T-M strikes. I may use different strikes for the same stock. For example, if I sell five contracts for company XYZ, I may sell three I-T-M strikes and two O-T-M strikes. In a favorable market environment, I will lean towards more O-T-M. In a volatile or declining market, I tend to sell more I-T-M strikes. Accordingly, laddering is another tool we can use to throw the odds of consistently earning profits in our favor. Though there are no guarantees in investing, laddering is another smart, sophisticated approach to covered call writing that few others even think about, much less actually employ.

Conclusion

In determining the best strike price to utilize for covered call writing, we must factor in several parameters (the three factors discussed above). By doing so, we will increase our chances to maximize the profits that this wonderful strategy will provide for us. If someone brazenly confronts you with the assertion that covered call writing cannot outperform index funds, ask this person what fundamentals he looks at prior to purchasing securities in his portfolio; ask him what forms of technical analysis he employs to ensure these securities are the right choices; ask him about market tone, risk tolerance, or the laddering of strikes; ask him about exit strategy utilization; ask him about earnings report avoidance. Then watch him walk quietly away!

More on the I-T-M strike

The principles behind selling the in-the-money strike

Successful covered call writing does not entail selecting an obvious choice based on a magical formula that can be employed in every situation. There are many factors to incorporate into our investment decisions, and no two scenarios are precisely the same. We can, however, use the Blue Collar Investor mission statement, in addition to our own common sense, to incorporate sound fundamental and technical principles to make informed conclusions and intelligent decisions. Think of yourself as the artist who incorporates his well-thought-out strokes into an eventual masterpiece. How many Picassos are created with a paint-by-the-numbers kit?

When to Use an I-T-M Strike

I view an I-T-M strike as an *option with an insurance policy*. Although this is a free insurance policy (paid for by the option buyer), it does eliminate the opportunity for share appreciation. So when would the odds favor us to sell an I-T-M strike as opposed to an O-T-M or A-T-M strike? The BCI system views the following situations as favorable for the potential sale of an I-T-M strike:

1- An extremely volatile or declining market.

2- Technical analysis of the stock demonstrates mixed indicators.

3- An uptrending but volatile chart pattern (the Scouter Rating will eliminate many of these volatile patterns).

4- Part of my laddering of strikes procedure: even in normal markets I will incorporate some I-T-M strikes as a way to diversify strikes. For example, even in a bull market my portfolio may consist of 10% - 20% in-the-money strikes.

Real-life example- PZZA: Real-life Example of the strike selection process

Here is an example of the thought process that goes into strike selection for our option sales:

Papa John's International, Inc. (NASDAQ:PZZA) is a stock with no upcoming earnings report. The technical indicators (Moving averages, MACD, stochastic oscillator and volume) recently turned positive after a positive earnings report (see recent volume spike circled in red on the right side of the chart below (Figure 43) :

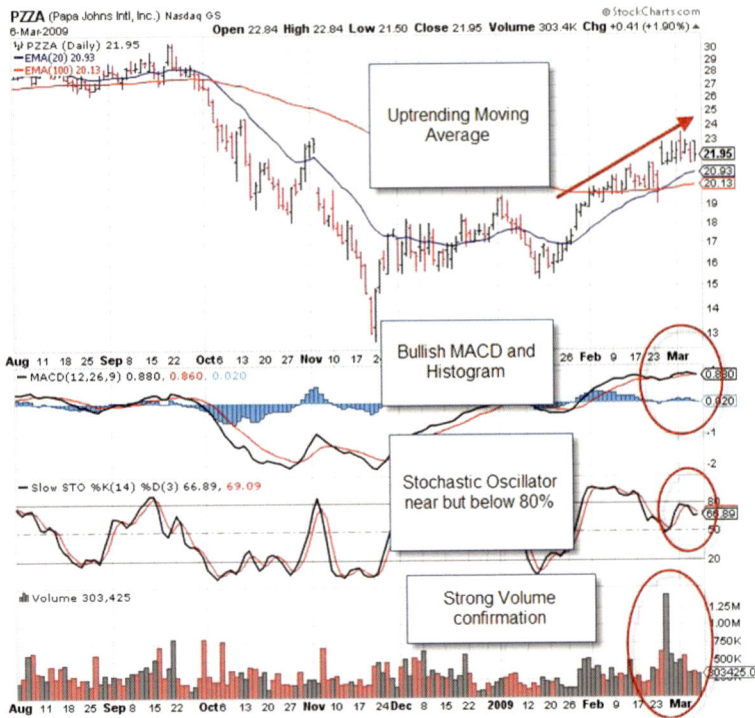

Figure 43- PZZA as of 3-6-09

The current market value of PZZA is $21.95, which is between the I-T-M $20 strike and the O-T-M $22.50 strike prices referenced on PZZA's option chain. The stock technicals are positive (as seen in chart 43)) but the market tone was volatile (The CBOE volatility index was above 50 and the S&P 500 was just bouncing off a multi-year low) at the time of this chart. Those with low risk-tolerance (I'm guilty as charged) may opt for the $20 I-T-M call. Let's work out the calculations. Since there were only two weeks remaining until the March options expire, let's look at the April calls:

1- *Out-of-the-money strike:*

- Buy 100 shares of PZZA @ $21.95 per share ($2195 total investment)

- Sell one $22.50 call option @ $1.25 ($125 total option

premium received)

- ROO = 5.7% six week return ($125 / $2195), or 49% annualized

- Upside potential (appreciation of $21.95 purchase price to $22.50 strike price) is 2.5% ($55 / $2195)

- There is no downside protection (of the option profit) because this is an O-T-M call option

2- *In-the-money strike*:

- Buy 100 shares of PZZA @ $21.95 per share ($2195 total investment)

- Sell one $20 call option @ $2.60 ($260 total option premium received, $195 of which is intrinsic value, and $65 which is time value)

- ROO = 3.3% six-week return (65) / [(21.95 − 1.95], or 28% annualized

Downside protection = 8.9% ($195 / $2195) or exists down to the price point of $20 ($21.95 - $1.95). This is our insurance policy paid for by the option buyer; our ROO is protected as long as the price of PZZA does not depreciate by more than 8.9%!, or to under $20!

As an informed Blue Collar Investor, we must decide between selling I-T-M or O-T-M call options (in this case there is no listed at-the-money or near-the-money strike. As demonstrated in the foregoing example, the more bullish approach would be to sell the O-T-M strike and receive a neat 5.7% six-week return, with the possibility of another 2.5% if the stock appreciates beyond the $22.50 strike price

The safer, more conservative investment would be the I-T-M strike wherein we generate a lower 3.3% six-week return but have a huge 8.9% downside protection insurance policy. In other words, our 3.3% return is protected as long as our stock does not depreciate in value by more than 8.9% in the next 6 weeks.

Many of our readers have asked why I often favor selling I-T-M strikes. The reason has to do with market volatility (large and frequent price movements)) and the fact that I am a conservative investor with low risk tolerance. More aggressive investors might opt for the O-T-M strike despite these volatile scenarios. There is no right or wrong decision as long as you are making an informed determination which factors in all available information.

Note: *Remember that all the calculations discussed in this chapter are done for you automatically using the Ellman Calculator, which will be discussed in detail shortly.*

More on the O-T-M strike

As we have discussed, an O-T-M call option is an option whose strike price (agreed upon sales price of the underlying equity) is HIGHER than the current market value of the stock. If we buy a stock for $28 and sell the $30 call option, that strike price is out-of-the-money.

When to use out-of-the-money strikes

Consider the O-T-M strike the most bullish of our covered call positions. The greatest benefit in using this strike is seen in situations where the stock appreciates in value from the time of purchase to expiration Friday. The closer the underlying stock price comes to the option's strike price (or surpasses it), the more money we realize; indeed, the returns in such situations can potentially be eye-popping! So let's take a common-sense look at some of the factors that would encourage us to favor the O-T-M strike:

- A bullish overall market with low volatility
- The stock chart is technically sound (most or all of the four indicators are bullish)

- The positive technical indicators are all on high volume

- The positive price momentum is continuous and not the result of a quick spike which could snap back.

- The stock's industry is also technically strong (this is screened in the SmartSelect IBD screen where the group RS rating showed a "green circle").

Advantages of the O-T-M Strike

- We can benefit from both the option premium AND the stock appreciation; one-month returns can easily end up between 10-20% if the strike price is reached.

- Less chance of assignment if we plan to hold the stock

- Time decay works in our favor since the premium consists only of time value. This means that as we approach expiration Friday, if the strike is still O-T-M, the time value (decreases as we approach expiration Friday) will approach zero.

Disadvantages of the O-T-M Strike

- Offers no downside protection (of the option profit)
- May be a poor choice for those with low risk tolerance
- The initial option premium is lower than at-the-money strikes, so the one-month return may not be impressive if the stock does not appreciate in value
- This strike has a low *delta* (amount an option value changes in relation to a $1 change in stock price. Delta is discussed in greater detail later in this chapter). If the stock drops in value, the corresponding option will not change as much, thereby making it more expensive to buy back the option for an exit strategy. *I-T-M strikes have the highest deltas.*

Conclusion

O-T-M strikes have an important place in our portfolios. Those with greater risk tolerance will tend to use these strikes more than those who are risk-averse. No matter who is writing these calls, they must be used to our greatest advantage, which entails selecting the strongest stocks in the strongest industries that have been uptrending with low implied volatility (avoid violent whipsaws on the charts). When constructing your portfolio for the month, you can mix or *ladder your strikes* using a higher percentage of these O-T-M strikes the more bullish you are on the market, and you can likewise decrease that percentage if you turn bearish. By employing these techniques, we are not guaranteeing success; however we are dramatically throwing the odds in our favor of winning more frequently than we lose.

Philosophy of strike selection- putting it all together

You're sitting at a blackjack table and looking at two eights...a sixteen, not too good! Then the dealer shows a ten and you realize that you are in BIG trouble. He probably has a twenty so you take a card and pray.

Next hand…two eights again. The dealer now shows a five (probably has fifteen) and could go "bust" (over 21) on his next hit. So you split your eights hoping to benefit from the dealer's lousy hand.

Next hand, two eights again (I guess it's time to head to the buffet!) Dealer shows a two, not great, not bad. You decide to stand pat, not take a card, not split and hope the dealer goes "bust".

The above demonstrates three identical situations which each dictated different decisions because of dissimilar surrounding circumstances. In much the same way, selecting a strike price based on differing conditions is an art and a science that must be mastered to elevate profits to the highest possible levels. In this section, we will look at an options chain and the I-T-M, A-T-M and O-T-M strikes. We will discuss in further detail the pros and cons of each of these three strikes, the role delta plays in choosing the strike we sell, and the rationale for each approach.

To begin, let's look at the options chain for HITK (Figure 44), which has three days remaining in the February option contracts:

Hi-Tech Pharmacal Co., Inc. (NASDAQ: HITK) Optionable

Last: (22.34) Chg: +1.48 (+7.07%) Open: 20.68 Avg Vol: 367,139 Volume:

Bid: 22.35 Ask: 23.23 High: 22.41 Low: 20.68 W%Chg:

After Hours Data Last: 22.36 Chg: +0.02 %Chg: +0.07% Volume: 6,458

Option Tools: Covered Calls Calculator Selling Pu

View: All Months

		Calls				Feb 10
Last	Intrinsic Value	Bid	Ask	Vol	Open Interest	Strike
7.30	7.34	7.00	7.60	0	0	15.00
4.85	4.84	4.70	5.00	0	22	17.50
2.42	2.35	2.30	2.55	97	285	20.00
0.50	0.00	0.45	0.55	55	402	22.50
0.05	0.00	0.05	0.05	0	460	25.00
0.05	0.00	0.05	0.05	3	726	30.00
0.05	0.00	N/A	0.05	0	560	35.00
0.10	0.00	N/A	0.10	0	0	40.00

Spreads for Fri Feb 19 21:00:00 PST 2010 Options: Bull Call Spreads | Bull F

		Calls				Mar 10
Last	Intrinsic Value	Bid	Ask	Vol	Open Interest	Strike
7.45	7.34	7.30	7.60	0	0	15.00
5.15	4.84	5.00	5.30	0	17	17.50
3.25	2.35	3.10	3.40	1	115	20.00
1.77	0.00	1.70	1.85	22	217	22.50
0.88	0.00	0.80	0.95	8	129	25.00
0.17	0.00	0.10	0.25	0	119	30.00
0.10	0.00	0.05	0.15	0	20	35.00

Figure 44- Strike selection for HITK

Here is the information we glean from the chain:

- HITK is currently trading at $22.34 (see red circle at top)
- March strikes to consider are $20, $22.50 and $25 (highlighted in yellow- generally we select the closest strikes to the current market value but others can be examined as well
- The I-T-M $20 strike returns $3.10 (red arrow)
- The A-T-M (near the money) strike returns $1.70 (blue arrow)
- The O-T-M $25 strike returns $.80 (green arrow)
- The only strike with intrinsic value is the $20 strike (green circle and green arrow to left)

Next, let's feed the information for the three different HITK strikes discussed directly above into the "single tab" of the Ellman Calculator, which will subsequently calculate (1) the initial return on the option or ROO; (2) the amount of downside protection of the option profit or ROO, if any; and (3) the amount of upside potential, if any. Figure 45 graphically depicts entry of this information into the Ellman Calculator:

THIS OPTION PAGE WILL ALLOW YOU TO COMPARE THE RETURNS ON UP TO FOUR DIFFERENT OPTIONS CHOICES FOR ONE STOCK PURCHASE

1) ENTER THE STOCK NAME, SYMBOL AND PRICE PER SHARE

Stock name >>	Hi-Tech
Stock symbol >>	HITK
Stock share price >>	$ 22.34

2) ENTER THE SYMBOL, STRIKE PRICE, EXPIRATION DATE AND OPTION PRICE PER SHARE

	Symbol	Strike Price	Exp Date	Price / share
Option choice #1 >>		20.00	03/19/10	3.10
Option choice #2 >>		22.50	03/19/10	1.70
Option choice #3 >>		25.00	03/19/10	0.80
Option choice #4 >>				

Figure 45 - HITK Info Fed into the Ellman Calculator

After the information obtained from the HITK options chain is entered into the blue fields depicted in Figure 45, the results will appear on the right side in the white cells, as depicted in Figure 46:

Option selected	HITK MAR 20.00	HITK MAR 22.50	HITK MAR 25.00
Today's date	02/16/10	02/16/10	02/16/10
Days to expiration	31	31	31
Cost for 100 shares of stock	$ 2,234.00	$ 2,234.00	$ 2,234.00
Proceeds from one contract	$ 310.00	$ 170.00	$ 80.00
IN / OUT OF THE MONEY	IN	OUT	OUT
INTRINSIC VALUE	$ 2.34	$ -	$ -
UPSIDE AMOUNT	$ -	$ 16.00	$ 266.00
UPSIDE POTENTIAL	0.0%	0.7%	11.9%
DOWNSIDE AMOUNT	$ 234.00	$ -	$ -
DOWNSIDE PROTECTION	10.5%	0.0%	0.0%
RETURN ON VARIOUS OUTCOMES			
Proceeds from option sale	$ 310.00	$ 170.00	$ 80.00
Amount of buy-down	$ 234.00	$ -	$ -
Actual option profit	$ 76.00	$ 170.00	$ 80.00
Option profit	$ 76.00	$ 170.00	$ 80.00
Upside profit	$ -	$ 16.00	$ 266.00
Total profit	$ 76.00	$ 186.00	$ 346.00
Cost of shares	$ 2,000.00	$ 2,234.00	$ 2,234.00
Return On Option (ROO)	3.8%	7.6%	3.6%
Return on Upside	0.0%	0.7%	11.9%
Total return	3.8%	8.3%	15.5%
Annualized return	44.7%	97.7%	182.5%

Figure 46- Calculation results for the 3 strikes for HITK

Let's review the information for each strike:

1- $20 I-T-M Strike- in RED:

- The only strike with intrinsic value: $2.34 or 10.5% downside protection of the option profit
- There is NO upside potential
- The return on the option (ROO) is 3.8%, or 44.7% annualized

2- The $22.50 A-T-M (near-the-money) Strike- in Green:

- Minimal upside potential and NO downside protection for the option premium
- The ROO = 7.6%, with the potential to reach 8.3% if the upside (upside potential) is realized
- Annualized return is 97.7%

3- The $25 O-T-M Strike- in Blue:

- 11.9% upside potential with NO downside protection of the option premium
- The ROO = 3.6%, with the potential to reach 15.5% if the upside is realized
- A possible 182.5% annualized return if upside is realized

What these calculations (and others like them) tell us

- The time value or option profit for I-T-M strikes offer lower returns than the near-the-money call but the greatest protection for the option premium.
- A-T-M (near-the-money) calls provide the highest ROO but offer little or no upside potential or downside protection <u>of the option premium.</u>
- O-T-M calls offer less option profit than the A-T-M calls,

but <u>do offer</u> the greatest total profit potential should the upside be realized or substantially realized.

The role of delta in our decisions

Delta is the amount an option value will change for every $1 change in the price of a stock. The greater the chance of the strike ending up I-T-M, the higher the delta. Delta values for call options run from 0 to 1. I-T-M strikes have deltas of 0.75 to 1.00. This means that if a stock declines in value, it will cause the option to simultaneously drop by the same amount (close to dollar for dollar), thus making a re-purchase of that option cheaper. For example, with respect to call options, a delta of 0.7 means that for every $1 the underlying stock decreases, the call option will decrease by $0.70. A-T-M strikes have deltas near 0.50%, and O-T-M strikes have deltas in the neighborhood of 0.25%. For these O-T-M strikes, if a stock drops in value, the corresponding option will not drop in step (dollar for dollar) with that equity, making it more expensive to unwind the position.

When to use each strike

- I-T-M strikes are the most conservative and the easiest to unwind because they are associated with high deltas. Use these strikes when technicals are mixed and/or the market is bearish or volatile.

- A-T-M strikes can be used when technicals are good and market conditions are positive.

- O-T-M strikes are best used when you are extremely bullish on the stock and general market conditions are favorable.

Laddering the strikes

There is no law that says you must use the same strike when you have multiple contracts. As discussed earlier, you can use some of each, favoring a particular strike based on the overall environment.

Conclusion

Whether you're sitting with a sixteen while playing blackjack or selling a call on an equity, one size DOESN'T fit all! Evaluate the stock and market parameters and then make a Blue Collar decision that has the best chance to maximize your returns.

The BASIC Ellman Calculator (aka ESOC-Ellman System Options Calculator)

Over the past few years, when giving my seminars, computing option returns has been the major challenge for Blue Collar Investors. Fortunately, that problem is no longer an issue, as we have the Ellman Calculator (formerly called the ESOC). I developed this calculator along with Owen Sargent, an outstanding accountant and seasoned stock market investor. The calculations depicted in Figure 46 provided an initial glimpse at the relative ease all our major calculations can be computed using the Basic Ellman Calculator. In this section I will provide you with more specific information about the calculator to ensure your covered call calculations are computed with ease and efficiency for the remainder of your financial career!

The *basic calculator* is set up with four tabs on the lower left portion of the first page:

- Intro tab - Highlights general information about the calculation process.

- Single tab- Allows you to evaluate returns from different strikes for the same stock.

- Multiple tab - Compares returns, upside potential, and downside protection for many stocks, all on the same page.

- What now tab - Calculates the returns for a package

transaction where an option is bought back and another is sold. It is used for expiration Friday exit strategies.

Intro Tab (Figure 47)

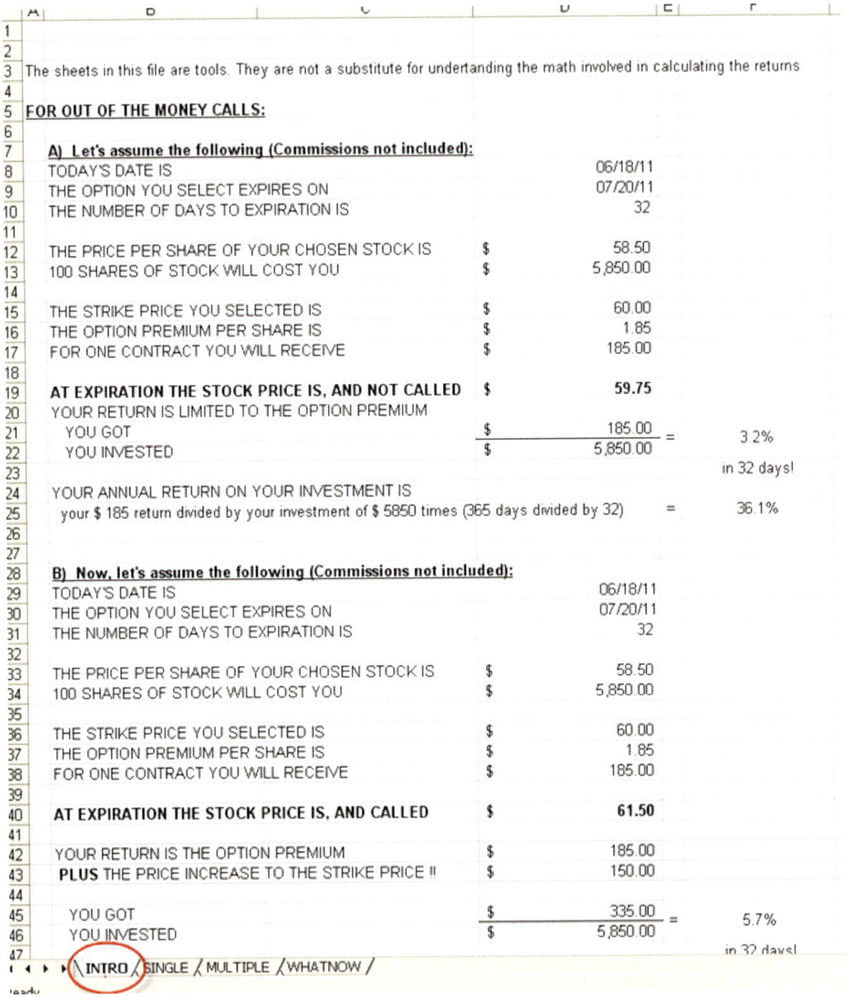

The sheets in this file are tools. They are not a substitute for undertanding the math involved in calculating the returns			
FOR OUT OF THE MONEY CALLS:			
A) Let's assume the following (Commissions not included):			
TODAY'S DATE IS		06/18/11	
THE OPTION YOU SELECT EXPIRES ON		07/20/11	
THE NUMBER OF DAYS TO EXPIRATION IS		32	
THE PRICE PER SHARE OF YOUR CHOSEN STOCK IS	$	58.50	
100 SHARES OF STOCK WILL COST YOU	$	5,850.00	
THE STRIKE PRICE YOU SELECTED IS	$	60.00	
THE OPTION PREMIUM PER SHARE IS	$	1.85	
FOR ONE CONTRACT YOU WILL RECEIVE	$	185.00	
AT EXPIRATION THE STOCK PRICE IS, AND NOT CALLED	$	59.75	
YOUR RETURN IS LIMITED TO THE OPTION PREMIUM			
YOU GOT	$	185.00	= 3.2%
YOU INVESTED	$	5,850.00	in 32 days!
YOUR ANNUAL RETURN ON YOUR INVESTMENT IS			
your $ 185 return divided by your investment of $ 5850 times (365 days divided by 32)		=	36.1%
B) Now, let's assume the following (Commissions not included):			
TODAY'S DATE IS		06/18/11	
THE OPTION YOU SELECT EXPIRES ON		07/20/11	
THE NUMBER OF DAYS TO EXPIRATION IS		32	
THE PRICE PER SHARE OF YOUR CHOSEN STOCK IS	$	58.50	
100 SHARES OF STOCK WILL COST YOU	$	5,850.00	
THE STRIKE PRICE YOU SELECTED IS	$	60.00	
THE OPTION PREMIUM PER SHARE IS	$	1.85	
FOR ONE CONTRACT YOU WILL RECEIVE	$	185.00	
AT EXPIRATION THE STOCK PRICE IS, AND CALLED	$	61.50	
YOUR RETURN IS THE OPTION PREMIUM	$	185.00	
PLUS THE PRICE INCREASE TO THE STRIKE PRICE !!	$	150.00	
YOU GOT	$	335.00	= 5.7%
YOU INVESTED	$	5,850.00	in 32 days!

INTRO / SINGLE / MULTIPLE / WHATNOW /

Figure 47- Intro Tab on the Basic Calculator

This tab gives a general explanation of the calculation process for both I-T-M and O-T-M calls.

Single Tab (Figure 48)

This tab allows you to view up to four different strike prices for the same equity.

1- Procedure for the single tab:

Simply input the information required into the blue cells on the left side of the single tab page, as shown in Figure 48. All of these figures are gleaned from the option chain:

	A	B	C	D	E
	THIS OPTION PAGE WILL ALLOW YOU TO COMPARE THE RETURNS ON UP TO FOUR DIFFERENT OPTIONS CHOICES FOR ONE STOCK PURCHASE.				
	1) ENTER THE STOCK NAME, SYMBOL AND PRICE PER SHARE				
	Stock name >>	Sandisk			
	Stock symbol >>	SNDK			
	Stock share price >>	$ 46.62			
	2) ENTER THE SYMBOL, STRIKE PRICE, EXPIRATION DATE AND OPTION PRICE PER SHARE				
		Symbol	Strike Price	Exp Date	Price / share
	Option choice #1 >>		45.00	06/18/10	3.50
	Option choice #2 >>		47.00	06/18/10	2.40
	Option choice #3 >>		50.00	06/18/10	1.15
	Option choice #4 >>				
	3) PRESS THE PRINTER ICON OR CLICK ON THE "FILE" MENU, SELECT "PRINT" AND CLICK "OK"				

Figure 48- Entering Options Chain Info into the Single Tab of the Basic Calculator

By way of example, assume we viewed the options chain for SNDK, and learned the stock is currently trading at $46.62 with three weeks remaining until expiration Friday. We will look at the in-the-money $45 strike, the near-the-money $47 strike and the out-of-the-money $50 strike. Figure 48 depicts where the foregoing information is entered within the Single Tab.

2- Information Generated From the Single Tab of the Basic Calculator:

For each strike price submitted, the Basic Calculator specifies the ROO (option profit), upside potential, downside protection (of the option premium), share buy down (I-T-M strikes), proceeds, cost basis and annualized returns. All of this information appears in a split second and can be printed to facilitate the best possible investment decisions. Figure 49 shows these results for SNDK:

RETURN ON OPTION (ROO) CALCULATOR - SINGLE STOCK

Stock name >>	Sandisk				
Stock symbol >>	SNDK		Stock share price >>	$	46.62

	Symbol	Strike Price	Exp Date	Price / share
Option choice #1 >>		45.00	06/18/10	3.50
Option choice #2 >>		47.00	06/18/10	2.40
Option choice #3 >>		50.00	06/18/10	1.15
Option choice #4 >>				

Option selected	SNDK JUN 45.00	SNDK JUN 47.00	SNDK JUN 50.00
Today's date	05/30/10	05/30/10	05/30/10
Days to expiration	19	19	19
Cost for 100 shares of stock	$ 4,662.00	$ 4,662.00	$ 4,662.00
Proceeds from one contract	$ 350.00	$ 240.00	$ 115.00
IN / OUT OF THE MONEY	IN	OUT	OUT
INTRINSIC VALUE	$ 1.62	$ -	$ -
UPSIDE AMOUNT	$ -	$ 38.00	$ 338.00
UPSIDE POTENTIAL	0.0%	0.8%	7.3%
DOWNSIDE AMOUNT	$ 162.00	$ -	$ -
DOWNSIDE PROTECTION	3.5%	0.0%	0.0%

RETURN ON VARIOUS OUTCOMES			
Proceeds from option sale	$ 350.00	$ 240.00	$ 115.00
Amount of buy-down	$ 162.00	$ -	$ -
Actual option profit	$ 188.00	$ 240.00	$ 115.00
Option profit	$ 188.00	$ 240.00	$ 115.00
Upside profit	$ -	$ 38.00	$ 338.00
Total profit	$ 188.00	$ 278.00	$ 453.00
Cost of shares	$ 4,500.00	$ 4,662.00	$ 4,662.00
Return On Option (ROO)	4.2%	5.1%	2.5%
Return on Upside	0.0%	0.8%	7.3%
Total return	4.2%	5.9%	9.8%

Figure 49- Single Tab Results

- Only the I-T-M strike ($45) offers 3.5% downside protection (of the option premium), as seen in the cell highlighted in yellow.

- The cells highlighted in green show the actual return on the option when initially sold.

- The cells highlighted in blue show upside potential if shares appreciate in value.

- The cells highlighted in red show maximum possible profit percentage for each strike price.

Depending on your market outlook, risk tolerance and stock technicals, you can use the information generated by the Ellman Calculator to select the strike price that best meets your needs.

Multiple Tab (Figure 50)

This spreadsheet allows you to evaluate multiple equities and multiple strike prices all on one page. Figure 50 depicts a typical page with information filled in and results shown:

Stock Name or Symbol	Stock $/sh	Option $/sh	Strike $	Expires	Intrisic	Upside	ROO	Up Potential	Down Protect
nflx	$ 75.00	$ 4.70	$ 75.00	05/21/10	$ -	$ -	6.3%	0.0%	0.0%
nflx	$ 75.00	$ 2.60	$ 80.00	05/21/10	$ -	$ 5.00	3.5%	6.7%	0.0%
swks	$15.49	$ 1.15	$ 15.00	05/21/10	$ 0.49	$ -	4.4%	0.0%	3.2%
db	$ 59.11	$ 1.95	$ 60.00	05/21/10	$ -	$ 0.89	3.3%	1.5%	0.0%
netl	$ 29.40	$ 1.65	$ 30.00	05/21/10	$ -	$ 0.60	5.6%	2.0%	0.0%
ipxl	$ 17.94	$ 1.20	$ 17.50	05/21/10	$ 0.44	$ -	4.3%	0.0%	2.5%
prgo	$ 59.08	$ 5.50	$ 55.00	05/21/10	$ 4.08	$ -	2.6%	0.0%	6.9%
prgo	$ 59.08	$ 2.40	$ 60.00	05/21/10	$ -	$ 0.92	4.1%	1.6%	0.0%
ctrp	$ 40.29	$ 4.00	$ 38.00	05/21/10	$ 2.29	$ -	4.5%	0.0%	5.7%
ctrp	$ 40.29	$ 2.90	$ 40.00	05/21/10	$ 0.29	$ -	6.5%	0.0%	0.7%
ctrp	$ 40.29	$ 2.00	$ 42.00	05/21/10	$ -	$ 1.71	5.0%	4.2%	0.0%
urbn	$ 37.84	$ 2.75	$ 36.00	05/21/10	$ 1.84	$ -	2.5%	0.0%	4.9%
urbn	$ 37.84	$ 1.60	$ 38.00	05/21/10	$ -	$ 0.16	4.2%	0.4%	0.0%
urbn	$ 37.84	$ 0.80	$ 40.00	05/21/10	$ -	$ 2.16	2.1%	5.7%	0.0%
shoo	$ 48.98	$ 1.95	$ 50.00	05/21/10	$ -	$ 1.04	4.0%	2.1%	0.0%

Figure 50- The Multiple Tab of the Ellman Calculator

1- Procedure for the Multiple Tab of the Basic Calculator:

Enter the required information in the five left-most columns (light blue). Once again, all of these statistics are derived from the options chain.

2- Information Generated from the Multiple Tab of the Basic Calculator

This is the tab that I use the most. When deciding on which financial soldiers you will send out into the investment battlefield for a particular month, this page allows you to compare a myriad of stocks and their corresponding potential option returns, upside potential and downside protection. In this example, one glance of the page will show us:

- Option sales with the greatest returns (ROO), or the option premiums with the most time value
- Highest upside potential (from stock price to strike price)

- Best downside protection of the time value of the option premium or the intrinsic value of I-T-M strikes

We then make our decisions based on market tone and technical analysis. In Fig 50, we see, highlighted in yellow, O-T-M strikes which offer excellent initial option returns and the possibility of significant additional profit from share appreciation. The areas shaded in green represent I-T-M strikes which also provide outstanding one-month returns with no upside potential, but significant downside protection. It is important to note again that when I refer to "downside protection," I am referring to protection of the time value of the option premium (ROO), not the overall position. When we sell an option, the protection of the total position, or breakeven point, is the entire option premium.

Favor yellow highlighted stocks:

- Bull markets
- Outstanding technical picture for the stock

Favor green highlighted stocks:

- Slightly bearish or volatile market tone
- Mixed technicals for that equity

This page can be printed and brought to your computer when you are ready to start generating cash into your accounts.

What Now Tab (Figure 51)

This tab will be used on or near expiration Friday when the current market value of the stock is higher than the strike price sold. We know that unless we invoke an expiration Friday exit strategy our shares will be sold. This tab will calculate the option returns, downside protection and upside potential for a "package trade," wherein we buy back the current option and sell the next month's same or higher strike. This is referred to as *rolling out* or *rolling out and up* and will be discussed more fully in Chapter 10,

As in the single and multiple tabs, the information found in the option chain will be entered in the blue cells as shown in Figure 51 below:

OKAY, YOU BOUGHT YOUR STOCK LAST MONTH AND SOLD AN OPTION AGAINST IT. TOMORROW IS EXPIRATION FRIDAY. WHAT DO YOU DO NOW? BELOW YOU WILL FIND SOME CHOICES FOR VARIOUS SITUATIONS.						
1) IS THIS COMPANY REPORTING EARNINGS NEXT MONTH? (Y or N)				N		
2) ENTER THE STOCK NAME, SYMBOL AND PRICES PER SHARE OF YOUR STOCK.						
Stock name >>	Blue Collar Investor Corp.					
Stock symbol >>	BCI			Stock share price you paid >>	$	78.00
Number of shares you bought >>	100			Stock share price today >>	$	83.00
3) ENTER THE INFORMATION BELOW FOR THE OPTION YOU SOLD.						
	Symbol	# Contracts	Strike Price	Exp Date		Price / share
Option you sold >>	80 call	1	80.00	08/20/10		2.90
Today's option price is >>						3.10
4) ENTER THE INFORMATION FOR THE NEW OPTION CHOICES YOU MAY SELL.						
	Symbol	# Contracts	Strike Price	Exp Date		Price / share
Roll out >>	80 call	1	80.00	09/17/10		6.00
Roll out and up >>	85 call	1	85.00	09/17/10		3.00
Roll out and down >>	See note on printed results page.					
5) PRESS THE PRINTER ICON OR CLICK ON THE "FILE" MENU, SELECT "PRINT" AND CLICK "OK"						

Figure 51- "What Now" Tab of the Ellman Calculator

1- Procedure For the "What Now" Tab of the Basic Calculator:

Enter the information in the blue cells obtained from the options chain. In the example in Figure 50, the stock was originally purchased for $78 per share and the $80 call option was sold. On or near expiration Friday, the current market value of this equity was $83. If we still want to retain the stock, and assuming it passes our fundamental and technical screens for the next contract month, we calculate our potential returns by rolling out to the next month's $80 call option or rolling out and up to the $85 call (again, these exit strategies will be discussed in detail in Chapter 10). Figure 52 depicts the results:

WHAT IF I LET THE STOCK GET CALLED AWAY?		
Do not count last month's return again.		
Your proceeds from the expiring option premium were:	$	290.00
Your stock basis (for comparison) today would be:	$	8,000.00

The basis of the stock appearing on this page is for comparison purposes ONLY. It is the lower of the expiring option strike price or the current stock price. If you allowed the stock to be called away the amount you would have to invest on Monday is the proceeds. DO NOT USE THE FIGURES BELOW FOR TAX PURPOSES.

WHAT IF I ROLL OUT?	w/o upside pot.
The proceeds for 1 BCI SEP 80.00 is:	$ 600.00
The cost to buy back 1 BCI AUG 80.00 is:	$ (310.00)
Your net return will be:	$ 290.00
Your comparative basis in the stock is:	$ 8,000.00
Your comparative returns are:	3.63%
You downside protection is:	$300.00

WHAT IF I ROLL OUT AND UP?	w/upside pot.	w/o upside pot.
The proceeds for 1 BCI SEP 85.00 is:	$ 300.00	$ 300.00
The cost to buy back 1 BCI AUG 80.00 is:	$ (310.00)	$ (310.00)
Your net loss on this option position is:	$ (10.00)	$ (10.00)
The "bought up" value in the closing option is:	$ 300.00	$ 300.00
Your upside potential return is:	$ 200.00	
Your net return will be:	$ 490.00	$ 290.00
Your comparative basis in the stock is:	$ 8,000.00	$ 8,000.00
Your comparative returns are:	6.13%	3.63%
You downside protection is:		$0.00

Figure 52- Results from the "What Now" tab of the Basic Calculator

2- Information Generated from the "What Now" tab of the Ellman Calculator:

- The ROO obtained if you roll out (3.63%).

- The downside protection we get when selling this I-T-M strike ($300).

- The ROO without upside potential when rolling out and up to an O-T-M strike (3.63%). There is a $10 loss on the option side of the trade and a $300 share appreciation generated from the sale of a higher strike. Prior to rolling out and up we are obligated to sell our shares @ $80.

By moving the "ceiling" to the new $85 strike our shares are now worth the current market value of $83.

- The ROO with upside potential when rolling out and up to an O-T-M strike (6.13%).

For a FREE Copy of the Basic Ellman Calculator

Contact me @ alan@thebluecollarinvestor.com

For a FREE Introductory CD, join my mailing list:

http://www.thebluecollarinvestor.com/joinlist.shtml

To read my journal articles:

http://www.thebluecollarinvestor.com/blog/

For additional educational products, visit my store@

http://www.thebluecollarinvestor.com/store.shtml

Owen Sargent can be contacted @ (osargentcpa@aol.com) to answer any questions relating to the calculator or tax consequences from options trading.

The Elite Calculator

In 2010, the Ellman Calculator was expanded to include two more tabs and this enhanced version was titled the Elite Calculator. The two new tabs are the "Unwind Now," tab which provides calculations used when unwinding your covered call position mid-contract, as well as the corresponding Schedule D computations (Schedule D, which is discussed more fully below, is a U.S. income tax form used by taxpayers to report their realized capital gains or losses). At the time this book was written, the Elite Calculator was available to BCI Premium Report subscribers at no cost, and to general members for a nominal fee.

Let's explore the tabs and other enhanced features of the Elite Calculator in the context of real-life examples. The following two tabs are not part of the Basic Ellman Calculator (original ESOC) but are an integral part of the expanded Elite Calculator:

The Unwind Now Tab

From time to time, you will buy a stock, sell the call and your equity will subsequently dart straight for the moon! That will leave your strike price deep, deep in-the-money. Even if you sold an O-T-M strike, if the stock price appreciates dramatically it could surpass the strike price, leaving it now I-T-M. One way of looking at this situation is that you made a significant profit and now that cash is protected by the difference between the share value and strike price of the option. For example, if you bought a stock for $38 and sold the $40 call and now the stock is trading at $45, you have generated a significant one month profit which is protected from $45 down to the $40 strike. In this case, you will just allow assignment and enter a new position the next contract cycle. There may be, however, an opportunity to generate even more cash in many of these situations, particularly when there is still time left until expiration.

When a strike price becomes *deep I-T-M, the time value of that option premium declines and approaches zero*. As we have learned, an I-T-M option premium consists predominantly of intrinsic value (stock price – strike price) when the strike is deep I-T-M. The amount of cash it takes to buy back the option is greatly offset by the share appreciation we would realize by eliminating the option obligation (closing the options position by buying back the call option) and selling the stock. There is nothing like a real-life example to clarify and I'll use PRGO, a stock that has been in my portfolio for months, as of the time this chapter was written. Thus, assume 300 shares of PRGO were purchased @ $51.10 per share on March 22nd, the start of the April options contract cycle. A week later, the price of PRGO rose to $56.79, as illustrated in Figure 53, which depicts PRGO's pricing activity for the month of March:

138 | Complete Encyclopedia for Covered Call Writing

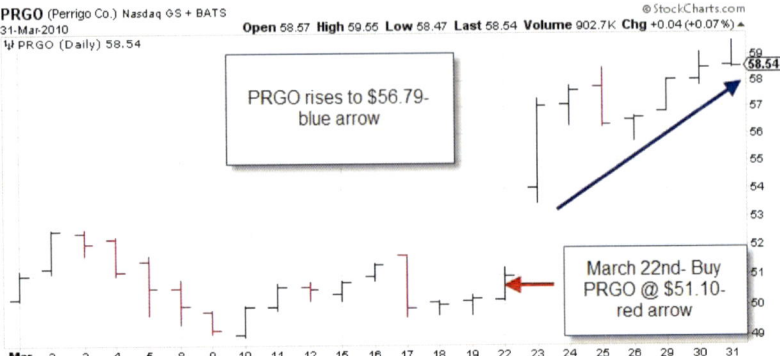

Figure 53 PRGO Heads to the Moon!

Assume further that the $50 call option was originally sold for $2.10, and that a week later (after PRGO's price spiked) was valued @ $6.90, as detailed in Figure 54:

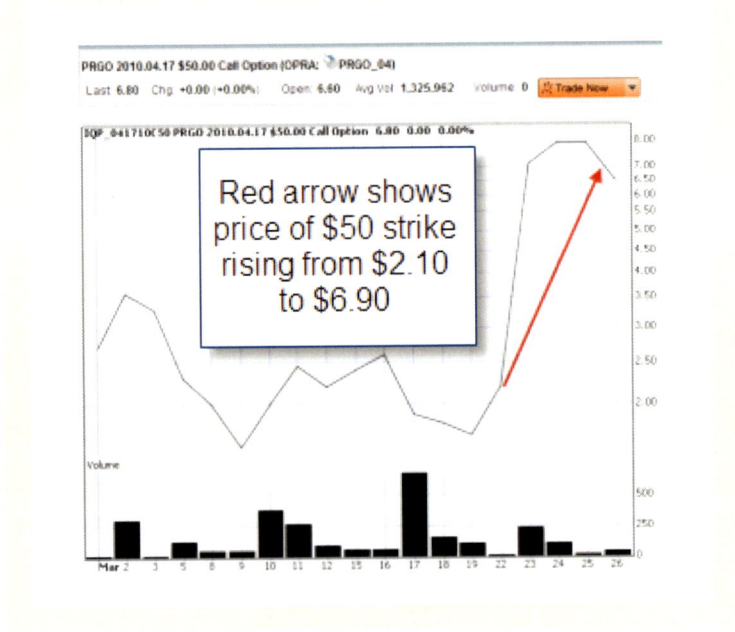

Figure 54 - PRGO Option Value

Let's see if there is a cash-generating opportunity by unwinding our position in the middle of option contract cycle (mid-contract). We must first explore the current option chain, an example of which is depicted in Figure 55:

Last	Intrinsic Value	Bid	Ask	Vol	Open Interest	Strike
16.75	16.79	16.60	16.90	0	23	40.00
11.75	11.79	11.60	11.90	0	18	45.00
6.80	6.79	6.70	6.90	0	1,011	50.00
2.78	1.79	2.70	2.85	0	824	55.00
0.53	0.00	0.45	0.60	0	266	60.00
0.10	0.00	0.05	0.15	0	0	65.00
0.10	0.00	N/A	0.10	0	0	70.00

Calls — Apr 10

Figure 55- PRCO Unwind - Options Chain

In the yellow-highlighted area, we see that the cost to close our short call option position is $6.90, and the intrinsic value is $6.79, leaving $0.11 in time value, or $11 per contract. We may be able to close our short position at a cheaper price by *playing the bid-ask spread*, a subject discussed in Chapter 9. Assuming commissions are *negligible* (and thus will not factor into our calculations) if we can use the cash generated from the sale of the stock, and thus generate a higher return than $11 per contract, we have made some additional profit. This is what Blue Collar Investors do as long as it makes sense and is relatively safe. Let's view the "Unwind Now" tab of the Elite Calculator (Figure 56). Note how the original profit of $100 per contract ($210 – $110) has now dipped by $11 to $89 (Figure 57).

First, as depicted in Figure 56, we enter the information into the "Unwind Now" Tab of the Elite Calculator:

1) ENTER THE ORIGINAL TRADE INFORMATION BELOW		
Stock name >>	Perrigo	
Stock symbol >>	PRGO	
Date of transaction >>	03/22/10	Today's date >>
Stock purchase price >>	$ 51.10	
Option STRIKE price >>	$ 50.00	
Option sale price/share >>	$ 2.10	

2) ENTER TODAY'S INFORMATION	
Current stock price >>	$ 56.79
Current option price/share >>	$ 6.90

3) PRESS THE PRINTER ICON OR CLICK ON THE "FILE" MENU, SELECT "PRINT" AND CLICK "OK"

Figure 56- PRGO Info Entered Into the "Unwind Now" Tab (blue cells on left)

Next, we view the results generated by the Elite Calculator after the requisite information is entered into the "Unwind Now," as illustrated in Figure 57 (white cells on right):

RETURN ON OPTION (ROO) CALCULATOR - UNWIND NOW

Stock name >>	Perrigo		
Stock symbol >>	PRGO	Today's date >>	03/29/10

RETURN IF I UNWIND THE POSITION TODAY

Cost of shares	$	5,110.00
Option premium received	$	210.00
Option close-out		
Cost to buy back the option	$	690.00
Premium received on sale	$	210.00
Gain (loss) on close-out	$	(480.00)
Stock close-out		
Proceeds from sale of stock	$	5,679.00
Cost of shares	$	5,110.00
Gain (loss) on close-out	$	569.00
Net Gain (Loss) to UNWIND	$	**89.00**
NET RETURN ON POSITION		
Net gain (loss) to unwind position today	$ 89.00	
Net cash to open position	$ 4,900.00 =	1.80%
Number of days position was open		7
Annualized return		89.00%

Figure 57- PRGO Final Unwind Results
(Elite Calculator- white cells on right)

Sometimes, we may feel that we can generate the extra cash by rolling up; however, there are two reasons in general why this may not be a prudent decision:

- The price of the stock may not be in a favorable position to generate a decent return

- Since the price appreciated so much, so fast, it could decline due to profit-taking

Instead, let's look for a new financial soldier to send out into the investment battlefield (this has all been decided prior to unwinding the original position). Enter BUCY (Figure 58):

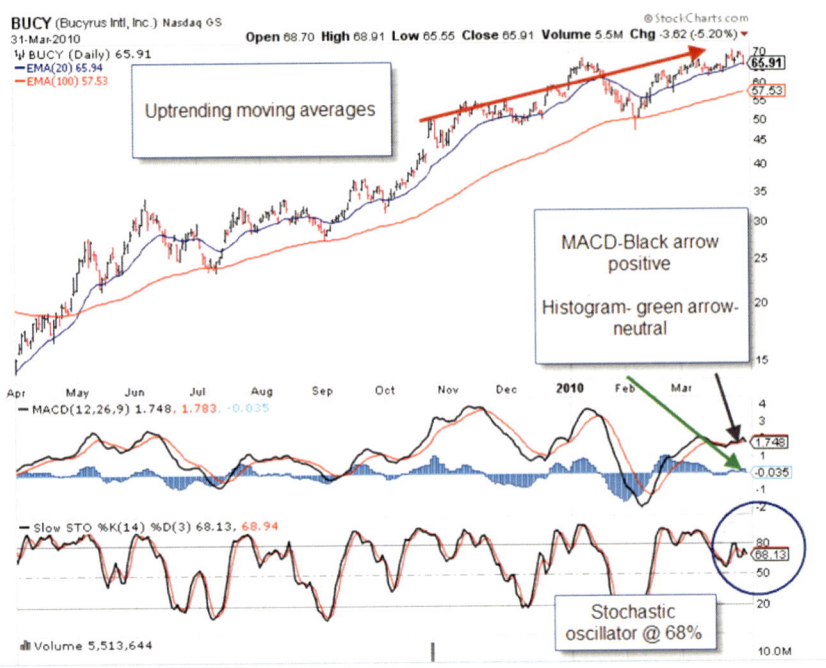

Figure 58- BUCY Chart as of 3/29/10

We approve the fundamentals and technicals by checking the system screens and the price chart above. This is a chart showing a bullish moving average trend with neutral to positive confirming technicals. Next we look to the option chain, which is depicted in Figure 59:

22.45	22.48	22.20	22.70	0	254	45.00
21.45	21.48	21.20	21.70	0	65	46.00
20.45	20.48	20.20	20.70	0	109	47.00
19.50	19.48	19.30	19.70	0	62	48.00
18.50	18.48	18.30	18.70	0	188	49.00
17.50	17.48	17.40	17.60	0	670	50.00
12.60	12.48	12.50	12.70	0	1,213	55.00
7.95	7.48	7.00	8.10	0	1,659	60.00
4.00	2.48	3.90	4.10	0	4,280	65.00
1.50	0.00	1.45	1.55	0	4,541	70.00
0.40	0.00	0.35	0.45	0	3,302	75.00
0.10	0.00	0.05	0.15	0	1,802	80.00
0.05	0.00	0.05	0.05	0	70	85.00

Figure 59- BUCY Options Chain

With the stock currently priced @ $67.48, we can sell the $65, I-T-M strike for $3.90, which, after entry into the Ellman Calculator, yields the calculations detailed in Figure 60 in the yellow highlighted area):

		RETURN ON OPTION (ROO) CALCULATOR - MULTIPLE STOCKS							
Stock Name or Symbol	Stock $/sh	Option $/sh	Strike $	Expires	Intrisic	Upside	ROO	Up Potential	Down Protect
BUCY	$ 67.48	$ 3.90	$ 65.00		$ 2.48	$ -	2.2%	0.0%	3.7%
MCRS	$ 44.43	$ 1.40	$ 45.00		$ -	$ 0.57	3.2%	1.3%	0.0%
ULTA	$ 31.01	$ 0.40	$ 35.00		$ -	$ 3.99	1.3%	12.9%	0.0%
MSB	$ 42.34	$ 1.75	$ 45.00		$ -	$ 2.66	4.1%	6.3%	0.0%
MOS	$ 68.39	$ 2.70	$ 70.00		$ -	$ 1.61	3.9%	2.4%	0.0%

Figure 60- -BUCY Multiple Tab Results of the Basic Calculator

As demonstrated in Figure 60, an additional 2.2% return is generated with a huge 3.7% downside protection ($2.48/$67.48). That calculates to a $115 per contract "bonus" ($390 - $248 - $11 - commissions) for instituting a *mid-contract* unwind exit strategy.

Conclusion:

When a stock appreciates in value over a short period of time, and there are still two weeks or more remaining in the cycle, unwinding your position may offer an opportunity to generate additional cash into your account. The unwind tab will show you how much profit (loss) you generated at that point in time, and how much time value (option profit) you are spending to unwind. If you can generate more cash per contract (in this case more than $11 per contract) by entering a new position, a second stream of income can be generated in the same contract cycle with the same cash investment. *The key is for the time value to be near zero and the new position to generate more cash than the amount of time value paid to close the original position.*

Schedule D

In non-sheltered accounts, if you sold a stock or option, regardless of whether you made or lost money on it, you have to file a *Schedule D* tax form. This two-page form, with all its sections, columns and special computations, looks complicated and it certainly can be. However, your extra work will be greatly reduced by the Schedule D tab of the Elite Calculator. In addition, the Schedule D tab will also assist you with your tax savings. For example, if you lost money, this form will help you use those losses to offset any gains or a portion of your ordinary income. However, if you profited from your transactions, the Schedule D tab will help ensure you don't overpay the government for your gains.

When you make money on a sale, the Schedule D requires

you to report the transaction using some basic information, including when you bought the asset and when you sold it. This is critical, because the length of time you hold an asset determines its tax rate. For example, if you own a security for one year or less, the security is considered a short-term asset, and any gains thereon are considered short-term capital gains, which will result in higher capital gains taxes. These short-term assets are taxed at the same rate as your regular income, which could be as high as 35% on your return. Short-term sales are reported in Part 1 of the Schedule D. Alternatively, if you own a security for 366 days or more, the security is considered a long-term asset and is eligible for a lower capital gains tax, which can range between 15% and 0%, depending upon your income level. Sales of long-term assets are reported in Part 2 of the Schedule D form.

Information Required for the Schedule D:

- Name of asset
- Date purchased
- Date sold
- Price sold
- Cost basis
- Gain/loss

The gain or loss that you enter on the Schedule D form is figured by subtracting your basis from the sales price.

Schedule D Information Tab on Elite Calculator

Figure 61 on the next page shows the Schedule D Information tab from the Elite Calculator, which is accessed by clicking on the icon highlighted by the red arrow.

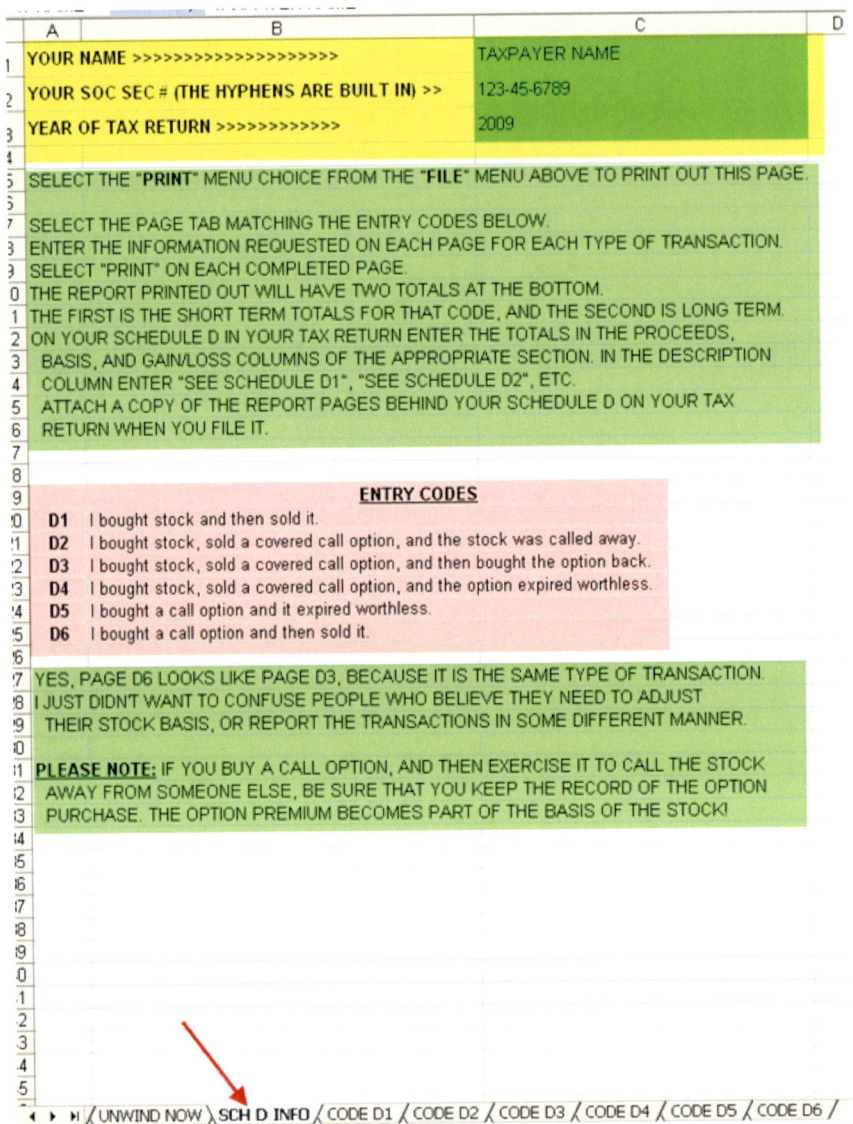

Figure 61 - Schedule D Information Tab on Elite Calculator

The following areas on Figure 61 have been highlighted:
- Yellow-personal information to enter

- Green- user information
- Pink- six entry codes or different pages of the Schedule D specific for the type of trade

Covered call writers will predominantly use Schedule D entry code tabs D2, D3 and D4.

Schedule D Entry Code Tab D2 on the Elite Calculator

We use the D2 entry code when we buy a stock, sell the call and our shares are assigned. In all entry tabs, information is entered in blue areas only as shown in Figure 62:

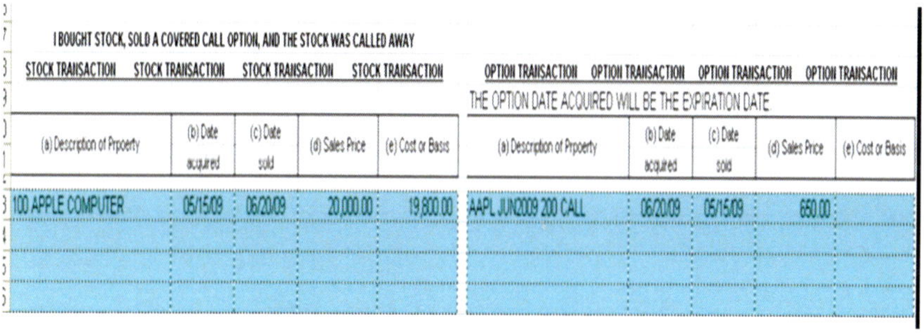

I BOUGHT STOCK, SOLD A COVERED CALL OPTION, AND THE STOCK WAS CALLED AWAY

STOCK TRANSACTION STOCK TRANSACTION STOCK TRANSACTION STOCK TRANSACTION

(a) Description of Prpoerty	(b) Date acquired	(c) Date sold	(d) Sales Price	(e) Cost or Basis
100 APPLE COMPUTER	05/15/09	06/20/09	20,000.00	19,800.00

OPTION TRANSACTION OPTION TRANSACTION OPTION TRANSACTION OPTION TRANSACTION

THE OPTION DATE ACQUIRED WILL BE THE EXPIRATION DATE

(a) Description of Prpoerty	(b) Date acquired	(c) Date sold	(d) Sales Price	(e) Cost or Basis
AAPL JUN2009 200 CALL	06/20/09	05/15/09	650.00	

Figure 62- D2 Entry Code

In this example, we bought 100 x AAPL for $198 and sold 1 x $200 call for $650. The calculations will appear in the right side of the tab in the "white areas," as depicted in Figure 63:

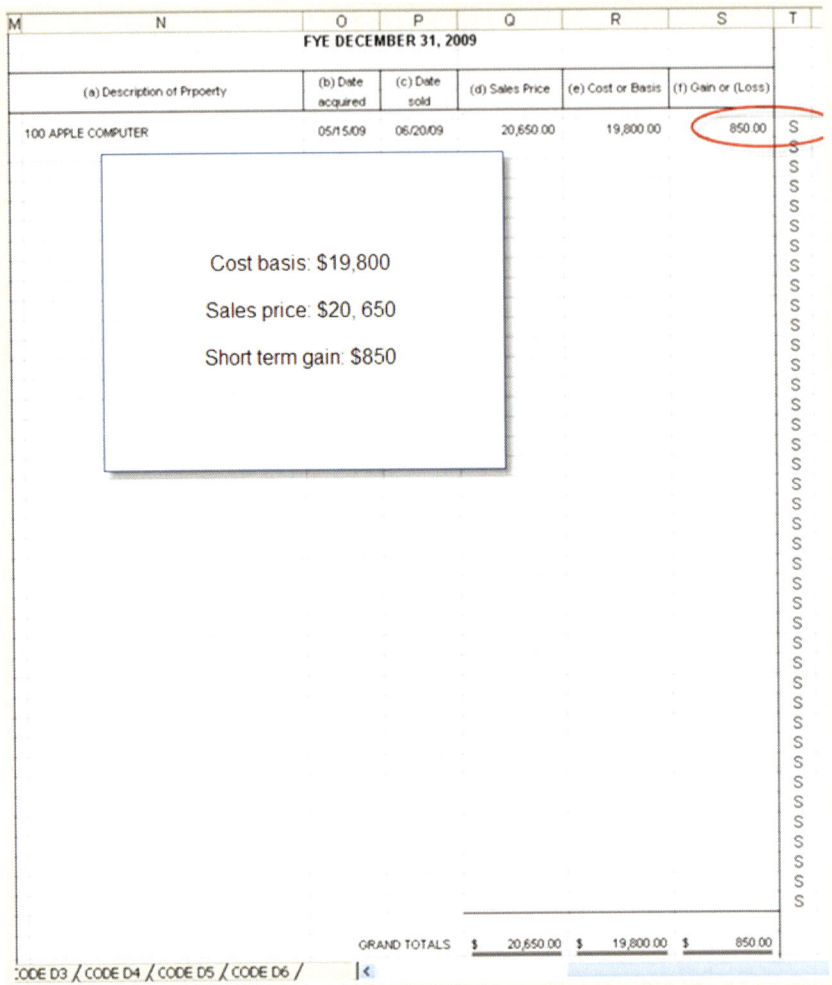

Figure 63

The red encircled area in Figure 63 shows a short-term profit ("S") of $850. $650 was from the option sale and $200 was from share appreciation (purchased @ $198 and sold @ the $200 strike price).

Schedule D Entry Code Tab D3 on Elite Calculator

We use the D3 entry code tab when we buy a stock, sell the option and then buy back the option. This is known as closing

Calculations | 149

your short position. Note that the "acquiring date" is later than the "sales date". Once again, the information is entered in the blue areas, as illustrated in Figure 64:

IGNORE THE STOCK TRANSACTION IN THIS CASE.				
I BOUGHT STOCK, SOLD A COVERED CALL OPTION, AND THEN BOUGHT THE OPTION BACK.				
OPTION TRANSACTION OPTION TRANSACTION OPTION TRANSACTION OPTION TRANSACTION				
(a) Description of Prpoerty	(b) Date acquired	(c) Date sold	(d) Sales Price	(e) Cost or Basis
AAPL JUN2009 200 CALL	06/10/09	05/15/09	650.00	124.00

Figure 64

The calculations generated after the requisite information is entered in the D3 tab will appear in the white areas on the right side of the tab, as displayed in Figure 65:

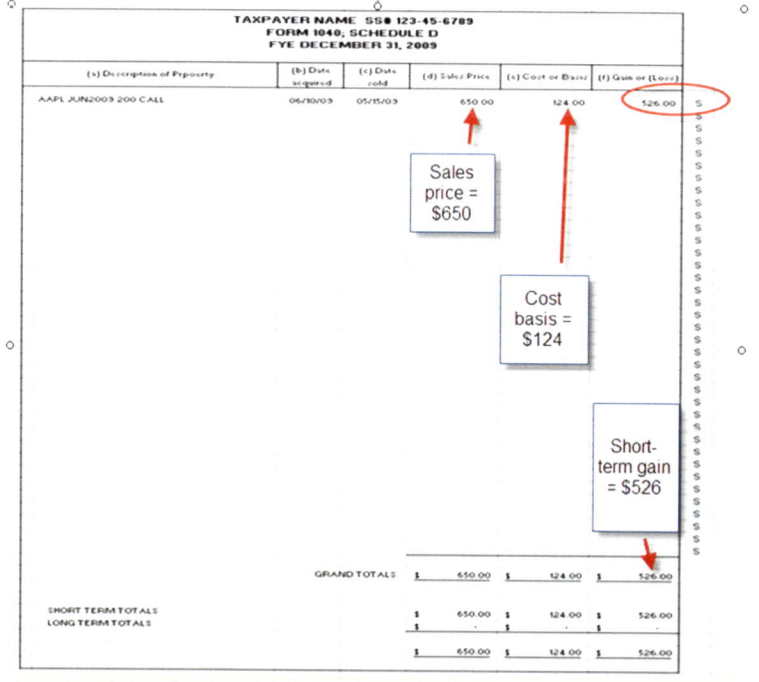

Figure 65

Since the option was sold for $650 and repurchased for $124, the spreadsheet shows a short-term capital gain of $526 (red circle and arrow).

Schedule D Entry Code Tab D4 on Elite Calculator

We use the D4 entry code tab when we buy a stock, sell the call and the option expires worthless. The blue cells are filled in manually as shown in figure 66:

(a) Description of Prpoerty	(b) Date acquired	(c) Date sold	(d) Sales Price	(e) Cost or Basis
AAPL JUN2009 200 CALL	06/10/09	05/15/09	650.00	
AAPL JAN2009 200 CALL	01/20/09	05/15/07	1,100.00	

IGNORE THE STOCK TRANSACTION IN THIS CASE. I BOUGHT STOCK, SOLD A COVERED CALL OPTION, AND THE OPTION EXPIRED WORTHLESS. OPTION TRANSACTION OPTION TRANSACTION OPTION TRANSACTION OPTION TRANSACTION THE OPTION DATE ACQUIRED WILL BE THE EXPIRATION DATE.

Figure 66

Note that the option on line 1 was originally sold in 2009 (for $650), while the option on the second line was sold (for $1,100) in 2007. Next we view the calculations, located on the right side of tab D4 in the white areas, as depicted in Figure 67:

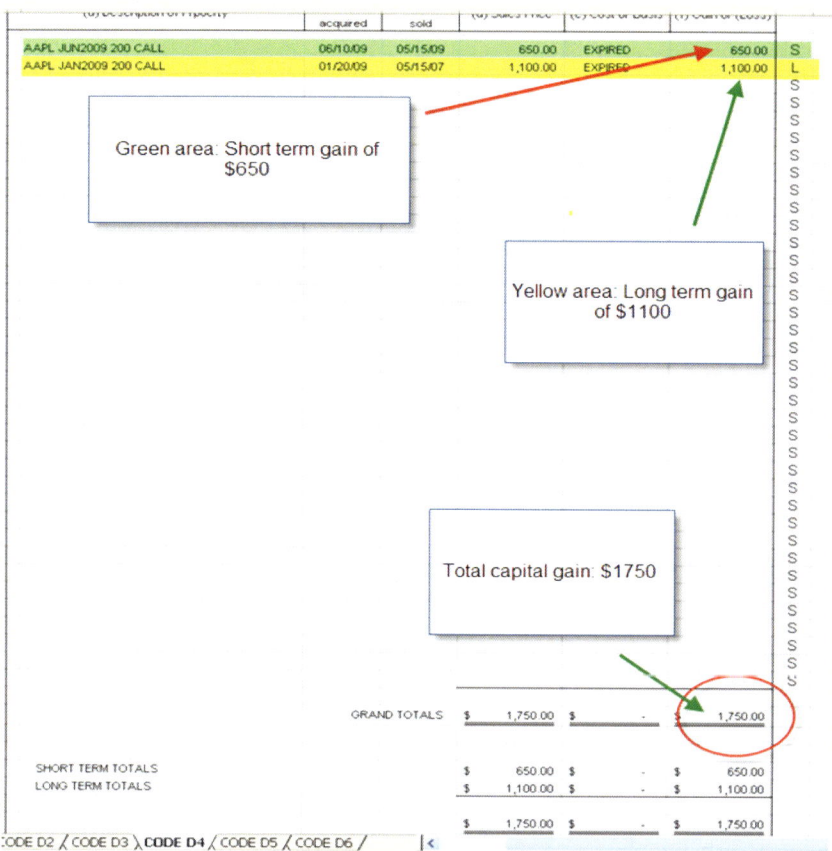

Figure 67

The green area shows a short-term capital gain of $650 ("S") and the yellow area shows a long-term capital gain of $1100 ("L"). The total capital gain of $1750 (red circle) is broken down into short and long-term gains at the bottom of the page (see figure 67).

The remaining entry code tabs on the Elite Calculator relating to Schedule D computations should be used either for stocks only or for options only, however not a combination of stocks and options (as we use for covered call writing).

***The Schedule D can also be used to calculate your final option return results.

***The information gleaned from the Schedule D of the Elite Calculator should be used in consultation with your tax advisor

Owen Sargent can be contacted @ (osargentcpa@aol.com) to answer any questions relating to the calculator or tax consequences from options trading.

Test your knowledge of key points

1- The formula for ROO for an I-T-M strike is _____.

2- The "breakeven" for all covered call positions is _____ _____.

3- When viewing an options chain, we sell at the _____ and buy at the _____.

4- Volume is a daily statistic whereas open interest is a _____ statistic.

5- The strike price that is the most conservative because it offers the greatest protection is the _____ strike.

6- The strike price that generates the largest initial ROO is the _____ strike.

7- The _____ strike has the potential for the largest overall return.

8- A mixed technical chart pattern in a mildly bearish overall stock market will call for favoring _____ strikes.

9- The strikes with the highest deltas are the _____ strikes which make it less expensive to _____ your short option positions in a declining market.

10- The Schedule D will allow you to process both _____ capital gains or losses and _____ capital gains or losses.

11- The single and multiple tabs of the Ellman Calculator will generate the following three calculations: _____.

Answers:

1- ROO for In-the-Money Call Options = time value of option premium x 100 / (price per share – intrinsic value of premium) x 100

2 Breakeven Point = Purchase Price of Stock – Total Option Premium

3- Bid, ask

4- Cumulative

5- In-the-money

6- At-the-money

7- Out-of-the-money

8- In-the-money

9- In-the-money, close

10- Long term and short term

11- ROO, downside protection of the ROO (if any) and upside potential (if any).

Chapter 7

Factors that Influence the Value of Our Option Premiums

Chapter outline

1- Option premium equation

2- Factors that influence time value

3- The Greeks

- Delta
- Gamma
- Theta
- Vega
- Rho

4- Implied volatility of our option premiums

5- The case for one month options

6- Beta

7- Stock option expiration cycles

8- The one point strike program

9- Open interest and volume

10- Non-standard options

11- Quarterly expiration option contracts

12- Weekly expiration option contracts

Option premium equation

You just sold an options contract for $380 and generated a 3.5% one-month return. Did you ever wonder how the market determined the value of that contract to be $380? The answer starts with the following equation, which should be a familiar one at this point:

$$\text{Option premium} = \text{Intrinsic Value} + \text{Time Value}$$

Let's briefly review intrinsic value and time value, the two components of an option premium.

Intrinsic Value – This is the value of an option if the option were to expire immediately with the underlying stock at its current price. Stated alternatively, intrinsic value is the amount by which the underlying stock is in-the-money. For call options, this is the positive difference between the stock price and the strike price. Call options only have intrinsic value when the price of the underlying stock is trading above the strike price of the call option (i.e. when the option is I-T-M).

For example, let's say that Dell Computer is trading for $22.50. The DELL $20 call option would have an intrinsic value of $2.50 ($22.50 – $20 = $2.50) because the option buyer can exercise his option to buy DELL shares @ $20, and then turn around and sell them at the market price of $22.50, thereby generating a profit of $2.50 per share. If we had sold the DELL $25 call (assuming Dell is trading at $22.50), the intrinsic value would be zero ($22.50 – $25 = -$2.50) because the intrinsic value cannot be a negative number. Therefore, *only in-the-money call options have intrinsic value*

Time Value – This is the portion of the option premium that is attributable to the amount of time remaining until the expiration of the option contract. Time value is whatever the value the option has in addition to its intrinsic value. Since all options (excluding quarterly contracts of some exchange-traded funds and the newer weekly options) expire on the third Friday of the month (expiration Friday), and because time value varies significantly from stock to stock, let's examine the *factors that determine the time value of our call options.*

Factors that influence time value

1- *Time until expiration*- When trading options, time is opportunity. The longer the time frames until expiration Friday, the greater the chance that the options will expire in-the-money. Therefore, an option buyer is willing to pay more for the increased opportunity for the option to expire in-the-money, and the seller will similarly demand more for the increased risk (seller will be forced to sell shares at strike price if option expires in-the-money) that the additional time requires him to assume. The time component of an option premium decays exponentially as expiration Friday approaches. Approximately 1/3 of its value is lost during the first half of its life; 2/3 during the second half of its life.

2 - *Volatility*- This is the fluctuation, not direction, of a stock's price movement. Volatility represents the deviation of day-to-day price changes of an option's underlying equity; it measures the speed and magnitude at which the underlying equity's price changes. There are two types of volatility:

- *Historical volatility* - the actual price fluctuation as observed over a period of time.
- *Implied volatility* - a forecast of the underlying stock's volatility as implied by the option's price in the marketplace. More on this topic later in this chapter.

Time to expiration and volatility are the primary factors that influence the time value of your option premiums. Two additional, but less significant factors are interest rates and dividends.

3- *Interest Rates*- As interest rates rise, the value of the call option will increase. Cash spent on owning the underlying stock is opportunity (interest) lost, thereby increasing the value of the option.

4- *Dividends-* As dividends increase, the call or option value decreases. This is because it is the option seller (who owns the underlying security) who collects the dividend distribution, not the option buyer.

The following is a brief summary of the factors that affect the value of our option premiums, and the type of affect each factor has on these premiums:

- Time to expiration decreases.................Call value decreases.

- Volatility increases..............................Call value increases.

- Volatility decreases.............................Call value decreases.

- Dividend increases.............................Call value decreases.

- Dividend decreases............................Call value increases.

- Interest Rate increases........................Call value increases.

- Interest Rate decreases.......................Call value decreases.

- Share price increases..........................Call value increases

- Share price decreases.........................Call value decreases

The complicated mathematical formulas that determine the precise option premium are not critical to our successful investing. I do feel, however, that having a basic understanding of the components that influence this price can only make us better investors and get us closer to our goal of becoming CEO of our own money.

The Greeks- Factors that Influence our Option Premiums

There are several factors that allow us to estimate the risks associated with our option positions. Together, they fall under the heading of the "Greeks" because *most* of these factors are named after Greek letters.

Factors that Influence the Value of Our Option Premiums | 159

Delta (price sensitivity)

The most commonly used Greek, Delta, measures the sensitivity of an option's price to a change in the price of the underlying stock, or in other words, how much the theoretical value of an option will change if the underlying value of the stock moves up or down $1. The delta of a call option can range from 0.00 to 1.00. The closer an option's delta is to 1.00, the more the option price will rise with every $1 rise in the underlying stock price. If an option has a delta of .50, for every $1 rise/fall in the underlying stock price, the option will rise/fall $0.50. For example, if company BCI is trading at $38 per shares and the $40 call is selling for $2 and has a delta of .50, the following would be true if all other factors remain constant:

- If BCI increases to $39 per share, the $40 call would increase in value to $2.50

- If BCI decreases in value to $37/share, the $40 call would decrease in value to $1.50

- For every $1 change in BCI's share price, the option value will change by one half that amount.

Gamma (second order price sensitivity)

Gamma indicates how the delta of an option will change relative to a $1 change in the underlying asset, or in other words, gamma represents the option delta's sensitivity to market price changes. Gamma is essentially second order price sensitivity; think of it as "the delta of the delta." When an option is deep in-the-money (strike price several points below current stock price) or deep out-of-the-money (strike price several points above current stock price)), its gamma is small. When the option is near-the-money or at-the-money, gamma is the largest. Gamma is used to gauge the price of an option relative to the amount it is either in-the-money or out-of-the money.

Theta (time sensitivity)

Educated covered call writers know that it is critical to sell our options early in the one-month cycle. I always try to sell my options in the first week of a four week expiration cycle, and no later than the beginning of the second week of a five week cycle. The reason has to do with the time value of the option premium and the erosion of its value over time. This is known as *theta*. As Blue Collar Investors, we view the sale of our call option as selling time value, or theta.

Definition

Theta is an estimate of how much the theoretical value of an option declines when there is a *passage of one day* while there is no change in the stock value or volatility. Theta is expressed as a negative number since the passage of time will decrease time value. For example, if the time value of an option premium falls by $0.05 each day, its theta is said to be (-) 0.05. Because intrinsic value only changes with the movement of the stock price, theta does not affect the intrinsic portion of the option premium. However, theta does have a major impact on time value, and covered call writers should be aware of this relationship.

Theta's role in reducing option value

As an option approaches expiration Friday, theta has a greater impact on the option value. Figure 68 depicts a one-month graph of a hypothetical option value:

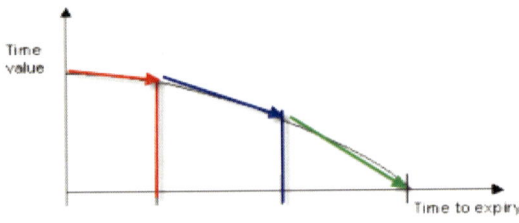

Figure 68- Theta- One-Month Chart

Notice how the decline in time value starts off gradual (red), accelerates (blue), and then "falls off a cliff" (green).

Theta and strike prices:

Since A-T-M strikes have the greatest time value (ROO), they have the most to lose over time. Therefore, theta is highest for A-T-M strikes and lower as options go deeper I-T-M or O-T-M.

Theta and volatility:

As volatility increases, theta increases and vice-versa. Higher volatility means greater time value so each day's decay will be greater if there is no movement.

Theta and days to expiration Friday:

Theta increases as there are fewer days to expiration Friday.

Theta and covered call writing:

It is important to understand the general concept that theta plays a major role in devaluing option premiums, especially for one-month contracts. This favors our strategy in three ways:

- Allows us to capture a generous option premium shortly before its dramatic time value decline.

- Allows us to close our positions profitably during the week of expiration Friday (if we chose to do so) because the cost to buy the call option back (close our short options position) has dramatically declined, especially if the stock price has not changed.

- Allows us to execute a mid-contract exit strategy (discussed in Chapter 10) at a reduced price.

Understanding theta also assists us in determining the ideal time to sell our options; not too early, and not too late.

Conclusion on theta

It is not necessary to analyze the specific theta of options we have sold, however understanding the principles of theta and the impact it has on our options values will make us more informed, and consequently, better investors.

Vega (volatility sensitivity)

Vega measures the change in the price of an option that results from a 1% change in volatility. Higher volatility means higher option prices because the greater volatility coincides with larger price swings, and thus, a higher likelihood that the option will be profitable, whichever side of the trade you are favoring. . Vega is highest for A-T-M calls and lessens as options delve deeper I-T-M or O-T-M. Vega also declines as Expiration Friday nears.

Rho

Not considered a major Greek, Rho measures the change in the option price due to a change in interest rates. As stated earlier, call value increases as interest rates increase.

Practical Application of the Greeks

1- *Delta and Gamma* are first and second order price sensitivity measures. When an option is deep in-the-money, delta is approximately 1.00, which indicates that a $1 increase in the price of the underlying security will represent another dollar of downside protection. We can only start losing profit from the time value of the original option sale if the stock price dips below the strike price. Likewise, a decline in share price of $1 will decrease our protection by that same amount. If we are especially concerned about a declining share price or market volatility, we may want to get as deep in-the-money as possible (still receiving a decent return) because protection erodes dollar for dollar of intrinsic value at these levels. To review the option premium formula:

Premium = Intrinsic value (amount in-the-money) + time value (including volatility)

2- *Theta* represents time sensitivity. Since, in the BCI system, we are selling predominantly one-month options, time is limited to begin with. During the final two weeks of a contract period, option value literally falls off a cliff. It's difficult to generate the kinds of returns we are seeking if we wait to sell our option deep into the one month cycle; let's say for the final two weeks. Because of the threat of theta, we should look to sell our options during the first week of a four-week contract period, and for a five-week contract period, we should sell our options during the first two weeks. Theta is also the reason I created the guideline of paying less to buy back an option during the later, rather than the earlier, part of the contract cycle when executing exit strategies (see Chapter 10).

3- *Vega* represents volatility sensitivity. We all love great, big, juicy returns. The more the better, right? WRONG!

If delta, gamma and theta remain constant but the option premium returns much more than the 6% per month for an at-the-money call option (initial ROO), we know that Vega is rearing its ugly head. Volatility means risk. The stock can go up a lot but it also can decline dramatically in a short period of time. When I see a 7% or greater one-month return for a one-month option (discounting share appreciation), I check the chart and usually see a major roller coaster pattern. No thank you, I'll pass for the steady uptrending safer moving averages.

 The bottom line is that it's not essential to memorize the definitions of the Greeks (unless you're going to appear on *Jeopardy*). It is helpful, however, to understand the concepts of how price, time and volatility factor into the value of our option premiums and of the corresponding effects on the underlying equities.

4- *More on Delta and Covered Call Writing:*

As previously discussed, the Greeks measure an option's exposure to risk. Those of us who study options are constantly reading and hearing that *delta*, one of the Greeks, is one of the most powerful influences over option value. For this reason, I thought it would be prudent to discuss this subject in greater detail.

Definition:

Delta measures the amount an option price will change as a result of a $1.00 price change the underlying security (stock, exchange traded fund). Other major factors that impact option value include the price of the stock, implied volatility and time to expiration. Since call options rise and fall *directly* with the price of the stock, they are assigned deltas between 0 to 1. Look at delta as a bet: What is the percentage chance that the option will expire in-the-money (strike price lower than the market value of the stock) or be exercised by expiration Friday? The higher the delta value, the greater the chance of this happening. A delta of .9 or 90%, for example, means that the strike price will almost definitely end up I-T-M. For example, if we sold a $50 call option and the underlying security is trading @ $70 with one week remaining, the delta would be at or near 1, meaning that for every $1 change in the price of the stock, the option will also change by approximately $1. This is typical of *deep I-T-M strikes.*

For *at-the-money strikes,* deltas will be closer to .5 or 50%. In this scenario, for every $1 change in the price of the underlying security, the option value will change by $0.50, which translates to a 50-50 chance that the option will expire I-T-M.

For *deep out-of-the-money strikes,* deltas would be quite low, between .1 to .2 or 10% to 20%, for example. If we sold the $50 call and the stock was trading @ $30, the chances of that $50 strike ending up I-T-M are quite low. If the stock price moves up or down by $1, the option value will change by perhaps $0.10 because of the low delta.

Figure 69 summarizes the *approximate* deltas for the one-month options we predominantly sell when writing covered calls:

APPROXIMATE DELTAS FOR OUR 1-MONTH OPTIONS

Strike	Delta	Percentage
Deep O-T-M	0.1	10%
O-T-M	0.3	30%
A-T-M	0.5	50%
I-T-M	0.7	70%
Deep I-T-M	0.9	90%

Figure 69- Approximate Deltas for One-Month Options

RULE:

Delta values increase as the strike moves further I-T-M and decrease as the strike moves deeper O-T-M, as illustrated in Figure 70.

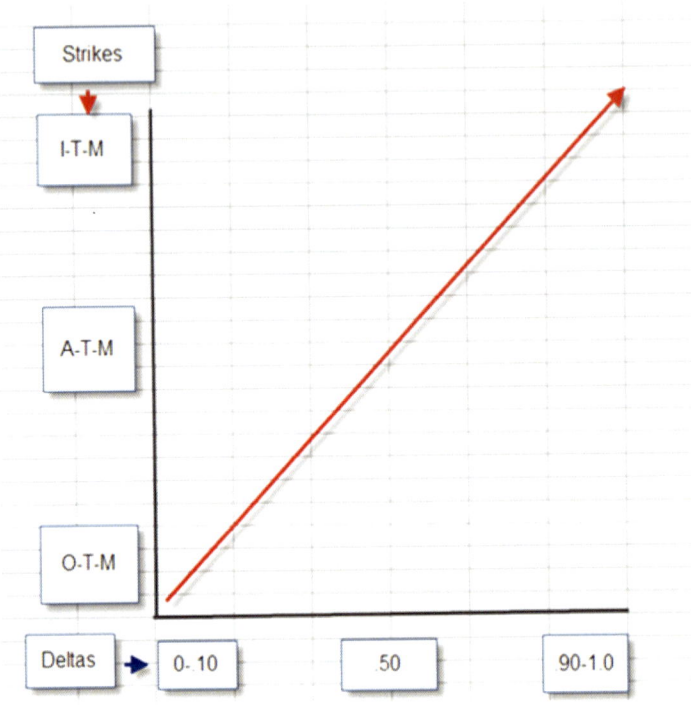

Figure 70 - Delta vs. Strike Prices

Factors Influencing Delta:

- Stock price- As we can see in Figure 70, an increase in stock price (red arrow) moves the strike towards I-T-M as delta increases.

- Time- Delta will change as we approach expiration Friday. I-T-M strikes will show increasing deltas because of the higher likelihood of the option expiring with intrinsic value (less time to move O-T-M). O-T-M strikes will show decreasing deltas because of the lower likelihood of turning things around and expiring I-T-M.

- Implied volatility (IV) - If all others factors remain constant an increase in IV will increase the time value of the option premiums. This will have little or no impact on the deltas of A-T-M strikes which should remain at about .50 but O-T-M strikes should show increased deltas and I-T-M strikes should show lower deltas. O-T-M strikes are impacted the most because IV affects only time value, not intrinsic value of our premiums and O-T-M strikes are ALL time value.

What Delta Teaches Us About Risk When Selling Covered Call Options:

Delta explains why selling O-T-M call options presents more risk. These calls have low deltas. If the stock drops in value, the option price will decline at a much slower pace (because of the low delta). This will make it more expensive to buy back the option if we are looking to institute an exit strategy and/or close our position.

Summary regarding delta:

Delta measures the probability of an option expiring I-T-M, or stated differently, the probability the option will expire with intrinsic value:

- I-T-M strikes- highest deltas
- A-T-M strikes- deltas near 50% or .5
- O-T-M strikes- low deltas

Strike selection based on delta:

- I-T-M strikes- if bearish or conservative, because option premiums decline faster with decreasing share price making it easier to B-T-C (buy-to-close).
- A-T-M strikes- for maximum premium return.
- O-T-M strikes- if bullish so option premium AND share appreciation can be realized.

Conclusion:

Understanding the relationship of delta to our option premiums will make us sharper investors as it will allow us to select the best strike price for a given situation.

Implied Volatility and our Option Premiums

What makes some options premiums worth so much more than others? Let's say we have two stocks, A and B. Both are trading @ $25/share. We look to sell the same month A-T-M $25 strike, yet one (stock A) returns 2%, while the other (stock B) returns 4%. WHY? The answer lies predominantly in the mysterious world of implied volatility. The volatility of an option reflects the fluctuation in the price of the underlying stock, both up and down. It does NOT predict a trend but rather predicts a range of price change that the equity is expected to have. In this case, stock B has a much higher implied volatility than does A.

Let's go back to our equation of the factors that determine the value of an option premium:

Intrinsic Value + Time Value = Premium Value

The Intrinsic value for call options is the amount of money the strike is below the market value of the equity, nothing more or less. It is not affected by anything other than the value of the underlying security. Therefore, volatility of the stock relates only to *time value*.

Now take a big gulp of high-octane coffee as we review some key definitions that relate to volatility:

Key definitions

- *Historical Volatility (Statistical Volatility)*: A statistic or statement of fact based on the closing prices over the past year. If a stock has had a trading range between

$30 and $40 and has an average price of $35, we can say the historical volatility is $5 in either direction. A stock that moves up or down $5 from its average of $35 is said to have a historical volatility of 14.3% (5/35). Historical volatility does not predict a future direction.

- *Implied Volatility*: This is the market's *estimate* of future volatility and is based on the option's last traded price. Stated differently, it is the volatility that the market as a whole is expecting that is giving the option premium its current value. If the historical volatility is @ 14.3% and the current implied volatility is @ 30%, that option is considered by some to be overpriced.

Common Sense Formulas for Implied Volatility

> As implied volatility increases = Call premium increases
>
> As implied volatility decreases = Call premium decreases

Causes of implied volatility changes:

- changes in stock volatility
- supply and demand
- earnings reports
- rumors
- news
- market psychology and volatility
- world events
- political events

Mathematics of Implied Volatility

In statistics, we often hear the term standard deviation. This means that a certain event will occur based on a statistical model, a certain percent of the time. Let's clarify this with an example:

Blue Collar Investor Corp (BCI) is currently trading @ $60 per share (I wish!). A pricing model such as Black-Scholes, determines that, based on the current market value of the call option ($60 strike, for example), the implied volatility is 25%. This means that the market is anticipating a price change of $15 (25% of $60) either up or down. (Remember, implied volatility does not identify a trend). The expected price range for the implied volatility of BCI is between $45 and $75 (plus or minus 25% of $60). The likelihood the latter range is accurate is 1 standard deviation, or 68% of the time (In statistics, about 68% of the values lie within 1 standard deviation of the mean). When implied volatility percentages are quoted, they are based on the current option value and on 1 standard deviation.

Where to Access Historical and Implied Volatility Statistics

To access historical and implied volatility statistics, use the following link, found on *iVolatility.com:*

http://www.ivolatility.com/options.j?ticker=SPX&R=0

You must join first (it's free). Use the category "basic options". Then type in the ticker symbol and you will see the historical volatility of the stock and implied volatility of the option. When implied volatility is much higher than the historical volatility, the market is anticipating an event that could move the equity price dramatically in either direction. Take a look at the right side of the screen...you will see a chart with both IV and HV plotted. By drawing a rough trend line across the highs and lows, you can get a rough idea of how the volatility has been playing out over time. These high IV scenarios are situations I try to avoid (earnings reports being the main one).

Factors that Influence the Value of Our Option Premiums | 171

How Implied Volatility Impacts the Different Strikes

In-the-money strikes
- The LEAST TIME VALUE
- Smaller % changes
- Conservative (which is why I use this strike so often in volatile markets).

At-the-money strikes
- The MOST TIME VALUE
- Largest DOLLAR changes
- More aggressive.

Out-of-the money strikes
- All time value.
- Largest PERCENT changes
- Most aggressive; great for uptrending markets.

Covered Call Examples Using Implied Volatility

1- Option premiums when stock price declines:

- Buy BCI @ $62 and sell the $65 call @ $1.50 with implied volatility currently @ 25%
- Then BCI drops to $57 two weeks later
- If implied volatility = 20%; premium may be $.05
- If implied volatility = 25%; premium may be $.10
- If implied volatility = 30%; premium may be $.15
- These figures will impact our B-T-C exit strategies

2- Option premiums when stock price increases:

- Same as above but stock price moves up to $67
- If implied volatility = 20%; premium may be $2.90

- If implied volatility = 25%; premium may be $3.20
- If implied volatility = 30%; premium may be $3.60

3- *No price change but option premium moves up:*

- Buy BCI @ $30 and sell the $30 call @ $1.50
- The next day BCI trades between $25 and $35 but closes @ $30.
- The same option is now trading @ $2.00 due to the increase in implied volatility.

4- *Stock price increases but option value decreases:*

- Same as above however the stock moves up slowly the next day to $31.
- Fears of an imminent price decline have been calmed.
- Option value has diminished to $1.20 due to the decrease in implied volatility.

The Case for One Month Options

I sell predominantly one-month options. This decision was NOT based on anything I read or was told, but rather on experience and common sense. Most stocks with options have at least four expiration cycles (discussed later in this chapter) affiliated with them at any point in time…the current month, the next month and two more months further out based on the particular option cycle that particular equity has been assigned to. Stocks that also have *LEAPS* (long-term options) have more than four cycles. Using the options chains and the Ellman Calculator, I will make my case for selling mainly one-month options.

Three Reasons to Sell One-Month Options

1- It facilitates adhering to a core BCI guideline of never selling an option in a contract cycle that has an upcoming earnings report. Since earnings reports are made public on a quarterly basis for U.S. companies, selling short-term options allow us to move our stocks in and out of our portfolios (yet keep them on our watch lists if they still meet our system criteria).

2- Stocks have no loyalty to us. They can be our best friends one month and our worst enemies the next. Although we do have exit strategies to help control a negative situation, the shorter the commitment we have to an equity, the less risk we incur.

3- We make the most money selling one-month options. I'm sure I have your attention now, so allow me to demonstrate via an options chain for Netlogic Microsystems (NETL), currently trading for $53.22 as shown in Figure 71:

Netlogic Microsystems, Inc. (NASDAQ: NETL) Optionable
Last: 53.22   Chg: -0.90 (-1.66%)   Open: 54.23   Avg Vol: 760,930   Volume: 563,157
Bid: 52.45   Ask: 53.31   High: 54.50   Low: 52.67   W%Chg: -25.99%
After Hours Data Last: 53.31 Chg: +0.09 %Chg: +0.17% Volume: 23,213

NETL- Current Price

Figure 71- NETL: current price

The option chain is shown in Figure 72:

Calls — Mar 10

Last	Intrinsic Value	Bid	Ask	Vol	Open Interest	Strike
23.15	23.22	22.80	23.50	0	0	30.00
18.05	18.22	17.70	18.40	0	32	35.00
13.15	13.22	12.80	13.50	0	42	40.00
8.40	8.22	8.10	8.70	0	365	45.00
4.45	3.22	4.30	4.60	39	1,101	50.00
1.73	0.00	(1.65)	1.80	300	441	55.00
0.45	0.00	0.40	0.50	720	40	60.00

Spreads for Fri Mar 19 22:00:00 PDT 2010 Options: Bull Call Spreads | Bull P

Calls — Apr 10

Last	Intrinsic Value	Bid	Ask	Vol	Open Interest	Strike
28.15	28.22	27.80	28.50	0	10	25.00
23.10	23.22	22.70	23.50	0	24	30.00
18.15	18.22	17.80	18.50	0	1,084	35.00
13.35	13.22	13.00	13.70	0	1,777	40.00
9.00	8.22	8.80	9.20	2	1,839	45.00
5.30	3.22	5.20	5.40	67	4,090	50.00
2.62	0.00	(2.55)	2.70	31	1,720	55.00
1.10	0.00	1.05	1.15	9	186	60.00
0.40	0.00	0.35	0.45	0	41	65.00

Spreads for Fri Apr 16 22:00:00 PDT 2010 Options: Bull Call Spreads | Bull P

Calls — Jul 10

Last	Intrinsic Value	Bid	Ask	Vol	Open Interest	Strike
28.35	28.22	27.50	29.20	0	1	25.00
23.20	23.22	22.70	23.70	0	10	30.00
18.65	18.22	18.20	19.10	0	117	35.00
14.25	13.22	13.80	14.70	0	249	40.00
10.65	8.22	10.50	10.80	0	658	45.00
7.35	3.22	7.20	7.50	3	3,559	50.00
4.80	0.00	(4.70)	4.90	2	399	55.00
2.98	0.00	2.85	3.10	0	170	60.00

Figure 72- NETL Options Chain

This information was captured after the February contracts expired. We will hone in on the March (one-month out), April (two-months out) and July (five-months out) contracts. Here is the information we glean from the options chain and will feed into the Ellman Calculator (single tab):

- The stock is trading @ $53.22 so we will look at the $55 call options

- The March $55 call returns $1.65/share (red circle)

- The April $55 call returns $2.55/share (blue circle)
- The July $55 call returns $4.70/share (green circle)

It may be tempting to opt for the higher dollar returns of the longer-term options; however we must factor in the time frame and logically deduce how to best put our money to work so as to generate the most profits. So let's feed this information into the single tab of the Ellman Calculator, as illustrated in Figure 73):

1) ENTER THE STOCK NAME, SYMBOL AND PRICE PER SHARE

Stock name >>	Netlogic
Stock symbol >>	NETL
Stock share price >>	$ 53.22

2) ENTER THE SYMBOL, STRIKE PRICE, EXPIRATION DATE AND OPTION PRICE PER SHARE

	Symbol	Strike Price	Exp Date	Price / share
Option choice #1 >>		55.00	03/19/10	1.65
Option choice #2 >>		55.00	04/16/10	2.55
Option choice #3 >>		55.00	07/16/10	4.70
Option choice #4 >>				

Figure 73- NETL- Info into single tab of the Ellman Calculator

Now, in Figure 74, let's examine the results of these calculations:

Option selected	NETL MAR 55.00	NETL APR 55.00	NETL JUL 55.00
Today's date	02/17/10	02/17/10	02/17/10
Days to expiration	30	58	149
Cost for 100 shares of stock	$ 5,322.00	$ 5,322.00	$ 5,322.00
Proceeds from one contract	$ 165.00	$ 255.00	$ 470.00
IN / OUT OF THE MONEY	OUT	OUT	OUT
INTRINSIC VALUE	$ -	$ -	$ -
UPSIDE AMOUNT	$ 178.00	$ 178.00	$ 178.00
UPSIDE POTENTIAL	3.3%	3.3%	3.3%
DOWNSIDE AMOUNT	$ -	$ -	$ -
DOWNSIDE PROTECTION	0.0%	0.0%	0.0%
RETURN ON VARIOUS OUTCOMES			
Proceeds from option sale	$ 165.00	$ 255.00	$ 470.00
Amount of buy-down	$ -	$ -	$ -
Actual option profit	$ 165.00	$ 255.00	$ 470.00
Option profit	$ 165.00	$ 255.00	$ 470.00
Upside profit	$ 178.00	$ 178.00	$ 178.00
Total profit	$ 343.00	$ 433.00	$ 648.00
Cost of shares	$ 5,322.00	$ 5,322.00	$ 5,322.00
Return On Option (ROO)	3.1%	4.8%	8.8%

Figure 74 - NETL- 1, 2 and 5 Month Returns

The ROO or percentage returns generated does NOT include the upside potential. Although the Ellman Calculator does give this information, I left it out of this graphic because all choices have the same upside, and I want to concentrate just on the initial option profit. Here are the ROO figures derived from the Ellman Calculator:

- The March $55 call returns 3.1% (green arrow)

- The April $55 call generates 4.8% (blue arrow)

- The July $55 call generates 8.8% (red arrow)

Once again, upon first glance it appears that the July $55 call will be the most lucrative for us until we annualize these percentages. To do so, we must convert these figures to a monthly return and multiply by 12, as follows:

- March: 3.1%/1 x 12 = 37.2%
- April: 4.8%/2 x 12 = 28.8%
- July: 8.8%/5 x 12 = 21.1%

The one-month options outperformed the two-month options by more than 29% and the five-month options by more than 76%! I rest my case.

Beta: Another Tool to Enhance our Returns

When we defined the Greeks, we discussed the price sensitivity of the option premium as it relates to the underlying equity, time and other factors. One of the principal tenets discussed was that (all other factors being equal) an increase in share *volatility* will increase an option premium. Thus, an equity with greater volatility will be associated with an option premium which generates greater profit but also carries greater risk.

One way to measure the volatility or *systemic risk* (market risk) of a security is to compare it to the market as a whole; the S&P 500 being the most commonly used benchmark. This is known as **beta**. This number is calculated using a process known as *regression analysis* wherein the "market" is assigned a number of "1". *Beta is the tendency of a stock's returns to respond to changes in the market.*

The Numbers

- Beta =1: the equity price will move in conjunction with the market. If the market is up 2%, so will the stock.

- Beta < 1: the stock will be less volatile than the market. Utility stocks typically have a beta of less than 1.

- Beta > 1: the security price will be more volatile than the market. Tech stocks typically have a beta of greater than one.

Bearing the foregoing in mind, if a stock has a beta of 1.5, it is considered 50% more volatile than the S&P 500. If the market appreciates by 8%, the expected return of that equity, based on its beta, would be 12%. On the other hand, if the market declines by 8%, that equity would be expected to decline by 12%. There you have the two faces of enhanced volatility… greater potential returns with enhanced risk. If an equity has a beta of .5 and the market was up 8%, one would expect that security to appreciate by 4%.

Negative betas

A stock with a negative beta tends to move in the opposite direction of the market. An equity with a beta of (-) 2 would decline by 10% if the market appreciated by 5%, and would increase by 10% if the market declined by 5%.

Problems with Beta

There is no such thing as a panacea in the stock market; beta does have its flaws and should not be solely relied upon in determining the risk of our investments. The following are some of the drawbacks in using beta:

- Beta does not account for business changes such as a new line of products.

- Beta looks backwards, and history is not always an accurate predictor of future events.

- Beta ignores the price level of a stock.

- Beta makes the assumption that the volatility is equal in both directions..

The drawbacks are more significant for longer-term investments. Beta can be extremely useful to us as one-month covered call investors. For our purposes of selling one-month call options, beta is a good measure of risk.

Implementing Beta into Our Decision-Making Process

High beta stocks will outperform the uptrending stock market and underperform the downtrending market. Low beta equities will underperform the uptrending market and outperform the downtrending market. In a bullish market, I lean towards high beta stocks and sell O-T-M strikes. In a bearish market, I favor low beta stocks and sell I-T-M strikes. In neutral markets, I "ladder" (use a mix) my beta stocks in much the same way that I "ladder" my strikes. At the time this book was written, the BCI Premium Report included beta information on all stocks on the premium watch list ("running list").

Conclusion:

Beta is simply a tool in our arsenal. Market conditions will dictate whether we should lean towards high or low beta stocks. It should be used in conjunction with all the BCI system criteria. No one factor will make our investment decision evident. By continually throwing the odds in our favor by using sound fundamental and technical analysis, in addition to common sense, we will watch our profits rise as success dominates our portfolios.

Related Information

Stock Option Expiration Cycles

Everyone likes when things make sense. When we understand why things are the way they are it has a calming effect on us. When we look at the different expiration months available for our stock options, an explanation is required and demanded by the curious investor. On first glance it makes no sense at all! Different stocks have different expiration months! How can that be? We want uniformity, not chaos. Like most things, there is a reasonable explanation.

All options are defined by an expiration month and date (the third Friday of the month, except for some quarterly and weekly expirations of some securities) after which the contract becomes invalid and the right to exercise no longer exists. When options began trading in 1973, the CBOE (Chicago Board Options Exchange) decided that there would be only four months at a time when options could be traded. Stocks were then randomly assigned to one of three cycles:

• January cycle- options available in the first month of each quarter (Jan., April, July and Oct.)

• February cycle- options available in the middle month of each quarter (Feb., May, Aug., and Nov.)

• March cycle- options available in the last month of each quarter (March, June, Sept., and Dec.)

The foregoing cycles proved to be a workable concept until options gained in popularity, increasing the demand for shorter-term options. In 1990, the CBOE decided that each stock (with options) would have the current and following months to trade, PLUS the next two months from the original cycle (hope your head isn't starting to spin). Let's simplify things by looking at the chart in Figure 75:

Current (Front) Month	Next Month	Third Option	Fourth Option
January Cycle			
January	February	April (1st month)	July (1st month)
February Cycle			
January	February	May (2nd month)	August (2nd month)
March Cycle			
January	February	June (3rd month)	September (3rd month)

Figure 75- Expiration Cycles

<u>If the current month is January</u>, we see that all options are available for both the current (January) and next month (February). The last two option expiration months available will depend on their original placement in one of the three cycles:

- January cycle- will also have April and July expirations
- February cycle- will also have May and August expirations
- March cycle- will also have June and September expirations

Now, if your head has stopped spinning and you're feeling a bit better, I ask you NOT to put away the Tylenol, at least not yet! Here come the *LEAPS* (Long-term Equity Anticipation Securities), which are options with longer-term expirations. Only heavily traded securities such as Microsoft have these types of derivatives. LEAPS will have options with more than four months of expirations, with some having up to seven months. LEAPS can further complicate these cycles, however, those of you who follow the BCI system of selling predominantly one-month call options need not be concerned with these extended expiration periods. However, intelligence does breed curiosity, so for those of you interested in learning more about LEAPS and potentially using these longer-term options as part of your covered call writing strategy, a more detailed discussion of same is included in Chapter 15. For purposes of this chapter, simply take note that the vast majority of stock options will fall into the four month cycle depicted in Figure 75.

One Point Strike Program

In 2009, the options exchanges received SEC approval to expand and make permanent the ability to list strike prices in $1.00 increments. Initially, the program allowed the exchanges to list dollar strike prices on equity options for up to five individual stocks, provided that the strike prices were $20.00 or less, but greater than or equal to $3.00. Under the recently approved program, each exchange can elect to list dollar strike prices on equity options for up to 150 individual securities, provided that the strike prices are $50.00 or less but greater than or equal to $1.00. Additionally, no $1 strike price may be listed that is greater than $5 from the underlying stocks closing price in its primary market on the previous day. For example, if a stock closed at $40 we can have strikes of $41, $42, $43, $44 and $45 but not $46, $47 etc. The options exchanges are also restricted from listing any options series[1] that would result in strike prices being $0.50 apart.

The options exchanges are also restricted from listing any options series[2] that would result in strike prices being $0.50 apart.

Note: As of November 4, 2009, the current participants in the $1.00 dollar strike program are as follows:

---

1   An options series is a specific set of calls or puts on the same underlying security, in the same class and with the same strike price and expiration date.
2   The participating securities may change.

- A – Agilent Technologies Inc.
- AA – Alcoa, Inc
- ABT – Abbott Laboratories
- ABX – Barrick Gold Corporation
- ACH – Aluminum Corp. of China Ltd.
- ACI – Arch Coal
- ADBE – Adobe Systems Incorporated
- ADM – Archer Daniels Midland Co
- ADP – Automatic Data Processing
- ADSK – Autodesk Inc
- AEP – American Electric Power Inc
- AET – AETNA Inc.
- AFL – Aflac, Inc.
- AIG – American International Group
- AKAM - Akamai Technologies Inc
- AKS - AK Steel Holding Corp.
- ALL - The Allstate Corporation
- ALTR - Altera Corporation
- AMAT - Applied Materials
- AMD - Advanced Micro Devices
- AMR - AMR Corporation
- AMSC - American Superconductor
- AMX - America Movil
- ANF - Abercrombie and Fitch
- ANR - Alpha Natural Resources Inc.
- AONE - A123 Systems Inc.
- APC - Anadarko Petroleum
- ARNA - Arena Pharmaceutical
- ARO - Aeropostale Inc.
- ATI - Allegheny Technologies Inc
- ATVI - Activision Blizzard Inc
- AUY - Yamana Gold
- AVP - Avon Products Inc.
- AXL - American Axle & Mfg Holdings Inc
- AXP - American Express Company
- BA - Boeing Company
- BAC - Bank of America Corp.
- BBBY - Bed Bath & Beyond Inc.
- BBT - BB&T Corporation
- BBY - Best Buy Company
- BHI - Baker Hughes

- BJS - BJ Services Company
- BK - Bank of New York Mellon Corporation
- BMY - Bristol Myers Squibb
- BP - BP Plc
- BRCD - Brocade Comm Sys
- BRCM - Broadcom Corporation
- BSX - Boston Scientific Corp
- BTU - Peabody Energy Corp
- BUCY - Bucyrus International Inc
- BX - Blackstone Group(The) L.P.
- C - Citigroup Incorporated
- CAL - Continental Airlines
- CAT - Caterpillar Inc.
- CBS - CBS Corporation
- CCJ - Cameco Corporation
- CCL - Carnival Corp
- CECO - Career Education
- CELG - Celgene Corp
- CHK – Chesapeake Energy Corporation
- CI - Cigna Corp
- CIEN - Ciena Corp
- CIT - CIT Group Inc New
- CLF – Cliffs Natural Resources
- CMCSA – Comcast Corporation
- CMCSK – Comcast Corporation
- CMI – Cummins Inc
- CNO – Conseco, Inc.
- CNQ – Canadian Natural Resources
- CNX – Consol Energy
- COF – Capital One Financial
- COH – Coach Inc
- COP – ConocoPhillips
- CRM – Salesforce.com
- CROX – Crocs, Incorporated
- CSCO - Cisco Systems Incorporated
- CSIQ - Canadian Solar Inc.
- CSX - CSX Corp.
- CVS - CVS Caremark Corporation
- CX - Cemex S.A.B. de C.V.
- CY – Cypress Semiconductor
- CYOU – Changyou.com

- DAL – Delta Airlines
- DD – Dupont
- DE – Deere & Co.
- DELL – Dell Incorporated
- DFS – Discover Financial Services
- DHI – D.R. Horton, Inc.
- DIS – Walt Disney Company
- DISH – Dish Network Cl. A
- DLTR – Dollar Tree Inc.
- DNDN – Dendreon Corp.
- DOW – Dow Chemical Company
- DPTR - Delta Petroleum Corp
- DRI – Darden Restaurants
- DRYS – DryShips, Inc.
- DTV – DirectTV Group Inc
- DUK – Duke Energy Corp
- EBAY – eBay Inc.
- EK – Eastman Kodak Co.
- ELN - ELAN Corporation PLC
- EMC - EMC Corp
- EMR - Emerson Electric
- ENER - Energy Conversion Devices, Inc.
- EP - El Paso Corporation
- ERTS - Electronic Arts, Inc.
- ESLR - Evergreen Solar Inc.
- ETFC - E Trade Financial Corp
- EXM - Excel Maritime Carriers, Ltd.
- F - Ford Motor Company
- FCX - F/M Copper & Gold
- FITB - Fifth Third Bancorp
- FNM – Fannie Mae
- FRE - Freddie Mac
- FUQI - FUQI International Inc.
- FWLT - Foster Wheeler AG
- GCI – Gannett Inc
- GE – General Electric
- GFI – Gold Fields Limited
- GG – Goldcorp Inc
- GILD – Gilead Sciences
- GLW – Corning Incorporated
- GME – Gamestop Corp

- GNK – Genco Shipping & Trading Ltd.
- GNW – Genworth Financial Inc
- GPS – Gap Inc
- GRMN – Garmin Limited
- HAL – Halliburton Company
- HANS – Hansen Natl Corp
- HBAN – Huntington Bancshares
- HBC – HSBC Holdings plc
- HD – The Home Depot Inc.
- HGSI – Human Genome Sciences Inc
- HIG – Hartford Financial Services
- HK – Petrohawk Energy
- HL – Hecla Mining Co
- HMY – Harmony Gold Mining Co. Ltd.
- HNZ – Heinz H J Co
- HOG – Harley-Davidson Inc
- HON – Honeywell International Inc.
- HOT – Starwoods Hotel & Resorts
- HPQ – Hewlett-Packard Company
- HRB – H&R Block Inc.
- HUM – Humana Inc.
- HUN – Huntsman Corporation
- IBN – ICICI Bank Limited
- IDCC – Interdigital Inc
- IGT – International Game Technology
- INTC – Intel Corporation
- IP – International Paper Company
- IPI – Intrepid Potash
- IVN – Ivanhoe Mines Limited
- JAVA - Sun Microsystems
- JBLU - Jetblue Airways Corp
- JCP - J.C. Penney Company, Inc.
- JDSU - JDS Uniphase
- JNPR - Juniper Network
- JOYG - Joy Global
- JPM - JP Morgan Chase & Co.
- JWN - Nordstrom Inc.
- KBH - KB Homes
- KBR - KBR, Inc.
- KEY - Keycorp
- KFT - Kraft Foods Inc.

Factors that Influence the Value of Our Option Premiums | 187

- KGC - Kinross Gold Corporation
- KLAC - KLA Tencor Corp
- KSS - Kohl's Corporation
- KWK - Quicksilver Resources Inc
- LCC - US Airways Group Inc
- LDK - LDK Solar Co
- LEN - Lennar Corporation
- LLTC - Linear Technology Co
- LLY - Lilly Eli & Co
- LM - Legg Mason
- LNC - Lincoln National Corp.
- LOW - Lowe's Corporation
- LUV - Southwest Airlines
- LVS - Las Vegas Sands Corp
- M - Macy's, Inc.
- MAR - Marriott Intl Inc
- MBI - MBIA Incorporated
- MCO - Moody's Corp
- MDR – McDermott International Inc
- MDT – Medtronic Inc
- MEE – Massey Energy Co
- MER – Merrill Lynch & Co., Inc
- MET – Metlife Inc
- MGM – MGM Mirage
- MO – Altria Group Inc.
- MOT - Motorola
- MRK - Merck & CO., Inc.
- MRO - Marathon Oil Corporation
- MRVL - Marvell Technology Group Ltd.
- MS – Morgan Stanley
- MSFT - Microsoft Corp.
- MT - ArcelorMittal
- MTW - Manitowoc Company
- MU - Micron Technologies
- MYGN - Myriad Genetics Inc
- MYL - Mylan Inc
- NAT - Nordic American Tanker Shipping, Ltd
- NBR - Nabors Industries Limited
- NDAQ - Nasdaq OMX Group
- NE - Noble Corporation
- NEM - Newmont Mining

- NLY – Annaly Capital Management
- NOK – Nokia Corporation
- NOV – National Oilwell Varco
- NSC – Norfolk Southern Corp
- NSM – National Semiconductor Corp
- NTAP – NetApp Inc
- NTES – Netease.com Inc
- NUE – Nucor Corporation
- NVAX – Novavax, Inc.
- NVDA – Nvidia Corporation
- NVLS – Novellus Sys Inc
- NYB – New York Comm Bancorp
- NYX – NYSE Euronext
- ODP - Office Depot Inc
- ONNN - ON Semiconductor Corp
- ORCL - Oracle Corporation
- PAAS - Pan American Silver Corp
- PALM - Palm Inc.
- PBR - Petroleo Brasileiro S.A.
- PCAR - Paccar Inc
- PCX - Patriot Coal Corporation
- PEI - Pennsylvania Real Estate Invest Trust
- PFE - Pfizer Inc.
- PFG - Principal Financial Group
- PHM - Pulte Homes, Inc.
- PLD - Prologis
- PM - Philip Morris
- PNC - PNC Financial Services
- PRU - Prudential Financial, Inc.
- PXP - Plains Exploration & Prod Co
- QCOM - Qualcomm Inc.
- RCL - Royal Caribbean Cruises
- RF - Regions Financial Corp
- RMBS - Rambus Inc.
- RRI - Reliant Energy Inc.
- RTN - Raytheon Company
- RYL - The Ryland Group, Inc.
- S - Sprint Nextel Corporation
- SAP - SAP AG
- SBUX - Starbucks Corporation
- SCHW - Charles Schwab Corp

Factors that Influence the Value of Our Option Premiums | 189

- SD - Sandridge Energy Inc
- SGR - Shaw Group
- SHLD - Sears Holding Corp
- SII - Smith Intl Inc
- SINA - Sina Corp
- SIRI - Sirius Satellite Radio
- SLM - SLM Corporation
- SLW - Silver Wheaton Corp
- SMH - Semiconductor Holders Trust
- SNDK – SanDisk Corporation
- SO – Southern Company
- SPG – Simon Property Group Inc.(New)
- SPLS - Staples Inc
- SPWRA - Sunpower Corp
- SQNM – Sequenom Inc.
- SSRI – Silver Standard Resources Inc.
- STI – SunTrust Banks Inc.
- STEC – STEC Inc.
- STI – SunTrust Banks Inc.
- STLD – Steel Dynamics Inc.
- STP – Suntech Power Holdings Co., Ltd
- STSI – Star Scientific Inc
- STT – State Street Corporation
- STX – Seagate Technology
- SU – Suncor Energy
- SUN – Sunoco, Inc.
- SVNT – Savient Pharmaceuticals Inc.
- SWN – Southwestern Energy
- SYK – Stryker Corp.
- SYMC - Symantec Corp
- SYNA - Synaptics Inc.
- T - AT&T Inc.
- TCK - Teck Resources Ltd
- TEX - Terex Corp
- TGT - Target Corporation
- THC - Tenet Healthcare
- TIF - Tiffany & Co.
- TOL - Toll Brothers Inc.
- TRA - Terra Industries Inc.
- TSL - Trina Solar Ltd. (ADS)
- TSO - Tesoro Petroleum Corp

- TWX - AOL Time Warner
- TXN - Texas Instruments
- TXT - Textron Inc.
- TYC - Tyco Intl Ltd
- UAUA – UAL Corp.
- UBS – UBS AG
- UNH – Unitedhealth Group
- UNP – Union Pacific Corp
- UPL – Ultra Petroleum
- URBN – Urban Outfitters
- USB – U.S. Bancorp
- USU – USEC, Inc.
- VALE - Companhia Vale Do Rio Doce
- VLO – Valero Energy Corporation
- VMW – VMware
- VRSN – Verisign
- VZ – Verizon
- WAG – Walgreen Co.
- WB – Wachovia Corporation
- WDC – Western Digital Corp
- WFC – Wells Fargo & Company
- WFMI – Whole Foods Market
- WFR – MEMC Electronic Material
- WFT – Weatherford International
- WHR – Whirlpool Corp
- WY – Weyerhauser Co
- WYNN – Wynn Resorts Limited
- X - United States Steel Corporation
- XL - XL Capital LTD
- XLNX - Xilinx Inc
- XRX - Xerox Corp
- XTO - XTO Energy Inc.
- YGE - Yingli Green Energy Holding Co.
- YHOO - Yahoo!
- YRCW - YRC Worldwide, Inc.
- YUM - Yum Brands
- ZION - Zions Bancorp

Open Interest and Volume

We are now all familiar with option chains, which is where we determine how much cash will be generated into our accounts when we sell our call options. It's fun! To recap, we first inspect the current price of the underlying security (stock or ETF). Next, we check the call options with the closest strike prices (I-T-M, A-T-M and O-T-M) and note the bid and ask prices for each option. For I-T-M strikes, we also look at the amount of intrinsic value that the option premium consists of. If we are interested in a particular option, we take note of the option symbol, usually found on the left side of the options chain. The inquiry, however, should not end there. Volume and open interest, two important yet often overlooked columns, should also be considered by all BCI investors during the strike price selection process. Accordingly, the purpose of this segment is to discuss that distinction between these two figures and the significance of each

Let's look at a typical options chain for MELI (Figure 76), an equity that was in my portfolio at the time this chapter was written (note the original option symbolgy, which was replaced by the option chain depicted in Figure 42, supra). Assume for purposes of Figure 76 that the current market price of MELI is $48.59:

Calls							
Symbol	Last	Intrinsic Value	Bid	Ask	**Vol**	**Open Interest**	Strike
QMB-LA	43.6	43.59	43	44.2	0	1	5
QMB-LT	40.8	41.09	39.9	41.7	0	0	7.5
QMB-LB	38.3	38.59	37.4	39.2	0	0	10
QMB-LV	35.8	36.09	34.9	36.7	0	0	12.5
QMB-LU	33.5	33.59	32.8	34.2	0	20	15
QMB-LW	30.8	31.09	29.9	31.7	0	0	17.5
QMB-LY	28.3	28.59	27.4	29.2	0	563	20
QMB-LX	25.95	26.09	25.2	26.7	0	814	22.5
QMB-LE	23.6	23.59	23	24.2	0	475	25
QMB-LF	18.45	18.59	17.7	19.2	0	671	30
QMB-LC	16.3	16.09	15.9	16.7	0	1,087	32.5
QMB-LG	13.4	13.59	12.5	14.3	10	642	35
QMB-LH	8.9	8.59	8.5	9.3	27	2,952	40
QMB-LI	4.6	3.59	4.4	4.8	76	1,789	45
QMB-LJ	1.55	0	1.45	1.65	202	2,282	50
QMB-LK	0.35	0	0.3	0.4	0	270	55
QMB-LL	0.08	0	0.05	0.1	0	211	60

Figure 76 - Options Chain for MELI (Using the Original Option Symbology)

Volume

Volume measures the amount of times a particular options contract has been bought or sold in a *particular day*. The higher the volume for a particular options contract, the more "liquid" that option is, or the easier it will be to buy or sell that option without materially affecting its price. A contract with zero volume is NOT necessarily "illiquid" because it takes time to build up volume during the day, and additionally, an exchange specialist or market maker is often obligated (pursuant to certain exchange-mandated volume and price-point thresholds) to provide liquidity, or step in and take the other side of a bid or offer. With respect to the options chain depicted in Figure 76, the volume for the MELI O-T-M $50 call is 202 contracts bought or sold as of the time that options chain was generated/viewed.

Open Interest

Open interest is the number of option contracts that are open or outstanding (i.e. have not yet been exercised, closed by an offsetting position or expired) on a particular day, and is an additional measure of an option's liquidity. This number is cumulative. Options with large open interest have a secondary market of buyers and sellers, which allow that option to be traded at a reasonable bid-ask spread. The open interest for the MELI $50 strike in Figure 76 is 2,282 contracts

The Mathematics of Open Interest

There are four types of options transactions that will affect the open interest of MELI. As summarized directly below and illustrated in Figure 77, opening transactions will increase MELI's open interest, while closing transactions will decrease this figure:

- Buy to Open (BTO)- Increases open interest by creating a new long position

- Sell to Open (STO)- Increases open interest by creating a new short position

- Buy to Close (BTC)- Decreases open interest by closing an existing short position

- Sell to Close (STC)- Decreases open interest by closing an existing long position

Trading Activity and Open Interest

TRADING ACTIVITY	CURRENT OPEN INTEREST	VOLUME
Trader A: B-T-O 6 contracts	6	6
Trader B: B-T-C 2 contracts	4	8
Trader C: S-T-O 8 contracts	12	16
Trader D: S-T-C 3 contracts	9	19

Figure 77 - Mathematics of Open Interest

As you can see, open interest is not the same as volume. With volume, both entries (opening positions) and exits (closing positions) cause volume to increase, however in the case of open interest, entries will cause an increase in overall open interest, while exits result in a decrease in the same. Open interest is generally a higher number than volume because it is cumulative, whereas volume is reset to zero at the beginning of each trading day.

Significance of Open Interest

Increasing open interest shows strength in the current price movement of an option in much the same way a volume spike enhances the significance of a change in a technical indicator such as the MACD. A decreasing open interest figure shows a weakening of the current price movement. Thus, if the price of an option is increasing on increasing open interest, the likelihood of continued price increases is greater, while a decrease in open interest is indicative that upward price movement is starting to weaken. Also, as mentioned earlier in this chapter, the greater the open interest, the more favorable the bid-ask spread is likely to be. *Open interest of 100 contracts or less is thought to have relatively thin liquidity. I like to see an OI of at least 100 contracts and/or a reasonable bid-ask spread ($.30 or less).* Keep in mind that a bid-ask spread of greater than $.10 can oftentimes be negotiated down by "playing the bid-ask spread".

Non-Standard Options- What They Are and Why We Should Avoid Them

You do your due-diligence and select a great performing stock in a great performing industry. Once you have determined that this equity meets all of our system requirements, you head off to the option chain to check the calculations. Since the stock is trading at $39 per share, you check the $40 call. This can't be...there are two call options with a $40 strike price and the same expiration date. They have different symbols, volume, open interest and bid-ask prices. One has a bid of $1, and the other a bid of $12. You think to yourself that the market makers must have been out late last night partying and made a huge mistake. "I'll sell the $12 option and make a huge profit," you think. "Better yet, I'll buy thousands of contracts of the cheaper option and sell the same number of the more expensive, offset my positions and pocket a fortune. I'm going to be rich!" However, the truth of the matter is, NO YOUR NOT! You have entered the world of non-standard options.

What Are Non-Standard Options?

Non-standard options do not have the standard terms of an options contract, namely, the right to buy or sell 100 shares of the underlying asset. Thus, the owner of a non-standard option has the right to buy or sell an amount *other than* 100 shares of the underlying asset. These option types are normally created as a result of a specific event, such as a merger, acquisition, spin-off, extraordinary dividend or stock split. As a result of the changing circumstances, the contract is adjusted to be equitable to both the option buyer and seller by equating the new underlying asset(s) of equal value as the owner of 100 shares. The *Depository Trust Company* (DTC) determines how the shares will trade pre-event, while the *Options Clearing Corp.* (OCC) decides how these changes will be reflected in the options. Each situation is unique and therefore *non-standard*. This makes non-standard options difficult to understand and therefore risky to most investors. In the hypothetical scenario detailed in the preceding section, one contract was a standard options contract, the other non-standard. The standard contract represents 100 shares of the underlying, while the non-standard contract does not. As an example, when Bank of America (BAC) took over Merrill Lynch, the owner of 100 shares of Merrill received 85 shares of BAC stock plus $13.71 in cash. Non-standard contracts of BAC now would deliver 85 shares of BAC plus the cash, as opposed to the standard contracts which represented the right to buy or sell 100 shares of BAC. The obvious rule is as follows: avoid all non-standard options; if an option value seems too good to be true, it is. Non-standard option contracts will oftentimes be associated with odd strike prices and premiums, as illustrated in Figure 78:

Real-life Options Chain for BAC Showing Standard and Non-Standard Options

Symbol	IV	Delta	Open Int	Vol	Change	Last	Bid	Ask	Strike
BYO DB	245.22	1.000	395	0	0.00	5.85	5.30	5.40	2.0
JLW DZ	0.00%	0.999	2,531	181	-0.11	3.89	3.80	4.15	2.5
BYO DC	172.31	0.997	5,211	786	-0.15	4.45	4.30	4.40	3.0
BYO DD	164.04	0.976	34,851	164	-0.20	3.45	3.35	3.45	4.0
JLW DA	0.00%	0.905	19,802	209	0.05	1.80	1.60	1.79	5.0
BYO DE	153.59	0.905	25,487	3,990	-0.25	2.50	2.50	2.54	5.0
BYO DF	140.25	0.779	45,811	7,008	-0.22	1.73	1.71	1.75	6.0
BYO DG	131.05	0.621	90,565	13,961	-0.16	1.11	1.08	1.11	7.0
JLW DU	64.26	0.541	21,236	1,813	-0.11	0.40	0.38	0.40	7.5
BYO DH	125.59	0.464	94,648	29,867	-0.12	0.65	0.64	0.65	8.0
JLW DM	78.26	0.329	11,987	600	-0.03	0.13	0.10	0.13	9.0
BYO DI	122.56	0.329	51,165	14,116	-0.09	0.35	0.35	0.37	9.0
JLW DB	87.03	0.225	22,265	355	0.00	0.09	0.04	0.08	10.0
BYO DJ	121.15	0.225	64,372	5,032	-0.05	0.19	0.19	0.20	10.0

BANK OF AMERICA CORPORATION (BAC) Last 7.34 Change -0.24 Bid 7.40 Ask 7.41

April 09 Calls   BAC @ 7   20 Days to

Figure 78 - Options Chain for BAC with Non-Standard

Options

The two $5 strike options for BAC are highlighted in the green encircled area in Figure 78. BYO DE (original option symbology) is the *standard* April 2009 call option, which represents the right to purchase 100 shares of BAC for $5, while JLW DA is the *non-standard* option, representing the right to purchase 85 shares of BAC for $5 plus cash. An uninformed investor looking to buy an option would think the non-standard option is a much better deal, costing $179 per contract as opposed to $254 per contract. The caveat, however, is that the former will deliver only 85 shares (+ cash), not 100 shares.

Liquidity of Non-Standard Options

Non-standard option contracts are often *illiquid and difficult to trade.* In Figure 78, we see that the volume of the standard contract is 3990, while the non-standard contract has a volume of only 209. In this regard, Figure 78 also highlights the importance of considering *both* open interest *and* volume when evaluating option liquidity. Specifically, if one were to evaluate the liquidity of the non-standard April 2009 call option for BAC based solely on its open interest figure, one might easily be deceived into thinking this option was much more liquid than it really was. The reality, however, is that many of the holders of those non-standard options had open positions in their contracts pre-merger, and that most likely, there had been little activity in these options since that time, as indicated by the significantly lower volume figure.

Timing of Contract Adjustments

When a contract adjustment is needed as a result of a merger, acquisition, spin-off, extraordinary dividend or stock split (as in the BAC example above), the standard ("plain vanilla") options are adjusted accordingly. When a new option comes into existence after the event, it will appear as a standard option. ****Check with your brokerage company to make sure that you will be notified, prior to execution, if attempting to trade a non-standard option.

Free information on contract adjustments

http://www.cboe.com/tradtool/contracts.aspx

Conclusion

Non-standard options result from an asset-changing event such as a merger or spin-off. They are difficult to understand because each is unique to its particular situation. When we see an option premium with two similar strike prices that doesn't appear to make sense, avoid the non-standard option and stick to the one we know and understand-the standard call option that gives the owner the right to purchase 100 shares of the underlying asset

Quarterly Expiration Options Contracts

There are a few heavily traded Exchange Traded Funds (ETFs) that, in addition to standard monthly expiration contracts, also have quarterly expiring contracts. These unusual contracts will expire *at the end of the month* in March, June, September or December. Many of the strike prices in these months will show different premiums for the same strike prices. For example, PowerShares QQQ Trust, Series 1 (QQQ) may have two $45 strike prices, one expiring on the third Friday of the applicable expiration month, and the other expiring at the end of the quarterly trading month. The latter will show a slightly higher premium due to the additional time value. Other ETFs that have quarterly contracts include SPDR S&P 500 (SPY), SPDR Dow Jones Industrial Average (DIA) and iShares Russell 2000 Index (IWM).Additional ETFs with quarterly contracts are expected to be added in the future.

Weekly Expiration Options Contracts

At the time this book was written, a relatively new options product called the *Weekly Options Series (weeklys)* became available. . These weekly expiration options are generally

Factors that Influence the Value of Our Option Premiums | 199

listed on a Thursday or Friday and expire the following Friday, however, they are not traded the week of expiration Friday, and therefore do not list new weeklys on the second Thursday of the month (the week before expiration Friday). The next new weekly series is thus listed on the Thursday prior to expiration Friday. An investor needs to carefully examine the option symbols to determine the precise expiration date of an option and if the option is a weekly. It has yet to be determined if weeklys will have a place in our world of covered call writing.

The following represents the list of available weeklys for stocks and ETFs as of September 2010:

Ticker Symbol	Name	Product Type
OEX	S&P 100 Index (American style)	Index
XEO	S&P 100 Index European-style	Index
DJX	Dow Jones Industrial Average	Index
SPX	S&P 500 Index	Index
NDX	NASDAQ 100 Index	Index
EEM	iShares MSCI Emerging Markets Index	ETF
FAS	Direxionshares Daily Financial Bull 3X Shares	ETF
FAZ	Direxionshares Daily Financial Bear 3X Shares	ETF
GLD	ishares SPDR Gold Trust	ETF
GDX	Market Vectors Gold Miner ETF	ETF
IWM	iShares Russell 2000 Index Fund	ETF
QQQ	Nasdaq-100 Index Tracking Stock	ETF
SPY	S&P 500 Depositary Receipts	ETF
USO	United States Oil Fund	ETF
XLF	Financial Select Sector SPDR	ETF
TLT	iShares Barclay's 20+ yr Treasury Bond ETF	ETF
VXX	iPath S&P 500 VIX Short-Term FT	ETN
AAPL	Apple Corporation	Equity
AMZN	Amazon.com Inc	Equity
BAC	Bank of America Corp	Equity
BIDU	Baidu, Inc.	Equity
BP	British Petroleum	Equity
C	Citigroup	Equity
CSCO	Cisco Systems Inc.	Equity
F	Ford Motor Company	Equity
GE	General Electric Company	Equity

GOOG	Google Inc	Equity
GS	Goldman Sachs Group, Inc.	Equity
MSFT	Microsoft Corporation	Equity
NFLX	NetFlix Inc.	Equity

What if a security has both weekly and quarterly expiration dates, such as QQQ, IWM and SPY? For a week when the quarterlys and weeklys expire on a different day (quarterlys do not expire on a Friday) the date in the ticker will differ and the two will be easy to distinguish.

When both the quarterlys and weeklys expire on the same day, the exchanges will not create a weekly the week before expiration because the quarterly will serve the same parameters on that week as a new weekly would. In other words, both would have the same premium value (intrinsic and time value). Bottom line: when the weekly and quarterly dates are the same, there is only one option available per strike price.

Test your knowledge of key points

1- Option premium = _____ + _____.

2- The major factors that influence the time value of an option premium are _____ and _____.

3- The five Greeks that impact the value of an option premium are_____ _____.

4- The most commonly used Greek measures how much the theoretical value of an option will change if the underlying value of the stock moves up or down $1 is called _____.

5- _____ is an estimate of how much the theoretical value of an option declines when there is a passage of one day while there is no change in the stock value or volatility.

6- The amount that the price of an option changes compared to a 1% change in volatility is called _____.

7- Delta values increase as the strike moves further _____ and decrease as the strike moves deeper _____.

8- It will be less expensive to buy back an option for _____ strikes due to their higher _____.

9- As implied volatility increases = Call premium _____.

10- Between one month options and longer term options, the one that produces the highest initial returns is _____ while the one that generates the best annualized returns is_____.

11- One way to measure the volatility or systemic risk (market risk) of a security is to compare it to the market as a whole; the S&P 500 being the most commonly used benchmark. This is known as _____.

12- In a bullish market, favor _____ beta stocks and sell _____ strikes. In a bearish market, I favor _____ beta stocks and sell _____.

13- The three option expiration cycles are known as the _____, _____, and _____ cycles.

14- All option expiration cycles have options available in the _____ month and the _____ month.

15- The SEC program that permitted exchanges to make strike prices available in one dollar increments for many individual stocks is called the _____.

16- Relating to an options chain, volume is a _____ statistic while open interest is a _____ figure.

17- A merger, acquisition, spinoff or stock split may result in _____ which are options that don't have the standard terms of an options contract, namely 100 shares as the underlying asset.

Answers:

1- Intrinsic, time

2- Time until expiration, volatility

3- Delta, gamma, theta, vega and rho.

4- Delta

5- Theta

6- Vega

7- In-the-money, out-of-the-money

8- In-the-money, deltas

9- Increases

10- Longer term options, one month options.

11- Beta

12- High/ out-of-the-money; low/ in-the-money

13- January, February and March

14- Current, next

15- One point strike program

16- Daily, cumulative

17- Non standard options

Chapter 8

Common Sense Considerations

Chapter outline

1- Earnings reports

2- Same store monthly retail sales reports

3- Minimum daily trading volume

4- Stock and industry diversification

5- Cash allocation

6- Summary of book to this point

Thus far we have learned to select underlying stocks using fundamental and technical analysis, how to utilize the stock's option chain and perform calculations to determine which call options and strike prices to select, and how to create organized lists of our securities, options and calculations. This is the foundation for our stock and option selection process. There are, however, a few more critical considerations we must factor into our final decisions which I will call "common sense considerations" that fall into the following five categories:

- Earnings reports
- Same store monthly retail sales reports
- Minimum trading volume
- Stock and industry segment diversification
- Cash allocation

Earnings Reports

Earnings reports are quarterly filings made by public companies to report their performance. They include items such as net income, earnings per share, earnings from continuing operations and net sales. Most companies report earnings in January, April, July and October. Certain foreign companies that trade on U.S. exchanges (American Depository Receipts or ADRs) are not required to report quarterly (They are likely to have their earnings announcements and calls coordinated with the schedule required in the country where their shares are traded). Prior to the publication of these reports, analysts make predictions regarding the earnings and revenues to be reported via a company's earnings report, and the market reacts according to these estimates. This overall prediction is called the *market consensus. A positive earnings surprise* occurs when a company's earnings report beats the market consensus, which usually is accompanied by a dramatic increase in the company's stock price. Alternatively, *a negative earnings surprise* occurs when a company's earnings report falls short of the market consensus, and generally is associated with a significant decrease in stock price. Sell-side firms (e.g. broker-dealers) and buy-side firms (e.g. mutual funds and hedge funds) both estimate the earnings for public companies, and these estimates are averaged together to form the *consensus estimate* for a stock (also called market consensus). Usually, however, there is one analyst who is considered to be the leader for a particular company; he or she is called the *high man* or the *ax man*. If the ax's estimates are higher than the consensus estimates, then a stock usually has to beat the ax's higher estimate, or otherwise risk a decline in its price.

There is also something called a *whisper number.* The whisper number is an unofficial earnings per share forecast that circulates among professionals on Wall Street. Thus, if a company's earnings report satisfies the market consensus but fails to satisfy the whisper number, the company's share price may nevertheless suffer a severe price decline.

In addition to market consensus and the whisper number, many earnings reports will include *earnings guidance.* This is information that a company provides as an indication of future earnings. These guidance reports can influence analysts' stock ratings and investor decisions to buy or sell an equity.

The primary reason for discussing earnings reports is to emphasize the tremendous increase in stock and option volatility leading up to and after an earnings report announcement. This enhanced volatility will increase our option premium value, which would *appear* to be a favorable circumstance to many. However, this increased volatility is also accompanied with a higher risk that the stock will suffer a major decline in share value if the "market" is unhappy with the report in any way. What good is a 4% option return if the stock plummets 15% following an earnings report disappointment? Therefore, the BCI system strictly adheres to the common sense rule to **never sell a covered call option on a stock about to report earnings in the current contract period.** Many ask if you can just own the stock and not sell the option. From time to time I will own a stock during the same month the company is due to report earnings and refrain from selling the call option; however I must have a lot of faith in the company, which, at a minimum, I require to have a history of positive earnings surprises. Bear in mind, however, owning the stock of a company which is about to report its earnings is NOT part of the BCI covered call writing system.

Two free websites where earnings report dates can be accessed are:

http://www.earningswhispers.com/

https://finance.yahoo.com/calendar/earnings

These dates can change from time to time so recheck them prior to entering a position.

Holding a Stock through an Earnings Report

You own a stock and love it! Hopefully, your admiration for the stock is predicated upon non-emotional reasons and sound fundamental and technical principles, in addition to common sense. If you adhere to the BCI methodology, you know **never** to sell a covered call option on a stock which is about to report earnings. In most cases, we would sell this equity prior to the report and then re-purchase the stock after earnings are announced, assuming, of course, that the security still meets the BCI system criteria. However, what if you really believe in this company and feel that it most likely will continue to appreciate in value? In such a situation, one can own the stock through earnings and then sell an option after earnings are reported and the price settles down. In other words, you can capture the best of both worlds: the share appreciation from a positive earnings report surprise (what we are anticipating) plus the cash generated from the sale of the option. Before I continue with a real-life example, let me again re-state that this is **not part of the BCI System**. However, it is something I have done from time to time in the past. Any time you own a stock through an earnings report there is the likelihood of volatility and the direction can be positive or negative. We refrain from selling the call because we would limit the upside of a positive surprise (by the option strike price) without downside protection, notwithstanding the option premium which could pale in comparison to the potential price decline in the underlying equity if there was a negative surprise.

That being said, there are limited situations wherein I do retain ownership of the stock through earnings, and thereafter sell the call option when the price of the underlying equity settles, as noted. Let's look at a real-life example where I used this strategy with positive results. The following is a brief outline of the six key aspects that existed and affected my decision to retain ownership of RVBD through earnings:

- I bought RVBD and sold the July call
- I closed the short option position when the stock and

option price declined, in preparation to execute an exit strategy (discussed more fully in Chapter 10)

- I re-sold the same option in the same contract period when RVBD increased in price
- The option expired worthless and the stock was retained prior to the earnings announcement
- The earnings report positively surprised and the share price accelerated
- An option was sold on the next higher strike price after the earnings report was published

For purposes of clarity, I have constructed a line chart (Figure 79) depicting the aforementioned six key aspects, which are numbered accordingly on the graph, inclusive of a red arrow indicating the execution of each trade that was effected. Please review this chart and the explanation that follows (trading commissions not included but should be non-events):

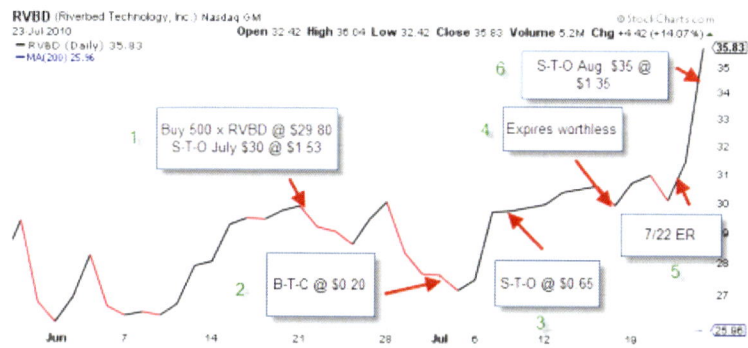

Figure 79- RVBD: Hold Through Earnings Report

The following numbers reference the numbers shown in the chart:

1- Initial covered call trade:

- Buy 500 x RVBD @ $29.80 (cost basis = $14,900)

- Sell 5 x July $30 calls @ $1.53 (initial profit = $765)
- Initial return = $765/$14,900 = 5.1%

2- Close short call position (buy-to-close):

- B-T-C 5 x July $30 @ $0.20
- Creates a debit of $100

3- Re-sell the same call in the same contract month:

- S-T-O 5 x July $30 @ $0.65
- Creates a credit of $325
- Exit strategy (2 and 3, I call "hitting a double") credit = $225 ($325 − $100)
- Total profit to date = $765 + $225 = $990

4- Stock price closes below the $30 strike on expiration Friday:

- Option expires worthless allowing the stock to be retained
- one-month profit = 6.4% ($990/$14,900)

5- Earnings report is announced:

- On July 22nd the earnings report is made public
- The market reacts favorably to a positive earnings surprise (I'm a genius....this time!)

6- Sell the next month call option at a higher strike price:

- The stock appreciates to near $35 per share and the slightly O-T-M $35 call is sold for $1.35
- S-T-O 5 x August $35 calls @ $1.35 = $675
- I compute my returns based on share value at that point in time: $675/$17,400 = 3.9%

- At the time this chapter was written, the price of RVBD = $36.80, making the stock worth $35 per share (to me) due to the option obligation

For the fun of it:

Although this contract cycle was far from over as this chapter was being formatted, let's compute our returns to date starting with the first covered call sale:

Profit:

$765- initial option profit for the July contracts

$225- net credit for "hitting a double" (exit strategy discussed later in the book) with the July $30 calls

$675- initial option profit for the August contracts

$2600- share appreciation from $29.80 to $35 for 500 shares

Total profit = $4265

Initial investment = $14,900

2-month return = 28.6% ($4265/$14,900)...I'm not even going to annualize that!

Conclusion:

The foregoing example was provided primarily in response to the myriad of inquiries I have received in connection with retaining a favored equity through an earnings report. Although this strategy is not part of the BCI system for selling covered call options, I do occasionally utilize same, (especially in bull markets) as detailed above. Bear in mind, however, that the positive results yielded in above-referenced example detailed are the exception, not the rule. Had earnings disappointed, we'd be looking for a box of Kleenex! The main point here is to be prepared; holding a stock through an earnings report is for investors with a higher risk tolerance and works best in bull market environments.

Same Store Monthly Retail Sales Reports ("Banned Stocks")

Some stores report sales figures on a *monthly basis*, thereby creating similar volatility and risk as earnings reports. The common sense rule we just discussed with respect to earnings reports applies with equal force to companies that report monthly same store sales (compare revenues from the same stores from time period to time period): never sell options on stocks that report monthly same stores sales statistics. Figure 80 lists the companies which, as of the penning of this chapter, reported same store sales on a monthly basis, and thus are considered "banned stocks" in the BCI system:

Stocks that Report Same Store Monthly Retail Sales

"Banned Stocks"

Definition
Monthly sales volumes from individual department, chain, discount, and apparel stores are usually reported on the first Thursday of each month. Chain store sales correspond with roughly 10 percent of retail sales. Chain store sales are an indicator of retail sales and consumer spending trends.

2011 Release Schedule
Released On: 1/6 2/3 3/3 4/7 5/5 6/2 7/7 8/4 9/1 10/6 11/3 12/1
Released For: Dec Jan Feb Mar Apr May Jun Jul Aug Sep Oct Nov

AEO	DDS	MW
ANF	DEST	NWY
ANN	DG	PLCE
ARO	DLTR	PSUN
BEY	FD	RAD
BEBE	FDO	ROST
BIG	FINL	RVI
BJ	FRED	SBUX
BKE	GOTT	SCVL
BONT	GPS	SHRP
BWS	GYMB	SKS
CACH	HOTT	SMRT
CBK	JAS	SSI
CHRS	JCP	TGT
CHS	JOSB	TJX
CLE	JWN	TLB
CMRG	KSS	WAG
CTR	LDG	ZUMZ
CVS	LTD	
DBRN	M	

Recent additions: APP, CATO, WTSLA, COST, PIR, WMAR.

http://prnwire.com/industryfocus/ret/retailreports/

Figure 80 -"Banned Stocks" in the BCI System

This list will be updated regularly on the BCI premium site, or, if you email me directly I'll be pleased to forward you the latest list.

Minimum Trading Volume

Stocks that are highly illiquid (i.e. have extremely low daily trading volume) with wide bid-ask spreads are susceptible to market manipulation (to be addressed later in this book). For this reason, our common sense rule is to never buy a stock with an average trading volume lower than 250,000 shares per day. With respect to the sale of the call option, I prefer to sell call options associated with a minimum open interest of 100 contracts at the time of trade execution and/or a bid-ask spread of $0.30 or less.

Stock and Industry Diversification

Investing a high percentage of your cash into one stock or in industry is risky; if that security or industry falls out of favor with the institutional investors, your wallet will undoubtedly suffer the consequences! By diversifying in non-correlated underlying securities, we can significantly reduce this risk. In this regard, the common sense rule is to invest in a minimum of five different stocks in five different industries, so that no one security or group will represent more than 20% of your portfolio.

Cash Allocation

In addition to stock and industry mixing, we must also allocate equal cash to each segment of our portfolios in order to effectively diversify our portfolios. For example, if we had five stocks in our covered call portfolio, it wouldn't make sense to have 100 shares of a $15 stock, and 100 shares of a $150 stock. To carefully balance a portfolio by cash, I have found adhering to the following two principals a successful approach:

- Determine how many stocks will fit your portfolio needs. A $50k portfolio will probably best be suited for about five stocks.

- Leave a small percentage (2-4%) of cash for potential exit strategy execution (to be discussed in detail in Chapter 10) and divide the balance by the number of stocks. For example, if you have $52,000 and decided to purchase five stocks for your portfolio, allocate approximately $10,000 per stock, and leave the remaining cash balance for exit strategies, with the understanding that it may not be needed.

- Divide the current price per share into the amount allocated per stock, and round that number off to the nearest one hundred (because you need 100 shares per options contract). This figure will dictate the number of shares to purchase and the number of contracts to sell.

Figure 81 illustrates cash allocation across five hypothetical stocks using the foregoing principals as guidelines. For purposes of analyzing Figure 81, assume you have $52,000 to purchase the five hypothetical securities, or a $10,000 allocation toward each stock:

A	B	C	D	E	F	G	H
STOCK		Price	# shares/10k		Rounded off		# contract
A		$10	1000		1000		10
B		$20	500		500		5
C		$30	333		300		3
D		50	200		200		2
E		100	100		100		1

Figure 81 - Cash Allocation @ about $10,000 per Stock

Notice how we can purchase 333 shares of stock "C" with the allocated $10,000 but we round down the 333 figure down to 300, as we can only use 300 shares (to cover the sale of 3 call options) for purposes of selling call options.

Summary of book to this point

Let's take a deep breath and summarize what we have accomplished to this point:

- Developed a watchlist of the greatest performing stocks in the greatest performing industries.

- Placed our securities in an organized list in our portfolio manager.

- Determined which stocks to purchase and the number of shares per equity using sound fundamental and technical analysis, calculations and common sense parameters.

The next step is to sit down in front of our computers and start generating cash into our accounts by executing our covered call trades.

Test your knowledge of key points

1- _____ are quarterly filings made by public companies to report their performance. They include such items as net income, earnings per share, earnings from continuing operations and net sales.

2- The major reason we avoid stocks about to report earnings and all stocks that report same store monthly retail sales is the increase in price _____ which also increases the _____ in our covered call positions.

3- Since some stocks with very low daily trading volume can be easily manipulated and may also have wide bid-ask spreads, our common sense rule is to never buy a stock with a trading volume lower than _____ per day.

4- Invest in a minimum of _____ different stocks in _____ different industries where no one security or group will represent more than _____ of your portfolio.

5- A portfolio of $105k and ten securities should have approximately _____ allocated per security with some cash remaining for potential _____.

Answers:

1- Earnings reports

2- Volatility, risk

3- 250k

4- Five, five, 20%

5- $10k, exit strategies

Chapter 9

Executing a Covered Call Trade

Chapter outline

1- Legging-in

2- Buy-Write order

3- Playing the bid-ask spread

4- Types of customer orders

5- Should we use stop loss orders?

6- Protective puts/ collar strategy

7- Penny pilot program

8- Online discount brokerages

There are several ways of entering a covered call position. You may already own a stock in your portfolio in which case you enter the position by selling the call option on the appropriate number of shares. This is called *overwriting*. For example, if you own 500 shares of BCI Corp., you can then sell up to 5 contracts. Another situation is when you are currently in a covered position and institute an exit strategy where the option is bought back (B-T-C or buy-to-close) and a new covered call position is initiated by selling a different call option (roll out, roll down etc). These latter choices will be discussed in the Chapter 10, covering exit strategies. Most commonly, covered call writers specifically purchase a stock for purposes of then selling the call option. This can be accomplished in two ways.

Legging-in

Legging in: The stock is first purchased with a market or limit order and once this trade is executed, the call option is then sold (generally) with a limit order. Legging-in is the more conventional way of executing a covered call trade; however this method of execution requires you to be at your computer during the entire process. If we already own the stock, we can execute our covered call trade by simply selling the option. However, if we do not own the underlying equity, we must first purchase the same prior to selling the call option, as depicted in Figure 82, which illustrates what your online form would look like when purchasing 300 shares of VMware, Inc. (VMW):

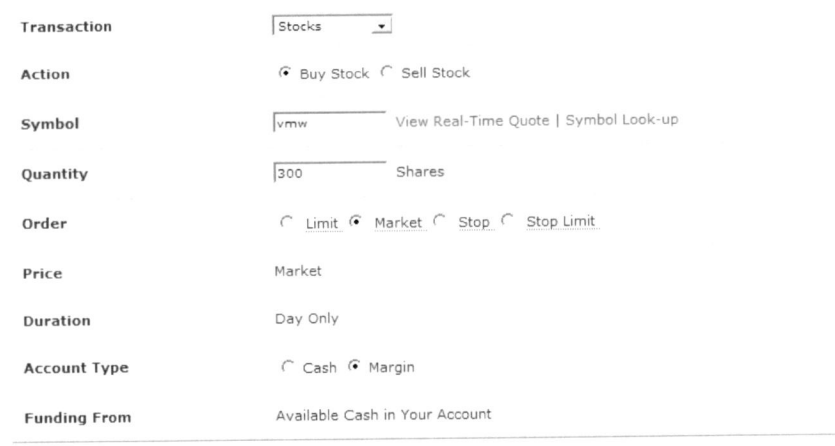

Figure 82 - Stock Purchase

The transaction is to "buy stocks." We enter the ticker symbol (in this case, VMW) and the number of shares. In this example, I chose to purchase all 300 shares of VMW "at the market," as indicated by selection of "market order" in the row titled "Order." Generally speaking, I prefer to use market orders for stock purchases in heavily traded stocks, where the bid-ask spread is typically small, thus enabling a good brokerage company to effect my orders at favorable prices. For stocks that have larger bid-ask spreads, I prefer to use "limit orders" which I always use for option sales and buy-backs. The duration is "day only," as these trades are executed in seconds or minutes and the account type is noted (margin or cash). After entry of the above-referenced information, we confirm on our online brokerage account that the order in fact has been executed. On my USAA brokerage account, trade execution confirmation can be obtained under the "activity" link, which is depicted in Figure 83:

Date	Transaction	Description	Quantity	Price	Net Amount	Realized Gain\Loss[1]
12/02/2009	Cash Disbursement	1015	0.000		($140.00)	N/A
11/30/2009	Money Market Interest	.15813%11/02-11/30 1110	0.000		$.14	N/A
11/27/2009	Sell	KIRKLANDS INC (QQJ 12/19/2009 C 15.000)	(3.000)	$.85	$246.79	N/A
11/27/2009	Buy	KIRKLANDS INC	300.000	$15.36	($4,613.05)	N/A
11/24/2009	Sell	UNITED STATES NATL GAS FUND LP	(500.000)	$9.02	$4,505.33	($2,134.22)
10/30/2009	Money Market Interest	.285% 10/01-11/01 1045	0.000		$.26	N/A

Figure 83 - Activity Showing Trade Execution Confirmation

In Figure 83, we see highlighted the execution of a different stock, Kirkland's Inc. (KIRK) wherein 300 shares were purchased for $4,613.05, or for $15.36 per share plus commission. Some online brokerages also have an "order status" option, which can be checked prior to this activity link and will read as "open" if the trade has NOT been executed and "executed" if it has.

Once we own the shares we can immediately sell the corresponding option, as illustrated in Figure 84, which depicts how a typical execution will appear on your online brokerage account:

Transaction	Options
Action	Sell Covered Call
Underlying Symbol	KIRK Symbol Look-Up | Get Option Chain | View Real Time Quote
Expiration Date	17-JUL-2010
Strike Price	15.0
Quantity	3 Contracts
Order	⦿ Limit ○ Market ○ Stop ○ Stop Limit
Limit Price	1.15
Duration	⦿ Day Only ○ Good-Until-Canceled (30 Days)
Qualifiers	☐ All or None
Account Type	○ Cash ⦿ Margin
Proceeds To	Available Cash in Your Account

Cancel > NEXT

Figure 84 - Selling the Call Option

In this example, we are selling the call option for KIRK. The call expires on July 17th, 2010. The strike price is $15, and three contracts are to be sold at a limit order of $1.15. This means we will receive $1.15 or better (higher) if the trade is executed. Once again, this is for the day only and the type of account is defined (most of us will have cash accounts; a margin account is shown above). Note that I did NOT check the "All or None" box. This is an important concept and will be explained more fully in this chapter when we discuss the *Show or Fill Rule*. Once the information is entered, we click on "next" and check the *order status* and/or *activity* link as we did after entering the stock trade.

Your account statement when opening a covered call trade

Cash balances are decreased by the cost of the stock plus commissions minus the profit from the sale of the option.

Account values, however, will reflect a debit regarding the sale of the option, and will appear with a minus sign (-). This is because the calls may eventually be bought back, and thus are considered a liability until the option is exercised (causing you to sell your stock), bought back (closed) or the option expires worthless.

Buy-Write order

Buy-Write (Net Debit) Order: Some brokerages (OptionsXpress.com, for example) have set up a special combination order type to allow all elements of a covered call trade to be entered at one time. This order type is called a *buy-write* or net debit order. With this order type, we enter a *limit order* (execution at a specific price or better is specified) in the form of a net debit. Net debit simply means that WE owe the brokerage money, we pay them. For example, if we buy a stock for $20 and sell the call option for $1, the net debit is $19, excluding commissions. Since the order is specified as a limit order, we pay $19 per share/option combination (or less/better) for the order to be executed. The commission for this trade may be slightly less than the cumulative commission charged for each of the two executions warranted to affect a trade by legging in.

Opening a Covered Call Position Using a Buy-Write

Let's look at an example of such a buy-write order (Figure 85). In this hypothetical, we will purchase 300 shares of Blue Collar Investor Corp. (BCI) and sell the next month's call option. Here are the current statistics for this hypothetical example:

- Current (Ask) price for BCI Corp. is $28.20
- Current (Bid) price for BCI- January $30 call is $0.70
- Net debit is $27.50

Covered Call Order Form			
Account No:	Password:		
Stock Symbol: [BCI]	Quantity: [300]	Action: (•) Buy ( ) Sell	Price: ( ) Market ( ) Limit Net Credit [ ] (•) Limit Net Debit [27.50]
Option Symbol: [BCI-AF]	Quantity: [3]	Action: (•) Sell to Open ( ) Buy to Close	
Duration: (•) Day Order ( ) Good until cancelled	Advanced Order: (•) None ( ) Contingent order		

Figure 85 -Entering a covered call position with a net debit

Achieving a more favorable fill (execution) for your order can be accomplished when using this combination order type by slightly lowering your limit net-debit order. Thus, in the example detailed in Figure 85, you may use $27.45 or $27.40, depending on the spread of the option bid-ask price. *The larger the bid-ask spread of the option, the better the chance of getting a more favorable fill.*

Let's look at the entries on this combination form to *open a covered call position:*

- Buy 300 shares of BCI
- Sell-to-open 3 contracts of the January $30 call option
- Limit net-debit order for $27.50 (or less, if playing the bid-ask spread, described in further detail below)
- *Select Day Order*-this order is good for the day only, as opposed to "good until cancelled" order, which stays

active until specifically cancelled by the investor A day order is the best duration for covered call writers. If our order is not filled the day it is placed, we can re-evaluate the trade returns the following day, as implied volatility may change. This then could impact the option premium and our calculations will need to be re-evaluated.

- *Do not select Advanced Order*. This order is not dependent on any other event.

- *Preview-* Check to make sure the order is correct, and if so, place the order.

Closing a Covered Call Position Using a Buy Write Combination Order

Next, let's turn our attention to Figure 86 to see how we can use a combination order type to close our covered positions. For purposes of Figure 86, assume the following:

- Two weeks later, BCI is trading @ $28.50 per share (bid)
- BCI- Jan. $30 is trading @ $0.10 (ask)
- Net Credit is $28.40

Covered Call Order Form			
Account No:	**Password:**		
Stock Symbol: [BCI]	**Quantity:** [300]	**Action:** ( ) Buy	**Price:** ( ) Market
		(•) Sell	(•) Limit Net Credit [$28.40] ( ) Limit Net Debit [ ]
Option Symbol: [BCI-AF]	**Quantity:** [3]	**Action:** ( ) Sell to Open (•) Buy to Close	
Duration: (•) Day Order ( ) Good until cancelled	**Advanced Order:** (•) None ( ) Contingent order		
	[Preview Order]	[Clear]	

Figure 86
Closing a covered call trade using a combination form

Let's look at the entries detailed on Figure 86 wherein we use this combination order form to *close our covered call position:*

- Sell 300 shares of BCI

- Buy-to-close (buy back) the 3 January $30 call option contracts

- Limit net-credit order for $28.40 (or more, if playing the bid-ask spread)

- *Select Day Order-*

- *Do not select Advanced Order*

- *Preview-* Check to make sure the order is correct, and if so, place the order.

Mathematics of closing the position:

Net credit – net debit = *Net Profit:* $28.40 – $27.50 = $0.90

Percentage return = Net Profit/Cost basis = $.90/$27.50 = 3.3%

Conclusion

Legging-in and buy-write combination orders are the two order types by which a covered call position can be established when the underlying equity is not yet owned. Buy-write order types are particularly useful when you can't get to your computer to affect trades on a regular basis. Bear in mind, however, that not all online brokerage firms offer the buy-write order type.

Playing the bid-ask spread and the show or fill rule

Would you like to earn $50 in 50 seconds? Why not learn how to play the bid-ask spread?

Blue Collar Investors throughout the world are always looking for ways to generate additional profits into our portfolios. This includes the use of some of the more esoteric maneuvers that may produce small returns of $40, $50 or more. One of the main philosophical approaches to Blue Collar Investing is that by generating small but consistent, low risk returns and then compounding those profits, we can become financially independent.

In my previous books and DVDs, the following phrase appears on numerous occasions:

Sell at the "bid", the lower price; buy at the "ask", the higher price. This references the price lists found in the options chains. Before we discuss some common sense applications to maximizing profits by playing the bid-ask spread, let's review some definitions (stay awake now, this can make you some cash!).

Definitions as they apply to options

BID: An offer made by an investor, a dealer or a trader to buy an option. It will usually stipulate the price the buyer is willing to purchase the option and the quantity to be purchased.

ASK: The price a seller is willing to accept for an option, also called the offer price. The "ask" will always be higher than the bid.

BID/ASK SPREAD: The difference in price between the highest price that a buyer is willing to pay for the option and the lowest price a seller is willing to sell it. If the bid is $2.80 and the "ask" is $3.00, then the bid-ask spread is $ 0.20.

Theoretical Value: The hypothetical value of an option as calculated by a mathematical model such as the *Black-Scholes Option Pricing Model*.

Black-Scholes Option Pricing Model: A model used to calculate the value of an option, by factoring in stock price, strike price and expiration date, risk-free return, and the standard deviation of the stock's return.

How the bid-ask spread is set

There may be several bid prices and several ask prices at any point in time. However, only the highest bid and lowest ask are used to calculate the spread. These are the figures you see when accessing the options chains. Utilizing an estimate of the volatility of the underlying stock, a theoretical option value is calculated using an option pricing model, such as the Black-Scholes model. A market maker will then set the *bid below* this theoretical value and the *"ask"* above this theoretical price. This is the spread and is determined mainly by liquidity. For example, the highly liquid ETF, QQQ, can have bid/ask spreads as low as $ 0.01. This is one of the reasons I require all stocks owned in our portfolios and on our watchlist trade at least 250,000 shares per day. Lightly-traded stocks tend to have wide bid-ask spreads. Market makers derive their profit from bid/ask spreads. The greater the spread, the more money they make. Playing the spread will decrease their profits and increase ours.

Market order vs. limit order

If you use a market order when executing a trade, you will sell at the published bid price and buy at the published ask price (this is called "lifting" the offer or "hitting" the bid). This may be okay for the purchase and sale of stocks where the spread is *tight* (small), but for options, which have a wider bid/ask spread, a limit order is more appropriate and beneficial.

The Show or Fill Rule

This is also called the *Limit Order Display Rule* or technically the Exchange Act Rule 11Ac1-4. This regulation requires *the market makers to show or publish any order that improves the current bid or ask prices unless it is filled.* Any order between the current bid-ask spread will improve the market.

Practical Application

Most exchanges have a policy in place that requires market makers to fill AT LEAST 10 contracts at the quoted price. For many equities and ETFs the number of contracts required is a lot more and varies from security to security. These players want to buy securities at the lowest price (bid) and sell at the highest price (ask or offer). Now it's time for Blue Collar Investors all over the world to become annoying and take out our slingshots in much the same way that David approached Goliath. As long as the bid-ask spread isn't too tight or close together, we place our order between the two quoted prices. If the market maker (MM) does not fill the order, he will be required to publish it and then be obligated to fill at least 10 contracts, perhaps more, at that price. Since most of us are selling small numbers of contracts, let's say up to 5 per stock, it is in the best interest of our friends on the other side to just fill our orders and settle for a lower amount on 5 contracts rather than be obligated for twice that amount and for many more traders. We got them right between the eyes….I mean between the bid-ask spread.

Example

In this hypothetical the bid is $2.50 and the "ask" is $3.00. That's a spread we can work with. As covered call writers, we sell at the bid or in this case, $2.50 per share or $250 per contract. That's the price at which the MM wants to buy our options. Instead our *offer* will be $2.65. That betters the current published offer of $3.00. Therefore, our friend on the other side has a dilemma: Do I fill these 5 contracts @ $2.65 or publish the new, improved offer and be responsible to fill 10 or more as required by the Show or Fill Rule? In most cases, we will get our $0.15 and the MM will get rid of us. This little maneuver will pay for our commissions and buy us lunch at Wendy's. $75 becomes hundreds, becomes thousands, and becomes tens of thousands and so on. The market makers? They're gazillionaires anyway...they'll be alright.

****<u>DO NOT CHECK THE ALL OR NONE (AON) BOX ON YOUR TRADE ORDER FORM:</u>

For most of us this is redundant, not necessary because the MM is required to fill at least 10 contracts. *If this box IS checked the MM is no longer required to publish our offer* and we will lose our leverage when playing the bid-ask spread.

A market order should always get filled as you are buying a said number of shares "at market" so you will hit offers until you have a fill. Limit orders will only fill at your specified limit price or better. If you don't want partial fills you can use the all or none order. They will fill the whole order or nothing. However, this will be counterproductive when playing the bid-ask spread.

Conclusion

To take advantage of the *show or fill rule* we must:

- Improve the market (bid-ask spread)
- Sell 10 contracts or less

- Not check the *all or none* box on the trade execution form

Blue Collar Investors have certain tools available that will somewhat level the playing field with the MMs. Taking advantage of the *Show or Fill Rule* is an important one especially when selling a small number of contracts. Although each trade will generate small amounts of cash, over time this will add up to significant dollars that will help to secure our financial future. Unlike David, though, we are not looking to injure our adversaries, just annoy them.

Types of customer orders

When instructing our online discount broker as to the actions we want taken, we submit a customer order. These orders can take several different forms depending on our investment strategies and objectives. We can buy or sell; request a specific price or simply the best available price; we can stipulate an action given a particular circumstance; and we can use combinations of orders. Let's look at the most common of these orders and the situations when we may utilize them.

Market Order

This is the most common of customer orders where we ask the broker to buy or sell a stock at the best available price. It is also called an "unrestricted order" and will always be executed.

Limit Order

This is an order to buy or sell a specific number of shares at a certain price or better. A *buy limit* order can only be executed at the limit price or lower. A *sell limit* order must be executed at the limit price or higher. These are particularly useful on low-volume or highly volatile stocks.

Stop Order

An order to buy or sell a security when its price surpasses a specific price called the *stop price*. At that point the stop order becomes a *market order*. A *sell stop order* is placed below the current market value of the stock and is used to prevent or limit a loss or to protect a profit on a long stock position. For example, you may have purchased a stock for $20 per share and it has appreciated to $30. A sell stop order @ $25 will guarantee at least a profit of $5 per share (barring a gap-down in the price of the stock). A *buy stop order* is always placed above the current market price of the stock. It is typically used to protect a profit or limit a loss on a short sale (selling a stock you didn't own by borrowing it). For example, if you sell short a stock @ $30 expecting to buy it back at a lower price but it starts going up in value instead, a buy stop order can limit your loss. It may kick in @ $32 thereby minimizing losses to $2 per share. Once the *buy stop price* is reached, the order becomes a market order.

Stop Limit Order

This is a combination of a *stop order* and a *limit order*. Once the stop price is reached the order turns into a limit order, meaning that it can only execute at or better than the specific limit price. The benefit of using a stop limit order is that the trader has precise control over when the order should be filled. The disadvantage, however, is that the order in fact may never get filled. A *sell stop-limit order* is always placed below the current market price of the equity, and is used to limit the loss or protect the profit on a long stock position. Once the stop price is reached, the order effectively turns into a limit order. For example, let's assume that XYZ is trading at $50 and an investor has put in a stop-limit order to sell with the stop price at $45 and the limit price at $44. If the price of XYZ moves below $45 stop price, the order is activated and turns into a limit order. As long as the order can be filled above $44 (the limit price) then the trade will be filled. If the stock gaps down below $44, the order will not be filled. A *buy stop-limit order* is always placed above the current price of the stock and is used to limit a loss or protect the profit on a short stock position. Once activated, it becomes a limit order. For example, suppose you are looking to buy 100 shares of MicroSoft Corp (MSFT) currently trading at $30 per share. You place a Buy Stop Limit Order for $33 on MSFT, with a Limit (maximum you're willing to pay) at $33.50. Let's assume MSFT then proceeds to trade up to $33. At that time, your order would become a Buy Limit Order and your order would be filled as long as the stock still trades below your specified limit price of $33.50.

Trailing Stop

A trailing stop adjusts the stop price at a fixed percentage or number of points below the market price of a stock. The purpose of the trailing stop is to protect against a move by the stock or option price in the opposite direction than what was expected. When the price of your stock rises, the trailing stop rises with it, helping to protect against a larger loss, and eventually capturing a portion of your profit. With a trailing stop, you continue to hold the stock and thus still receive dividend payments, assuming any such payments are made. Should the stock plunge past your stop price your shares are sold at the *next available price*, not necessarily the stop price, assuming you have not placed the stop order with a limit price.

Example of a trailing stop order

Assume the current price of a stock is $50. You have instructed your broker to institute a 10% trailing stop. Thus, the trailing stop order will be triggered if the market price reaches $45 per share ($50 – 10% of $50). The trailing stop moves in accordance with the price increase. Thus, if the price increases to $54, the trailing stop will be $48.60 ($54 –10% of $54).

The trailing stop order has no effect if the price of the stock keeps rising or stays at the same level. On the other hand, if the price of the stock falls, the trailing stop order is triggered when the specified level is reached and your broker is required to sell the stock.

Summary of Orders Entered Above the Market (above current price of security)

- Buy Stop-Limit
- Buy Stop
- Sell Limit

Summary of Orders Entered Below Market (below current price of security)

- Buy Limit
- Sell Stop
- Sell Stop-Limit

Should We Use Stop Loss Orders?

You're boarding a jet to fly from California to New York to attend a BCI seminar. A JetBlue flight attendant greets you and asks the following question: "Would you like this plane put on auto-pilot, or would you prefer that it be flown by an experienced, educated and motivated pilot?" You think of the myriad of weather and other factors that could affect the journey and immediately opt for a human pilot, not Robby the Robot. In much the same way, there are multiple factors that impact our covered call positions that need our management, the human element if you will, to maximize the results. That is why I prefer NOT to implement stop-loss orders when trading covered call options.

*Complications from Using Stop-Loss Orders
When Selling Covered Calls*

1- If we were to place a stop order on the underlying equity and it was executed, we still would have a short call on the table. Fortunately, our brokerage firm generally will not allow such a scenario UNLESS we have approval for naked call writing.

Most Blue Collar Investors cannot get (nor do they even want) this type of approval. It's actually better for most retail investors NOT to have this approval so as to avoid a scenario wherein the underlying equity gets sold accidentally, leaving the unfortunate investor to deal with the immense risk that accompanies a naked short call position. The bottom line is as follows: in order to close our long stock position, we must first close our short call position.

2- What if we place a stop-loss order to close the short option position first and then request notification if and when this trade is executed? The second leg of unwinding this position, the sale of the stock, can now be accomplished. The issue with this approach is to predict the relationship between the option price and the stock value. This is virtually impossible to do because the call premium is dependent on many factors such as implied volatility and the type of strike (I-T-M, A-T-M or O-T-M). Therefore, placing a stop on the option price with the expectation to then sell the stock may not be the appropriate action to take.

3- Placing a "one triggers other" order (OTO order):

A "one triggers the other" order is when you instruct your broker to close your entire position (is essence, placing a stop on both positions) by first buying back the short call option, and then selling the underlying security. The problem here is that many brokers do not permit these order types simply because their trading platform software is not programmed to accommodate such trades. Even if brokers do accommodate such contingency trades, the same dilemma detailed in # 2 above nevertheless remains

4- We may lose an opportunity to generate additional income:

Great performing stocks will sometimes consolidate or "take a breather", profit-taking if you will. If the stock is still trading above its moving average and no negative news has come out, why not buy back the option and look to *resell the same option when the stock recovers* (discussed in the chapter 10 on exit strategies). Hastily selling a stock without properly evaluating chart technicals, market tone and current news will cost us money. Stop-losses cannot do this analysis for us. Our brains are required to participate in the process if we want to maximize our profits.

Some say to enter stop-losses when leaving for vacations. I have a better idea. Purchase a netbook or a laptop for a few hundred dollars and take it with you. You'll make your money back quickly and the time spent will be minimal. If you want to vacation and not think about the market, close your positions before you leave (or don't enter them to begin with) and get back in the game when you return.

Now That We Know What NOT to Do, What SHOULD We Do?

I've written an entire book on this subject, titled *Exit Strategies for Covered Call Writing*, which is also discussed in Chapter 10 of this book. You absolutely should not allow a falling stock to continue to decline without taking any action. That's what uneducated investors do, not us. As discussed more fully in Chapter 10, the BCI system adheres to a series of guidelines with respect to the utilization of exit strategies in the face of declining stock value. Choosing the correct action requires our brains and common sense, not our friend Robby the Robot. We evaluate stock technicals, market tone and check for changing equity news. It won't take much time. When we are ready to act, our decisions will CRUSH those of Robby and we'll have a lot more cash in our pockets for it.

Conclusion

Setting stop-loss orders is more appropriate for long-term investing than it is for covered call writing in the eyes of this author. Becoming educated, active and proficient in position management will prove to be both a time-efficient and wealth-enhancing approach to covered call writing. Just as the savvy, experienced pilot guides his jet across the country, so should we guide our portfolios to positions of great wealth.

Protective Puts/ The Collar Strategy

As safe a strategy as covered call writing is there is some risk; the risk is in purchasing the stock, not in selling the option. For this reason, some investors who sell covered calls also buy *protective puts* to alleviate some of the risk. Remember, the owner of a put option has purchased the right, but not the obligation, to SELL 100 shares of the underlying stock at the strike price on or before expiration Friday. A put option is considered in-the-money if the strike price of the put option is higher than current market value of the underlying stock. Likewise, a put option is considered *out-of-the-money* if the strike price of the put option is lower than the current market value of the underlying equity. You will note that the *in-the-money and out-of-the-money strike/ share value relationships are opposite for calls and puts.*

A protective put is a put option that is purchased for an underlying stock that is already owned by the put buyer. A *protective put* defends against a decrease in the share price of the underlying security. When a protective put is used in conjunction with covered call writing, the strategy is referred to as a *collar strategy*. A *collar* is the simultaneous purchase of a protective put option and the sale of a covered call option. In a true collar strategy, the puts and calls are both out-of-the-money and have the same expiration dates and an equal number of contracts. Thus, we sell an out-of-the-money call and add additional downside protection for the underlying equity by purchasing a protective put option.

Example of a Collar

- Buy 100 shares of XYZ @ $48
- Sell 1 $50 (O-T-M) call option for $2
- Buy 1 $45 (O-T-M) put option for $1
- Net gain on the option buy and sale is $100 ($200 – $100)
- This brings our cost basis down to $4700 ($4800 – $100)

Possible outcomes

1- Outcome if stock price surpasses the $50 strike price:

- Shares are sold for $5000 ($50 strike price × 100 shares)
- Results in a profit of $300 ($5000 − $4700)
- ROO = 300/4700 = 6.4%

2- Outcome if stock prices falls below the $45 put strike price to $43:

- Shares are sold for $4500 (not $4300) because of the protective put
- Net loss is $200 ($4700 − $4500) = (-) 4.3%

3- Outcome if stock price remains @ $48:
- ROO = $100 ($100/$4700) = 2.1%

Figure 87 depicts the risk profile and possible outcomes of the collar for this particular example:

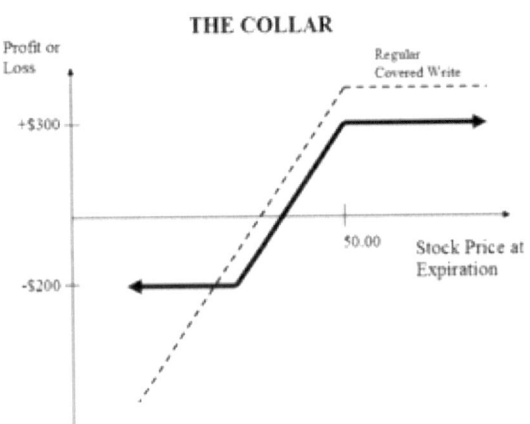

Figure 87-Risk Profile of a Collar

As demonstrated in Figure 87, the profit potential of an otherwise normal covered call position (dotted line) is muted due to the additional cost of purchasing the protective put (solid line); however, the protective put also gives us downside protection at the strike of the put. If you exit the covered call position early, you can sell the remaining protective put, thus slightly improving your return.

Tax Treatment of Protective Puts

When the protective put is purchased on the same day as the underlying stock, it is referred to as a *married put* for tax purposes. To calculate capital gains or losses, the investor adds the premium paid for the option to the purchase price of the stock to calculate the tax basis of the stock. For example, assume you buy 200 shares of stock ABC for $30 per share On the same day you purchase two $25 puts options at $2 per contract. The tax basis of the stock is $6400 ($6000 + $400).

The Case against Protective Puts

Let me premise the following remarks by briefly noting that there is nothing wrong with purchasing protective puts. I feel, however, that we can get our insurance for free by educated, well-calculated and common sense investing. Here is what the Blue Collar Investor System does to alleviate risk without the need to spend additional cash for the added insurance afforded by protective puts:

- Select only the greatest performing stocks
- Select equities in the best performing industries
- Avoid earnings reports, the most likely cause of a radical price decline in the underlying equity
- Avoid companies that report monthly same store retail sales
- Sell I-T-M strikes when market tone and/or stock technicals

are compromised. In this case, the option buyer is paying our insurance
- Use technical analysis to determine buy-sell points
- Implement exit strategies when needed
- Sell predominantly one-month contracts for better control

In the Blue Collar Investor system, the only time a protective put will benefit us (over and above the inherent protection already built into the system), is when a stock drops precipitously in a short period of time. This can occur after an earnings report, however, as we now know, we are already looking to avoid owning the underlying equity during the announcement of these reports. The latter scenario notwithstanding, situations involving precipitous price declines are few and far between (but possible). Therefore, in my judgment, it doesn't pay to purchase a put every time you sell a call option. Simply stated, you're just not getting enough bang for your buck assuming you do your due diligence and follow all the BCI system criteria.

Related Information

Penny Pilot Program

Do you get frustrated when something doesn't make sense? Me too! Here's a prime example taken from my own personal experience that is similar to the episode I shared earlier with non-standard options: You're viewing an options chain of a great-performing stock in a great-performing industry, and you notice that the option premiums are trading in $.05 increments. As discussed earlier in this chapter, this is important information to have when playing the bid-ask spread. You then check the same options for the following month, and see that the same strike options are now trading in $.10 increments. What's up with that? As you scratch your head in frustration, you type in another ticker and find that these same strike option premiums are trading in $.01 increments! These situations are not inexplicable aberrations, but rather the result of the *Penny Pilot Program*.

Prior to 2007, most options traded with minimum price variations (MPVs) of $.05 for premiums below $3.00, and $.10 for premiums above $3.00. Beginning in January of 2007, the SEC initiated an industry wide (on six option exchanges) pilot program entitled the *Penny Pilot Program*, in which MPVs were reduced for certain equity options. This program reduced the MPVs to .01 for premiums below $3.00, and to .05 for premiums above $3.00. An exception to this was the ETF QQQ, which already traded in $0.01 increments. The reason the SEC initiated this program was to reduce trading costs for investors by reducing the potential for market makers to earn a larger spread between option prices thereby allowing investors to trade options at better prices.

This six-month program, which started with 13 option classes (equities), has been renewed and expanded several times. Here is a list of the stocks that were participating in the Penny Pilot Program at the time this book was being written:

Mini-SPX (XSP/XSP)
SPDR S&P 500 (SPY/SPY)
NYSE Euronext (NYX/NYX)
Apple Inc. (AAPL/AAQ)
Cisco Systems (CSCO/CYQ)
Altria Group, Inc. (MO/MO)
Financial Select Sector SPDR (XLF/XLF)
Dendreon Corp. (DNDN/UKO)
AT&T, Inc. (T/T)
Amgen Inc. (AMGN/AMQ)
Citigroup, Inc. (C/C)
Yahoo! Inc. (YHOO/YHQ)
Amazon.com Inc. (AMZN/ZQN)
Qualcomm Inc. (QCOM/QAQ)
Motorola Inc. (MOT/MOT)
General Motors (GM/GM)

Research in Motion Ltd. (RIMM/RUL)
Energy Select Sector SPDR (XLE/XLE)
Freeport-McMoRan Copper & Gold, Inc. (FCX/DPJ)
Dow Jones Industrial Average(DJX/DJX)
Diamonds Trust (DIA/DIA)
ConocoPhillips (COP/COP)
Oil Services HLDRS (OIH/OIH)
Bristol-Myers Squibb Co. (BMY/BMY)

Goldman Sachs Group, Inc. (GS)
Countrywide Financial Corporation (CFC)
Bank of America Corporation (BAC)
iShares MSCI Emerging Mkts. Index Fund (EEM)
Merrill Lynch & Co., Inc. (MER)
Vale (RIO)
EMC Corporation (EMC)
Exxon Mobil Corporation (XOM)
Wal-Mart Stores, Inc. (WMT)
The Home Depot, Inc. (HD)
Valero Energy Corporation (VLO)
Alcoa Inc. (AA)
Dell Inc. (DELL)
SanDisk Corporation (SNDK)
The Bear Stearns Companies, Inc. (BSC)
Pfizer Inc. (PFE)
eBay Inc. (EBAY)
Halliburton Company (HAL)
Lehman Brothers Holdings Inc. (LEH)
JPMorgan Chase & Co. (JPM)
Washington Mutual, Inc. (WM)
Ford Motor Company (F)
Target Corporation (TGT)
American International Group, Inc. (AIG)
Newmont Mining Corporation (NEM)

Verizon Communications Inc. (VZ)
Mini-NDX Index Options (MNX)
Starbucks Corporation (SBUX)

*How to use the Penny Pilot Program
When Playing the Bid-Ask Spread*

When the *bid-ask spread* is small, I simply sell at the current bid. For example, if the bid-ask is $1.35- $1.40, I will sell my call option for $1.35. For higher priced premiums, we move to the higher increments. Thus, if the spread is $6.60 – $6.70, I will put in offer to sell my call option for $6.60 because of the tight spread. If, however, there is a larger spread, we may be able to put some additional cash in our pockets by playing the bid-ask spread. As I note in my writings and seminars, we don't want to insult the market makers, but rather, we want to be "mild pests." For example, assume the spread for a particular option is $1.10 – $1.40. I compute the midpoint of the spread, which in this case is $1.25, and then place an offer to sell my call option slightly below that midpoint. If we are trading in .05 increments (normal increments for this price range) that figure will be $1.20, which likely won't be taken as an insult (too expensive) to the market maker, and he very well may pay us the more favorable price just to get rid of us. If so, we've just put an additional $10 per contract in our pockets, which, assuming successful repetition could turn into perhaps a few hundred dollars per month, a few thousand per year and tens of thousands over an investment lifetime. If an option is a participant in the Penny Pilot Program, you can place a limit order to sell your call option between $1.20 and $1.24. In other words, with the penny pilot program we may be able to place our limit order a few cents higher than the $1.20 and achieve a slightly higher return. I like to look at returns in terms of percentages rather than dollar amounts (see Chapter 6 on calculations to review my calculation equations). By understanding the Penny Pilot Program and playing the bid-ask spread, if we generate $1.20 per contract rather than $1.10, we have increased our returns by 9% (10/110)!

Conclusion

The Penny Pilot Program is another tool Blue Collar Investors can use to level the playing field with Wall Street insiders. I know that there are those who view the small amount of returns generated in playing the bid-ask spread as miniscule, but I bet these same folks are cutting $0.50 coupons out of the newspaper to get a "great deal" on a bar of soap. The simple fact remains that the extra cash we can generate in playing the bid-ask spread will go either in our pockets or in those of the market makers. It's a no-brainer. Understanding the Penny Pilot Program and knowing how to play the bid-ask spread will make us significant profits over the long run.

Online Discount Brokerages- What to Look For

In the early 1990s when I started investing in the stock market, trade commissions were a major factor impacting our bottom line results. Commissions of $50, $100 and even $200 per trade were common debits seen on our brokerage account statements. The internet has nurtured a change in trading costs through an explosion of online discount brokers. We can now trade at significantly reduced commissions, but in return, we receive no personalized advice from our broker. This is the perfect scenario for Blue Collar Investors who have educated themselves to the point where we don't need the assistance of others. After all, *nobody cares more about our money than we do!* Furthermore, selling predominantly one-month covered call options requires many trade executions, thus the need for low commissions is essential to maximizing our returns. When deciding on which online discount broker to use, consider the following factors:

- Low trade commissions
- Efficient trade executions
- Watch out for hidden fees and minimum requirements

- Prompt and courteous phone service should be available if a problem arises
- Depending on your volume, you may be able to get access to their "advanced platforms."

I started using USAA Brokerage Services in the early 1990s as I was an officer in the military (in the 70s), and at the time, military service was a prerequisite to becoming a USAA member. Since that time, USAA has relaxed this requirement, and currently, everyone (in the U.S.) is eligible to use their brokerage service, which I recommend without hesitation. There are other brokerages that charge slightly lower commissions and others that have more sophisticated research tools. Over the years, fellow Blue Collar Investors have recommended other online discount brokers to me and other members of the BCI community. Although I have no first hand knowledge of these other brokerages, I have included them on the following list of online brokers (current as of June 2010) so that you can do your due-diligence and determine which service best meets your personal needs:

USAA: www.usaa.com
$5.95 PER TRADE + $0.75 PER OPTION CONTRACT
(platinum members)

This is for the top tier of service (lowest commissions) for those who execute 25 trades per quarter and accept online statements.

ALLY: www.ally.com/invest/
$4.95 per trade + $.065 per option contract. Lower prices available with a balance over $100,000. and at least 30 trades per quarter.

TD AMERITRADE: www.tdameritrade.com
$7.00 per online trade with no account maintenance or inactivity fees, and low balance requirements. While phone and broker

assisted trades do cost more, they can be easily avoided by simply sticking with online trades exclusively.

E*TRADE: www.etrade.com
$9.99 per equity trade for those who make at least thirty trades a month or maintain $50,000 in account assets. A standard rate of $12.99 per trade is charged if less than thirty trades per month are made.

CHARLES SCHWAB: www.schwab.com
On-line trades for $8.95 per equity trade, plus $0.75/options contract. You can negotiate lower prices based on your account and trade volume.

Other sites to consider:
www.thinkorswim.com
www.interactivebrokers.com/ (this may be the least expensive of all the brokerages)

It is important to do your own research to assure that you receive the lowest possible commissions without sacrificing quality of service.

Test your knowledge of key points

1- A two-stage transaction where you first buy a stock and then sell a call option to enter a covered call position is called _____.

2- For most liquid stocks with a tight bid-ask spread a _____ order can be placed to buy the security but a _____ order should always be placed when selling the call option.

3- On your account statement the option sale will reflect a _____ regarding the sale of the option and will appear with a minus sign (-). This is because the calls may eventually be bought back and thus are considered a liability until the stock is sold or the option expires worthless.

4- A _____ will allow all elements of a covered call trade to be entered at one time. We enter a limit order (executed at a specific price or better) in the form of a _____.

5- When using a combination form, closing a covered call position will result in a _____.

6- The _____ requires the market makers to show or publish any order that improves the current bid or ask prices unless it is filled. Any order between the current bid-ask spread will improve the market.

7- When playing the bid-ask spread never check the _____ box on your trade execution form.

8- When playing the bid-ask spread, a good place to enter your limit order is slightly below the _____ of the published bid-ask spread.

9- Stop loss orders are most appropriate for _____.

10- When a protective put is used in conjunction with covered call writing, the strategy is referred to as a _____. The put aspect of the collar is known as a _____ put.

11- The _____ permits the exchanges to trade options, on specified equities, in $0.01 increments.

12- To keep trading commissions to a minimum when using the strategy of covered call writing, it is essential we use a reliable _____ brokerage.

Answers:

1- Legging-in

2- Market, limit

3- Debit

4- Buy-Write order form, net debit

5- Net credit

6- Show or Fill Rule (Limit Order Display Rule)

7- All or none (AON)

8- Midpoint

9- Long term investing

10- Collar strategy, protective

11- Penny Pilot Program

12- Online discount

Chapter 10

Exit Strategies

Chapter outline

1- Definitions

2- Exit strategies prior to expiration Friday

    Key parameters

        Time to expiration and option value
        Market tone
        Technical analysis of the underlying security
        Calculations

    Exit strategy choices

        Rolling down
        Take no immediate action and look to "hit a double"
        Convert dead money to cash profits
        No action taken
        Mid-contract unwind

    Managing stocks that have gapped down

3- Exit Strategies on or near expiration Friday

    Key parameters

        Market tone
        Technical analysis of the underlying security
        Earnings reports

Calculations

Exit strategy choices

> Rolling out
> Rolling out and up
> Take no action

4- Multiple exit strategies with the same stock in the same month

5- Early exercise and assignment of options

Savvy investors know that when you enter ANY investment position, plans should be in place to exit that position for ALL possible circumstances. When I purchase an investment property I have decided whether to rent it, flip it, do a 1031 exchange to defer taxes, to refinance to pull out equity or any other choice that would yield the best results. In much the same way, when we enter a covered call position, we must be prepared for all possibilities:

- What if a stock drops in price?
- What if the stock increases in price exponentially?
- What if the market deteriorates or accelerates unexpectedly?

All these scenarios represent situations where we may need to execute an exit strategy to reduce losses or enhance profits. By being prepared, knowing the best choices for a given situation and making non-emotional decisions based on fundamental and technical parameters as well as common sense, we will maximize our bottom line profits. The exit strategy choices that follow will be broken down into two time frames: *prior to expiration Friday* and *on or near expiration Friday*. Before we address the specifics of these strategies, we need to define certain terms:

Key Definitions and Core Principals:

1- *Exit Strategy-* A plan by which a trader intends to get out of an investment position. In other words, an exit strategy is a mechanism by which a trader "cashes out" or closes his or her position. With respect to writing covered call options, unless your plan is to do nothing (allow the option to expire, or allow assignment of your shares), all exit strategies begin with buying back the call option you initially sold.

2- *Assignment-* The receipt of an exercise notice by the option seller (that's us) that obligates us to sell our underlying stock shares to the option buyer at the specified strike price. Since we are selling *American-style options,* assignment can take place at any time from the sale of the call option through expiration Friday.

3- *Expiration Friday* - The last day on which an option may be exercised. This date is the third Friday of the expiration month. If the third Friday of the month is an exchange-recognized holiday, the last trading day the option can be exercised is the Thursday immediately preceding this holiday. Some heavily traded ETFs have quarterly expirations on the last Friday of the quarter.

4- *Rolling Down-* Closing out an options position at one strike price, and opening (in our case, selling a call option) another options position at a lower strike price in the same contract month.

5- *Rolling Out or Forward-* Closing out an option contract at a near-term expiration date and opening a same strike contract at a later date.

6- *Rolling Up-* Closing out an option contract at a lower strike price and simultaneously opening another options position at a higher strike price in the same contract month.

7- *Rolling Out and Down-* - Closing out an option contract at a near-term expiration date, and opening a lower-strike contract at a later date. I have found very little use for this strategy (of rolling out and down) in covered call writing, as there is no need to buy back the option if the price of the stock has declined

8- *Rolling Out and Up* - Closing out an option contract at a near-term expiration date, and opening a higher strike contract at a later date. This is a bullish strategy.

9- *Online Discount Broker-* An online stockbroker who carries out *buy and sell orders* at a reduced fee, but offers no investment advice.

10- *The Ellman Calculator* (formerly the ESOC or Ellman System Option Calculator)- an excel calculator used to compute option returns specifically for Alan Ellman's *Cashing in on Covered Calls* system. For exit strategies, the fourth tab, called the "What Now" tab, will be particularly useful in calculating expiration Friday exit strategy returns. The "Unwind" tab of the *Elite Calculator* (expanded version of the Ellman Calculator) will give information for unwinding your positions mid-contract when the stock price accelerates dramatically. The Schedule D of the *Elite Calculator* computes long and short-term capital gains (losses), and additionally allows for final profit and loss computations.

11- *Buy-to-Close-* A term used by many brokerages to represent the closing of a short position (the option sale) in option transactions (buying back the original call option that was sold).

12- *American-Style Option-* An option contract that may be exercised at any time between the date of purchase and the expiration date.

13- *Convert Dead Money to Cash Profits-* An exit strategy (BCI term) wherein an option is bought back and the underlying equity sold. The cash generated from the sale of the underlying equity is then used to buy a better performing stock, which itself is used to sell another covered call.

14- *"Hit a Double"-* A BCI term and exit strategy wherein an option is bought back and then resold at a higher premium in the same contract period.

15- *"Hit a Triple"-* A BCI term and exit strategy wherein an option is bought back twice and resold twice in the same contract period.

16- *Contract Cycle or Contract Period-* The period of time, starting with the first trading day after expiration Friday, through the end of the following expiration Friday (4 p.m. EST, unless there is an exchange recognized holiday). Most contract cycles consist of 4 weeks or 20 trading days (less any holidays), however some cycles will consist of 5 weeks and 25 trading days (less any holidays).

17- *S&P 500 (Standard and Poor's 500)* - index consisting of 500 stocks chosen for market size, liquidity, and industry grouping, among other factors. It is designed to be a leading indicator of U.S. equities and is meant to reflect the risk/return characteristics of the large-cap universe.

The foregoing definitions are the definitions you need to know and master for covered call exit strategies. For a complete list of all definitions used in the *Cashing in on Covered Calls Strategy (BCI)*, see the glossary in the back of this book.

Exit Strategies Prior to Expiration Friday

Key Parameters to Consider

1- Time to Expiration, Share Price Decline and Option Value:

Since we are dealing with predominantly one-month options, there are 4 weeks or 20 days of time value inherent in those option premiums. Some contract periods will last 5 weeks or 25 trading days. The decay of time value starts off slowly the first week, begins to increase in the second week, and virtually falls off a cliff during the last 2 weeks.

Figure 88 depicts time decay in one-month option premiums:

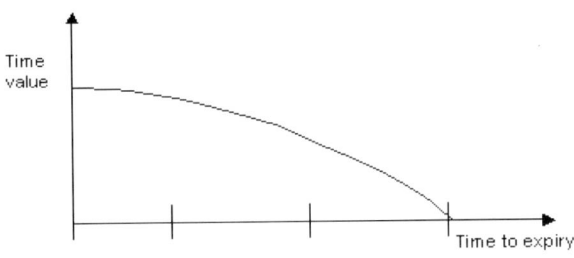

Figure 88-Time Decay in One-Month Option Premiums

As can be seen from Figure 88, there is greater opportunity to make money on an option by buying back and *re-selling* the option earlier in the contract period, as opposed to the last 2 weeks. For example, if we sell an option, then buy it back at the end of week 1, we still have 3 weeks remaining for the option value to go back up and re-sell that very same option. For this reason, I am willing to pay slightly more to close my option position earlier in the contract period. As time value erodes and expiration Friday nears, it becomes increasingly more difficult to profit by closing (buying back) your open option position and reselling another option during the same contract period, given that the premium you will obtain from selling the option for the second time (the *sell-to-open* premium) is lower at this point in the contract cycle (due to a decrease in the time value portion of the premium), and likely will not be significantly more than the cost of buying back the option (the *buy-to-close* premium). This concept of garnering additional income through exit strategies also emphasizes the importance of using an online discount broker to minimize trading commissions.

Using the above-referenced common sense approach *vis a vis* the pricing implications associated with *time to expiration*, I have developed the following *exit strategy guidelines* for the BCI system, which provide specific parameters detailing when to

buy back an option in a given contract cycle:
- During weeks 1 and 2 of the contract cycle (or also week 3 if we are in a 5-week contract cycle), buy back the option when the *"ask"* is 20% or less of the original option premium. Thus, if we see an option value on our watch list decline to 20% or less of the original sale price, we will almost always buy it back. This relieves us of our obligation to sell 100 shares of the underlying equity at the option's strike price, and sets up the possibility of generating additional cash into our accounts. As an example, assume we paid $40 per share (investment of $4000 for every call option sold) and sold the *out-of-the-money* $42 call option for $1.50 ($150 per contract), which gives us a 3.75% one-month return. To calculate the options price that would trigger this exit strategy, we multiply the original option premium by 20%, or $1.50 x .20, which gives us $0.30. This means that *if the option's asking price depreciates to $0.30 or less during weeks 1 or 2 (assuming a standard 4-week contract period),* we buy the option back. The rationale for this parameter, like all our BCI guidelines, is simply predicated upon common sense. In the event the premium drops to .30, we are left with exactly 20% of the <u>original</u> option premium (i.e. $0.30/$1.50), which represents the highest price point our option premium would have to decline to in order to trigger this exit strategy. In this scenario, I am still willing to give up 20% of my original profit by buying back the option because of the possibilities of creating even more profit by selling another call option; at worst (even if another option is not sold), my one-month option profit is 3% (80% of the original 3.75%). So as guideline #1 above dictates, during the first two weeks of the contract cycle, buy back the option when its value declines to 20% of the <u>original</u> option premium or less. This will expand to the first 3 weeks in a 5-week contract cycle.

- During week 3 of the contract cycle (week 4 if we are

in a 5-week cycle), buy back the option when the ask is 10% or less of the original option premium. Since this is the second half of the contract period, at which time the time value erosion of the premium begins to decline precipitously, we are not willing to spend as much as we were during the first two weeks.

- During week 4 of the contract cycle (week 5 if we are in a 5-week cycle), buy back the option at any price if we feel the <u>necessity</u> to sell the underlying equity immediately. If you still plan to hold onto the underlying stock, there is not enough time left in the contract period to realistically expect to generate an exit strategy profit so taking no action would be appropriate in that scenario. However, if the technicals, news or any other factor is cause for concern that the stock price may drop dramatically, buy back the option and sell the stock immediately.

- If <u>at any time</u> during the contract cycle you have reason to believe that a stock could be in serious danger of dropping dramatically in price, buy back the option <u>at any price</u>, sell the stock, and immediately move the cash into another position.

If we sell an *at-the-money or out-of-the-money strike,* the calculations are easy; we simply take 20% or 10% of the original premium derived from the sale in order to determine the option price range that triggers our exit strategy. But what about *in-the-money strikes*? How do we calculate these option percentages? Unlike our ROO calculations, *the 20%-10% guideline works the same for both in-the-money and out-of the-money strikes.* The reason this exit strategy parameter applies equally to both *in-the-money* and *out-of-the-money* strikes has to do with the different deltas associated with each option type. As discussed earlier, delta measures the amount of change in an option value for every $1 change in share price. In-the-money strikes have the highest deltas (between .8 and 1.0), *out-of-the-money* strikes have the lowest deltas (.2 to .3) and *at-the-money* strikes are in between the latter and the former. This is why it works to calculate the 20%/10% guideline for I-T-M strikes which have intrinsic value as well as time value.

The following *hypothetical examples* compare the 20%-10% calculations for an *in-the-money strike* with those for an *out-of-the-money strike,* and will assist in clarifying the aforementioned point. Bear in mind, however, that the figures used in these examples are general, hypothetical numbers, which in reality, can vary from stock to stock and situation to situation. Overall, however, the rationale demonstrated by these examples has significant application to most scenarios:

- We own a stock @ $53 and sell the *in-the-money* $50 call option for $4. Assume this call option has a delta of .8, which means the option will drop (or rise) $.80 in value for every $1 of share depreciation (or appreciation). Thus, because of delta, if the stock drops by $4 to $49, the option value would depreciate to $.80 (i.e. $4 - $3.20), which meets our 20% guideline To calculate the options price point which would trigger the 20% exit strategy for this *in-the-money* strike, note that we multiplied the *original, entire* option premium (not just the ROO or time value portion of the premium) by 20% ($4 x .20 = $0.80). Because delta is higher for in-the-money strikes, the 20%/10% guidelines are generally applicable to the entire option premium for all strikes.

- We own a stock @ $48 and sell the *out-of-the-money* $50 strike @ $1.50. Assume a delta of .3 for this option. If this stock, like the stock for the in-the-money strike in the example directly above, also dropped $4 in value to $44, the corresponding option value will be $.30 (i.e. $1.50 - $1.20) which also meets our 20% guideline. Note that $0.30 (i.e. $1.50 x .20), the 20%

exit strategy price point for this out-of-the-money strike, was calculated using the same formula that we used to calculate the 20% exit strategy price point for the *in-the-money* strike in the first example directly above.

Bear in mind that the above-referenced examples are purely hypothetical, and the calculations therein will not always be exact. In other words, given the same amount of share depreciation, the in-the-money and out-of-the-money strikes will not always depreciate to the exact same figure but they will be in the same "ballpark". That said, these examples were created to make a point; thus, the deltas are accurate for each strike price and the resulting option returns and protection calculations are figures which could reasonably be expected under similar circumstances. The point isn't to examine these figures in detail, but rather, to understand the relationship between strike price and delta, and why these option components make the 20%-10% guidelines applicable in most situations.

Let's now move on to the effect of a significant acceleration in share price, the next exit strategy parameter considered in the BCI system.

2- Significant Acceleration of Share Price:

In the above-referenced situations, we saw how a decline in the share and option price initiated an exit strategy maneuver. But what if the share price increases to the point where the option premium has no time value, and we can unwind our position at very little or no cost? In these cases we may be able to use the cash from unwinding one position to initiate another position, thereby generating a second income stream with the same cash in the same month. Examples of this strategy will be given later in this chapter.

3- Market Tone:

The direction and strength of the general market should play a key role in our investment decisions. When the stock market is declining precipitously, making profits is analogous to riding a bicycle uphill. If, on the other hand, the market is appreciating dramatically, generating great profits is as easy as riding the bicycle downhill. In an uptrending market, we are more likely to base our investment decisions on the likelihood that equities will be driven higher as they get caught up in the momentum of an appreciating equities market. In a market trending downward, our decisions will be based on the greater possibilities of declining stock values. Once again folks, this is not rocket science, simply common sense. *A BCI rule of thumb is that 70+% of a stock move is due to the general market trend.* Therefore, the price of a specific equity will, in large part, be influenced by overall market conditions.

So how do we go about determining market tone? Most of the time, information can be gleaned by following the news of the day and watching our portfolios. Picking up a newspaper or turning on our TVs and computers will oftentimes provide the knowledge to make this determination. Many investors prefer to rely on the charting patterns of certain indexes in order to quantify the tone and mood of the market. The S&P 500 Index ($SPX) and the CBOE Volatility Index® (VIX®)[3] are two of the more popular indexes used to gauge market sentiment. A strong chart pattern for the S&P 500, coupled with a declining or sideways trading pattern for the VIX at a low volatility level, is viewed as bullish signals by stock traders. Plotting the moving averages on the S&P 500 or its companion ETF commonly referred to as the "Spiders" (SPY) will provide a good visual indication of the major market trend.

4- Technical Analysis of the underlying security:

When making our exit strategy decisions, a positive chart with all confirming indicators would be extremely bullish. A mixed technical pattern would be neutral in which case I would tend to be more conservative. If all indicators had turned negative

---

[3] The CBOE Volatility Index® (VIX®) is a key measure of market expectations of near-term volatility conveyed by S&P 500 stock index option prices.

from the initial purchase of the stock and subsequent sale of the option, I would consider buying back the option and selling the stock immediately.

5- Calculations:

As we evaluate time to expiration, cost to *buy to close*, market tone and technical analysis we are formulating the first part of our plan. The second part encompasses computing our returns or potential returns. Further along in this chapter we will explore exit strategy opportunities where we will utilize these parameters to guide us to our ultimate preference. Although the calculations are important, I use this final parameter as the least significant of the four (with the exception of the case when the stock appreciates dramatically). If the other factors are describing a stock that will probably continue to depreciate in value, I will opt for an exit strategy that factors that into consideration, even if it is at the expense of a potential higher return. We will go into detail with calculations in this chapter where examples are given for ALL possible scenarios. The Ellman Calculator will be particularly helpful when calculating Expiration Friday Strategies and Mid-contract unwind situations (this last tab is included in the Elite Calculator).

Exit Strategy Choices Prior to Expiration Friday

In the first few weeks of a contract cycle there are several exit strategy possibilities we must be prepared for. Which choice, if any, is most appropriate will depend on the parameters discussed above.

1- Rolling Down:

Rolling down occurs when we buy back a previously sold option (buy-to-close our short position) and simultaneously sell another option at a lower strike price in the same contract month (open a new short position). Let's say we purchase Company XYZ @ $38 per share. We then sell the $40 call option, which trades in a standard contract cycle, @$2, or a total of $200. This represents a one-month 5.3% return ($200/$3800). One week later, the price of XYZ drops to $35 per share, and the corresponding option value also declines to $0.40. Thus, during the first two weeks of the contract cycle, the option premium has declined to 20% of its original value ($2 x .20 = $0.40). In accordance with the 20%-10% guidelines discussed above, we close our open position by buying back the call option for $0.40, and look to increase our profits by selling another call option. Assume that at the same time, the $35 strike is selling for $2. Here, we can "roll down" by selling the $35 strike for $2. This is a defensive play that allows us to garner an additional $160 per contract ($200 - $40 = $160 for the 100 shares). This will also result in a probable loss of $3 per share, or $300 per contract, on the share depreciation, because our initial purchase was for $38 per share, and we are now required to sell our shares for $35 per share due to the option obligation. If the value of the stock is below $35 at expiration Friday, the shares will not be assigned and sold. Assuming, however, that the shares are sold, here's how to calculate the result:

- Income from two option sales: $200 (original option sale) + $160 ($200 premium from the second sale minus the $40 cost of the initial option buyback) = $360 profit.

- Loss from stock depreciation: $3800 (100 shares @$38) - $3500 (sold @ $35/share) = $300.

- Our net gain from option and stock sales is $360 - $300 = $60 profit

Therefore, by instituting a rolling down exit strategy, we generated a $60 profit despite the fact that our asset (stock) depreciated in value by $300 per contract.

We lean towards implementing a rolling down strategy when the market tone and technicals are mixed to negative. I would also be more inclined to use this strategy later, rather than earlier, in the contract period (late in week 2 and week 3, rather than week 1).

Real-life example of rolling down:

Figure 89 depicts an actual example of a rolling down exit strategy I previously implemented in connection with a covered call position I had in Hasbro, Inc. (HAS):

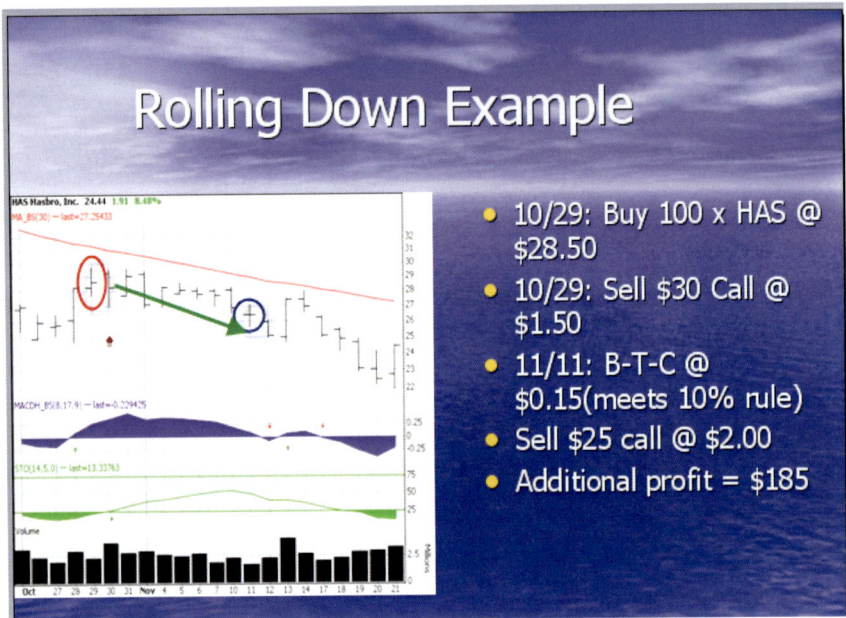

Figure 89- Rolling Down with HAS

Figure 89 is an example taken from one of my seminar slides and also found in my second book, *Exit Strategies for Covered Call Writing*. The stock was purchased and the first option ($30) was sold on 10/29 (red circle) for $1.50. On 11/11 the option was bought back for $0.15, or 10% of the original option premium which meets our 10% guideline and signaled me to buy back the original option. Accordingly, on 11/11, I bought back or bought-to-close (B-T-C) the $30 call option for $0.15 and implemented a rolling down exit strategy by selling-to-open (S-T-O) a $25 call option (blue circle) for $2.00. This generated an additional $185 per contract into my account ($200-$15), as the stock closed the cycle just below the $25 strike price and my shares were not assigned and not sold. The green arrow on Figure 89 highlights the downtrending price of HAS, a typical condition seen in connection with rolling down exit strategies. *Please note that at this point there IS a paper loss on the share value ($2850 – 2500 = $350) which is almost fully compensated for by the original option sale and exit strategy profit generated ($150 + $185 = $335).*

2- Take No Immediate Action after Buying Back the Option

Create an Opportunity to "Hit a Double":

Can you tell that I'm a baseball fan? It's my book, so I can call my exit strategies whatever I want! When we "hit a double," we buy back the option (buy-to-close) assuming it meets our 20%-10% guidelines, and simply watch the stock price without taking additional *immediate* action. Here, the goal is to wait for the underlying equity to appreciate in value in a relatively short period of time after the initial buy-back of the option, thereby driving up the option value. If this occurs, we can sell the exact same option (same strike and expiration date) and generate a second income stream from the same option, or, in other words, "hit a double." Over the years, I have actually also hit a few "triples," wherein the same option was sold *three* times prior to its expiration!

As a rule of thumb, we attempt to "hit a double" when the market tone and stock technicals are mixed to positive earlier in the contract period (especially during the first week or early in the second).

Real-life example of "hitting a double:"

Figure 90 depicts an actual example of when I "hit a double" with respect to a prior covered call position in Blue Coat Systems, Inc (BCSI), which ultimately generated an additional $868 into my account. Bear in mind that the additional $868 does NOT include the original $992 I "earned" when I sold the option for the first time. First, let's look at the chart for BCSI as it existed at the time this exit strategy was implemented:

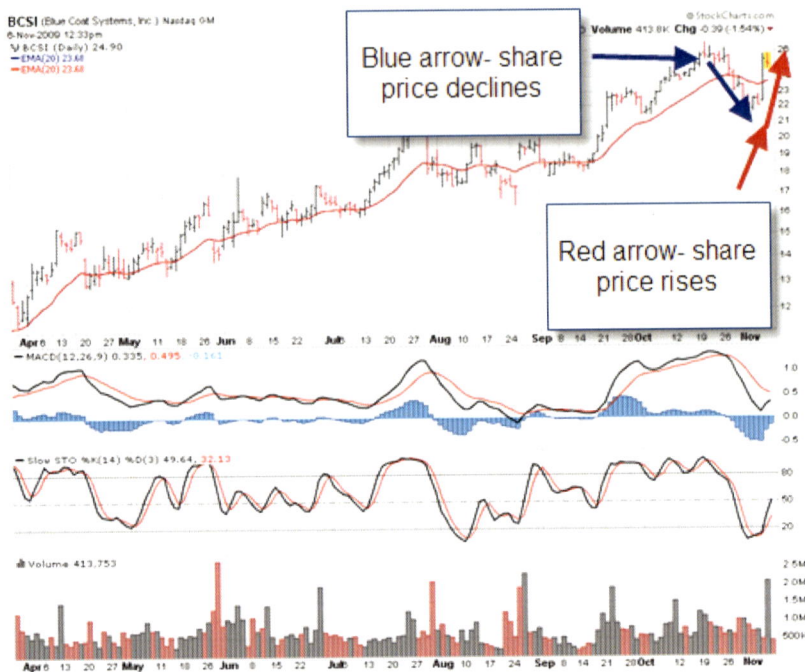

Figure 90- Hitting a Double in BCSI

Note how BCSI took a big plunge (blue arrow) and then recovered quickly over the next two weeks (red arrow). Here are the four prongs of this one-month investment:

- 10/26/09- Purchased 1000 shares of BCSI @ $25.35

- 10/26/09 – Immediately sold 10 contracts of the slightly *in-the-money* November $25 call option for $1.35, generating a profit of $992 (I deducted the intrinsic value of $0.35, as well as commission, in calculating the latter $992 figure). Should I be happy and complacent and head for the mall? Not Blue Collar Investors!

- 10/30/09 – Took advantage of a market dip and bought back the 10 contracts for $0.25 per contract ($250 in total) in accordance with our 20% guideline, thereby creating a loss of $262, inclusive of commissions.

- 11/5/09 – Took advantage of a price upswing (red arrow) and re-sold the EXACT SAME 10 OPTIONS for $1.15. This generated an additional $1130 into my account, inclusive of commissions. Thus, my net gain in connection with the utilizing the "hitting a double" exit strategy in this example is $868 ($1130 - $262). It took me less than 5 minutes to buy back the option, and less than 5 minutes to re-sell the option a few days later. Now, if that doesn't put a smile on your face, let's add in the initial option profit of $992, for a *total profit* of $1860 ($992 + $868). Our original investment was $25,000 using the intrinsic value of the first option premium to "buy down" the cost of the stock from $25.35 to $25 (use the Ellman Calculator or review Chapter 6 if this part troubles you). As such, our one-month profit or ROO is: $1860/$25,000 = 7.4%. So now it's time to head to the mall, right? Nope, still two more weeks until expiration Friday!

As demonstrated in the above-referenced example, the "hitting a double" exit strategy is best utilized when the underlying equity, and thus, the option premium, will appreciate in value in a relatively short period of time. If, however, the price of the underlying equity does not appreciate in this manner, we can then look to roll down, or alternatively, to possibly implement our third exit strategy, which involves selling the stock and "converting dead money to cash profits."

3- Convert Dead Money to Cash Profits:

This strategy should be considered when there is a dark cloud hanging over our stock. We worked so hard to properly identify one of the greatest performing stocks in a strong industry, however assume, for whatever reason, this equity is not behaving as predicted. This *will* happen. You may have even allowed this stock to remain in your portfolio an additional contract period (perhaps against your better judgment). The price has dropped, the technicals are deteriorating and you are losing patience with this financial soldier. <u>There is nothing wrong with selling a stock that is not performing.</u> This is one of the most difficult concepts for investors to accept. Many assume that if they sell, they are losing money and if they don't, there is no loss.

Here is my common sense approach to the foregoing situation, with which I hope you concur: the cash in that stock is what is important; the stock itself is merely a vehicle that is temporarily bringing that cash out into the investment battlefield with the hopes of coming home with friend$ (no misprint). If the price of that equity is not behaving as predicted, it needs to be replaced with a stronger warrior. This point can be clarified by asking yourself the following question: "at this point in time, is the cash tied up in this underperforming stock more likely to generate profit in a stock with poor technicals and declining market value, or in different stock with great technicals and an uptrending share price?" Granted, the laggard stock may turn around and head back up. The new stock we buy may change direction as well. There are no guarantees. However, we are throwing the odds to profit in our favor by using sound fundamental and technical principles, in addition to a whole lot of common sense.

Since options are priced based on the value of the corresponding stock, if a stock has been depreciating in price, so has its option value. When we convert dead money to cash profits, we buy back the option at any price, sell the poor-performing underlying equity, purchase a new, healthier stock and proceed to sell the option on that healthier gladiator. We make every effort to generate a profit on this exchange, and quite often we will in fact succeed. Keep in mind, however, that the main purpose behind this maneuver is to avoid a major loss on the value of the underlying equity. *Bearing the foregoing in mind, the rule of thumb for converting dead money to cash profits is as follows: we utilize this strategy when the stock technicals are negative and the stock price has dropped with little sign of near-*

term improvement. This choice can be utilized at any time during the contract period prior to expiration Friday.

Real-life situation where converting dead money to cash profits may be a viable exit strategy:

Figure 91 below shows a typical chart pattern of an equity wherein converting dead money to cash profits is potentially a viable strategy. The red arrow in Figure 91 highlights what appears to be a downtrend that has little hope of recovery, at least in the short-term. We see a downtrending price pattern with bearish MACD and stochastic oscillators on high volume (this is a 1-month chart but a similar pattern appeared on a 6-month chart):

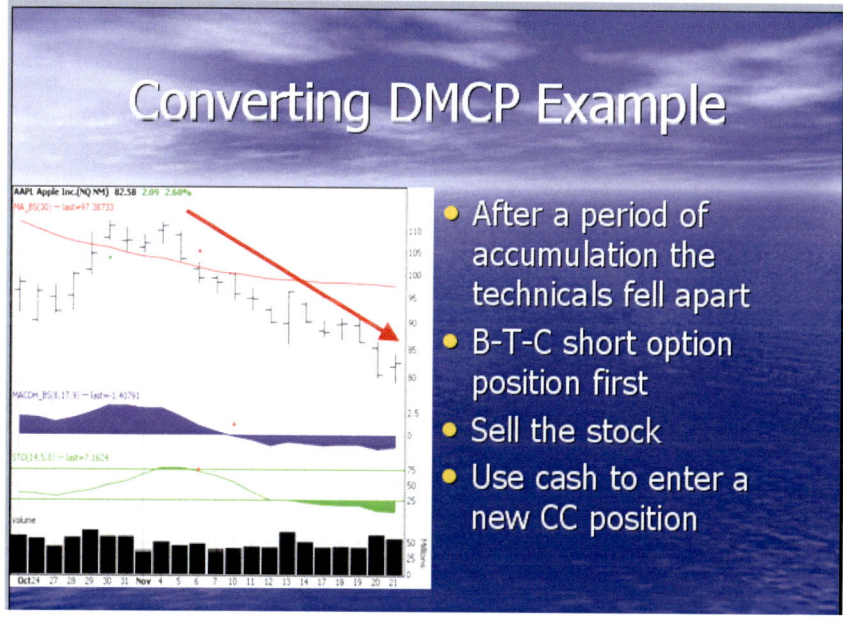

Figure 91- Convert Dead Money to Cash Profits

4- No Action Taken:

As free-thinking Blue Collar Investors, taking no action should always be considered. Assume there is no clear cut choice from the three exit strategies mentioned above. Perhaps the calculations don't impress you, or maybe you just want to see how things turn out by the end of the contract cycle; after all, we are only talking about a one-month obligation. The *No Action Taken* is a choice I tend to favor in the later stages of the contract cycle when the possibilities of creating exit strategy profits have declined. As long as you have appropriately evaluated the other choices and excluded each as a viable option, feel free to take no action. It could turn out to be the best decision.

5- Mid-Contract Unwind:

From time to time, you will buy a stock, sell the call option and your equity will subsequently dart straight for the moon! That will leave your strike price deep *in-the-money*. One way of looking at this situation is that you made a significant profit, and now that cash is protected by the difference between the share value and strike price of the option, or the intrinsic value of the option premium. In this case, you will just allow assignment and enter a new position the next contract cycle. There may be, however, an opportunity to generate even more cash in such a scenario, especially when there is still time left until expiration Friday.

When a strike moves *deep in-the-money, the time value of that option premium declines and approaches zero*. This means that the option premium consists predominantly of intrinsic value. The amount of cash it takes to buy back the option is greatly offset by the share appreciation we would realize by eliminating the option obligation (closing our short option position by buying the option back) and selling the stock. Always consider a mid-contract unwind exit strategy when the time value of the option premium approaches zero and there is enough time remaining in the current contract cycle to generate additional profit with another position.

Real-life example of a mid-contract unwind exit strategy:

There is nothing like a real-life example to clarify the utilization of the mid-contract unwind exit strategy. Figures 92 through 96 depict the primary stages that occurred when I utilized this strategy in a covered call position for the underlying security, Perrigo Company (PRGO). Initially, 300 shares of PRGO were purchased @ $51.10 on March 22nd, the start of the April contract cycle. At this time, three $50 call option contracts were sold for $2.10, yielding a profit of $100 per contract given that this premium consists of $1.00 of time value ($2.10-$1.10). A week into the contract cycle, PRGO had appreciated in value to $56.79, and the premium for the corresponding $50 call option had likewise appreciated to $6.90, as illustrated in Figures 92 and 93, respectively:

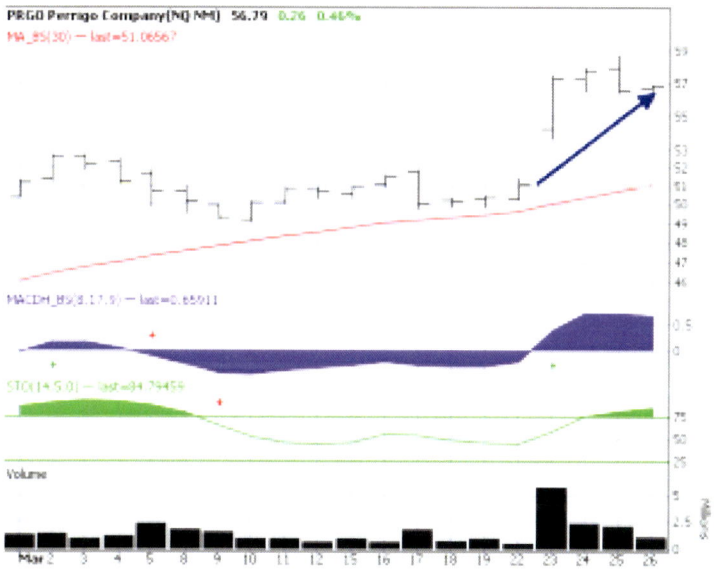

Figure 92- PRGO Heads to the Moon!

Figure 93 – PRGO $50 Call Option Premium Heads to the Moon!

The drastic increase in PRGO share price and its corresponding option premium in such a short period of time prompts us to explore the potential to generate more profits by unwinding the initial position mid-contract and then selling the stock. In order to examine the viability of this cash-generating opportunity, we must first explore the current options chain for PRGO, depicted in Figure 94:

	Calls					Apr 10
Last	Intrinsic Value	Bid	Ask	Vol	Open Interest	Strike
16.75	16.79	16.60	16.90	0	23	40.00
11.75	11.79	11.60	11.90	0	18	45.00
6.80	6.79	6.70	6.90	0	1,011	50.00
2.78	1.79	2.70	2.85	0	824	55.00
0.53	0.00	0.45	0.60	0	266	60.00
0.10	0.00	0.05	0.15	0	0	65.00
0.10	0.00	N/A	0.10	0	0	70.00

Figure 94 - PRGO - Unwind Options Chain

In the yellow-highlighted area enclosed by the red circle, we see that the cost to close our short position for the $50 *in-the-money* call option is $6.90 (we may pay less by playing the bid-ask spread), and that this premium consists of $6.79 of intrinsic value, leaving a time value of $0.11, or $11 per contract. Discounting our miniscule commissions, if we can use the cash from the sale of the stock and generate a higher return than $11 per contract, we have made additional profit. Using the "Unwind Now" tab of the Elite Calculator we can see how the original profit of $100 per contract ($210 – $110) has now dipped by $11 to $89. To do this, we first we enter the options chain information for PRGO into the blue cells of the "Unwind Now Tab" spreadsheet of the Elite Calculator (Figure 95):

1) ENTER THE ORIGINAL TRADE INFORMATION BELOW		
Stock name >>	Perrigo	
Stock symbol >>	PRGO	
Date of transaction >>	03/22/10	Today's date >>
Stock purchase price >>	$ 51.10	
Option STRIKE price >>	$ 50.00	
Option sale price/share >>	$ 2.10	
2) ENTER TODAY'S INFORMATION		
Current stock price >>	$ 56.79	
Current option price/share >>	$ 6.90	
3) PRESS THE PRINTER ICON OR CLICK ON THE "FILE" MENU, SELECT "PRINT" AND CLICK "OK"		

Figure 95 - PRGO Options Information Entered Into the Unwind Now Tab of the Elite Calculator

Next, we view the results generated from the entry of the foregoing information in the "Unwind Tab of the Elite Calculator, which is depicted in Figure 96:

RETURN ON OPTION (ROO) CALCULATOR - UNWIND NOW

Stock name >>	Perrigo		
Stock symbol >>	PRGO	Today's date >>	03/29/10

RETURN IF I UNWIND THE POSITION TODAY

Cost of shares	$	5,110.00
Option premium received	$	210.00
Option close-out		
Cost to buy back the option	$	690.00
Premium received on sale	$	210.00
Gain (loss) on close-out	$	(480.00)
Stock close-out		
Proceeds from sale of stock	$	5,679.00
Cost of shares	$	5,110.00
Gain (loss) on close-out	$	569.00
Net Gain (Loss) to UNWIND	$	**89.00**

NET RETURN ON POSITION

Net gain (loss) to unwind position today	$	89.00	= 1.80%
Net cash to open position	$	4,900.00	
Number of days position was open			7
Annualized return			89.00%

Figure 96 - Unwind Results for PRGO Generated by the Elite Calculator

This shows that the original $100 profit was reduced by the $11 to $89. Now if we can use the cash from the stock sale to generate more than $11 (not that challenging to accomplish) we can establish a second income stream in the same contract month with the same cash!

Perhaps, some *may* feel that we can generate the extra cash by rolling up, however, the following two reasons may render the decision to utilize this strategy an unwise one:

- The price of the stock may not be in a favorable position to generate a decent return

- Given the drastic share appreciation over a short period of time, the possibility exists that profit-takers (sellers) could cause the price to experience a drastic decline in value.

Instead of rolling up, let's look for a new financial soldier to send out into the financial battlefield (this has all been decided prior to unwinding the original position). To do this, we look to our watch list, which contains 40-60 fundamentally sound equities, and (in this example), Bucyrus International, Inc. (BUCY) surfaces as a viable candidate. This stock was selected from our watch list which was established with the fundamental, technical and common sense principles addressed earlier in this book. We then put BUCY through our technical screens, which (in this example) it passed, as depicted in Figure 97:

Figure 97 - BUCY Chart as of 3/29/10

Next, we look to the options chain for BUCY (Figure 98) in order to obtain the relevant figures necessary to perform our ROO calculations via the Ellman Calculator:

22.45	22.48	22.20	22.70	0	254	45.00	
21.45	21.48	21.20	21.70	0	65	46.00	
20.45	20.48	20.20	20.70	0	109	47.00	
19.50	19.48	19.30	19.70	0	62	48.00	
18.50	18.48	18.30	18.70	0	188	49.00	
17.50	17.48	17.40	17.60	0	670	50.00	
12.60	12.48	12.50	12.70	0	1,213	55.00	
7.95	7.48	7.80	8.10	0	1,659	60.00	
4.00	2.48	3.90	4.10	0	4,280	65.00	
1.50	0.00	1.45	1.55	0	4,541	70.00	
0.40	0.00	0.35	0.45	0	3,302	75.00	
0.10	0.00	0.05	0.15	0	1,802	80.00	
0.05	0.00	0.05	0.05	0	70	85.00	

Figure 98 - BUCY Options Chain

With BUCY currently priced at $67.48, we can sell the $65, in-the-money strike for $3.90, which yields a 2.2% ROO. Figure 99 illustrates the foregoing calculations as generated via the Ellman Calculator:

RETURN ON OPTION (ROO) CALCULATOR - MULTIPLE STOCKS

Stock Name or Symbol	Stock $/sh	Option $/sh	Strike $	Expires	Intrisic	Upside	ROO	Up Potential	Down Protect
BUCY	$ 67.48	$ 3.90	$ 65.00		$ 2.48	$ -	2.2%	0.0%	3.7%
MCRS	$ 44.43	$ 1.40	$ 45.00		$ -	$ 0.57	3.2%	1.3%	0.0%
ULTA	$ 31.01	$ 0.40	$ 35.00		$ -	$ 3.99	1.3%	12.9%	0.0%
MSB	$ 42.34	$ 1.75	$ 45.00		$ -	$ 2.66	4.1%	6.3%	0.0%
MOS	$ 68.39	$ 2.70	$ 70.00		$ -	$ 1.61	3.9%	2.4%	0.0%

Figure 99- ROO Calculations for BUCY (yellow highlighted area)

As depicted in Figure 99, an additional 2.2% return is generated (by buying the stock @ $67.48 and selling the in-the-money $65 call option) with a huge cushion of 3.7% in downside protection ($248/6748). This 2.2% figure translates to a $115 per contract "bonus" for instituting a mid-contract position unwind exit strategy.

Conclusion:

When a stock appreciates in value over a short period of time, and there are still two weeks or more remaining in the cycle, unwinding your position may offer an opportunity to generate additional cash into your account. *The keys are that the time value of the option premium must be close to zero, and the new position must generate more cash than the amount of time value paid to close the original position.*

Managing Stocks that Have Gapped Down

In the preceding example wherein a mid-contract unwind strategy was implemented, the stock moved up in price substantially. However, what if the stock gaps down unexpectedly? A gap is a break between prices on a chart that occurs when the price of a stock makes a sharp move up or down with no trading occurring in between. Gaps can be created by factors such as regular buying or selling pressure, earnings announcements, changes in analyst's outlook, or any other type of news release. If there are many more sellers than buyers, a stock will gap-down. A "gap up" occurs when the current price bar's low is above the previous day's high. A "gap-down" occurs when the current price bar's high is below the previous day's low. Stock gaps occur as a result of excessive buy or sell orders which forces prices either up or down. Figure 100 depicts a chart of BCSI which gapped down after a disappointing earnings report was announced:

Figure 100 - BCSI Gaps Down

As depicted in Figure 100, beginning at $29 per share, this stock gapped down to $22 per share. Now, for those Blue Collar Investors who follow my system, you would not have been hurt by this precipitous drop because we avoid earnings reports for this very reason. However, a stock can gap down for some of the other reasons mentioned directly above.

When a stock gaps down, human nature is such that most investors want to get their money back with the same equity; psychologically, the "loss" will no longer be perceived as a loss. As a result, many investors will choose not to unwind their position, but rather, leave the position as is and ride it to wherever it goes. This approach is misguided in some instances. Think back to stocks such as Enron, Tyco, WorldCom, Citi, Bear Stearns, Lehman and many others. Holding positions in these companies spelled disaster, even though these corporations were once considered pillars of our economy. Circumstances change, and so we must be willing to change our perspectives as well. When a stock drops from $29 to $22 (as it did in Figure 100), we now have $2200 in cash per options contract (100 shares of the underlying equity). In other words, we no longer have $2900 per contract, as we did when we initially opened the position. The question then becomes, "where do we want the $2200 in cash to be placed, so as to give us the best chance for a successful investment?" Simply put, it may or may not be with this same security. So step one in determining whether to leave our cash in the same equity is to determine what caused the equity to gap down. We must check the news to see what caused this unexpected turn of events. If it is a serious matter (e.g. corporate fraud, the departure of a key officer of the company, the loss of a patent, an announcement that the FDA has rejected a company's new drug, new legislation that negatively impacts the company or other events that dramatically alter the prospects for that company), it's time to hand that cash over to a new financial warrior. If, on the other hand, the gap-down was caused by a less serious matter (e.g. a single analyst downgraded his or her rating of the stock) and a market over-reaction followed, we may opt to stay with the same equity.

For those of you familiar with casino blackjack, the following example may serve as useful guidance. Assume you hold a "15" hand and your prospects look bleak. This position is analogous to the stock after it has gapped down. The dealer's hand represents the circumstances that will dictate how to manage the gap-down. Now, do you stay with the "15" or do you make a change? Well, that depends on the cause of the event, or, for purposes of this blackjack example, the dealer's hand. If the dealer has a "5," this "event" should not be considered a serious one. Therefore you hold your position, as there is a good chance the dealer will "go bust" or go over "21" with his next card. In other words, your investment outlook by leaving your hand as is looks positive. If, however, the dealer is showing a "10," you face a more precarious situation, as there is high statistical chance the dealer has a "20," which would effectively destroy your hand. Therefore, you must change your "financial soldiers" by selecting another card to increase your chances of winning the hand. In other words, given the same hand but different conditions, we must make different decisions. In much the same way, if a few analysts cause a gap-down by downgrading their ratings in a particular stock, this "non-serious" event should not alter your view that continued ownership of that equity will likely result profitable returns. A more serious event, on the other hand, should signal that new stock and options positions are likely warranted in order to increase our chances of yielding successful returns on our investments. .

When we decide to hold a stock that has gapped down, we are employing a strategy I like to call *technical nullification*. As with jury nullification, where a jury ignores the facts and opts for an atypical conclusion, in *technical nullification*, we ignore technicals indicators such as chart patterns and retain ownership of the equity regardless. Let's look at a chart of BCSI (Figure 101) three weeks after a gap-down, at which time BCSI begins to consolidate (i.e. trade sideways) and form a base from which it may head back north:

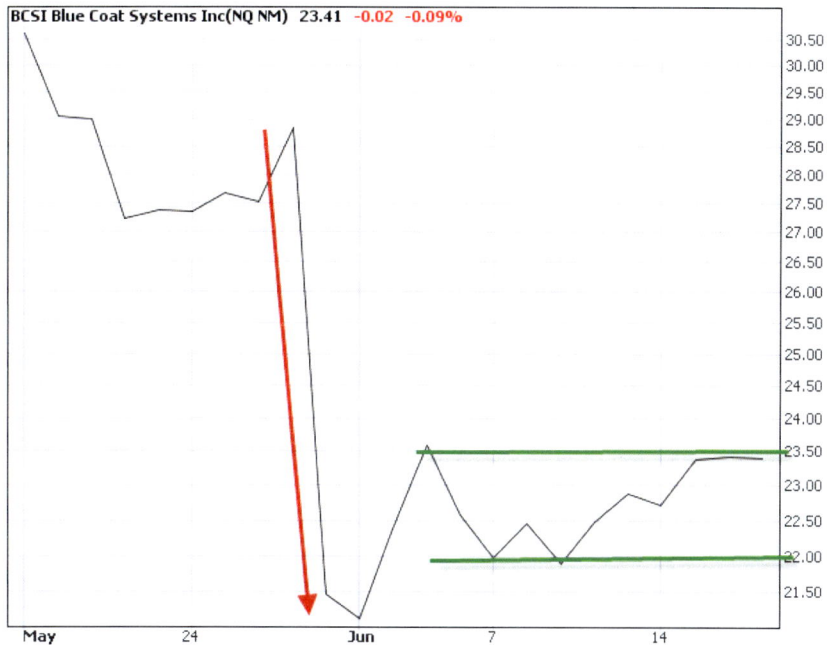

Figure 101- BCSI after Gap-Down

Notice that after the huge gap-down (red arrow), BCSI began trading sideways between $22 and $23.50. Using technical nullification in conjunction with the expectation that BCSI will return to its previous pre-gap-down price level leads us to selling the *out-of-the-money* calls, which in this example, is the $25 call option. The option chain for BCSI (Figure 102) shows a return of near 2% for the next month *out-of-the-money* $25 call option:

Options

View By Expiration: Jun 10 | Jul 10 | Oct 10 | Jan 11 | Jan 12

CALL OPTIONS — Expire at close Friday, July

Strike	Symbol	Last	Chg	Bid	Ask	Vol	O
17.50	BCSI100717C00017500	5.50	0.00	5.50	6.00	0	
20.00	BCSI100717C00020000	3.50	0.00	3.30	3.70	6	
22.50	BCSI100717C00022500	1.50	↓ 0.20	1.50	1.70	181	
25.00	BCSI100717C00025000	0.50	↓ 0.05	0.40	0.50	248	
30.00	BCSI100717C00030000	0.04	0.00	N/A	0.05	38	
35.00	BCSI100717C00035000	0.05	0.00	N/A	0.10	1	
40.00	BCSI100717C00040000	0.05	0.00	N/A	0.10	0	
45.00	BCSI100717C00045000	0.20	0.00	N/A	0.10	0	

Figure 102- BCSI- Option Chain

In addition to looking at the short-term technicals of a stock after a gap-down, we should also compare its price performance to that of the broad market. If the stock is consolidating but significantly underperforming the overall market, I would view same as a bearish signal and accordingly, would consider selling the stock. In Figure 103 however, we see that BCSI had matched the recent price performance of the S&P 500 after it gapped down, reinforcing the confidence we may have in this equity.

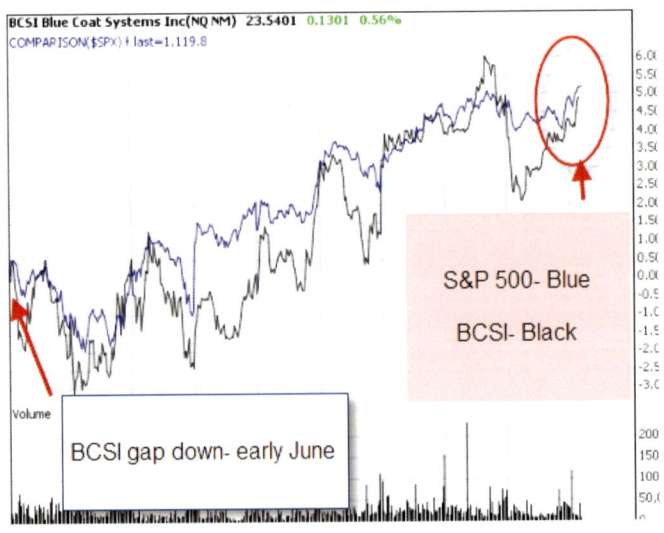

Figure 103 - BCSI after Gap Down vs. S&P: *You decide to keep the stock after a gap-down:*

If you decide that the cause of a gap-down was not serious and that retaining the equity is still a wise investment, we first buy back the option. Since the price of the equity has declined dramatically, the price of the option has similarly declined in value. If we are mid-contract or earlier, I generally prefer to wait for a bounce-back and resell the same strike to "hit a double." If the stock is slow to recover its value, we can roll down to a lower strike price *that is still above the current market value.* In the BCSI example above, selling the $22.50 strike for $1.50 will generate income to help offset the share value depreciation. If we are correct and the stock continuers to recover, we can nurture this security up by selling out-of-the-money strikes.

You decide to sell the stock after a gap-down:

If you feel that the cause of a gap-down was a longer-term issue, buy back the option and sell the stock. We then utilize the cash generated from this sale to enter a new covered call position.

Both management decisions can be re-evaluated as time progresses using the same exit strategy maneuvers discussed earlier in this chapter.

Exit Strategies On or Near Expiration Friday

Key parameters to consider

Of the four parameters we considered for pre-expiration Friday exit strategies, the first, *time to expiration and option value* is no longer a consideration as there is NO TIME VALUE to speak of on expiration Friday. Nor are we considering the current option value as an entity in and of itself as a factor. This is because on expiration Friday, we will be willing to buy back an option AT ANY PRICE if the concurrent re-sale of the next month's option makes that "package deal" a sensible one. In other words, if the package of the cost of the buyback and the subsequent sale of the next month's option yields a respectable return for an equity we are still interested in retaining, then we have an investment we will move forward with. Therefore, the *calculation parameter* becomes much more critical on expiration Friday than during the earlier weeks of the contract period. We are also adding in one additional parameter to consider, earnings reports. That being said, here is my list of key parameters to consider when evaluating expiration Friday exit strategies:

1- Market Tone:

There are several exit strategies to choose from. On expiration Friday, one such consideration will be which strike price to select when re-selling the next-month's option. A strongly positive or sometimes a mixed market tone (with concurrent positive stock technicals) will encourage a higher strike price so as to capture both the return on the option premium (ROO) and upside appreciation. A mixed (with concurrent mixed stock technicals) or negative market tone may direct us to the lower of the strike prices.

2- Technical Analysis of the Underlying Stock:

This parameter is important for two reasons. First, before employing an expiration Friday exit strategy, we are required to make sure that the equity is still fundamentally and technically sound. This is part of our original system requirement to only own the greatest performing stocks. If the security is sound technically, with either all confirming indicators positive or moving average positive and one or more confirming ones negative or neutral, that stock is eligible for an exit strategy maneuver. The second reason this parameter is important relates to the strike price. As with market tone, we are more likely to re-sell at the higher strike price if the technicals are all positive, rather than mixed. If the technicals are all negative, we are required to sell the stock. This is an unlikely scenario since the market price has exceeded the strike price (the only time we consider an expiration Friday exit strategy), so the chart pattern should still be quite healthy. If we do decide that the stock needs to be sold, *no action needs to be taken on our part.* Share assignment will occur over the weekend, after 4PM, on expiration Friday, and the cash from that sale will be in our account by the following Monday. This will cost us one commission (the sale of the stock) rather than two (close short option position and then sell the stock).

3- Earnings Reports:

As previously discussed in Chapter 8 of this book and in chapter 12 of Cashing in on Covered Calls it is critical to avoid earnings reports when selling covered call options. As we approach expiration Friday we need to check our portfolio manager list, premium report or ER Website (www.earningswhispers.com) to make certain that this equity will not be reporting in the upcoming contract period. If the equity will be reporting in the upcoming contract period we have three choices:

- Allow assignment and use the cash to purchase a different equity the following week.

- Buy back the option and own the stock through the earnings report without selling an option. This way, if the ER is positive, we can get the full appreciation of the stock without being limited by a strike price. This second choice is NOT part of my system of selling covered call options. I mention it because I am asked about this scenario at each and every one of my seminars. If you are sticking strictly to a covered call strategy, allow share assignment if the ER is going to be announced the upcoming contract period.

- If the ER is reported early in the next contract period, allow the shares to be sold, and buy them back a day or two after the report assuming all system criteria are still in place. At this point you are again free to again start cashing in on covered calls with that same equity.

4- Calculations:

Let us review the list of circumstances that need to materialize in order to be in a position to calculate potential expiration Friday option returns:

- The current market value of our stock is greater than the agreed upon strike price.

- The fundamentals and technicals of the equity still meet our system criteria.

- We have evaluated market tone and stock technicals to help guide us to an appropriate strike price determination. The more positive these indicators are, the more likely we are to roll out and up as opposed to rolling out only.

- There is no earnings report scheduled for the upcoming contract period.

If all four of these criteria are met, then we will do our calculations to determine if that stock will be in or out for the next contract period. We use the *What Now* tab of the Basic Ellman Calculator to determine our returns and compare those to the ones we would get from selling the stock and utilizing a different financial soldier.

Exit Strategy Choices On or Near Expiration Friday

1- Rolling Out:

In this strategy, we close out our option contract (buy-to-close) and immediately sell the <u>next month's same strike contract</u>. To get to this point, we have already determined that the fundamentals and technicals of the underlying equity are still sound and meet our system criteria. We have also ascertained that there is no upcoming earnings report to interfere with this deal. Finally, the calculations are such that we have come to the conclusion that the cash in this equity will be most productive by holding the stock. In other words, we still love the stock and the returns it generates.

<u>As a rule of thumb,</u> when we roll out, we always do so to an in-the-money strike. If we initially bought a stock for $38 and sold the $40 call option, and on expiration Friday the share price was $42, our call option would be $2 *in-the-money*, and we would thus consider a rolling out strategy. Here, if we choose to roll out to the next month's $40 strike, the call option would be *in-the-money* (i.e. lower than the market value) by $2 per share. Consequently, we are also gaining some downside protection when rolling out, given that we only roll out by selling *in-the-money* strikes. As we know, the amount an option is in-the-money is equal to the intrinsic value of the option premium. To calculate downside protection after rolling out, divide the option's intrinsic value by the current market value of the shares. In this scenario, downside protection would be calculated a follows:

$$\$42 - \$40/\$42 = 4.8\%$$

Remember, the "What Now" tab of the Ellman Calculator will calculate the dollar amount of downside protection present in an option that is *in-the-money*, which, in the example above, would be $200 per contract or $2 per share.

We use the rolling out strategy when the current market value is at or more than the previously sold strike price, market tone is mixed to positive, stock technicals are mixed to positive, there is no ER coming out in the upcoming contract period, calculations show a good return and you are uncertain about share appreciation.

Real-life example of rolling out on or near expiration Friday:

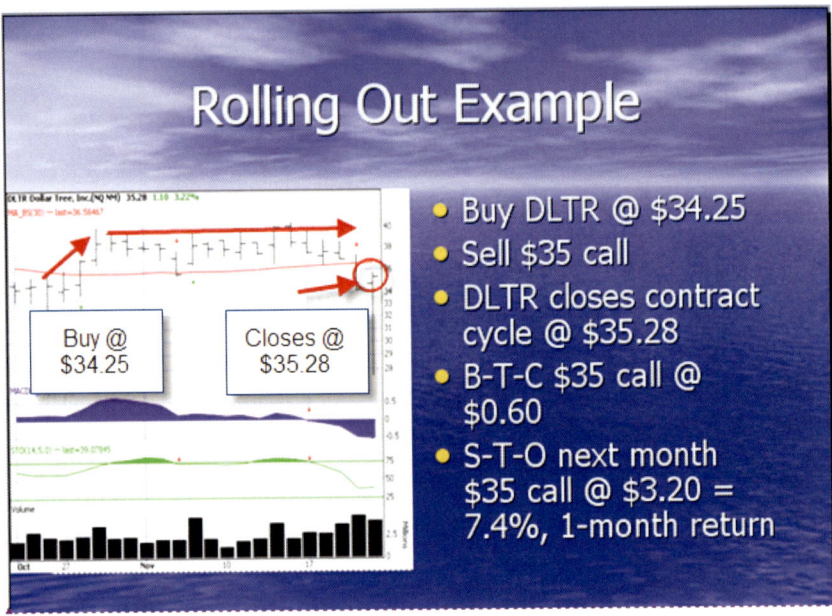

Figure 104 - Rolling Out On or Near Expiration Friday

Figure 104, which charts prices for Dollar Tree, Inc. (DLTR) on expiration Friday, demonstrates a typical rolling out chart pattern wherein the price of DLTR has risen and closed above the strike price of the call option that was initially sold (i.e. the call option is *in-the-money* on expiration Friday). The cost of buying back or buying-to- close (B-T-C) the call option in this example is $0.60 and we can generate $3.20 by selling-to-open (S-T-O) the next month's $35 call option. Accordingly, our option credit (option sale is greater than the option buy-back) is $2.60 per share ($3.20 - $0.60), and the cost basis or current value of our shares is $35 due to the original option obligation. The equation for calculating the one-month ROO we would generate by rolling out is thus: $260/$3500 = 7.4%.

For situations such as the one provided in the DLTR example above, I am often asked why I don't allow assignment, repurchase the shares the next week, and sell the call option the next week to avoid the cost of buying back the option. Here are my reasons:

- The time value to buy back the option is also incorporated into the next month's option premium. If we wait until the following week to sell the call option, the option premium will be worth less at that time and thus will garner less income.

- There is no guarantee as to what price the underlying equity and corresponding option will be trading at the following week. If the deal is there, take it.

- An additional, but relatively MINOR factor is that by rolling out, you are incurring two commissions (buying back this month's option, and selling next month's option), whereas if you allow assignment, three commissions are incurred (i.e. sell stock, buy stock, sell option).

Rolling out: step by step example:

July 16th represented the expiration of the July contracts. Given that most of the stocks on our watch list were due to report earnings during the August cycle, many of the corresponding equities were NOT eligible for an expiration Friday exit strategy such as rolling out or rolling out and up. However, Lululemon Athletica Inc. (LULU) was not scheduled to report. It had a mixed chart pattern and potentially was a viable candidate for such strategies due to its strong fundamentals. Initially, the $38 call option was sold. In order to determine whether LULU was in fact a viable candidate for an expiration Friday exit strategy, let's first look at the technicals:

Figure 105 - LULU on July 16th (Expiration Friday)

As demonstrated in Figure 105, LULU demonstrated mixed technical signals on July 16th (expiration Friday):

- The red circle highlights a recently ascending price pattern, which was still slightly below the 20-d EMA, a bearish but improving signal.

- The red arrow shows the MACD histogram just turning positive, a bullish signal.

- The blue arrow highlights the stochastic oscillator moving above the 20% and ascending, also a bullish signal.

Since this is a mixed technical picture, (which raises the question of whether LULU should be held or sold) I would lean towards rolling out, as we start the contract cycle with an in-the-money strike and also gain downside protection for our ROO. I will, however, also compute the ROO figures that can be generated by rolling out and slightly up as well. Prior to doing so in either case, however, we must first ensure that this equity is NOT reporting earnings in the August cycle. The projected date LULU was expected to announce earnings was on September 9th. Earnings report dates should be re-checked prior to trade execution because, although a rare circumstance, a corporation may change the date of an earnings announcement at the last minute. Figure 106, which was taken from www.earningswhispers.com, depicts such a projection:

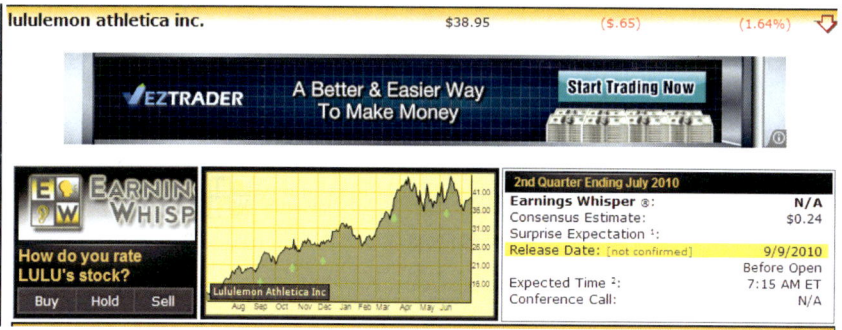

Figure 106 - Earnings Report for LULU on Expiration Friday

As can be seen in Figure 106, the scheduled earnings report date for LULU was 9/9/10 (highlighted in yellow), well after the end of the 8/20/10 date the next month's call option was due to expire. Now that we have ensured LULU will not be reporting earnings during the August contract cycle, we will calculate ROO for each prospective exit strategy (i.e. rolling out and rolling out and up) using the information obtained from the July and August option chains. We first check the July options chain (Figure 107) to obtain the cost of buying back the short options position we originally sold:

Lululemon Athletica Inc. (NASDAQ: LULU) Optionable
Last: 38.88 Chg: -0.72 (-1.82%) Open: 39.53 Avg Vol: 1,948,489 Volume: 2
Bid: 38.88 Ask: 38.89 High: 39.84 Low: 38.46 W%Chg: -(

| Option Tools: | Covered Calls Calculator | Selling Puts |

View: All Months

Calls — **Jul 10**

Last	Intrinsic Value	Bid	Ask	Vol	Open Interest	Strike
18.95	18.88	18.40	19.50	0	17	20.00
16.65	16.38	15.80	17.50	0	25	22.50
13.95	13.88	13.40	14.50	0	30	25.00
8.75	8.88	8.40	9.10	6	246	30.00
6.95	6.88	6.40	7.50	0	0	32.00
5.95	5.88	5.40	6.50	0	0	33.00
4.95	4.88	4.40	5.50	0	13	34.00
3.90	3.88	3.80	4.00	1	548	35.00
3.00	2.88	2.50	3.50	0	16	36.00
1.77	1.88	1.40	2.15	0	102	37.00
0.98	0.88	0.90	1.05	20	84	38.00
0.28	0.00	0.15	0.40	2	186	39.00
0.08	0.00	0.05	0.10	47	1,253	40.00

Figure 107 - July Call Options Chain for LULU on Expiration Friday (July 16th)

I have highlighted (in yellow) and circled (in red) the July contract with $1.05 asking price, which represents the cost to buy back the $38 call option that was initially sold. Note that it is possible to buy back this option back at price slightly below $1.05 if we were to play the bid-ask spread and place a limit to buy at a price slightly *below* the published asking price of

$1.05, as discussed in Chapter 9. Next, we look at the August options chain (Figure 108) to ascertain the amount of cash that can be generated from selling the August $38 or $39 contracts:

		Calls					Aug 10
Last	Intrinsic Value	Bid	Ask	Vol	Open Interest		Strike
16.80	16.38	15.90	17.70	0	0		22.50
14.10	13.88	13.40	14.80	0	0		25.00
9.00	8.88	8.60	9.40	0	0		30.00
7.25	6.88	6.90	7.60	0	0		32.00
6.40	5.88	6.10	6.70	0	0		33.00
5.65	4.88	5.30	6.00	0	0		34.00
4.80	3.88	4.50	5.10	0	505		35.00
4.10	2.88	3.90	4.30	0	22		36.00
3.40	1.88	3.20	3.60	0	81		37.00
2.78	0.88	2.60	2.95	0	90		38.00
2.35	0.00	2.25	2.45	10	217		39.00
1.77	0.00	1.65	1.90	13	1,325		40.00
1.43	0.00	1.35	1.50	0	116		41.00

Figure 108 - August Call Options Chain for LULU on Expiration Friday (July 16th)

As depicted in Figure 108, we will receive $2.60 to roll out to the $38 call option, and $2.25 to roll out and slightly up to the $39 call option. Once again, bear in mind that the large bid-ask spreads may allow us to generate even more cash by playing the bid-ask spread, or in this example, by placing a limit order to sell at a price slightly above the published bid of $2.60. Because of the mixed technical picture, I will generally lean to the in-the-money strikes. The information gleaned from the August call options chain is then fed into the *"What Now"* tab of the Ellman Calculator, as illustrated in Figures 109 and 110:

290 | Complete Encyclopedia for Covered Call Writing

1) IS THIS COMPANY REPORTING EARNINGS NEXT MONTH? (Y or N)					N		
2) ENTER THE STOCK NAME, SYMBOL AND PRICES PER SHARE OF YOUR STOCK.							
Stock name >>	LULULEMON						
Stock symbol >>	LULU			Stock share price you paid >>	$	38.00	
Number of shares you bought >>	100			Stock share price today >>	$	38.88	
3) ENTER THE INFORMATION BELOW FOR THE OPTION YOU SOLD.							
	Symbol	# Contracts	Strike Price	Exp Date		Price / share	
Option you sold >>	August $38	1	38.00	07/16/10		1.30	
Today's option price is >>						1.05	
4) ENTER THE INFORMATION FOR THE NEW OPTION CHOICES YOU MAY SELL.							
	Symbol	# Contracts	Strike Price	Exp Date		Price / share	
Roll out >>	Augsut $38	1	38.00	08/20/10		2.60	
Roll out and up >>	August $39	1	39.00	08/20/10		2.25	
Roll out and down >>	See note on printed results page.						
5) PRESS THE PRINTER ICON OR CLICK ON THE "FILE" MENU, SELECT "PRINT" AND CLICK "OK"							

Figure 109 - August Options Chain Detail Entered Into the Ellman Calculator for Rolling Out Calculations

Note the entries of $1.05 (red arrow), $2.60 (blue arrow), and $2.25 (green arrow). Once entered, the calculations will appear on the right page of this spreadsheet:

WHAT IF I ROLL OUT?		w/o upside pot.
The proceeds for 1 LULU AUG 38.00 is:		$ 260.00
The cost to buy back 1 LULU JUL 38.00 is:		$ (105.00)
Your net return will be:		$ 155.00
Your comparative basis in the stock is:		$ 3,800.00
Your comparative returns are:		4.08%
You downside protection is:		$88.00

WHAT IF I ROLL OUT AND UP?	w/upside pot.	w/o upside pot.
The proceeds for 1 LULU AUG 39.00 is:	$ 225.00	$ 225.00
The cost to buy back 1 LULU JUL 38.00 is:	$ (105.00)	$ (105.00)
Your net profit on this option position is:	$ 120.00	$ 120.00
The "bought up" value in the closing option is:	$ 88.00	$ 88.00
Your upside potential return is:	$ 12.00	
Your net return will be:	$ 220.00	$ 208.00
Your comparative basis in the stock is:	$ 3,800.00	$ 3,800.00
Your comparative returns are:	5.79%	5.47%
You downside protection is:		$0.00

Figure 110 - Rolling Calculations for LULU from the "What Now" Tab of the Ellman Calculator

Based on the calculations generated from the "What Now" tab (depicted in Figure 110), we now know the following:

- Highlighted in yellow is the 4.08%, one-month return for rolling out.
- The red arrow shows downside protection of $88 per contract
- The green highlighted area shows rolling out and up returns with upside appreciation (5.79%) and without upside appreciation (5.47%).

Conclusion:

When considering expiration Friday exit strategies, we must first check the stock's fundamentals and technicals. If technicals are mixed, we may want to garner the extra protection associated with an *in-the-money* strike by rolling out, NOT out and up. Consideration should also be given to general market tone. Additionally, we must also make sure that there is no earnings report announcement due in the upcoming contract cycle. Finally, the ROO calculations must meet our goals, which for me personally, are 2%-4% per month. Once one of these exit strategies are implemented and new positions are established, they must be monitored as with any other covered call position.

2- Rolling Out and Up

When we roll out and up, we close out our open options position (buy-to-close) and immediately sell the next month's higher strike call option. To get to this point, we have already determined that the stock fundamentals and technicals still meet all BCI system criteria. In addition, we have also ascertained that there are no upcoming earnings reports to interfere with this deal, and have determined that there is an excellent chance that the stock will continue to climb in value. Finally, our calculations are such that we have concluded that the cash in this equity will be most productive by staying in this same stock. In other words, we still love the stock and the returns it generates. When we roll out and up, the new, higher strike can be *at-the-money, in-the-money or out-of-the-money*. We will address the latter in the examples that follow.

Real-life example of rolling out and up to an out-of-the-money call option:

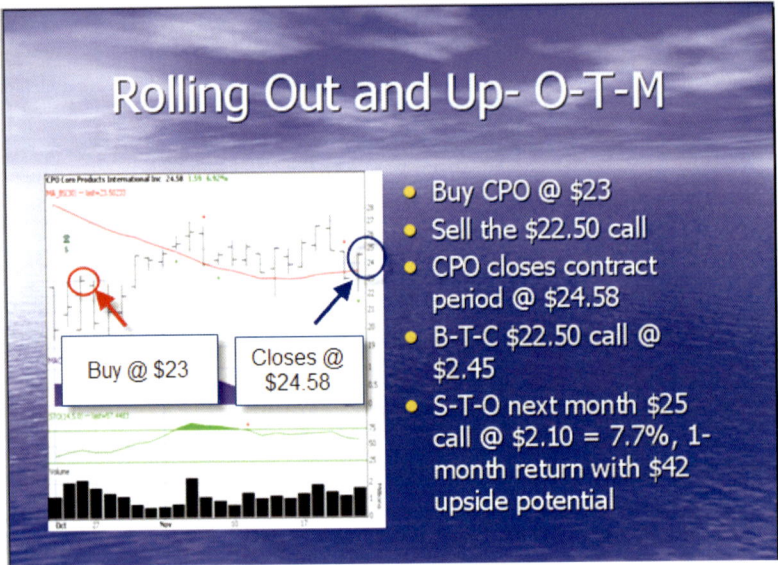

Figure 111 - Rolling Out and Up to an *Out-of-the-Money* Call Option

In Figure 111, we see the stock is purchased @ $23 (red circle) and closed the contract cycle @$24.58 (blue circle). Since the $22.50 strike price was sold, the shares would have been assigned if no exit strategy was invoked. By rolling out and up (to the $25 strike), share assignment was avoided with a strike that is slightly *out-of-the-money*. The calculations for rolling out and up are a little tricky, as there is often a loss on the option side and an unrealized gain on the share value side. In this example, our cost of buying back or buying-to close (B-T-C) the $22.50 call option is $2.45, and the credit of selling to open (S-T-O) the next month's $25 call option is $2.10. As such, we have a debit of $0.35 ($2.10 - $2.45) with respect to the options premiums, but our share value has now increased from $22.50 (our obligation to sell) to the current market value of $24.58, an unrealized price appreciation of $2.08. Thus, our initial profit (per contract) is calculated as follows: $208 - $35 = $173. Our cost basis is $2250 per contract, so the initial percentage return (ROO) is: $173/$2250 = 7.7%, with a possible additional share appreciation from $24.58 to $25.

Rolling out and up to an out-of-the-money strike offers upside potential in addition to the initial option returns.

Real-life example of rolling out and up to an in-the-money call option (Figure 112):

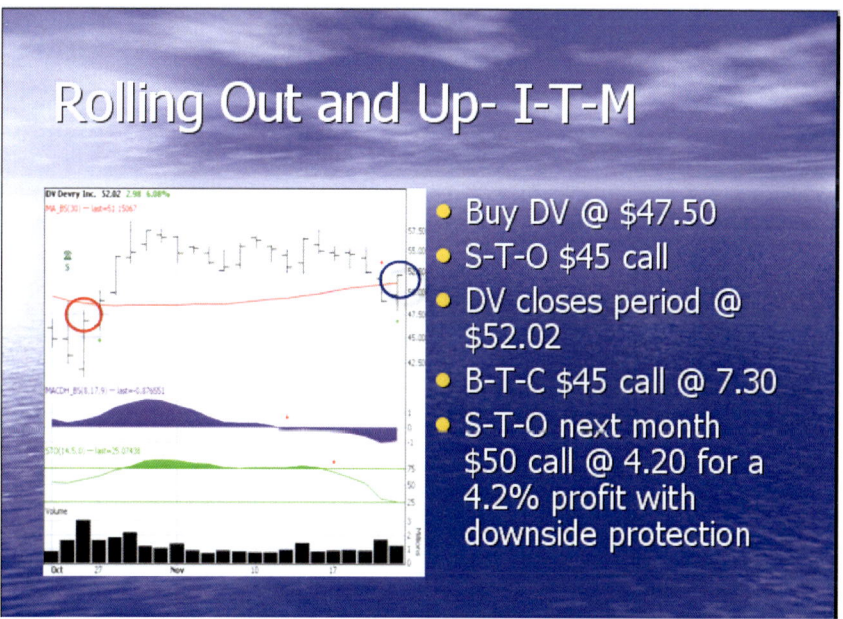

Figure 112 - Rolling Out and Up to an In-the-Money Call Option Example

In this example, we purchased the equity for $47.50 (red circle) and sold the in-the-money $45 strike. The stock closed the contract cycle @ $52.02 (blue circle). By rolling out and up to the in-the-money $50 strike, we have a debit of $3.10 ($4.20 - $7.30) or $310 per contract on the options side. However, by rolling out and up, our share value increases from $45 (our obligation to sell) to the new strike price of $50, which amounts to an unrealized increase of $5 per share, or $500 per contract. The one-month percentage return (ROO) is calculated as follows: $500 - $310/ $4500 = 4.2%, with 3.9% in downside protection ($202/$5202). This means that our 4.2%, one-month return is protected as long as our shares do not depreciate by more than 3.9% during the next month.

Rolling out and up to an *in-the-money strike* offers downside protection in addition to the cash generated from the initial option return.

3- Taking No Action:

When you take no action, you have essentially decided that it is best to allow your shares to be sold after option assignment. Perhaps there is an earnings report due in this next contract period, the technical indicators suggest you should sell the stock, or your calculations have caused you to conclude that the cash in that particular equity may be better utilized in a different stock that will generate more income. Whatever the reason (and it should be a valid one), in taking no action, you have decided to use the cash generated from the sale of the underlying equity to purchase another financial soldier to join your army the next month. If this is the path you decide to take, no action is required on your behalf. As long as your shares are above the strike price after expiration Friday, they will be sold. When you check your online account on Saturday or Sunday, you will see that you no longer own those shares, and that the cash generated from that sale will be available for use on

Monday. There will be one commission charged to you (a *de minimus* amount if you are using an online discount brokerage) for this transaction. Your next step is to plan how to best utilize this cash in the upcoming contract period. The quicker you put that cash to work (after intelligent, non-emotional analysis), the greater your profits will be.

Using multiple exit strategies with the same stock in the same month

By being prepared to utilize all the exit strategies discussed in this chapter, there will be times when we can actually invoke more than one strategy with the same covered call position to either enhance our returns or minimize our losses. In the example depicted in Figure 113, we *"hit a double"* and *rolled down*. In this example, we converted a huge loss in a position in Navistar International Corporation (NAV) into one that was much more palatable. Remember, losses will occur. One of the BCI mission statements is to minimize losses through the use of exit strategies.

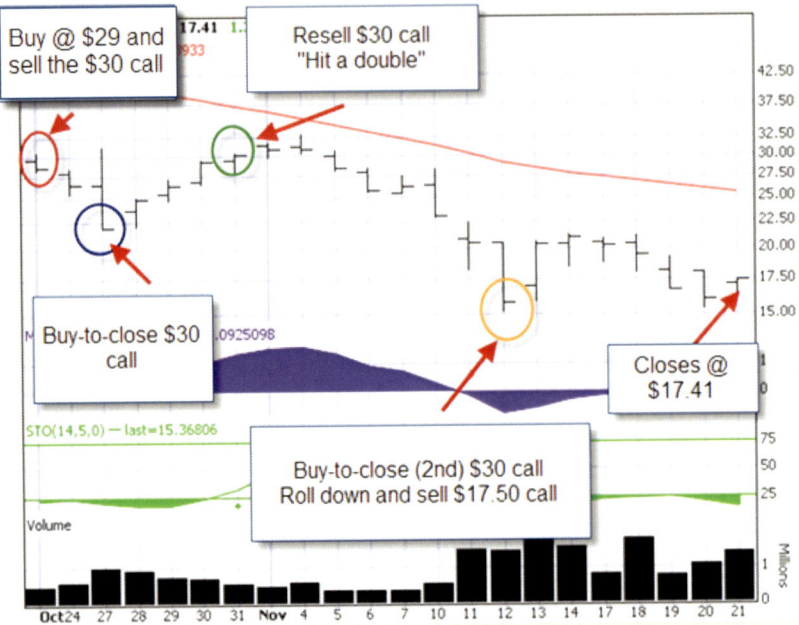

Figure 113 - NAV Chart Depicting a Scenario Where Invoking Multiple Exit Strategies to Minimize Losses May Be a Viable Option

Note the following information illustrated in Figure 113:

- 10/20/08- Buy 100 x NAV @ $29 (red circle)
- 10/20/08- Sell 1 x $30 call @ $2.75
- 10/27/08- Buy-to-close 1 x $30 Call @ .55 (meets our 20% rule) (blue circle)
- 10/31/08- Sell 1 x $30 Call @ $2.75 (green circle)
- 11/12/08- Buy-to-close 1 x $30 call @ .30 (approximates our 10% rule- orange circle)
- 11/12/08- Roll down and sell 1 $17.50 call @ $1.00

- 11/21/08- NAV closes the contract period @ $17.41 (red arrow)

If you were told that we both hit a double and rolled down, how would you expect the chart pattern to look? First, the stock would decline after the first option was sold. Subsequently, the stock would increase in value, at which time the strategy of "hitting a double" would be implemented. Thereafter, the stock would again decline in value, which would invoke the rolling down strategy. That is exactly what this chart shows: down-up-down.

Had we not sold options on the stock after the initial purchase, our loss would be $11.59 per share ($29 - $17.41) or $1159 per contract.....ouch! Let's see, however, how using multiple exit strategies partially mitigated this loss:

- Options credits per contract (sell to open): $275 + $275 + $100 = $650

- Option debits (buy-to-close): $55 + $30 = $85

- Net options credit: $650 - $85 = $565

- Total position loss: $1159 - $565 = $594

Losing $594 is no reason to celebrate but, when contrasted to a loss of $1159, highlights the benefits and importance of using exit strategies. To be a successful covered call writer and maximize your returns you must be prepared to execute any and all of the above exit strategies at the appropriate times. Be prepared and act!

Related information

Early Exercise and Assignment of Options

When we sell a covered call option, we are undertaking an obligation for which we are well paid. Should the option holder decide to exercise that option, we must sell our shares at the specified strike price at or prior to the expiration date. This is the nature of American-style options as opposed to *European style options,* the latter which can be exercised only on expiration Friday.

For the most part, share assignment will not occur until after expiration Friday, when the agreed-upon strike price is below the current market value. For example, if we sold the $50 strike and the current value of the stock is $52, the option holder or brokerage will exercise that option and achieve a $2 per share profit.

Why aren't most options exercised early?

Option value consists of intrinsic value plus time value. Early exercise will result in the holder surrendering this time value, so it rarely occurs. The option owner may sell the call option to capture the time value, however early exercise and purchase of our shares makes no sense if there is significant time value remaining ($0.25 or more). It's true that the shares can be purchased and then sold again at the market price to capture this value, but why not just sell the call? This concept applies to in-the-money and at or near-the-money strikes. Out-of-the-money strikes, however, would never be exercised.

How is it determined which shares are assigned if early assignment?

This is a completely random process whereby the Options Clearing Corporation (OCC) decides to which brokerage the assignment will be given, and that brokerage firm, in turn, will then pass the assignment on to one of its clients also randomly.

Why does early assignment occur?

As time value declines (below the aforementioned $0.25), the chances of early assignment increases. There are times when the call options trade below the intrinsic value. In these cases, the chances of early assignment are much greater. This will occur when the strike is deep *in-the-money*. Let's look at an options chain for VanceInfo Technologies Inc.(VIT) as an example:

Vanceinfo Tech Ads (NYSE: VIT) Optionable
Last: **15.75** Chg: **+0.06 (+0.38%)** Open: **15.50** Avg Vol: **670,981** Volume:
Bid: **15.35** Ask: **16.07** High: **15.81** Low: **14.79** W%Chg:

Option Tools: Covered Calls Calculator Selling Put

View: All Months

	Calls					Feb 10
Last	Intrinsic Value	Bid	Ask	Vol	Open Interest	Strike
5.35	5.75	4.80	5.90	0	10	10.00
3.25	3.25	3.10	3.40	5	37	12.50
1.20	0.75	1.10	1.30	33	133	15.00
0.22	0.00	0.15	0.30	106	896	17.50
0.08	0.00	0.05	0.10	75	1,355	20.00
0.05	0.00	0.05	0.05	1	2,726	22.50
0.10	0.00	N/A	0.10	0	52	25.00
0.10	0.00	N/A	0.10	0	0	30.00

Figure 114 - Early Assignment Possible for $12.50 Call Option in VIT

Note that the intrinsic value of the $12.50 call is @ $3.25 (since the stock price is $15.75), yet the "bid" or sale price of the option is $3.10 (red circle). Not only is there no time value for this option, but the premium is actually trading below the intrinsic value. Although the "ask" is trading at $3.40, institutional investors can often get pricing closer to the bid and take advantage of this situation. The $15 strike, on the other hand, has time value of $0.35 ($1.10 – $0.75).

As your strike moves deeper in-the-money, the chances of early assignment increase.

Other factors that may lead to early assignment

1- Dividends- When your equity is about to distribute a dividend, early assignment is possible for in-the-money strikes when that dividend value is greater than the time value remaining for that option. This will take place prior to the ex-dividend date; the date share ownership is required to be eligible to capture this dividend. The following is a link to a FREE site that tracks these dates:

http://www.dividendinvestor.com/tracker.php

2- *High Open Interest*- Thousands of open contracts in a particular option is a sign the institutional players are involved. Their trading costs are near zero, and their *arbitrage* opportunities (profitable trades effected by exploiting price differences of identical or similar financial instruments, on different markets or in different forms) are greater than ours when time value approaches zero.

3- *Pinning the strike* (pin risk) - this occurs when puts and calls are near the money on expiration Friday, and represents the tendency of a stock's price to close at the strike price of the option. This scenario may result in assignment (not early, but unexpected) after the bell and can also take place if there is a report or late news coming out the day on expiration Friday. I will discuss this topic in greater detail in Chapter 20.

How to avoid assignment

1- *To generate more cash (mid-contract)* - If there is little or no time value remaining in our option (sold), why not unwind our position? Buy-to-close the open call option and sell the stock, thereby re-capturing the intrinsic value. Now you can take that bundle of cash and reinvest it in another covered call position.

You can also roll the call out or up, assuming of course our calculations are favorable. Remember, covered call writers are tough "bosses;" no vacations or days off for our cash, which must be working at all times during normal market conditions!

2- *To avoid tax consequences-* If your cost basis is much lower than the current market value of your shares, assignment may result in unfavorable tax consequences. In these cases, you will want to close or roll your calls before assignment. If your shares are unexpectedly assigned, you can purchase new shares at the market and inform your broker that these new shares are to be the ones associated with the assigned option. Please check with your tax advisor and brokerage on these matters.

Conclusion

Early assignment of your shares is rare but possible. Understanding why and when early assignment may occur will further add to the bottom line of your investment success.

Test your knowledge of key points

1- A plan in which a trader intends to get out of an investment position made in the past and is a way of cashing out or closing a position and is called an_____.

2- All covered call exit strategies begin with_____.

3- Closing out an options position at one strike price and opening another at a lower strike price in the same contract month is called _____.

4- Closing out an option contract at a near-term expiration date and opening a higher strike contract at a later date is known as _____.

5- - A term used by many brokerages to represent the closing of a short position (the option sale) in option transactions is known as _____.

6- The four key parameters to evaluate when considering exit strategies prior to expiration Friday are _____ _____.

7- Consider buying back the option in the first part of the cycle when the premium declines to _____ of the original sale price; and to _____ of the original price in the latter part of the cycle.

8- The five main exit strategy choices we have prior to expiration Friday are_____.

9- The exit strategy we may consider when a stock gaps up significantly in the middle of a contract cycle is the _____.

10- When a stock declines in value early in the contract cycle and the option value meets the 20%/10% guideline we would consider which exit strategy if we are still bullish on the stock? _____ _____.

11- A key criteria examined for instituting the mid-contract unwind is for the time value of the option premium to _____.

12- If we were to consider keeping a stock that has gapped down, the critical information we would first need to determine is_____.

13- The four key parameters to evaluate when considering exit strategies on or near expiration Friday are_____ _____.

14- The three main exit strategy choices on or near expiration Friday are _____, the most bullish of which is _____.

15- Since we are dealing with _____ options, early assignment of our shares, although unlikely, is possible.

Answers:

1- Exit strategy

2- Buying back the option

3- Rolling down

4- Rolling out and up

5- Buy to close (B-T-C)

6- Time to expiration and option value, market tone, technical analysis of the underlying security and calculations

7- 20%, 10%

8- Rolling down, take no immediate action and look to "hit a double", convert dead money to cash profits, no action taken and mid-contract unwind

9- Mid contract unwind

10- Look to "hit a double"

11- Approach zero

12- The cause of the gap down

13- Market tone, technical analysis of the underlying security, earnings reports and calculations

14- Rolling out, rolling out and up and taking no action; rolling out and up

15- American style

Chapter 11

Dollar Cost Averaging and Exchange Traded Funds (ETFs)

Chapter outline

1- Definitions

2- Dollar-Cost Averaging

3- Exchange traded funds (ETFs) and covered call writing

4- Constructing a covered call portfolio using ETFs

5- The BCI Premium Report and ETFs

6- How ETFs operate

7- Leveraged ETFs

One of the most common questions asked of me is: "How do I get started if I don't have a lot of money to invest?" Another is "What is the most conservative way to start selling covered calls?" These questions evoke the same sentiments I had when I first began educating myself in this strategy:

- Fear of the unknown
- Excitement for the possibilities
- Preservation of capital

To address these questions we must review our requirements to be properly diversified.

Definitions

Diversification: A risk management technique that mixes a wide variety of investments in a portfolio. The rationale behind this strategy is that a portfolio of non-correlated investments will, on average, yield higher returns and present a lower risk than any one individual investment within that portfolio. We must be diversified in three areas:

- Stock
- Industry
- Cash allocation

Since we must own 100 shares of the underlying security in order to sell one contract, we must own at least 500 shares to be adequately diversified into five different stocks in five different industries. For those who are just starting to invest and may not be adequately capitalized or for those who want to start conservatively you may want to consider dollar-cost averaging into *exchange traded funds (ETFs)*. Let's define these terms first:

Dollar cost averaging: The technique of buying a fixed dollar amount of a particular investment on a regular schedule, regardless of the share price. The benefit of dollar cost averaging (as opposed to a lump sum investment) is that over time, more shares can be purchased at a lower price.

Exchange traded funds: A security that tracks an index, a commodity or a basket of assets like an index fund, but trades like a stock on an exchange, thus experiencing price changes during the course of a day as it is bought and sold. Think of ETFs as mutual funds that behave like stocks, with the additional benefit of providing instant diversification.

Dollar Cost Averaging and Exchange Traded Funds (ETFs)

Dollar-Cost Averaging
An Investment Technique for You?

Let's say you have $1200 to invest. Instead of investing it all at one time, you invest $100 on the 1st of every month (or whatever date you determine) for twelve months.

Does it go by any other names?

Dollar-cost averaging is also called **DCA** and **Constant Dollar Plan** in the U.S. and **Pound-Cost Averaging** in the U.K. and the currency neutral term of **Cost Average Effect**.

The Three Parameters:

- The fixed amount of money- in the above example, it's $100.

- The investment frequency- in the above example, it's once a month.

- Time horizon- in the above example, it's one year.

How it works:

The reason we dollar cost average into a security is to ultimately own more shares at a lower price, which protects us from losing maximum capital if there is price depreciation. For example, assume you have $1200 dollars to invest in stock XYZ, and decide to dollar cost average your investment by purchasing $100 of XYZ every month for a year, regardless of what price XYZ is trading at in any particular month. Assume further that the price of XYZ depreciates from $10 per share in January to $5 per in December, as depicted below:

- January: $10 per share buys 10 shares
- February: $9 per share buys 11 shares
- March: $7 per share buys 14 shares

- April: $5 per share buys 20 shares
- May: $6 per share buys 17 shares
- June: $9 per share buys 11 shares
- July: $10 per share buys 10 shares
- August: $11 per share buys 9 shares
- September: $12 per share buys 8 shares
- October: $10 per share buys 10 shares
- September: $9 per share buys 11 shares
- October: $7 per share buys 14 shares
- November: $6 per share buys 17 shares
- December: $5 per share buys 20 shares

Over this 1-year time frame, we purchased 182 shares. Had we invested the entire $1200 in January when XYZ was trading at $10 per share, we would have purchased only 120 shares. Yes, we still lost money, but not as much had we not dollar-cost averaged our investments:

- Money lost with a 1-time investment: $600 (120 shares x $5) = $600 remains from $1200 investment
- Money lost with dollar-cost averaging : $290 (182 shares x $5) = $910 left from $1200 investment

Disadvantages and criticisms:

Before investing our hard-earned money, it is critical to also understand the criticisms, both valid and invalid, commonly associated with dollar cost averaging, which include the following:

1- It is a marketing gimmick that lulls worried investors into investing more than they normally would have. I think this criticism was created by pundits who suggest that fear is somehow a positive. The market historically goes up, and in my view, no one has developed the skill to perfectly time the market, as there are way too many parameters that influence market direction. How can a computer software system or a great economic mind quantify market psychology, or ever-changing news or global influences? Even Warren Buffett lost a tremendous amount of wealth during the recession of 2008. If we can agree that accurate market timing is not possible, and that we will only invest what we can afford, dollar cost averaging can be a great strategy for most neophyte and conservative investors.

2- Dollar cost averaging ignores transaction fees: This is a valid concern, but one that can be easily avoided by using the appropriate investment vehicles. In our hypothetical example with stock XYZ, had we paid a $25 transaction commission fee for each of our monthly purchases, our bottom line would have been dramatically negatively impacted. That is why **dollar cost averaging works best with mutual funds or ETFs when using** extremely inexpensive online discount brokers, especially when investing modest amounts of money. A typical **no-load index mutual fund** can have an expense ratio (the cost to invest in a mutual fund, determined by dividing a fund's operating expenses by the average dollar value of its assets under management) of 20 basis points. This means that for a $100 investment, you would pay only 20 cents, and not the $10 to $25 fee typically charged by discount brokers to execute an individual stock purchase. When considering which underlying securities to purchase in contemplation of selling covered calls, dollar cost averaging into ETFs through an inexpensive (but quality) online discount broker, or into a no-load index fund, can prove to be a conservative cost effective strategy, and one particularly useful to the neophyte covered call writer, as noted above. In short, by investing with the appropriate investment vehicles and using a cost-efficient broker, transaction fees can become a non-event. <u>Note</u>: There are no transaction fees when you buy Schwab branded ETFs online, some of which are optionable. Some Schwab ETFs have a lower expense ratio than Vanguard, iShares, or SPDRs.

3- We will miss out on profits if the market appreciates dramatically from the time of the initial investment: Once again, this is a valid point. The hypothetical dollar cost averaging example detailed above (in stock XYZ) is a negative scenario, or one that we need to protect ourselves from. In that example, had the market took off like a rocket ship, we would have ended up buying shares at higher and higher prices. This potential drawback is the price we pay for risk management. Most of us who use the dollar cost averaging technique cannot afford to lose large amounts of money, and downside protection from large losses is precisely what this strategy offers. Although this downside protection comes at the potential cost of missing gains in an uptrending market, we accept that cost and sleep better at night.

Conclusion:

It pays to exercise caution when it comes to investing our hard-earned money. For those just starting out in the stock market, or for conservative investors in general, dollar cost averaging into a no-load index fund with a low expense ratio, or an ETF with a great online discount broker, may be a sensible choice. Many mutual funds also have automatic investment plans that allow you to invest a fixed amount automatically each month. Many times, the initial minimum investment needed to get started is much lower when automatic investing is set up. One excellent starting point to look for low expense ratio index funds is:

www.vanguard.com

Exchange traded funds (ETFs) and covered call writing

A critical requirement of my system is to be properly diversified by stock, industry and cash allocation. No one stock or industry should represent more than 20% of your portfolio holdings. Owning five different stocks in five different industries would require you to own at least 500 shares since each options contract represents 100 shares. This may require a cash allotment of $25,000 to $50,000, or more. Because each share of an ETF represents a basket of stocks, ETFs can provide its purchaser instant diversification, and therefore can play an extremely useful

Dollar Cost Averaging and Exchange Traded Funds (ETFs) | 311

role in covered call writing. ETFs are also extremely time efficient. When we write covered calls using individual equities, we must constantly change our portfolio mix and consider factors such as earnings reports, technical, and fundamental analysis. With ETFs, we merely need to track an index, which effectively is akin to tracking as little as one security. So, why not use ETFs all the time when writing covered calls? The answer lies in the greater returns you can garner by writing calls on individual equities. In normal market conditions a return of 2-4% is achievable when using individual equities in my experience, whereas ETFs typically yield an approximate 1-2% return.

Who should use ETFs?

Investors with limited cash to invest, with low risk tolerance, or with time restrictions should consider writing calls on ETFs.

Advantages of ETFs:

1- *Broad diversification-* by definition an ETF inherently provides diversification across an entire index.

2- *Lower costs-* Most ETFs are not actively managed, thereby decreasing marketing, distribution, and accounting expenses. For example, most ETFs do not have 12b-1 (advertising and distribution) fees.

3- *Tax efficiency-* ETFs have low capital gains because of the low turnover in their portfolios.

4- *No need for a financial advisor-* Why pay 1.5%-2% a year to do something you could manage yourself?

5- *Buying and selling flexibility-* ETFs offer all the transaction options typically associated with stock purchases/sales, including limit orders, short selling, stop orders, and options.

Types of ETFs - Most ETFs are index funds, which are the ones I will focus on. For informational purposes, there are also leveraged (short), commodity, currency, and actively managed ETFs, among others. Here are three of the more popular ETFs used for writing calls on heavily traded indexes:

- QQQ- follows a basket of 100 of the largest non-financial equities on the Nasdaq exchange.
- VTI- Vanguards security that tracks the total stock market.
- VV- Vanguards security that tracks the large cap universe.

I will provide more optionable ETFs later in this chapter.

Major issuers of ETFs:

- Barclays Global Investors issues iShares.
- State Street Global Advisors issues street Tracks and SPDRs
- Vanguard issues Vanguard ETFs, formerly known as VIPERs.
- Merrill Lynch issues HOLDRs.
- PowerShares issues ETFs and BLDRS (based on American Depository Receipts).

Did you know that there are <u>actively managed</u> ETFs based on Covered Call Writing?

There are several relatively new (at the time this book was written) ETFs that themselves incorporate the covered call strategy on different indices or types of securities in at least 50% of its portfolio. Here are a few: LCM, BEO, DPD, FFA, MCN, and BEP. Personally, I am not a fan of using these types of ETFS. First, these funds haven't proven themselves over time. Second, we aren't sure what's going on in the other 50% portion of the portfolio. My gut tells me that if I was gong with an investment vehicle that was actively managed, I'd prefer to manage it myself, thank you.

The CBOE S&P 500 *BuyWrite Index* (BXM): This is a benchmark index designed to track the hypothetical performance of a covered call strategy on the S&P 500 Index.

It is based on buying the index and selling a one-month out-of-the-money call, similar to the Blue Collar System, though our system considers all strikes. A study done by Ibbotson Associates in 2004 analyzing BXM over a 16-year period demonstrated BXM to have a 12.30% return, slightly higher than the 12.20% return of the S&P 500 over the same time period, but with two-thirds the volatility of the S&P 500. This means that by using the BXM, an investor can generate similar returns to the S&P 500 index but with less aggravation. I created the chart below (Figure 115) to show the comparison of the BXM Index (blue line) compared to the S&P 500 (black line) over the past five years:

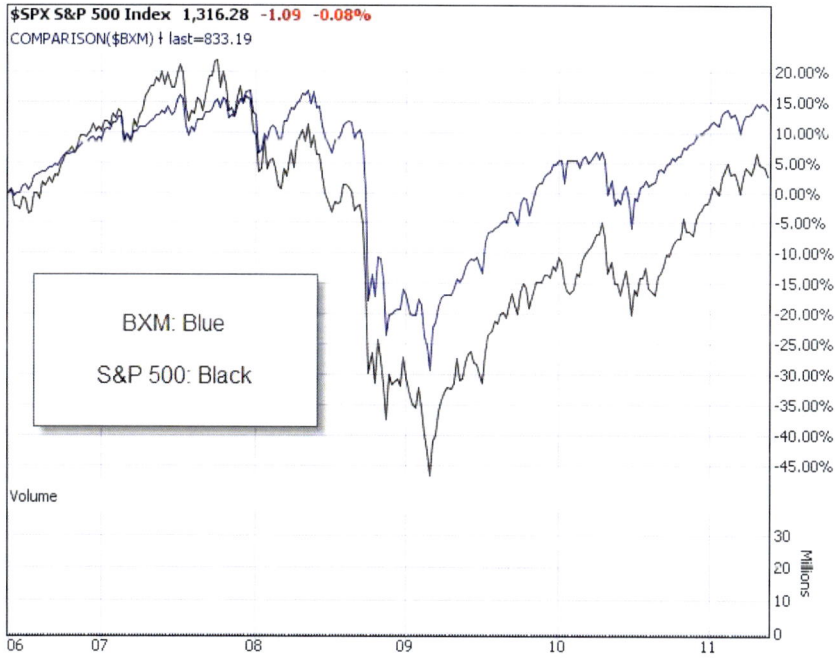

Figure 115- BXM vs. the S&P 500- 5 year chart

The Blue Collar System vs. the BXM Index:

Here are the reasons why the Blue Collar System generates

better returns than the BXM Index:

- We are not required to hold every stock in the index; we can select only the greatest performers in the greatest industries.
- We avoid earnings reports, which you cannot do with ETFs.
- We can utilize different strikes, and not just out-of-the-money strikes.
- We can initiate exit strategies, which give us greater control in elevating profits and minimizing losses.

Once again, let me mention that the advantages of the BXM Index and other ETFs are the lower time and cost requirements. The approach that is best for you can only be determined by you. But by having the knowledge and the ability to evaluate your positions unemotionally, you will have the opportunity to make the decision that makes the most sense for your portfolio.

Constructing a Covered Call Portfolio Using ETFs

How to select ETFs for your Covered Call Portfolio:

Since we are dealing with a basket of stocks with ETFs, fundamental analysis becomes less of a science. So I come back to what I consider the most critical factor to consider when selecting a security: What are the institutional investors doing regarding this security? To resolve this issue, I compare a 3-month chart of the S&P 500 ("the market") to various selected ETFs. I currently evaluate all of the Select Sector SPDRs, the "Qs" (QQQ) as well as the top-performing ETFs over a 3-month time span. All non-leveraged ETFs (with associated options) outperforming the S&P 500 and have a relative price strength (RS) rating of 70 or better are eligible. Here is a chart taken from our premium site that demonstrates such a screen:

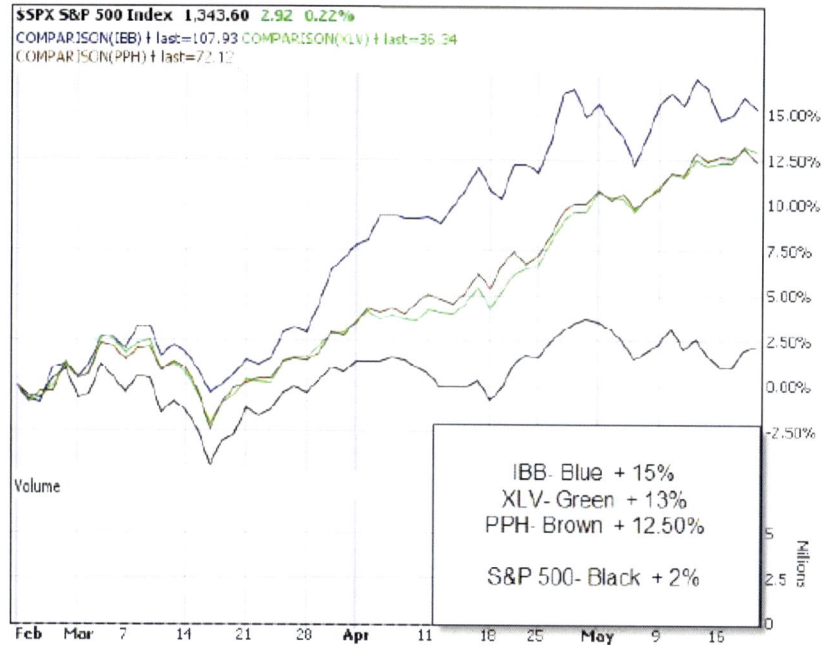

Figure 116- Top ETFs vs. S&P 500 (black line on bottom)

Next, let's assume a portfolio with cash available of $52,000. We will set aside $2,000 for possible future exit strategy execution. That leaves 5 securities and $50,000 to spend. We will give equal cash allocation of approximately $10,000 per security as we round off to the nearest 100 (we need to own 100 shares for each options contract we sell). Let's calculate:

SECURITY	PRICE	Shares/$10k	Rounded Off	COST
XLI	$32.62	306	300	$9,786
XLY	$34.83	287	300	$10,449
XLF	$16.98	588	600	$10,188
XLP	$28.03	356	300	$8,409
QQQ	$50.13	199	200	$10,006

Figure 117- ETF- Calculate Cash Allocation

Since we spent $48,838, we will have a cash balance of $3,162 from our original $52,000. Next, access the option chains and sell the May 2010 call options. Here is the options chain for XLY (Figure 118):

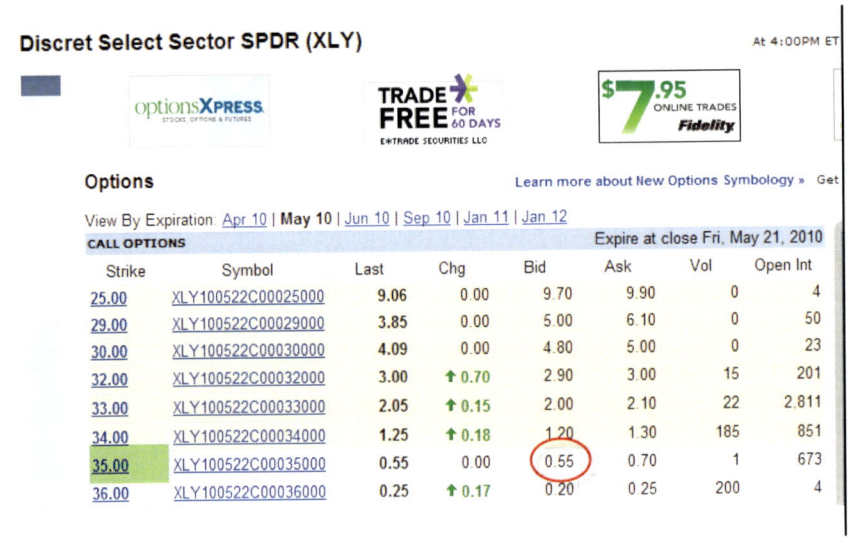

Figure 118- ETF- Options Chain

Next we will feed this information into the "multiple tab" of the Ellman Calculator as shown below in Figure 119:

Dollar Cost Averaging and Exchange Traded Funds (ETFs) | 317

After accessing the five chains, we will feed the information into the Multiple tab of the

A	B	C	D	E	F	
xli	$ 32.62	$ 1.01	$ 32.00	05/21/10	$ 0.62	$
xli	$ 32.62	$ 0.44	$ 33.00	05/21/10	$ -	$
xly	$34.83	$ 0.55	$ 35.00	05/21/10	$ -	$
xlf	$ 16.98	$ 0.46	$ 17.00	05/21/10	$ -	$
xlp	$ 28.03	$ 0.45	$ 28.00	05/21/10	$ 0.03	$
qqqq	$ 50.13	$ 1.64	$ 49.00	05/21/10	$ 1.13	$
qqqq	$ 50.13	$ 0.98	$ 50.00	05/21/10	$ 0.13	$
qqqq	$ 50.13	$ 0.49	$ 51.00	05/21/10	$ -	$

Figure 119- Multiple tab of the Ellman Calculator

Assuming we were mildly bullish on the market, we will sell the near-the-money and out-of-the-money strikes, as highlighted in yellow in Figure 119:

- XLI: 3 x $33 calls @ $0.44 = $132
- XLY: 3 x $35 calls @ $0.55 = $165
- XLF: 6 x $17 calls @ $0.46 = $276
- XLP: 3 x $28 calls @ $0.45 − $0.03 = $126
- QQQ: 1 x $50 call @ $0.98 − $0.13 = $85
- QQQ: 1 x $51 call @ $0.49 = $49

Note: Ticker symbol QQQQ has since been changed to QQQ.

The total initial profit = $833 on an investment of $48,838 = 1.7% one-month profit with significant upside potential. Had we been bearish on the market, we would favor the in-the-money strikes when possible (the $49 "Qs" and XLI).

Conclusion:

The use of ETFs in our covered call portfolios has its advantages and disadvantages. Understanding these pros and cons will help us determine how and when to utilize these securities.

The Premium Report and ETFs

At the time this book was being written, the Blue Collar Investor Corp. was providing a weekly report of the top-performing optionable ETFs over the previous 3-month time frame. The top five (or more) ETFs are charted in two graphs and compared to the broad market benchmark, the S&P 500. Sector and pricing information are also available, as are several other top ten ETFs. Figure 120 is an example of one of the pages included in such a report:

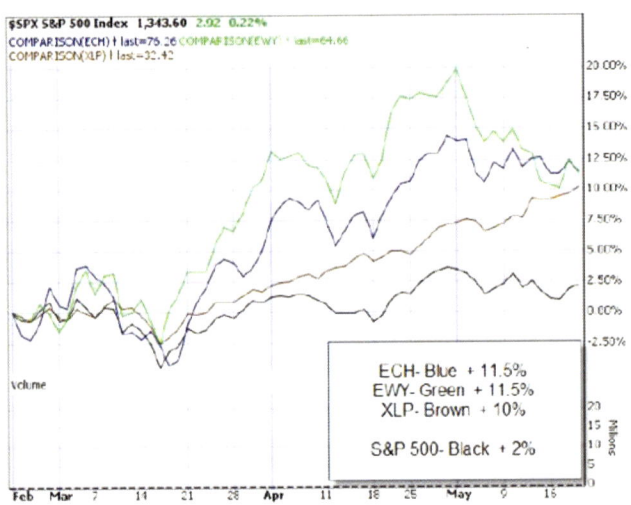

Top 5 ETFs (ticker, name, sector and recent price)

Top Chart

1- IBB- Blue- iShares Nasdaq Biotech/ $108
2- XLV-Green- Spdr Health Care/ $36
3-PPH- Brown- Holders Tr- Pharmaceutical/ $72

Lower Chart

1-ECH- Blue- Ishares Msci Chile Index/ $76
2- EWY- Green- Ishares Msci South Korea/ $64.50
3- XLP- Brown- Consumer Staples Select Sector SPDR Fund / $32.50

*** SEE BELOW FOR ADDITIONAL FUNDS TO CONSIDER

Figure 120- Premium ETF Report

This premium report is updated weekly, and one can construct a portfolio of the top-performing ETFs, and update this portfolio based on the most recent performance information. In addition, the top three S&P 500 Sector ETFs are charted with percentage returns over the past 3 months. More recently added to this report are Inverse ETFs which can be used in bear-market situations.

Related Information

ETFs- How they Operate and the Pros and Cons

When we buy one share of the "Qs" (Powershares Exchange-Traded Fund Trust – Powershares QQQ Trust, (NASDAQ:QQQ) for $45, we are purchasing a piece of all 100 shares in the fund. So how does that work? Are we applying $0.50 towards each stock? It's actually a bit more complicated than that

The Mechanics of an ETF:

These funds are continuously creating new shares or redeeming existing shares depending on market demand. The shares represent ownership interest in the underlying basket of securities. Only large institutional investors called **Authorized Participants (APs)** partake in this creation and redemption process. They will buy *creation units* or sell *redemption units* over sophisticated electronic platforms. Shares are created when the APs provide a basket of securities to the fund, which then creates ETF shares that are handed over to the AP. These ETF shares are then sold on the secondary market (exchanges) to us by the APs.

On the other hand, when an AP provides the fund with a number of ETF shares (redemption unit), they will receive from the fund the associated basket of securities.

What's in it for the APs?

Are they doing this to be nice guys and allow BCIs to take advantage of these funds? I don't think so either! They are doing it to take advantage of **arbitrage** opportunities. These are simultaneous purchases and sales of assets in order to profit from a difference in the prices. Here's how the game is played: The underlying securities in an ETF are priced every 15 seconds during the trading day. This value is similar to the NAV *(net asset value)* of a mutual fund, which is priced only after the market close. When there is a small difference between the intraday NAV and the actual share price of the fund, the AP can buy one and sell the other to generate a profit. This arbitrage process actually serves a useful function for us, in that it keeps the fund price and the NAV price very close.

Conclusion:

ETFs are vehicles that can benefit both institutional and retail investors. For writers of covered calls, the main benefit of ETFs is its instant diversification that permits a conservative approach to an already conservative strategy.

Leveraged and Inverse ETFs - buyers beware!

How would you feel if your best friend was metamorphosing into a monster? A Dr. Jekyll and Mr. Hyde, if you will. Could that be happening to our old friend, the exchange traded fund? The historical definition of an *ETF* is a security that tracks an index, a commodity or a basket of assets like an index fund, but trades like a stock on an exchange. As discussed in this chapter, ETFs provide the diversification of an index fund, and thus may be a viable avenue to explore for those with limited cash looking to get started in covered call writing.

Recently, however, the definition of an ETF has started to change. Some ETFs are actively managed and aren't required to follow the complexion and market capitalization of an index. These more aggressive funds offer the possibility of greater returns, but also represent a higher degree of risk and administrative costs. If your mission statement includes risk reduction, you need to be aware of the pros and cons of such ETFs.

Dollar Cost Averaging and Exchange Traded Funds (ETFs) | 321

Taking this Jekyll and Hyde analogy to a higher level, we now have the introduction of *leveraged and inverse exchange-traded funds*. Leveraged ETFs, sometimes called "ultra" or "2X" ETFs, use futures or derivatives to multiply the *daily* returns of an index. Inverse ETFs look to return the opposite of the index, or double or triple the opposite of the return of that index. Therefore, an inverse ETF on the SPY will benefit from a market decline. *A non-leveraged inverse ETF may be useful to us in bear-market scenarios and is discussed in more detail in chapter 20.*

After the impact that leveraging had on the real estate industry in 2007-2010, and its subsequent devastating impact on our economy, regulators appear to be voicing their concerns. On FINRA's (Financial Industry Regulatory Authority) website recently, brokers and investment advisors were reminded that these instruments are complicated and usually not suited for retail investors (that's us folks) who plan to hold them for more than one trading day! The notice continued, "Due to effects of compounding, their performance over longer periods of time can differ significantly from their stated daily objective."

Paul Justice, an ETF expert with Morningstar, stated that leveraged and inverse funds are appropriate for less than 1% of the investing community, but still have attracted billions of dollars. Wasn't there a lesson learned from leveraged real estate investing?

To demonstrate, let's look at the returns of two leveraged ETFs:

The Direxion Daily Financial Bear 3X Shares (FAZ) seeks daily returns of three times the inverse of the Russell 1000 Financial Services Index, was down 85% as of 6-26-09.

The Direxion Daily FinancialBull 3X (FAS) seeks daily returns of three times the Russell 1000 Financial Services Index, was down 67% in this same time frame. Figures 121 and 122 show the charts of these leveraged funds:

Figures 121 and 122: *Two leveraged ETFs (FAZ and FAS)*

These leveraged ETFs do have a place in the portfolio of some. It is important to understand the risks as well as the rewards and make an informed decision based on the facts, rather than getting carried away with profit potential alone.

The main point I want to make to all my fellow Blue Collar Investors is that some ETFs no longer represent the relative safety associated with the older generation of funds. The previous funds certainly still exist, but their offspring have had a genetic mutation that we must be aware of. FINRA seems to be all over this and so should we.

Dollar Cost Averaging and Exchange Traded Funds (ETFs)

Test your knowledge of key points

1- A risk management technique that mixes a wide variety of investments in a portfolio is called _____.

2- Diversification is critical in these three areas: _____ _____.

3- The three parameters considered when dollar-cost averaging are_____ _____.

4- Three major advantages of using ETFs for covered call writing are _____ _____.

5- The major disadvantage of using ETFs for covered call writing is that _____ due to _____.

6- _____use futures or derivatives to multiply the daily returns of an index.

7- _____look to return the opposite of the index, or double or triple the opposite of the return of that index.

8- Non-leveraged inverse ETFs may be of use to covered call writers in _____ _____ conditions.

Answers:

1- Diversification

2- Stock, industry and cash allocation

3- Fixed amount of money, investment frequency and time horizon

4- Less cash required, instant diversification and less management required

5- A lower option return is generated, lower volatility of this security

6- Leveraged ETFs

7- Inverse exchange-traded funds

8- Bear market

Chapter 12

Stock Splits

Chapter outline

1- Definition

2- A real life example

3- Pre and Post Split comparison

4- Reverse stock splits

Definition

A stock split is a change in the number of shares outstanding (in circulation). The number of shares is adjusted by the split ratio, e.g. 3 to 1. In this case, 100 shares splits to 300 shares, however the share price is cut in third. Thus, the cost and current value of the investment remains the same, however the number of shares owned increases, while the price per share decreases. This facilitates retail investors to own shares in round lots in that they can buy more shares for less money.

Is a stock split an asset or a liability?

There are those who feel that a stock split will automatically result in a share price increase. Research seems to disprove this theory. However, a split will oftentimes occur after a significant run-up in price, and a continuation of this trend is likely. I give credence to a stock split that occurs after such a price increase, and look at the company's chart to evaluate the momentum associated with this appreciation. When the technicals confirm the split as legitimate, I consider the event as another plus in that stock's column of assets.

On the other hand, if the chart paints an ugly picture and a split is announced, it is likely that the Board of Directors is desperate and looking to garner interest in a deteriorating asset. In this instance, the split should be viewed as a liability.

A real-life example: SHOO

Early in 2010, SHOO announced a 3-for-2 stock split. This means that for every 2 shares owned, 1 additional share would be distributed. The value of the shares will be worth 2/3 of the current value at the time of distribution so the *capitalization* (price x number of shares) remains the same. Let's look at the chart to evaluate whether this split represents an asset or a liability:

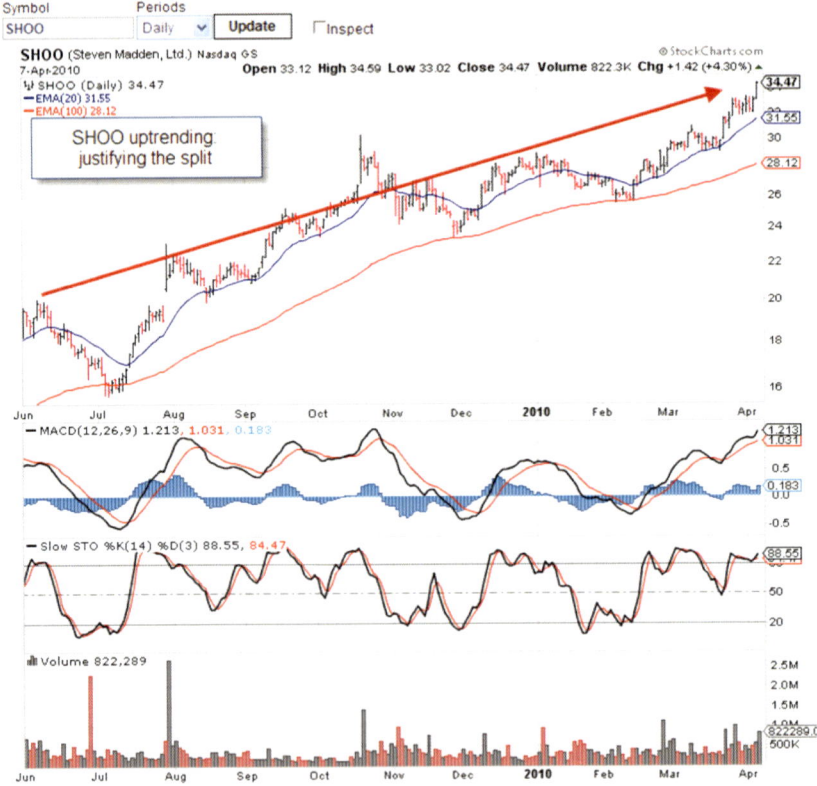

Figure 123- SHOO as of 4-17-10

Figure 123 is a beautiful chart, uptrending with confirming indicators, describes an authentic split and is an asset in the column of parameters for this equity

Next, let's view the current options chain. Assume we purchase 200 shares (that rounds off nicely!) and sell the May $55 calls as the stock is trading at $53 per share:

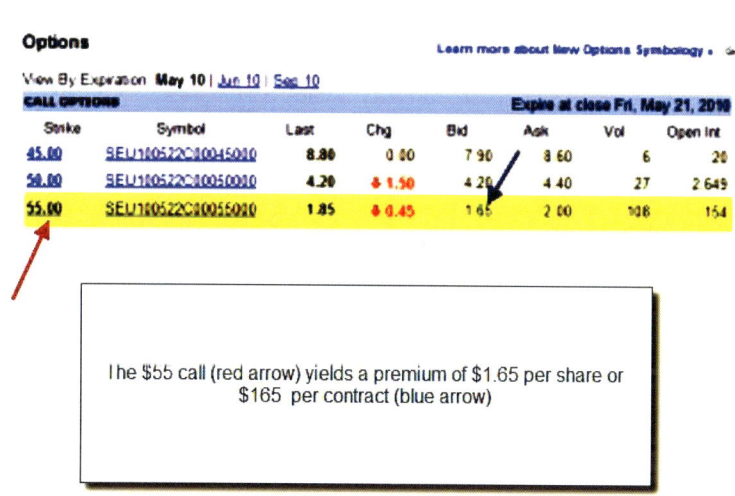

Figure 124- SHOO Options Chain 4-17-10

The $55 call generates $165 per contract, or a 3.1%, 1-month return ($165/$5300) with additional upside potential of 3.8% per share if the stock climbs from $53 to $55 and assignment occurs ($200/$5300). Let's next view the impact this split will have on our covered call position both pre- and post-split.

Pre- and post-split comparison

Pre and Post Split Comparison	
Pre-Split	**Post-Split**
$165 initial profit	$165 initial profit
Expires May 21st	Expires May 21st
Own 200 shares	Own 300 shares
Cost basis is $53	Cost basis is $35.33
Sold (2) May $55s	Sold (2) May $36.67s
Ticker is SHOO May 21, 2010 C 55000	Ticker is SHOO May 21, 2010 C 36670

Figure 125- SHOO- Pre- and Post-Split

The major difference is that prior to the split, each contract delivers the conventional 100 shares while post-split; each contract will deliver 150 shares. This is known as a non-standard contract and was discussed earlier in Chapter 7. If the split had been by an even number, such as 2 for 1, the number of contracts would simply double and would deliver the standard 100 shares. For example, if a $50 stock splits 2-for-1 and we sold one $50 call, after the split we would have sold two $25 calls and our cost basis would be $25, with each contract delivering 100 shares.

Conclusion:

When the economy is on the upswing and the stock market shows a bullish trend, stock splits are likely to become part of our covered call lives. It is important to recognize quality splits from imposters and to learn how the splits impact our option contracts.

Reverse Stock Splits and How they Affect our Option Contracts

In a filing with the SEC early in 2009, Citigroup said it was considering a reverse stock split as part of its effort to convert *preferred shares* (takes priority over common shares on earnings and assets in the event of liquidation) to common shares.

What is a reverse stock split?

A reverse stock split is a reduction in the number of a corporation's outstanding shares and a corresponding increase in the value of those shares. For example, if you own 200 shares of company XYZ at $5 per share, a 1 for 2 reverse stock split would result in your owning 100 shares at $10 per share. The total value of your holdings, however, remains the same:

$$200 \times \$5 = \$1000$$
$$100 \times \$10 = \$1000$$

Reasons why reverse stock splits are done:

- Reverse stock splits make corporate shares look more valuable, although there has been absolutely no change in terms of real worth.

- Many institutional investors have rules against purchasing a stock whose price is below a certain minimum level. For example, many institutional investors consider a stock trading at $5 or less to be a penny stock, and accordingly will refuse to purchase a stock at this price. Citigroup, in 2010, fell into the latter category.

- Fear of being delisted is another possible reason. If a stock falls below a certain price, it may no longer meet exchange requirements and could face being delisted or removed from trading on that particular exchange.

- Reducing the number of shareholders is a rare but possible explanation for a reverse split. If the split results in a shareholder owning less than a minimum required number of shares, they would receive a cash payment and no shares of stock. This may be beneficial to a company seeking to be put in a different regulatory category, such as an S-Corp, which is required to have less than 100 shareholders.

Typically, a stock will temporarily add a D to the end of its ticker symbol during a reverse stock split.

Citigroup situation:

Let's take a look at a chart of Citigroup as of May, 2011:

Figure 126- Reverse split for Citi

As can be seen in Figure 126, Citigroup went from a $50 per share stock to a $4 per share equity before the reverse split. To get this to a somewhat cosmetically acceptable scenario, a 1for10 split would be necessary. This would elevate Citi's share price to $40 per share. Thus, if you owned 1000 shares of Citi at $4 before the split, you would own 100 shares at $40 after the split.

What does a reverse split signal?

In 2008, Jim Rosenfeld, an associate professor of finance at Emory University's Goizueta Business School in Atlanta, did a study involving 1600 companies that did reverse stock splits. He found that the typical stock in his study underperformed the market by 50% on a risk-adjusted basis during the three year period after the action. He concluded:

"Reverse stock splits are a strong indicator the company is going to be a significant underperformer during the near future."

What if I sold covered call options on a stock that was subject to a reverse stock split?

Perhaps you were out partying the night before and had a bit too much to drink. You woke up the next morning and omitted your first cup of high-octane coffee that might have brought you out of your fog. Through no fault of your own, this drug-induced state caused you to ignore all the fundamental and technical requirements of the BCI system. Common sense was also tossed out the window, as you rationalize that Citigroup cannot possibly go any lower than $30! Okay, that's all water under the bridge. Here's an example that is simple to follow if you sold a covered call on a stock you never should have purchased:

You sold 10 contracts of the $5 call.

- After a 1for10 split, that would change to having sold 1 contract of the $50 call.

- Ticker symbols would change, but the expiration date remains the same as does the premium initially collected.

When the numbers don't break down as perfectly as these, it is much more complicated. The best way to handle these scenarios is to contact your broker or the CBOE Exchange. The split information can be obtained online at the following link:

www.cboe.com/contractadjustments

You can also call the CBOE (Chicago Board Options Exchange) for free information:

1-888-678-4667

* The Blue Collar System strongly encourages you to avoid all stocks that are forced to resort to reverse splits. They simply will never meet our fundamental and technical criteria.

Test your knowledge of key points

1- When a stock splits the total number of shares is divided into multiple shares but the _____ remains unchanged.

2- To determine if the split is an asset or a liability we must check the _____.

3- If a covered call option is sold on a stock that splits two-for-1 before expiration Friday, the following two parameters will not change: _____.

4- If a covered call option is sold on a stock that splits two-for-1 before expiration Friday, the following four parameters will change: _____ _____.

5- A reduction in the number of a corporation's outstanding shares and a corresponding increase in the value of those shares is called a _____.

Answers:

1- Total dollar value

2- Price chart technicals

3- Initial option profit, expiration date

4- Number of shares owned, cost basis per share, contract strike price and option ticker symbol.

5- Reverse stock split

Chapter 13

Tax Treatment for Covered Call Writing in Non-Sheltered Accounts

Chapter outline

1- Short term versus long term capital assets and gains or losses

2- Tax rules for covered call writers

3- Schedule D of the Elite Calculator (see chapter 6)

4- Updated tax information and definitions

As I type the first sentence of this chapter, let me state the obvious: *I am not a tax expert.* However, I do make every effort to be as informed as possible on issues that affect my hard-earned money. This article is a brief and highly simplified introduction to the tax issues; it is not tax advice, which should be addressed with your attorney, accountant or tax preparer.

Short-term versus long-term capital assets

Under current IRS regulations, both stocks and stock options are considered capital assets, and any gain on their sale is taxable. If the stock or option is held for *less than one year, then short-term capital gains* (STCG) apply. This rate would be your *ordinary income tax rate, up to 35%.* If the stock or option is *held for at least a year,* the gain is taxed at a long-term capital gains rate, which is *15%* for taxpayers in the 25%, 28%, 33% and 35%

tax brackets. For stocks, holding periods can be affected when selling deep in-the-money strikes. This discussion is beyond the scope of this chapter, and consultation with your tax advisor in this regard is appropriate.

Since we sell predominantly one-month options, short-term capital gains rates would apply in all non-sheltered accounts. As a matter of fact, most stock options have a duration of nine months or less, so tax rates will usually be at the short-term rates. The exception to this rule is LEAPS. As referenced in Chapter 7 and discussed in detail in Chapter 15, LEAPS are options contracts with expiration dates that are longer than one year. Structurally, LEAPS are no different than short-term options, but the later expiration dates associated with LEAPS offer the opportunity for long-term investors to gain exposure to prolonged price changes without needing to use a combination of shorter-term option contracts. The premiums from LEAPs are higher than the premiums received from selling standard options in the same stock because of the increased time value associated with LEAPS; LEAPS have later expiration dates than standard options, which gives the underlying asset more time to make a substantial move, and consequently, the investor more time to make a healthy profit.

What is a Capital Gain?

A capital gain is an increase in the value of a capital asset, such as a stock or an option, which gives it a higher worth than the purchase price. Capital gains must be claimed on income taxes in non-sheltered accounts.

Rules for Covered Call Writers

Premiums received for writing covered calls are not included as income at the time of receipt, but are held in suspense until the writer's obligation to deliver the underlying stock expires, or until the writer either sells the stock as a result of assignment or closes the option position (buy-to-close). With that in mind, here are three possible tax-related scenarios that may arise after the sale of the option:

1- An expired option (we sold the call, we didn't close the position by buying back the option, and the holder did not exercise the option) results in a short-term capital gain. For example, if we sell an Apple April 90 call for $4.50 in March, $450 in proceeds are garnered. Since the cost basis is $0, the short-term capital gain is $450. The acquisition date will be LATER than the sales date, and the word "Expired" should be written in column "e," the cost basis column.

2- If we buy back the same option in the above-referenced example to close the position (usually to invoke an exit strategy), the difference between the sale profit and the buy-back cost will represent a capital gain or a capital loss. Here, like the example above, the acquisition date will also be LATER than the sales date.

Capital gain example: We close our position by buying back the option for $250. The capital gain is $200 ($450 – $250).

Capital loss example: We close our position by buying back the option for $550. The capital loss is $100 ($550 – $450).

3- If the option is exercised, the option transaction becomes part of the stock transaction. The option premium is added to the strike price received, less commissions. If the stock has been held for less than one year, the entire transaction will be treated as short-term. If the stock had been held for *one year or more*, the entire transaction will be treated as long-term, as the *option holding period is ignored.*

Schedule D of the Elite Calculator (see chapter 6)

***The Schedule D of the Elite Calculator is designed to assist your tax advisor with these long and short-term capital gains (losses) issues.

The specific information referenced above can be found in IRS Publication 550 entitled Investment Income and Expenses, pages 57 – 58.

I avoid these tax issues by trading covered call stock options predominantly in tax-sheltered accounts.

Updated tax information and definitions (as of December, 2010 and contributed by Owen Sargent, CPA)

First, I strongly urge all BCI members to download IRS Publication 550, *Investment Income and Expenses*, from the Internal Revenue Service website, at:

http://www.irs.gov/pub/irs-pdf/p550.pdf.

You will recognize much of the following information when you read it. The page references below refer to the page in the 2009 Publication 550. Throughout this discussion I will refer to capital GAINS on the optimistic assumption that you will not incur a capital LOSS. However, where you read capital gain, generally you may also read it as capital loss, or capital gain/(loss).

Second, there are no reporting requirements for retirement account trading, so, if you are only trading in your IRA, most of this discussion does not matter. You just want your account balance to be bigger next month than it was last month.

Third, some important terms need to be defined:

Capital Asset (Pub 550 P.51): This is pretty much anything you own and use for personal, pleasure or investment purposes. The term includes such tangible assets as a boat, a coin collection, or a piece of real estate. It may also include intangible assets, such as a patent or copyright. The distinction between a capital asset and a non-capital asset is its use. Pretty much any capital asset becomes a non-capital asset if it is used in a trade or business, or is "for sale" to customers in a trade or business. (See the discussion on pages 49.and 50) Our discussion will be limited to corporate stocks and stock options.

Capital Gain (Loss) (Pub 550 P.51): A capital gain or loss is simply the difference between the proceeds of the sale and your cost basis of the asset sold. (The IRS has invented something

Tax Treatment for Covered Call Writing in Non-Sheltered Accounts | 339

called the "deemed sale" which will be discussed later) If you bought a stock for $25 and sold it for $30, you have a capital gain of $5. You can't have a capital gain or loss unless you have a sale of a capital asset. However, a sale of an asset does not necessarily mean you have a capital gain or loss. Why? Because every capital gain requires two parts of the transaction, a sale AND an acquisition or purchase (see Short Sale discussion below).

Short Sale (Pub 550 P.57): The normal progression of a trade is to buy the security, wait, and then sell it. Well, in the world of Wall Street, you are allowed to do the trade in the reverse. A short sale of a stock is where you borrow shares from your broker and sell them, with the understanding that you will purchase the stock at a future date and return the shares. When you sell a call option (either naked or covered by underlying stock shares) you are opening a short sale. The sale transaction does not constitute income or an adjustment to the basis of the stock. If the call is "bought to close" it becomes a reportable capital gain. If the call option is exercised by the buyer, the option premium becomes part of the stock sale (see Basis discussion below). You may be required to report the sale on your tax return as part of reconciliation to the Schedule D. New reporting requirements will have your broker reporting option sales to the IRS. If you sell a January call option in December, you may have to explain why you are not reporting a gain on the option sale. Make sure your tax preparer understands short sales.

New IRS reporting: From the instructions for 2011 Form 1099-B:

Short sales of securities: Do not report a short sale entered into after 2010 until the year a customer delivers a security to satisfy the short sale obligation. Disregard sections 1259 (constructive sales) and 1233(h) (short sales of property that becomes worthless). Report the short sale on a single Form 1099-B unless:

- There is both short-term and long-term gain or loss reported for the short sale (see page 1),

- The securities delivered to close the short sale include both covered securities and non-covered securities (see page 1), or
- There was backup withholding and other conditions apply (see below).

Report on Form 1099-B the relevant information about the security sold to open the short sale, with the exceptions described in the following paragraphs.

> In box 1a, report the date the security was delivered to close the short sale.
> In box 1b, report the acquisition date of the security delivered to close the short sale.
> In box 3, report the adjusted basis of the security delivered to close the short sale.

If the short sale is closed by delivery of a non-covered security, you may check box 6. In this case, you do not have to report adjusted basis and whether any gain or loss on the closing of the short sale is short-term or long-term. However, if you choose to report this information and check box 6, you will not be subject to the penalties under sections 6721 and 6722 for failure to report this information correctly.

In box 8, report whether any gain or loss on the closing of the short sale is short-term or long-term based on the acquisition date of the security delivered to close the short sale.

Also, the form is available on the IRS website:
http://www.irs.gov/pub/irs-pdf/f1099b.pdf

Basis (Pub 550 P.43): Basis (also referred to as "cost basis") is often a moving target. Generally, basis it is what you paid for a stock or option. There are adjustments which may be necessary to report the proper capital gain. These adjustments may include special dividends, stock splits and stock dividends, among others. It is highly recommended that you read the basis discussions in Publication 550. You should also keep an eye on your brokerage account, as the IRS will likely assume that your broker is providing the correct basis figures.

If you write a covered call which is ultimately exercised, the option premium is added to the proceeds of the sale of the stock. For example, assume you buy 100 shares of ABC stock for $3,800 and sell the JUL $40 call for $125. If the stock gets called away, the proceeds will be $4,125 ($4,000 + $125), and the basis will be the $3,800 you paid for the stock. Your broker will likely report this basis properly. However, to err on the side of caution, be sure your broker doesn't report the option sale, and then report the stock exercise, including the option premium as two separate entities.

Adjustments for call purchases or a put option transactions is beyond the scope of covered call writing, and thus will not be discussed. However, you can learn more about the tax implications in connection with these transactions by reviewing Pub 550, Page 60.

Wash Sale (Pub 550 P.58): A wash sale loss is not deductible. A wash sale occurs when you sell a stock for a loss and, within 30 days before or after the trade, buy the same stock, or substantially the same stock. This means that if you sell a stock at $35 for a loss, and buy a $35 call option, you have a wash sale and cannot deduct the loss on the stock.

Short-term vs. Long-term (Pub 550 P.53): One of the reasons to keep up to date on the tax rules is because they are subject to change. A long-term gain is currently a gain on a security held for more than one year. If you have owned a stock for more than one year which is called away in an option exercise, the gain is considered a long-term gain. It does not matter if the option was sold the day before yesterday

Schedule D: It would be wise for you to obtain a copy of Schedule D for Form 1040, including the corresponding instructions. Familiarize yourself with the reporting requirements so that you can ensure the information regarding stock and option transactions is correct.

Inherited Stock: The estate tax issue is still being discussed in Washington. At this point in time, if you inherit stock from someone who died in 2010, you inherit it at the deceased person's cost basis. If you received your inheritance before 2010, your cost basis is the average price of the stock as of the day the decedent died.

Owen Sargent is an outstanding CPA, an attorney and a seasoned stock investor. He helped me develop the Ellman Calculator and is a frequent contributor to the BCI blog forum. If you are in need of a tax advisor I recommend Owen without hesitation. Many thanks to Owen for his assistance with this portion of the book. Owen may be reached at (516) 938-3700, or at osargentcpa@aol.com.

Tax Treatment for Covered Call Writing in Non-Sheltered Accounts | 343

Test your knowledge of key points

1- Under the current IRS regulations, both stocks and stock options are considered _____, and any gain on their sale is taxable (unless in a sheltered account).

2- If the stock or option is held for at least a year, the gain is taxed at a _____ which is 15% for taxpayers in the 25%, 28%, 33% and 35% tax brackets.

3- Since we sell predominantly 1-month options, _____ capital gains rates would apply in all non-sheltered accounts.

4- Most stock options have a duration of _____ or less. The exception to this rule is _____.

5- Premiums received for writing a covered call are not included as income at the time of receipt, but are held in suspense until one of these three events occur: _____.

6- An expired option results in a _____.

7- A _____ occurs when you sell a stock for a loss and, within 30 days before or after the trade, buy the same stock, or substantially the same stock (like a call option)

Answers:

1- Capital assets

2- Long-term capital gains rate

3- Short-term

4- Nine months, LEAPS

5- The option expires, the shares are assigned as a result of the option obligation or the short option position is closed by buying back the option

6- Short-term capital gain

7- Wash sale

Chapter 14

Portfolio Overwriting: Selling Covered Calls on Stocks You Want to Keep

Chapter outline

1- Definition

2- Why a portfolio overwriter does not want his shares assigned

3- Advantages of portfolio overwriting

4- Strike selection for portfolio overwriting

5- Why some portfolio overwriters sell in-the-money strikes

6- How to manage early assignment

Most covered call writers purchase a stock specifically for the purpose of selling the corresponding call option. The investment time frame is one to two months, as earnings reports will end the "run" of even the best performing equities (assuming you agree with my guidelines). In many cases, share assignment is permitted by the seller, and even if early assignment occurs, our investment is still a successful one. In other words, losing (selling) the stock is no problem and really just part of the strategy. However, there are other investors who sell call options in a different manner, called portfolio overwriting. In this instance, a call option is sold on a stock that is already part of an existing portfolio. The call writer prefers NOT to have his shares assigned. That option is selected in a manner where the option is NOT expected to be exercised.

Why a Portfolio Overwriter does not want his shares assigned

This is basically a tax issue. The holding period for short-term versus long-term capital gains is one year, as discussed in Chapter 13. If the stock has been held for less than one year, the writer would prefer to retain the equity for a longer time frame, assuming share appreciation. In addition, if the shares have appreciated substantially from the cost basis, selling in any time frame may not be in the investor's best interest as the shareholder would not want to pay capital gains, short or long term

Another important tax issue:

If the underlying stock has not accumulated the full one year holding period for long-term capital gains, covered call writing may suspend or eliminate the current accumulated holding period. In other words, if you own a stock for ten months selling options may put a hold on the long term requirement or even eliminate the accrued ten month ownership. It is advisable to consult with your tax advisor on this matter.

Advantages of portfolio overwriting over stock ownership

- Achieve higher returns in declining, neutral and slightly bullish markets. We are generating additional capital on the option premiums while our shares may be flat or barely changing in value.

- Beat the returns of long-term holders of equities because of this additional cash generated.

- Increase portfolio downside protection, thereby minimizing risk as the premiums serve to lower the breakeven.

- Generate a monthly cash flow
- Use option profits to compound your returns

Strike selection for portfolio overwriting

Since our goals are to generate a monthly cash flow and NOT have our shares assigned, common sense dictates that we sell out-of-the-money strikes. This will benefit us because time decay is greatest for these strikes, and the option value will dissipate as we get closer to expiration Friday. Remember, we don't want our option strike price ending up in-the-money. If it does, that will increase the chance of assignment. Our mindset needs to be slightly different when selling these out-of-the-money strikes because our standard 2-4%, one-month return is too lofty a goal. I would set a more realistic goal of 1 - 1.5% per month, which will help ensure that the implied volatility of the option is not too high. A high implied volatility means that the market is anticipating a large price movement in the underlying security, which consequently corresponds to a higher possibility that the option will be in-the-money at or near expiration Friday. Simply put, settle for a lower premium (by choosing to sell an option with a lower implied volatility) which will decrease the chances of assignment. As a guideline, when I'm selecting options to sell for portfolio overwriting, I like to see the *underlying share price at least 5% lower than the strike price of the option contract I am going to sell.* For example, if I sold a $50 strike, at the time of the sale I would want that equity to be trading at $47.50 or less, with the option premium generating a 1 to 1.5% monthly return.

Why some portfolio overwriters sell in-the-money strikes

This is a riskier strategy if keeping the stock is important to the investor, although there is a case to be made for employing such a strategy. Portfolio overwriters generally sell in-the-money strikes when the stock, or market in general, is *declining*, and the in-the-money strikes will generate greater returns with more protection ("more protection" is afforded in this scenario because the market is declining, thus decreasing the chance the option will expire in-the-money and be assigned). In addition, the higher delta of the option (amount the option premium changes with a corresponding $1 change in the underlying stock price) will make it easier to close or roll the position (buy back the option). Portfolio overwriters also use the in-the-money approach in conjunction with technical analysis, specifically where support and resistance points are identified, and the in-the-money strikes can be sold at resistance (with the expectation that the stock will start to decline towards support) and closed or rolled if still in-the-money near expiration Friday.

What if early assignment occurs?

Early assignment will not occur often, but is likely to happen eventually. If and when it does, purchase an amount of shares equal to the obligation to deliver, and notify your broker that these newly acquired shares should be indentified as the shares delivered to meet the option obligation. *Before executing your transaction, seek your broker's advice as to the best way to manage such scenarios.*

Conclusion:

Portfolio overwriting provides many of the same advantages as the buy-write strategy, however because of the tax implications associated with portfolio overwriting, its income goals and strike management requirements differ, and therefore need to be fully understood before action is taken.

Test your knowledge of key points

1- _____ is a strategy when a call option is sold on a stock already part of a portfolio. A strike price is selected such that is unlikely that the shares will be _____.

2- When portfolio overwriting, our percentage return goals should be set slightly _____ and _____ strike prices should be favored.

3- A guideline for portfolio overwriting is for the share price to be at least _____ lower than the strike price.

4- A portfolio overwriter may select an in-the-money strike in a _____ stock market.

Answers:

1- Portfolio overwriting, assigned (sold)

2- Lower, out-of-the-money

3- 5%

4- Declining or bearish

Chapter 15

Covered Calls and LEAPS

Chapter outline

1- Definitions

2- The concept of selling calls on LEAPS

3- Advantages of LEAPS

4- Disadvantages of LEAPS

Wait a minute! What if I buy a call option instead of the stock and then sell a call option on that option? I'll be spending less money than the outright purchase of the equity and still generate cash from the sale of the call option! This idea has come to many astute covered call writers. Although not a true covered call write, purchasing a long-term option (more than one year out), which is called a *LEAPS*, and then selling call options against that the LEAPS is an alternate strategy *similar* to covered call writing. Technically, these trades are known as *calendar spreads.* Let's start out with a brief review of some of the core definitions germane to this strategy.

Definitions

LEAPS (Long-Term Equity Anticipation Securities) - These are option contracts with expiration dates longer than one year. LEAPS are generally associated only with the more heavily traded stocks and ETFs.

Calendar Spread- Simultaneously establishing long and short options positions on the same underlying stock with different expiration dates. For example, you buy the December 2010, $20 call and sell the April, 2010 $20 call on the same equity.

Horizontal Spread- A spread where both options have the same strike price (as in the above-referenced calendar spread example) but different expiration dates. *The terms calendar and horizontal spreads are interchangeable.*

Diagonal Spread- A long and short options position with different expiration dates AND different strikes. For example, you buy the December, 2010 $20 call and sell the April, 2010 $25 call.

Concept behind selling calls on LEAPS

An investor who sells covered calls using LEAPS usually establishes the long options position by purchasing in-the-money LEAPS, and establishes the short options position by selling near-term, slightly out-of-the-money calls. These positions are constructed such that, if assigned, the difference between the spread ($5 in the example above where the $20 call was bought and the $25 call was sold) and the short premium collected exceeds the cost of the long option. If unassigned (i.e. the price of the stock does not exceed the strike price of the short call), we can continue to write calls and generate a monthly cash flow. The problem in this second scenario (where the option is not assigned) is that if the stock price falls, the premiums generated from short-selling the call also drops unless we write for a lower strike, which may result in a loss for this long-term strategy as the spread (difference between the two strikes) declines.

Let's take a look at the options chain for a highly traded equity, INTC (figure 127):

Intel Corporation (NASDAQ: INTC) Optionable

Last: 20.43 Chg: +0.37 (+1.84%) Open: 19.96 Avg Vol: 73,688,865 Volume: 91,108,878
Bid: 20.44 Ask: 20.52 High: 20.68 Low: 19.79 W%Chg: +23.64%
After Hours Data Last: 20.51 Chg: +0.08 %Chg: +0.39% Volume: 9,556,421

INTC currently priced @ $20.43

With the stock priced @ $20.43 let's look for a deep I-T-M LEAPS:

		Calls				Jan 12
Last	Intrinsic Value	Bid	Ask	Vol	Open Interest	Strike
17.98	17.93	17.80	18.15	0	0	2.50
15.45	15.43	15.30	15.60	0	2	5.00
12.95	12.93	12.80	13.10	0	0	7.50
10.47	10.43	10.35	10.60	14	3,824	10.00
6.33	5.43	6.25	6.40	21	4,026	15.00
4.70	2.93	4.65	4.75	378	18,406	17.50
3.35	0.43	3.30	3.40	142	17,581	20.00
1.61	0.00	1.57	1.65	422	11,714	25.00
0.71	0.00	0.68	0.73	5	2,483	30.00

Figure 127- INTC- Deep In-The-Money Calls

The January, 2012 $10 strike is purchased for $10.60, $10.43 of which is intrinsic value, and only $0.17 is time value. *Minimal time value is a characteristic of deep in-the-money LEAPS options.*

Next let's check the near-term and slightly out-of-the-money strikes:

Calls						Mar 10
Last	Intrinsic Value	Bid	Ask	Vol	Open Interest	Strike
5.47	5.43	5.40	5.55	2	20	15.00
4.50	4.43	4.40	4.60	0	1	16.00
3.50	3.43	3.45	3.55	171	2,215	17.00
2.56	2.43	2.55	2.58	1,198	4,534	18.00
1.69	1.43	1.68	1.70	1,582	8,861	19.00
0.96	0.43	0.95	0.97	4,965	19,557	20.00
0.44	0.00	0.43	0.45	20,542	21,604	21.00
0.17	0.00	0.17	0.18	2,630	70,831	22.00
0.06	0.00	0.05	0.06	555	3,404	23.00
0.01	0.00	0.01	0.02	150	678	24.00
0.01	0.00	0.01	0.01	260	161	25.00

Figure 128- INTC- Near-Term, Out-Of-The-Money Options

The next month, $21 slightly out-of-the-money strike can be sold for $0.43.

Let's do the math, *if assignment occurs:*

We collect the difference in the spread ($21 – $10 = $11) + the short option premium ($0.43) for a total of $11.43. We deduct the cost of the long call ($10.60) for a profit of $0.83 per share, or $83 per contract. The percentage return is $83/$1060, or 7.8%. All calendar spreads are constructed such that a profit is generated in the event assignment occurs. If the shares are not assigned (price of stock NOT greater than the $21 strike of the short call, our profit is $43/$1060 = 4.1% and we're free to sell another option. As noted above, this strategy works well as long as the share price does not dramatically decline, thereby reducing the returns on the short options. We also must bear in mind that the long call (LEAPS) is a decaying asset and will ultimately expire, at which time we will no longer own the right to purchase INTC at the $10 strike. If we continue to generate monthly returns of $43, how long will it take us to retrieve the $1060 if assignment never occurs? Here's the math:

$1060/$43 = 24 months (not counting any difference in the spread)

Our LEAPS option is good for about 22 months, so if it ultimately expires worthless and the spread has decreased, we lose! Diagonal spreads work best for rising stocks, where we can take advantage of the difference in the original strike prices.

Advantages of using LEAPS

- Less costly than purchasing stock; remaining cash can be used to generate additional cash

- A declining stock will have time to recover

- Low time value of deep in-the-money LEAPS makes option ownership similar to stock ownership where intrinsic value changes dollar-for-dollar.

Disadvantages of using LEAPS

- You do NOT capture stock dividends.

- To stay active, you must sell options in cycles that report earnings, taking on additional risk

- LEAPS have a delta of approximately .50 to .60, making it difficult to close a position at a profit for at-the-money and out-of-the-money strikes (option value has not moved up in step with share value). This is less of a factor for in-the-money LEAPS

- A higher level of approval will be required by most brokerages to allow this type of trading

- The long calls will ultimately expire, stocks will not

- Forced assignment may not allow for a profitable trade
- You cannot use this strategy in *some* self-directed retirement accounts, depending on the brokerage company. While the calls being written are hedged, they are not considered to be "covered." In the event of assignment, because of the one-day lag between exercise and assignment, using the long-term call used to close out the position would require being short the stock for a day. Many brokerages do not allow short stock positions in retirement accounts under any circumstances.

Conclusion:

Purchasing LEAPS and selling a call option on that position is NOT a true covered call write. It is an alternate strategy that has its pros and cons. For most Blue Collar Investors, covered call writing is the better path to take. But to some investors who fully understand the nuances of diagonal spreads, this may be a viable alternative.

Test your knowledge of key points

1- Option contracts with expiration dates longer than one year are known as _____.

2- Simultaneously establishing long and short options positions on the same underlying stock with different expiration dates is known as a _____.

3- When selling call options against LEAPS, the investor usually establishes the long option position by purchasing _____ strikes on the LEAPS, and then selling a _____, the short position

4- All calendar spreads are constructed such that there is a _____ if assignment occurs.

Answers:

1- LEAPS or Long-Term Equity Anticipation Securities

2- Calendar spread

3- In-the-money: near term, slightly out-of-the-money call option.

4- Profit

Chapter 16

Margin Accounts and Covered Call Writing

Chapter outline

1- Definition of margin account

2- Cost to carry- interest

3- How much can you borrow?

4- Margin calculator

5- Maintenance margin

6- Minimum margin versus initial margin

7- Disadvantages of margin accounts

In real estate investing, the concept of leveraged investing is well known and documented in such best sellers as Robert G. Allen's *Nothing Down for the 2000s*, and Michael A. Lechter's OPM (Other People's Money). The idea of generating profit while using little or none of your own money down is enticing and exciting. It actually does make sense in certain scenarios. For example, when you own an investment property, you are using "OPM," as your tenant is paying off the mortgage. When it comes to the stock market, the use of options is a great example of leveraged investing. The option buyer (not us) is controlling shares of stock at a greatly reduced cost.

When we write covered calls, we are using the cash generated from the call premium sale to either reduce our cost basis, or to take the profit and re-invest it, thereby compounding our profits instantly (the next trading day or T +1, in the case of options). There is, however, another way to leverage our covered call investments, and that is to trade in a *margin account.*

Definition

Margin Account:

A margin account is a brokerage account that allows an investor to borrow money from the broker to purchase securities. This loan is then collateralized by the cash and securities in that specific account. Using this form of leverage can magnify both gains and losses. If and when the value of the security drops to a certain level, the investor will be required to put additional cash in the account, or alternatively, sell certain securities. This is known as a *margin call.* You are only allowed to borrow money to buy certain securities called *marginable securities.* You cannot buy options on margin. However, when writing covered calls, you can borrow money for the first leg of the trade, which is the purchase of the security.

Interest plays a factor

When money is borrowed from our broker in a margin account, interest is charged and needs to be calculated into our profit calculations. Expenses incurred while a position is being held, including interest paid on margin, are known as the *Costs to Carry,* and are usually associated with an annual interest rate charge ranging from 5% to 9%. However, as educated covered call writers, in normal market conditions we should easily be able to generate returns higher than the costs that will be incurred should we decided to purchase the underlying equity on margin.

How much can I borrow?

According to *Regulation T*, the SEC has set the maximum borrowing power to purchase a marginable security at 50% of either the current stock price or the call's strike price, whichever is lower (when using the covered call strategy). Note, however, that some brokerage firms require you to deposit more money One of the many benefits of covered call writing is that the cash generated from the option sale reduces the amount of cash that would otherwise be required (in accordance with Reg T's 50% rule noted above) to enter the position on margin.

Example of margin in a covered call trade:

Buy 200 shares of BCI at $40/share = $8000

Sell to open 2 $40 calls at $2/option =$400

Margin Calculator

Next, let's feed this information in to a margin calculator (http://www.cboe.com/tradtool/mCalc/default.aspx):

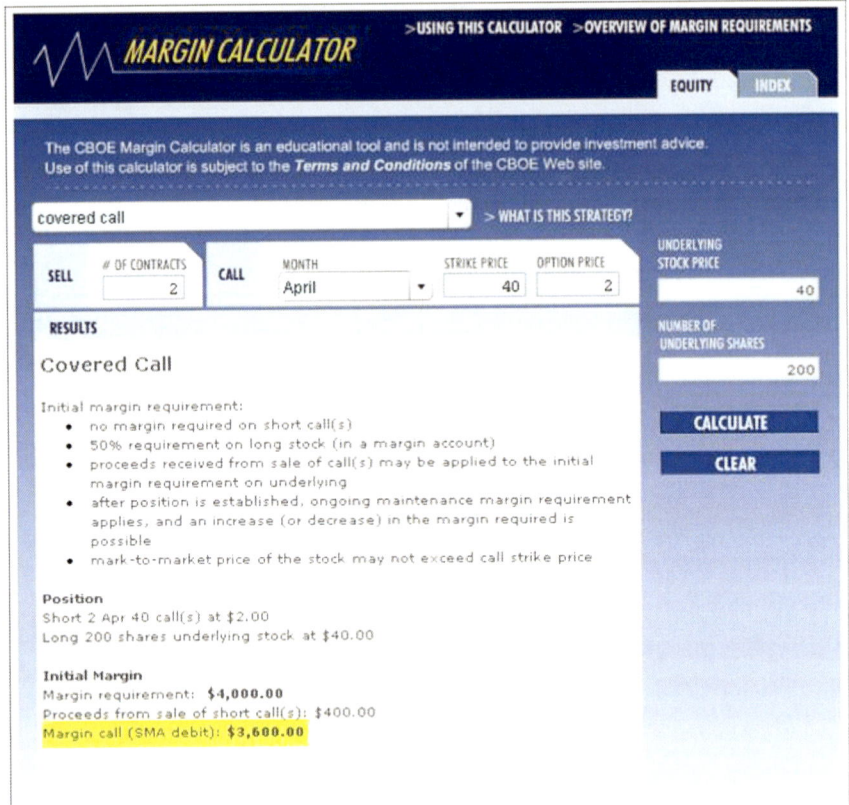

Figure 129- Margin Calculator

As depicted in Figure 129, the amount of cash required to invest is reduced from $8000 to $3600 by taking 50% of the $8000, and then subtracting the $400 generated from the sale of the short call. Let's assume our shares are assigned and calculate our returns with and without margin:

Cash Account:

ROO = $400/$8000 =5%, one-month return

Margin Account:

We will assume a 9% interest charge on the $4000 loan. This results in a one-month debit of $30 ($4000 x 9%/12).

ROO = $400 − $30/$4000 = 9.3%, nearly doubling the returns from the cash account. *Notice that I didn't deduct the $400 premium from the cost basis ($4000) because in the BCI system, we stress taking the profit and re-investing it, and thereby compounding our money instantaneously. Either way is correct, however, as this is simply a different philosophical approach to the strategy.*

Maintenance Margin

The rules of FINRA and the exchanges supplement the requirements of Regulation T by placing "maintenance" margin requirements on customer accounts. Generally speaking, FINRA requires a customer's equity (i.e. share value − amount borrowed) in the account to be at least 25% of the current market value of the securities in the account. If the customer's equity falls below this 25% threshold level, the customer may be required to deposit more funds or securities in order to maintain the 25% level. The failure to do so may cause the brokerage firm to liquidate the securities in the customer's account in order to bring the account's equity back up to the requisite level. This *minimum* 25% equity requirement is referred to as the *maintenance requirement.* Many brokerages choose to have requirements between 30-40%, but it cannot be less than 25%.

Maintenance Requirement Example:

- Buy 200 shares of BCI at $40/share = $8000
- Borrow $4000 in a margin account
- Market value of shares drop to $5000
- Equity falls to $5000 − $4000 = $1000
- A 25% maintenance requirement would be $5000 x 25% = $1250, leaving a shortfall of $250 ($1250 − $1000)

- Had the maintenance requirement been 40% of $5000 (or $2000), the shortfall would be $1000

- A shortfall will trigger a *margin call* where the investor would be required to add cash to the account or sell stocks. *It is possible that your broker can take it upon himself to sell some of your shares without notifying you with a margin call.*

Minimum Margin vs. Initial Margin

Minimum margin is FINRA's requirement that broker-dealers require its customers to deposit at least $2000 or 100% of the purchase price - whichever is less - *before* the customer is permitted to purchase a security on margin. Some broker-dealers may require an even higher deposit. Minimum margin should not be confused with FINRA's *maintenance margin requirement* (discussed above), which prohibits the equity in the account from falling below 25% of the current market value of the securities in the account after stock is purchased on margin. Initial margin is set forth by Regulation T (discussed above) of the Federal Reserve Board and currently allows up to 50% of the purchase price of marginable securities.

Disadvantages of Margin Accounts

- You may have to deposit additional cash or securities in your account on short notice to cover market losses

- To pay back the loan, your brokerage firm may sell some of your shares without consulting with you

- You may be forced to sell some of your securities to compensate for falling share prices

- The enhanced risk inherent in margin accounts can exacerbate losses

Conclusion:

Margin accounts are a form of leverage which can magnify investment results dramatically in both directions. I would advise that only experienced, savvy investors use margin accounts when writing covered calls.

Test your knowledge of key points

1- A brokerage account where the client can borrow money from the broker to purchase certain securities is called a _____.

2- True or false: Options are marginable securities. _____.

3- The interest charged in a margin account is called _____.

4- _____ is the SEC-mandated rule that sets the maximum borrowing power to purchase a stock at 50% of either the current stock price or the call's strike price, whichever is lower.

5- Once a stock has been purchased on margin, FINRA requires that you must maintain a minimum amount of equity in the margin account. This is known as the _____, which is set at _____%.

6- _____ is FINRA's requirement that we deposit at least $2000 or 100% of the purchase price, whichever is less.

7- True or False: Your brokerage may sell some of your shares without consulting with you to pay back the loan? _____.

Answers:

1- Margin account

2- False (stocks are marginable but not options)

3- Cost to carry

4- Regulation T

5- Maintenance requirement, 25%

6- Minimum margin

7- True

 # Chapter 17

Selling Naked or Cash-Secured Puts vs. Covered call Writing

Chapter outline

1- Definitions

2- Advantages of selling covered calls over cash-secured puts

A will is a legal document that expresses the wishes of the author with respect to the disposition of property after the author's death. So is a revocable trust. So they're the same, right? WRONG. On the surface they are similar, but when inspected closer there are differences that make one document more appropriate for a particular set of circumstances. The same is true of covered call options and cash-secured put options.

Some books and courses on options suggest that when you sell a covered call option, you are investing more money but getting similar returns as you would by selling a naked put. Therefore, the theory goes, the latter makes much more sense than the former. I must respectfully disagree. First some background information and definitions.

Definitions

Naked put- Here we are selling the right, but not the obligation, for the buyer of the put to sell a stock to us at a specified price, by a specified date. In return for undertaking this obligation, we also receive a premium. For example, a stock is trading at $30

per share and we sell a $30 put for $1.50, receiving a return of $150 per contract. The returns in these scenarios are generally similar to the returns of generated from selling covered calls, and if the put is exercised, we are required to buy the stock for $30, the same price the call seller paid for the underlying shares in the preceding covered call example. Note: *The put seller buys the stock at the strike less what he/she received from the put sale...some traders look at this as a way to get a stock you want to own at a discount.* For example, in the above scenario the stock is purchased for $28.50 ($30 - $1.50).

Cash-secured put- When a brokerage company requires us to have the cash in our accounts to purchase the shares we are obligated to buy, it is now known as a cash-secured rather than a naked put. Some investors will enter a covered call position by first selling a cash-secured put and if exercised, then sell a call on the stock put to us. Most retail investors will be required to sell cash-secured rather than naked puts.

*Advantages of covered calls
over naked or cash-secured puts*

So what's the difference, and why should we have to buy the stock and lay out all that cash for the covered call position? The following constitutes the primary reasons why, in my opinion, covered call writing is a more advantageous, profitable strategy than selling puts.

- Many brokerages want assurances that you have the ability to purchase the shares you are obligated to buy when selling the put. Therefore, they will require you to have an adequate amount of cash in your account to cover such an event. In this scenario, you have sold a *cash-secured put* by setting aside the same amount of cash the covered call seller would have to pay to purchase the underlying shares. The *covered call seller captures all dividends* distributed by the underlying corporation; the put seller does not capture any dividends, because he or she does not own the underlying shares. We're not talking about a huge windfall here, but the cash from these dividends is better in our pockets than someone else's.

- Selling covered calls allows the investor more flexibility. The most profit a put seller can generate is the premium from the option sale. A covered call writer can profit from the option premium PLUS additional share appreciation if an out-of-the-money strike is sold. That choice is available to the covered call writer but not to the naked or cash-secured put seller.

- Early assignment is not an issue for CC writers because the option premium is not affected and possible additional upside appreciation is incorporated into your profits if an out-of-the-money strike was sold. For naked put sellers, early assignment *could* be a disaster. Imagine (as a put seller) the price of the corresponding stock gaps down, and the stock is "put" or sold to the put seller at the strike price of the put option he sold, which is now higher than the price of the underlying shares. The put seller now owns the underlying stock, which is still plummeting and heading for the teens! The put seller wants to sell the stock before it loses more ground, but perhaps the shares haven't even hit his account yet. He or she may have to wait until the next day (after the stock is "put" or sold to him) to sell the shares. One way of getting around this issue is to sell the shares short (selling before actually owning them). The problem with this solution is that average Blue Collar Investors will have a difficult time getting "shorting privileges" from their brokerage firm, and may also lack the sophistication necessary to manage such situations. Besides, who needs such headaches?

- You are more likely to get permission from your broker to trade options in sheltered accounts when using covered calls although brokerages are beginning to allow additional low risk strategies.

Conclusion:

There are many ways to make a profit in the stock market, and selling naked or cash-secured puts is certainly one of them. The risk-reward profile for covered call writing and put selling are indeed similar, however like the will versus the revocable trust analogy referenced at the beginning of this chapter, important differences nevertheless exist. Each investor must be well-informed about all strategies and approaches before deciding which road to take with his or her hard-earned money.

Test your knowledge of key points

1- True or false: When a brokerage company requires us to have the cash in our accounts to purchase the shares we may be obligated to buy pursuant to an options transaction we effected, it is now known as a naked put.

2- Some covered call writers look to purchase the underlying security at a discount by _____.

3- When a brokerage requires the investor to have 100% of the put obligation cash in his account, the investor is said to have sold a _____.

4- True or false: The put seller captures all corporate dividends distributed prior to contract expiration. _____.

5- Early assignment is a greater disadvantage for covered call writing or put selling?

6- The options strategy that most brokerages will permit in self-directed IRA accounts is _____.

Answers:

1- False- When a brokerage requires a cash balance to accommodate the possible exercise of a sold put, it is known as a cash-secured put.

2- Selling a put

3- Cash-secured put

4- False- The put seller captures no dividends but a shareholder does.

5- Put selling

6- Covered call writing

# Chapter 18

Compounding and the Time Value of Money

Chapter outline

1- The time value of money: future value and internal rate of return

2- Compounding and the Rule of 72

The time value of money

A dollar received today is worth more than a dollar received tomorrow. This simple but powerful sentence sums up the concept of the *time value of money (TVM)*. In chapter 2, I listed the reasons why I sell options. One of those motives states "You can compound your profits in a matter of minutes." This means that when the cash is immediately generated into our accounts from the sale of the call options, we can turn around and immediately reinvest these profits. The sooner we put this money to work, the wealthier we become.

Future Value and Compounding:

Future value projects what an investment will be worth at some point in the future. For example, if we invested $10,000 for 5 years with a simple annual interest rate of 5%, a $500 per year profit would be gained each year for a total profit of $2,500. The future value of the investment is $12,500 ($10,000 + $2,500). Had we re-invested the $500 profit each year, thereby compounding our money, the resulting future value would be $12,762.82. Now let's expand our time frame to 30 years. With the same 5% simple annual interest rate, our future value comes to $25,000 ($10,000 + $500 per year for 30 years). By using the power of compounding and reinvesting each $500 interest payment, the future value balloons to $43,219.42. As compounding periods increase, so do our bottom lines.

Internal Rate of Return (IRR):

IRR is a way to analyze an investment using the time value of money. It is the rate of growth a project is expected to generate. Once you know this rate, you can compare it to IRR rates on other investment opportunities, or compare it to the actual cost of borrowing money for your investment. For example, if you borrow money and pay annual interest of 6%, your investment should show an IRR a lot higher than 6%. If we were able to increase our IRR from 5% to 6% in the above example (30-year, 5% compounded investment), our future value would grow from $43,219.42 to $57,434.91. A 2% increase to 7% would result in a future value of $76,122.55. Never underestimate the power of compounding. This is why I immediately re-invest my call premiums whenever possible and my strategy philosophy is to reinvest premium profits rather than to use them to reduce my cost basis (this is a philosophical accounting issue).

Compounding and the Rule of 72

The Rule of 72 states that in order to find the number of years required to double your money at a specific interest rate, you divide the *fixed annual rate of interest or growth rate* into 72. The result is the approximate number of years that it will take your investment to double. You can also calculate the interest rate required to double your money in a given amount of time. Here is a chart showing both calculations:

Growth Rate	Time Required to Double	Calculation
4%		72/4 = 18
6%		72/6 = 12
8%		72/8 = 9
9%		72/9 = 8
10%		72/10 = 7.2 (years)
	18	72/18 = 4
	12	72/12 = 6
	9	72/9 = 8
	8	72/8 = 9
	7.2	72/7.2 = 10

Figure 130- Compounding your money

If we could achieve a conservative 2% monthly return in normal market conditions, our annual rate of return would be 24%. That means the time it takes to double our investment would be 3 years (72/24). An investment of $100,000 could grow to $1.6 million in a 12-year time frame! That demonstrates how powerful compounding can be for our financial futures.

Covered Calls vs. Treasury Notes:

Let's first state the obvious. When comparing covered calls to treasury notes, we are comparing a low-risk investment to a no-risk investment. For undertaking the low covered call risk, we will be well paid in most market conditions. Contrasting the compounding advantages of covered call writing to other low-risk investment vehicles highlights what is, in my opinion, one of the greatest benefits afforded by the covered call writing strategy. When we purchase a treasury note or bond at its face value or "par", we are guaranteed a specific interest rate, referred to as the coupon or coupon rate, which is simply the amount of interest paid per year expressed as a percentage of the bond's face value. For example, assume we purchase a bond with a face value of $1,000 and a coupon rate of 5%. Each year we will receive $50 in interest which is paid in two installments (the first $25 of this is paid after the first 6 months of the year, and the second $25 is paid six months thereafter). In contrast, when we sell a covered call option, we don't need to wait a full year to collect our premium - the option premium is instantly generated into our accounts and available for reinvestment that same day or the day following the option sale. If the cash generated from the sale of our option is not needed, it behooves us to reinvest that income and begin our journey down the lucrative path paved by the geometric progression compounding offers us.

Conclusion:

Each investment strategy has its unique advantages and disadvantages. Treasury notes, for example, are essentially riskless investments. The safety of such low risk or no risk investments, however, does not come without a price. With Treasury notes, that price comes in the form (among other things) of being unable to immediately collect and reinvest the interest you are due to receive. Essentially, you are being forced to let your interest payments sit on the sidelines for months at a time. To that end, and as the old adage goes, compounding is the eight wonder of the world. It simply makes no sense to let cash sit idle in our accounts. One of the primary advantages to writing covered calls is that it is a *low risk* strategy that allows us to generate profits *instantaneously,* which in turn affords us the opportunity to immediately reinvest, and effectively compound our profits. The earlier that money goes to work for us, the sooner we will no longer need to go to work ourselves. That is the power of compounding…the eight wonder of the world. Thus, although there is more risk associated with covered call writing when compared to investing in Treasury notes, writing covered calls is nevertheless an extremely risk-averse strategy that if executed in the proper manner, can yield significantly higher returns than most no-risk, low-risk, and even some high-risk investment strategies.

These first eighteen chapters provide you with all the information you need to become a successful covered call writer. However, to be as comprehensive and thorough as possible, I have added two more chapters that contain peripherally-related topics. Since one of the mission statements of the BCI methodology is to be as educated as possible, I am hoping that you find this subject matter interesting, enlightening and time well spent.

Test your knowledge of key points

1- The concept that encourages us to put our money to work as soon as possible is known as the _____.

2- If $5000 was invested at a simple interest rate of 10% for three years without reinvesting the interest, the future value of that investment would be _____.

3- The _____ calculates the interest rate which is the equivalent of the dollar amount your investment will return.

4- According to the Rule of 72, if we invested $50k at an interest rate of 8%, how long would it take our account to grow to $100k? _____.

Answers:

1- Compounding

2- $6500.00

3- Internal Rate of return (IRR)

4- 9 years

Chapter 19

Other Factors Influencing Stock Performance

Chapter outline

1- Company news (aside from earnings reports)

2- Market psychology

3- Key economic indicators

4- Globalization

5- Interest rates

6- Yield Curves

7- Triple and quadruple witching Friday

8- Using leading economic indicators

9- Macroeconomics

Thus far we have discussed fundamental and technical analysis, along with several common sense principles to select the best 1-month covered call candidates. Upon first glance, it would seem that we almost can't lose by following these system parameters. Unfortunately, that is not the case. As I have stated throughout this book, there IS risk in the BCI system. This risk is low, but it nevertheless exists. It is important to remember that the risk is in the stock, not in the sale of the option, and there are factors other than stock fundamentals and technicals that can impact the performance of our financial soldiers Although we don't have control over many of these circumstances, it is important to be aware of them and have a plan of action should one or more negatively impact our investment positions.

Company news other than earnings reports

Negative news can rear its ugly head at any time and have a devastating impact on our share price. In early 2010, MED was a high-flying stock, and in fact had been named the "stock of the decade" due to its incredible share appreciation. It was on my watch list and was making sensational returns for me and many other Blue Collar Investors. Then it happened! One day news came out about potential corporate fraud and the price plummeted from the mid-thirties to the teens in a matter of a few days. I rolled down (see Chapter 10 to review this exit strategy in more detail) and then converted "dead money" to cash profits. That salvaged some of my losses, but only a small percentage.

Market psychology

Some of you may remember the dot.com explosion of the late 1990s. Internet stocks went one way only...north. Investors couldn't lose, and returns of 25% per year just didn't seem quite enough! If you remember those good old days, you probably also remember when the bubble burst and the NASDAQ plummeted from 5000 to 1300 - a perfect example of greed and fear. We saw a similar scenario unfold more recently with the sub-prime real estate debacle that ultimately led to the recession of 2008. The problem, or challenge if you will, that most of us have (including yours truly) is recognizing the impact that market psychology has, and taking timely appropriate action when it rears its ugly head, either by moving into another asset class, or cash, if necessary. Major market moving events such as those noted directly above are few and far between, but they do occur, and we must be accordingly prepared to act when they do. As I write this chapter, I have moved much of my stock allocation into cash because of the effect the European debt crisis in Greece and other parts of Europe is having on U.S. markets.

Key economic indicators

These are statistics that measure current economic conditions that can assist in forecasting market trends and predicting the future profit potential of public companies. These stats are publically available on a weekly basis, and nearly every day as well. Markets react favorably or unfavorably based on their interpretation of the numbers. Here are some of the indicators that influence our equity performance:

- Inflation data
- Housing starts
- Same store sales
- Interest rates
- Bond yields
- Income statistics, hours worked etc.
- Employment statistics
- Gross Domestic Product
- Consumer Price Index (CPI)
- Producer Price Index (PPI)
- Trade deficit
- Michigan Sentiment Index
- And many more

A free site where you can access much of this information is:

http://www.money-rates.com/indicators.htm

Globalization

Our economy is no longer an entity unto itself. We are tied to the economies all over the world. The financial standing of our trading partners does matter. Currencies of other countries are important to us. A successful industrial revolution in China will bode well for corporations that may supply basic materials for their infrastructure. In my first book, *Cashing in on Covered Calls,* I alluded to the Yen Carry Trade where interest rates in Japan can impact the direction of U.S. markets. Here's an example of a "yen carry trade": A trader borrows 1,000 Japanese yen from a Japanese bank, converts the funds into U.S. dollars and buys a bond for the equivalent amount. Let's assume that the bond pays 4.5% and the Japanese interest rate is set at 0%. The trader stands to make a profit of 4.5% as long as the exchange rate between the countries does not change. Point being, the world is becoming more complex, yet it is this same growth and expansion that will give our great corporations the opportunity to expand and grow, as Blue Collar Investors all over the world take advantage of this exciting time in our history. Of course, this doesn't require each of us to become expert economists. Rather, we can glean the current status of global market conditions by diligently tuning into the nightly news, or listening to CNBC or another financial network. If there is volatility, sell in-the-money strikes for protection (I move into cash rarely and only in extreme situations). If the market is bullish and the economy is showing positive signs, look to use out-of-the-money strikes and maximize your profits. There is no need to be a rocket scientist here. We just need to be educated, non-emotional investors and prepared to act when necessary.

Interest Rates and our Stock Market Investments

Few economic indicators have a bigger impact on the stock market than interest rates, which is simply the cost of borrowing money. As general rule of thumb, interest rate hikes weaken stocks, while a decrease in rates is generally associated with a strengthening stock market. But how are interest rates determined, and why do they impact our economy and the stock market? Answers to these critical questions are contingent upon an understanding of The Federal Reserve, or the "Fed," which is the central banking system of the United States, and is empowered to set interest rates. To be a fully informed investor, one must closely follow the actions and statements of the Federal Reserve. Let's take a closer look at typical actions undertaken by the Fed, and how these actions affect the economy, the stock market, and potential for BCI investors to cash in on covered calls.

The mission of the Federal Reserve is to promote economic growth and control inflation. One of the most powerful tools used in this regard is the *U.S. Federal Reserve's federal funds rate*. This is the cost that banks are charged for borrowing money from the Federal reserve banks, and is the main way the Fed attempts to control inflation (i.e. too much money chasing too few goods). By raising the federal funds rate, the Fed attempts to lower the supply or circulation of money in the economy by discouraging borrowing and encouraging savings.

When the Fed increases interest rates:

Consumers are now paying more for credit cards and mortgage interest rates, thereby decreasing the discretionary money they have to spend. This has a negative impact on business' income and profit. Businesses themselves are affected as well, as the higher cost of borrowing discourages the same. This slows down economic growth, and results in lower corporate profits. Another negative impact that higher rates have on companies and the stock market is related to the *Discounted Cash Flow (DCF)* method of evaluating equities. Analysts determine the value of a stock by projecting its future free cash flows, and then discount those figures back to the present. If a company is seen as cutting back on its growth spending, the price of the equity will likely decline.

When we invest in the stock market, we are incurring additional risk over treasury debt investment risk (actually considered risk-free). We do so because we anticipate a *risk premium* over and above the risk-free rate of return of (let's say) treasury bills. As the risk premium decreases, investors may decide to move their capital into *substitute investments.* Rising short-term interest rates tend to push up longer-term bond yields, making these less risky investments such as government bonds more attractive. This causes investors to take their money out of stocks, which puts additional downward pressure on stock prices.

Conclusion:

When the Fed *raises* the interest rates that it lends to banks (e.g. in an attempt to control inflation), the rate hike will have a negative impact on consumers, businesses and the stock market. As we approach a rate *cut* cycle (one we are in the midst of as I write this chapter), the opposite normally holds true; that is, safer investments such as bonds and bank certificates of deposits become *less* attractive, while the higher prospective rates of return offered by stocks become *more* attractive. In Figure 131, take a look at the how interest rate cuts affected the S&P 500 from March of 2009 through September of 2009:

Figure 131- S&P 500 as of September 2009

According to S&P Equity Research, the S&P 500 returns, on average, 8.2% per year. Twelve months after a rate *cut,* this average increases to 15.5% (as can be seen in Figure 131), while the figure declines to 6.2% twelve months following a rate *hike.* This, folks, is why we watch the actions and statements made by the Fed in connection with interest rates. For current data on the fed funds target rate use the following free link:

http://www.newyorkfed.org/markets/omo/dmm/fedfundsdata.cfm

The Yield Curve

Baseball fans know all about slow curves, knuckle curves and Uncle Charlie's curve, but a sports fanatic who invests in the market should also know about *Yield Curves*. The yield curve is a line that plots the interest rates of (most frequently) three-month, two-year, five-year and thirty-year U.S. Treasury debt (bonds and T-bills). The curve is also used to predict changes in economic growth and output. Usually, short-term bonds generate lower yields to reflect the fact that they carry less risk. After all, if the economy expands, there is an expectation of increased inflation, which may cause the Federal Reserve to tighten monetary policy by raising short-term interest rates to slow economic growth. If interest rates are greater in the future, your current investments may not look so good in the present time hence the interest rate risk factor. Therefore, we would expect a typical yield curve to resemble the one depicted in Figure 132

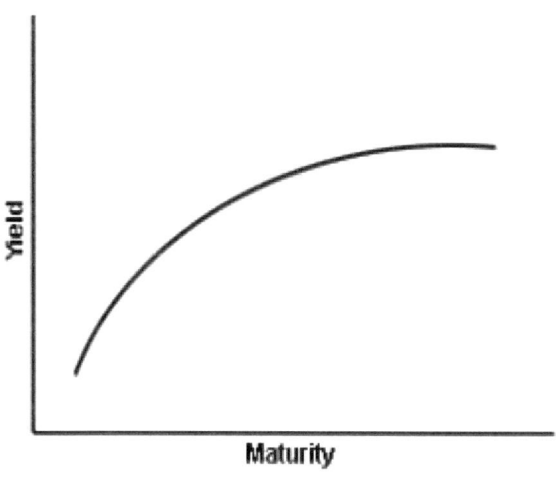

Figure 132- Yield Curve- Normal Expectation

There are, however, *several* shapes a yield curve can take. Here are some of the most important:

Normal Curve:

The normal yield curve (see Figure 132) reflects that fact that investors expect the economy to expand at normal growth rates without significant inflation or capital availability issues. This defines a period of economic and stock market expansion, which is good news for investors and economists. The yield curve slopes *gently* upward as bond (longer-term treasuries) investors demand more of a return to counterbalance interest rate risk in the future.

Steep Curve:

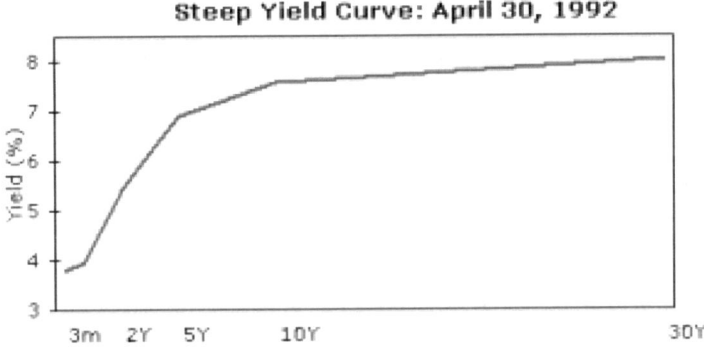

Figure 133- Steep Yield Curve- 1992

A steep yield curve results when we have a greater than normal gap or distance between the shorter and longer-term treasuries, as we did in April of 1992, depicted in Figure 133 above. A steep yield curb generally marks the beginning of an economic expansion shortly after a recession. By 1993, the GDP was expanding by 3% per year, and by the following year, short-term interest rates had increased by 2 percentage points. That's why investors were demanding greater long-term returns. Those investors who used this curve to increase their stock holdings were rewarded with a 20% return over the next two years (Russell 3000).

Inverted Curve:

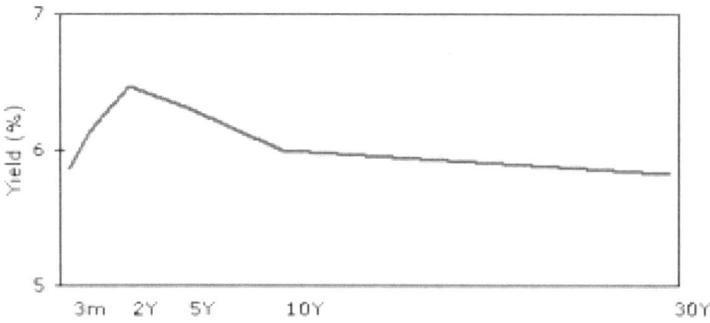

Figure 134- Inverted Yield Curve- 2000

An inverted yield curve occurs when long-term yields fall below shorter-term yields. Essentially this means that long-term investors are betting that the economy will decline in the future. The inverted yield curve has predicted a declining economy in five out of the six such instances since 1970. The Federal Reserve Bank of New York regards this yield shape to be predictive of recessions two to six quarters ahead. In short, these curves are rare, but are almost always followed by an economic slowdown or even a recession. Accordingly, stock investors should be extremely wary in the face of an inverted yield curve.

Flat or Humped Curve:

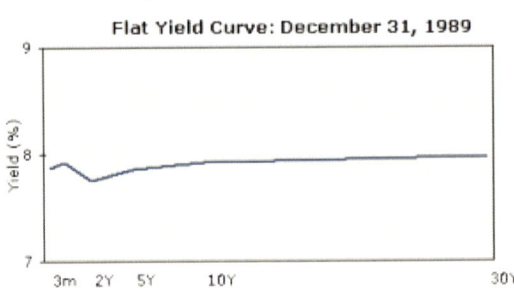

Figure 135- Flat Yield Curve-2008-09

In the case of a flat curve (shown above), all maturities have similar yields. For humped curves, short and long-term maturities are the same while intermediate maturities are higher. Humped yield curves are relatively rare. It is important to note that for a yield curve to become inverted, it must pass through this flat phase first. Now, not all flat or humped curves become inverted, but most are predictive of an economic slowdown and lower interest rates. Like inverted curves, both are red flags for stock investors.

Current Yield Curve (as of November, 2010):

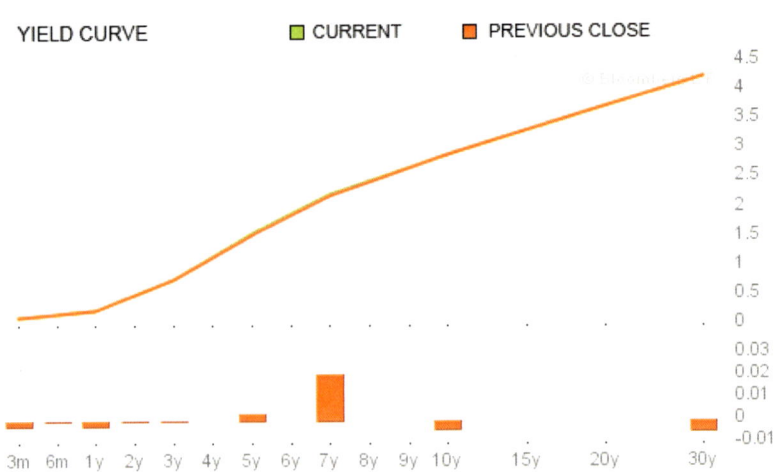

Figure 136- Yield Curve as of November 2010

Figure 136 depicts a steep yield curve which foreshadows economic expansion subsequent to the recession of 2008.

Here is a free website to access the current yield curve:

https://www.bondsupermart.com/main/market-info/yield-curves-chart

Triple and Quadruple Witching Friday

Triple Witching Friday.....what a scary term! Is it the day after Halloween? NO. Is it a hazing ritual for a college fraternity? Not even close.

Well then, what is it?

Triple Witching Friday (also referred to as *Freaky Friday*) is an event that takes place when stock index futures, stock index options and stock options all expire on the same day. *Triple witching* days occur four times a year on the third Friday of March, June, September and December. It is believed that the term triple witching originates from the three witches in Shakespeare's play *Macbeth*. More recently, single stock futures have been added to the trader's arsenal, and these securities also expire on the same four dates noted above, thereby giving birth to the term *Quadruple Witching Friday*. Because investors attempt to unwind (close out) their positions prior to contract expiration, the market can be particularly chaotic and unpredictable on these days, as market volatility and trading volume is significantly enhanced. The last hour of these trading days, from 3:00 to 4:00 PM EST, is referred to as *Quadruple Witching Hour*.

Increased volume and volatility:

Stock options that are exercised (i.e. the underlying stock is bought/sold) create large additional volume. When large volumes of stock are simultaneously unwound, there is an increase in index arbitrage (i.e. the simultaneous purchase of index futures and sale of a basket of stocks, or vice versa when the value of the index and underlying shares become "out of wack" with each other). At the same time, other investors are trying to exit their positions and/or assume different positions. There is one other reason for the increase in volatility. The composition of the Russell 2000 index, a barometer for small-cap stocks, is reconfigured each June by Frank Russell Co., which created the index. Thus, there is added trading activity in the delisted stocks (i.e. the stocks removed from the index) as well as those added to the index. Much of the latter buying and selling is the result of index funds selling the delisted equities and buying the new entries.

Conclusion:

Quadruple or Triple Witching Fridays create increased volatility due to greater trading volume and price fluctuations. This is similar in nature to the effect that earnings reports have on equity prices. Volatility means risk and we, as Blue Collar Investors do everything necessary to avoid risk. Now, I'm not suggesting that we stop selling options four months out of the year. However, wouldn't it make sense to stay in the market and opt for a *higher percentage* of in-the-money strikes during these months? This way, we will have the safety of the additional downside protection we may need if this volatility causes our shares to head south? *Whenever a contract period ends with a Quadruple Witching Friday, I tend to have a higher percentage of in-the-money strikes than out-of-the money strikes.* An exception to this guideline (or at least one that I personally adhere to) occurs when Quadruple Witching Friday coincides with an extreme bull market. The momentum of a raging bull market can mitigate the volatility risk of a triple witching Friday.

Using Leading Economic Indicators in our Covered Call Decisions

Understanding and staying current with certain fundamental economic indicators is crucial to successful covered call writing. The investment choices of nearly all successful investors are first grounded in common sense economics and an understanding of key economic indicators. A solid economic foundation also helps us avoid making poor investment choices. That said, I am entirely aware that loading this section with boring economic "mumbo-jumbo" is not the least bit helpful, nor is it useful to point you to hundreds of different economic resources, effectively making it virtually impossible to streamline pertinent key economic indicators. But wouldn't it be helpful if you could access a free, online resource that provides key economic indicators for you? If you're inclined to answer "yes" to this question, keep reading.

The S&P 500 and the CBOE Volatility Index (VIX) are great resources to gauge general market tone, as both are easily accessible and generally reliable. However, it behooves all BCI investors to keep current with more detailed, fundamental economic indicators and reports, which provide additional information that can help formulate our assessment of general market tone, and consequently, our covered call determinations relating to strike price and exit strategy decisions. Such detailed information regarding the status of the economy can be obtained by reviewing the data circulated by the *Conference Board.*

The Conference Board:

> The Conference Board (http://www.conference-board.org/) is a not-for profit (non-governmental) global business organization that disseminates objective, world-renowned economic data and analyses used by business and policy leaders across the world. More specifically, the Conference Board is responsible for publishing widely followed benchmarks called the Business Cycle Indicators, which is a composite of leading, lagging and coincident indicators used to forecast changes in the direction of the overall

economy. These indicators are composed of three indexes: the Conference Board Leading Economic Index® (LEI), the Conference Board Coincident Economic Index® (CEI), and the Conference Board Lagging Economic Index® (LAG). A brief overview of each index is instructive:

1- **Leading Indicators:** These are economic factors that change *before* the economy starts to demonstrate a particular trend. These indicators can be used to predict future behavior of our economy. The Conference Board Leading Economic Index® (LEI) is an index published by the Conference Board on a monthly basis. The LEI is widely used by economic participants to predict the short-term direction of the economy's movements. An increase in the LEI bodes well for the economy, while a decrease in this index provides a bleaker economic outlook. The LEI consists of the following 10 leading indicators:

- interest rate spread
- stock prices
- real money supply
- index of consumer expectations
- building permits
- manufacturers new orders for non-defense capital goods
- average weekly manufacturing hours
- average weekly initial claims for unemployment insurance
- manufacturers new orders for consumer goods and materials
- vendor performance

2- **Coincident Indicators:** Coincident indicators are economic factors that vary directly and *simultaneously* with the business cycle, thereby describing the current state of the economy.

The Conference Board Coincident Economic Index® (CEI) is widely used by economists and investors to determine the *current* phase of the economic business cycle, and consists of the following four coincident indicators:

- personal income
- manufacturing and trade sales
- industrial production
- employment

3- **Lagging Indicators:** Lagging indicators are economic factors that change *after* the economy has begun to follow a particular trend. Just like moving averages, lagging indicators are used to *confirm* long-term trends, but *cannot predict* them.

The Conference Board Lagging Economic Index® (LAG) consists of seven lagging indicators, and is one of the primary indexes used to confirm the direction of the economy's movements in past months. Also published on a monthly basis, the LAG is comprised of the following seven lagging indicators:

- average duration of unemployment
- commercial and industrial loans outstanding
- change in labor cost
- ratio of manufacturing and trade inventories to sales
- average prime rate charged by banks
- ratio of consumer credit to personal income
- change in CPI (consumer price index) for services

A continuing decline in these lagging indicators demonstrates a negative economic trend. For example, if the CPI (most important measure of inflation) was above expectations, it would have a negative impact on stocks and bonds.

As noted, although it is not necessary to become sophisticated economists, I believe that it is prudent to be aware of what the economic indicators are telling us so we can tailor our investment decisions accordingly. Here is a link to The Conference Board's Website: http://www.conference-board.org/

Using Our Understanding of Economics in Covered Call Writing

We now have a better understanding of economics and how to forecast potential economic trends. But what does this have to do with covered call writing? Here's my personal take on the economy and how it influences our covered call decisions: in a healthy economy, stocks are more likely to appreciate in value and we can then take a more aggressive posture with our investments. This means selling more out-of-the-money strikes and generating even higher investment returns. If we are experiencing economic woes (as we did in 2008), we either should consider moving our cash out of the market, into other asset classes such as real estate and bonds or taking a more defensive posture by selling in-the-money strikes. In a bear market, if you are not comfortable with either of the foregoing strategies and/or if all else fails, consider staying out of the market altogether to err on the side of caution. In this case you can keep your money in CDs, money markets, treasuries or other cash-equivalents.

If you were dreading reading a chapter dedicated solely to economics, hopefully this chapter has convinced you that we need not aspire to become expert economists, but having a general understanding of economic indicators and policies discussed will help us interpret key economic news, which in turn will assist us in making wiser and more informed investment decisions.

Test your knowledge of key points

1- Two of the major factors relating to market psychology that can impact the overall market are _____.

2- Inflation data, housing starts and the trade deficit are a few of the statistics that are examples of _____ _____.

3- The Yen Carry Trade is an example of how _____ can impact the US stock markets.

4- In general, when the Fed raises interest rates, it will have a _____ impact on our stock markets.

5- A _____ yield curve slopes gently upward as bond (longer-term treasuries) investors demand higher returns to counterbalance interest rate risk in the future.

6- A _____ yield curve marks the beginning of an economic expansion shortly after a recession.

7- Quadruple witching Friday marks the expiration of the following four contracts: _____.

8- _____ indicators are economic factors that vary directly and simultaneously with the business cycle, thereby describing the current state of the economy. Employment is an example.

9- Economic factors that change before the economy starts to demonstrate a particular trend are called _____, while those that tend to change after the economy participates in the trend are called _____.

Answers:

1- Greed and fear

2- Key economic indicators

3- Globalization

4- Negative

5- Normal

6- Steep

7- Stock options, index options, single stock futures and index futures

8- Coincident

9- Leading economic indicators, lagging economic indicators

Chapter 20

Related Topics of Interest

Chapter outline

1. Commingling of Asset Classes
2. Dividend Capture Strategy
3. Covered Calls to Increase Stock Value
4. Flash Trading
5. Pump and Dump Scams
6. S&P Futures and Fair Value
7. Money Market Accounts and Funds
8. Derivatives
9. Classification of Stock
10. Common Stock versus Preferred Stock
11. Dark Pools
12. CBOE Volatility Index- VIX
13. After Hours Trading
14. How our Trade Orders are Executed
15. Pinning the Strike
16. Using Covered Calls to Increase Dividend Yield

17. Inverse Exchange-Traded Funds and Covered Call Writing

Over the years, fellow Blue Collar Investors have expressed interest in subjects peripherally related to covered call writing, many of which I have addressed in my seminars and journal articles. Because one of my primary objectives when writing this book was to be as thorough and complete as possible, I decided to devote an entire chapter focusing solely on several of these topics.

Commingling of Asset Classes

Knowledge is Power. This segment demonstrates how I accumulated 1.2 million dollars worth of real estate without taking one penny from my savings account. I call this *Commingling of Asset Classes,* whereby I used my knowledge of the Stock Market and Real Estate Market to accumulate this wealth.

My story begins in 1999 when my son Craig was entering his first year at Brooklyn Law School. Looking to rent a studio apartment for him within walking distance to the Law School, I realized that it would cost the same to buy an apartment as it would to rent one. The only difference would be the down payment. Fortunately, this occurred at a time when I was honing my skills as a covered call writer. I had generated $35,000 profit at that point in time. I did this by investing $175k over an 8-month time frame. That cash was utilized as a down payment on a $90,000 co-op. Six years, one law degree, and one business degree later, that unit was valued at $350,000! During that time frame, I paid off the mortgage using the cash I generated from the sale of stock options.

Of course, the capital gains resulting form the covered call transactions and sale of the co-op left Uncle Sam hovering over my shoulders with a large empty sack labeled "Capital Gains Tax." Would I fill it for him? The answer was NOT YET! I used my knowledge of real estate investing to defer the capital gains tax.

Under Section 1031 of the Internal Revenue Code (26 U.S.C. § 1031), capital gains taxes due from the sale of an investment property may be deferred if the equity is *exchanged into another property or properties* of similar or greater value. This method of tax deferment is known as a "1031 Exchange." I did my due diligence in much the same way I do when I do when locating stocks for covered call writing, and decided to effect a 1031 Exchange by investing the proceeds from the sale of the Brooklyn co-op into three office condominiums in Austin Texas. At the time, the real estate market in Austin was smoking hot.

At this point, I owned 3 properties and still hadn't spent one cent from my savings account. But I still wasn't satisfied. I had too much cash in these properties. As a real estate investor, I normally try to limit the amount of cash I invest into each property to 20% of the total investment. I felt that if I did adequate due-diligence, each property should cash-flow (rent would take care of all expenses) with a 20% down investment. These properties had a lot more than 20% invested in them. So how was I going to get my hands on the extra cash while still deferring taxes? The answer was to refinance. Refinancing is a loan. You don't pay tax on a loan, only interest. I was able to generate $100,000 by refinancing these three properties. I put $50,000 down on a single-family home, and the other $50,000 on a residential condo. Now I own 5 properties in Austin-3 cash flowing positive covering all expenses plus generating a cash profit, and 2 that are breaking even but nevertheless appreciating in value.

Figure 137 is a flow chart which depicts how these deals specifically transpired:

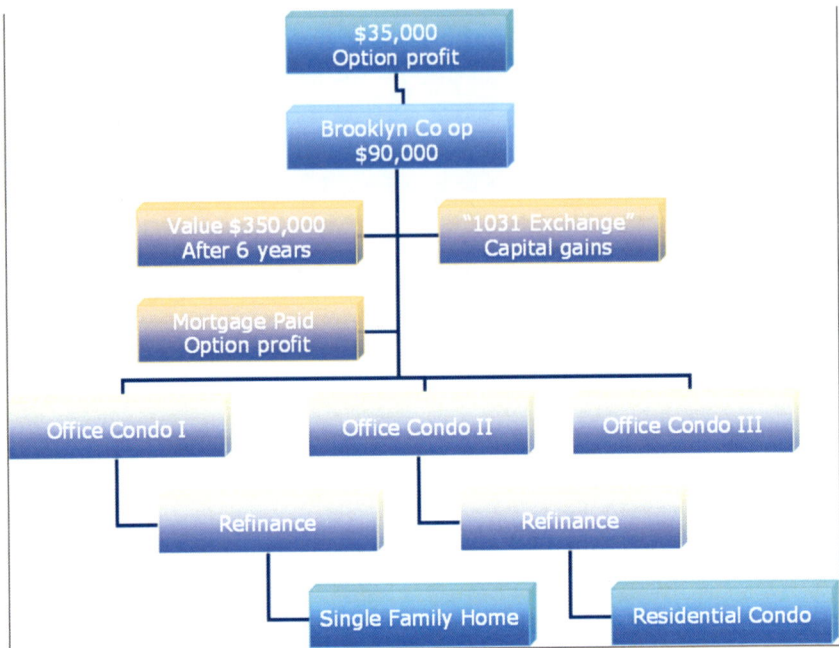

Figure 137 - Commingling of Asset Classes

The current market value of these 5 units is 1.2 million dollars, several hundred thousand of which is in real equity. Checking my savings account, I see that I still haven't taken out one penny to make these deals happen. Once the real estate market turns around (and it will eventually), I will look to do more 1031 Exchanges and continue to refinance my properties.

Knowledge is Power because it allows you to do things such as commingling asset classes, which can assist you in becoming CEO of your own money, and ultimately lead you to financial independence.

Dividend Capture Strategy

Your stock is behaving erratically and you have no clue why. You made sure to avoid the earnings report. It does not report same store monthly retail sales. The technical indicators meet the system criteria. You check the recent news posted for this equity and nothing turns up. Despite having done your due diligence, the recent chart pattern looks like a roller coaster, and volume is way up. Did this ever happen to you? What could possibly be causing this? One possibility is that your stock has fallen victim to the *dividend capture strategy.*

Definition:

> The dividend capture trading strategy is the act of buying a security for its dividend, capturing the dividend, and then selling the stock to buy another stock which is about to pay a dividend.
>
> *Key dates associated with stock dividends:*
>
> - *Dividend Declaration Date:* The date on which dividends are declared by the board of directors.
>
> - *Ex-Dividend Date:* Ex-dividend means "without dividend." Practically speaking, the ex-dividend date is the first day that the stock trades without the right to receive the current dividend that is announced by the company. On this day, the price of the stock (as of the last trade in the previous trading session) usually will be reduced by the amount of the dividend. To capture the dividend, you must purchase the stock BEFORE the ex-dividend date. If you purchase an equity one day before the ex-dividend date, and then sell the stock on the ex-dividend date, you are entitled to receive the dividend. If you purchase the stock on or after the ex-dividend date, you will not be on the company's books and records as owner of the shares, and thus will not be entitled to collect the current dividend.
>
> - *Record Date:* The date established by an issuer of a security for the purpose of determining the holders who are entitled to receive a dividend or distribution. Essentially, the record date is a cut-off date set by the company that allows it to determine which stockholders

qualify to receive the declared dividend. All investors who are official stockholders as of the record date are entitled to receive the declared dividend on the payment date. Dividend eligibility is automatic for shares purchased prior to the ex-dividend date.

- *Payment Date:* The date on which the dividends are deposited into your investment accounts or sent in the mail.

How to utilize the dividend capture strategy:

Investors start purchasing a stock after the declaration date but before the ex-dividend date. Once the dividend is captured, the *stock is held for 61 days so that the profit is taxed at a reduced 15% rate.* If the shares are sold prior to 61 holding days, dividends will be taxed as ordinary income up to 35%. After the 61-day holding period, the stock is sold and the cash is diverted to another security about to go ex-dividend.

Receive 6 dividend payments rather than 4:

Most companies pay dividends on a quarterly basis, so an investor who holds a particular stock for a year ordinarily will receive four dividend payments that year as owner of the stock. However, if we use the dividend capture strategy and assume a 61-day holding period, an investor would then generate six annual payments (365/61 = 6).

Problems with the dividend capture strategy:

- There is no guarantee that the stock price won't fall more than the amount of the dividend.

- This strategy requires you to hold the stock for 61 days after capturing the dividend in order to avoid the higher tax rate.

- The share price will go up before the ex-dividend date, and subsequently depreciate thereafter by, at least, the amount of the dividend. New buyers will not benefit from the dividend, a fact that tends to work against share appreciation. This may result in a higher buy price and lower sell price.

- Trading commissions and buy-sell spreads need to be overcome to make a profit.

Institutional investors play the dividend capture game in a different ballpark:

That's right....we play in the corner schoolyard, and the institutional investors play at Yankee Stadium. Market makers, sophisticated firms with good clearing relationships, and well-capitalized upstairs trading firms have virtually no transaction costs. As a matter of fact, many exchanges have instituted *cap fees* (i.e. a maximum ceiling on fees) that can be charged to these players to encourage them to participate in such a strategy and others. The big boys can now take a $0.31 dividend (for example), parlay that with hundreds of thousands of shares and negligible transaction costs, and make a nice profit. These institutional players also use a sophisticated options strategy to buy the shares at a lower price. By purchasing shares at a lower price and eliminating the bulk of the transaction costs, they have a much greater opportunity to succeed using the dividend capture strategy than the average Blue Collar Investor. That said, I do think that it is possible to succeed with this strategy in most bull market scenarios.

How the dividend capture strategy may effect our stock positions:

Because the institutional investors engage in this strategy by buying and selling hundreds of thousands of shares, the shares will rise in value prior to the ex-dividend date, and will decrease in value after the ex-dividend date. Subsequent to the ex-dividend date, the shares may or may not bounce back to their original price point. So if you see your stock behaving with unusual volatility, it may be the victim of the dividend capture strategy. A free website that allows you to access information on ex-dividend dates is:

http://www.dividend.com/ex-dividend-dates.php

Special dividends and option strike prices:

From time to time a company will announce a special, one-time dividend distribution over and above any regularly scheduled dividends. Such an announcement will devalue the price of the stock and the associated strike prices. For example, if a stock is trading at $30, and a one-time $.50 dividend is distributed, that stock will be worth $29.50 on the ex-dividend date. The associated $30 strike price of the corresponding option will also drop to $29.50. Note that a change in the strike price will not occur for regularly distributed dividends. For a strike to change in these circumstances, two criteria must be met:

- It must be a special one-time distribution AND
- The dividend must be for greater than 12 ½ cents

***The Blue Collar Premium Report will also provide information as to which stocks on the watch list provide dividends.

Using Covered Calls to Increase Stock Value (see also chapter 10)

If you had a $1000.00 more today than you did yesterday, is your net worth up $1000.00, or does it depend where that cash came from (this is not one of my trick questions). What if you earned it at your job? Investment income? Found it on the street? Gift from grandma? Got lucky at the casino? The way I see it, a thousand dollars is a thousand dollars, no matter the origination of that cash. The same can be said of the monetary growth of our portfolio when selling covered call options. Why just close our eyes to the option returns (great as they are) and not consider share appreciation generated by savvy execution of exit strategies? There are times during an options cycle that we can increase the value of our stock by taking advantage of the differences in the time value of options premiums from month to month. I am speaking, specifically, on or around expiration Friday when your share value is higher than the strike price, or in another words, when your short call option is in-the-money. We know that if no action is taken, our shares will be assigned and sold at the strike price. For purposes of realistically evaluating the worth of our portfolio, the shares are worth the strike price (our obligation to sell at that price) times the number of shares. Any share value above the strike price is NOT ours.

If the stock still meets all BCI system criteria (including the earnings report requirement), the next step is to do our calculations (the Ellman Calculator to the rescue). If we opt to execute a rolling out strategy, we buy back the option and sell the next month same-strike call. In this scenario, our profit or return on investment is the difference between the two premiums (i.e. the next month same strike call premium - the cost of closing/buying back the original call options sold) divided by our cost basis per contract (i.e. 100 x the strike price of the original contract). This strategy is relatively simple to understand and a big money-maker for Blue Collar Investors.

A strategy that will elevate our returns even higher is when we roll out and up, which occurs when we close (i.e. buy back) the original short options position and sell the next month's option at a higher strike price. This is a more bullish maneuver than simply rolling out, and is best utilized when market tone and stock technicals are positive. This exit strategy is also executed on or near expiration Friday when the original call option that was sold is in-the-money. The first step, closing the original options position, removes the obligation of selling the underlying shares at the original strike price. Here, there can be a small gain, or more frequently a small loss, in the option premium. However, closing the original options position is only one aspect of the "deal," as we then sell the next month's option at a higher strike price. In removing the obligation to sell our underlying shares at the original strike price and elevating that obligation to a higher strike price, we have enhanced the value of our stock to either the current market value of the underlying shares or the new strike sold, whichever is lower. This increase in equity value must be calculated into our portfolio worth, just as the $1000 in our bank account that came from good ole granny. Furthermore, if the new strike is higher than the share market value, there may be additional upside potential to sweeten the deal.

Let's clarify these comments with a real-life example taken from the option chain of SNDA as of the market close on July 2, 2009. Although there are two weeks remaining until expiration Friday, let's treat this as an expiration Friday exit strategy for purposes of this example.

- Previously purchased 100 shares of SNDA and sold the July $50 calls
- Current market value of SDNA is $53.15
- Buy-to-close the July $50 calls = $4.60
- Sell-to-open the August $55 calls = $3.80
- Option loss ($4.60 – $3.80) = (–) $0.80 = (-) $80 per contract

At this point, many covered call writers would be heading for the hills! Why lose $80 per contract? Should we be examining the deal or our heads? Let's evaluate this deal like a true Blue Collar Investor and factor in ALL facets of this strategy:

By removing the $50 ceiling on SNDA, we are allowing it to grow in value to the current market value of $53.15, thereby gaining $3.15 per share *(this technically is an unrealized gain; final calculations are made when the position is closed)* or $315 per contract....grandma just handed us all this cash - we must count it! In addition, the new ceiling is now $55, which means that our stock can potentially grow in value another $1.85 per share without restriction. Let's calculate these new improved numbers:

Loss on option premiums (from above) = (-) $0 .80 per share =

$80 per contract

Share appreciation – option loss = $315 – $80 = $235/contract

$235/$5000 = 4.7% return

Upside potential = $185/$5000 = 3.4%

POSSIBLE total profit on this deal = 8.1% (4.7% + 3.4%).

Once again, this is a bullish strategy best utilized when market conditions and stock technicals warrant a positive expectation of share appreciation.

Conclusion:

Many covered call writers buy a stock, sell the option, get down on their knees, clasp their hands and pray for positive results. Blue Collar Investors, on the other hand, manage their positions with educated, non-emotional decisions, factoring in every bit of information that others can't see. For more examples of this strategy, see Chapter 10.

Flash Trading

Generally speaking, if a limit order is routed to a particular exchange but is not marketable (i.e. cannot be executed) on that exchange, but is immediately marketable on another exchange, an SEC-mandate rule called Regulation NMS requires the exchange that initially received the order to route the order to an exchange where the order is marketable. For example, assume a limit order to buy 100 shares of XYZ at $50 is first routed to the Direct Edge Exchange, but that the best offer for XYZ at Direct Edge is $51. Because the order included the limiting instructions to buy XYZ at $50 or less, the order is not immediately marketable at Direct Edge. If, however, 100 shares of XYZ are immediately marketable at the NASDAQ (i.e. offered at the NASDAQ for $50 or less) at the time the order was entered, Regulation NMS requires the Direct Edge to route the order to the NASDAQ for execution.

Flash trading is a controversial computerized trading practice offered by some stock exchanges wherein certain traders can utilize sophisticated, high-speed technology to view orders which are about to be routed from one exchange or trading platform (where the order is not initially immediately marketable) to another venue quoting at the best price (where the order is immediately marketable). Before the order is routed to an away market, information about the order is "flashed" or displayed (typically for less than 30 milliseconds) on the initial venue's proprietary data feed to those traders who subscribe to feed. Put more succinctly, a "flash" order refers to an order that an exchange posts for a fraction of a second to a select group of traders before the order is published on a rival venue. Traders who are privy to flash order information have the advantage of recognizing market movement and sentiment before the broader market (that includes us!). Thus, one of the primary regulatory concerns in connection with flash trading is that these anointed preferred traders with ultrafast computer technology can trade ahead of these orders and artificially affect the price of a security. In other words, they will benefit from better pricing than you and me. For example, if a preferred trader sees (is flashed) a buy order for a large block of stocks he may buy "ahead" of this order benefitting from information that you and I didn't have. This is called front running and is strictly prohibited by the SEC. Many institutional investors who were benefitting (so they thought!) from Bernie Madoff's strategy concluded he was front running because they refused to believe that he was running a Ponzi scheme.

Flash orders also benefit high frequency traders who seek to profit from liquidity rebates. Many exchanges and ECNs (Electronic Communication Networks) pay liquidity rebates (about one-third of a penny per share) to traders who "post liquidity." This simply means that traders get paid to route non-marketable limit orders (orders which do not receive immediate executions) to the exchanges that offer such rebates. Because these limit orders are not immediately executed, the exchanges may post or quote these orders to the public, either as a bid or an offer. Not surprisingly, exchanges that offer liquidity rebates typically charge fees to traders who "take liquidity," or execute trades against these posted limit orders. With a flash order, a trading firm can keep its order on a certain exchange for up to half a second without matching an existing buy or sell order on another exchange, which puts it in a position of a liquidity poster rather than a liquidity taker. This dynamic boosts the chance the flash-order trader will complete the trade on the exchange and obtain the rebate before the order is routed to an away market with a better price, in which case it will likely receive an immediate execution and be considered a liquidity taker, not a poster. In the above example, there is an inquiry as to whether there is a trader willing to take the other side of the $50 trade. Perhaps there is someone who wants to "get rid" of his shares quickly and does take the other side. The poster gets the rebate, the buyer gets his price and the exchange keeps the trade at home.

The traders who put the order in allowing it to be flashed can benefit in another way other than rebates....they can send an order designed such that it immediately cancels after it is flashed, essentially guaranteeing it doesn't get executed. They do this because their computers can somehow see if there is interest in the order after it is flashed but before it is cancelled.... thus they can use the flash order as a way of gleaning market interest without risking execution.

It should now be readily apparent that traders aren't the only ones who benefit from flash trading. Exchanges and ECNs that offer liquidity rebates attract order flow from traders seeking to profit from those rebates. The more limit orders an exchange can quote in a particular stock, the tighter the bid-ask spread is for that stock. A tighter spread means better prices, and exchanges that offer better prices attract even more contra-side order flow, and thus make more money from the resulting executions. In short, exchanges and ECNS utilize flash trading to maintain or increase *market share,* something the exchanges are constantly in a vigorous battle over.

As of 2009, flash trading represented 2.8 percent of the 9 billion shares traded in the U.S. Recognizing the potential impact posed by flash trading to retail investors, Mary Shapiro, chairwoman of the S.E.C., stated "Flash orders may create a two-tiered market by allowing only selected participants to access information about the best available prices for listed securities." For these reasons, and in the wake of the recent financial crisis, in September 2009 the S.E.C. proposed banning flash trading to balance the interests of long-term investors and short-term traders. As of the penning of this article, these proposals have not been implemented, though some venues have voluntarily ceased engaging in the practice. Accordingly, it appears that one of the silver linings to come out of this sub-prime/Bernie Madoff Ponzi scheme debacle is that the SEC appears to be significantly more vigilant in protecting the rights of retail (Blue Collar) investors.

Pump and Dump Scams

I'll bet that each and every one of you has received an email that went something like this:

IMAGINE IF YOU HAD THE CHANCE TO BUY A WAL-MART FRANCHISE IN MEXICO RIGHT WHEN IT FIRST OPENED ITS DOORS, AND ALL YOU NEEDED WAS A SMALL STAKE TO GET IN.

HURRY, WE SEE THIS STOCK STARTING TO MAKE THE TURN NOW. BIG WATCH IN EFFECT FOR NOVEMBER, 15TH, 2009!!!!

What a great guy this must be to send me this information and to be so concerned about my financial well-being! The truth is that this email is a classic example of bait for a *pump and dump* scam.

Pump and Dump definition:

This is a form of microcap (companies with under $250 million in market capitalization) stock fraud which attempts to artificially pump up the price of an equity through false, misleading, or exaggerated statements. The perpetrators of this scheme, who already have a position in the stock, dump their securities after the hype has caused a higher share price. The victims then lose a considerable portion of their investment as the price subsequently plummets.

Perhaps that fellow who sent the email wasn't such a nice guy after all!

In the past, pump and dump schemes were initiated through cold calling, but the internet has opened the door for a new breed of fraudsters. The internet provides a cheaper, easier and faster avenue by which these scammers can reach huge numbers of unsuspecting victims. We must not let greed and temptation overtake our sense of reality. We know how to locate great investment opportunities through fundamental and technical analysis. This is a far superior approach than listening to "some guy" who we never met.

Oftentimes these scams take on multi-level, more sophisticated formats. There can be email and telemarketing campaigns supported by newsletters highlighting the company as a "hot stock pick." Chat rooms are flooded with pleas for investors to "hurry-up and buy this red-hot stock." Give me a _____ break (feel free to fill in the blank).

Why Micro Caps?

Pump and dump scams work best with small, thinly traded companies called "penny stocks." These are equities that trade at a low price (under $5 per share) and have a small market capitalization (# of outstanding shares x share price), generally under $250 million. Micro cap stocks usually trade over-the-counter through pink sheets and bulletin boards, and are considered high risk due to their lack of liquidity, large bid-ask spreads, and limited analyst following and disclosure. There is also a class of even smaller companies called *Nano Caps* which have market capitalization under $50 million.

Impact on crooks and victims:

It is estimated that 15% of spam email messages involve pump and dump scams. Spammers can make a quick 6% return, while victims typically lose 5% of their investment within 2 days, and could very well lose all of the money they invested. The SEC regards this problem as one of the most common investment frauds perpetuated over the internet. Accordingly, pump and dump schemes have encouraged the development of software programs designed to locate spammers before they hurt hard-working investors. John Stark, the head of internet enforcement at the SEC, put out the following statement: "This is basic lying, cheating and stealing, and the message to anyone engaging in these shenanigans is they are going to get caught."

Painting the Tape:

This is a related illegal action taken by some market manipulators wherein they buy and sell securities amongst themselves to create artificial trading activity which is then reported on the ticker tape. Unsuspecting investors may falsely perceive the seemingly high volume of activity as institutional interest and take positions in the stock. The fraudsters then sell their own stock after the price of the stock is artificially inflated, while the unsuspecting retail investors take the hit. The SEC is all over this one as well.

Conclusion:

Forget about that Wal-Mart in Mexico and let's stick to our system of fundamental and technical analysis to locate our investment candidates. This will protect our hard-earned money and force those con artists to get real jobs, just like the rest of us.

S&P Futures and Fair Value

You turn on CNBC early one morning:

The S&P Futures are UP 5 points.....GREAT!!!!!!!!!!

Fair Value is + 10.......what's that mean?

The market is expected to open DOWN…….ughhhh……why?

To understand how this works, we need to first understand the relationship between a financial index (in this case the S&P 500) and its index futures:

The S&P 500 Index- This is an index of 500 stocks chosen for market size (large cap), liquidity and industry grouping. It is one of the most commonly used benchmarks used to gauge the overall status of the U.S. stock market.

Index Futures- Index futures are contracts that specify a future date of delivery of the underlying shares (in the S&P 500 index). Buying or selling a futures contract represents a bet on the future direction of how an index will behave over time. Its value fluctuates according to what traders are willing to pay for it. The futures for the S&P 500 and the actual S&P 500 are NOT the same thing. Since stocks historically rise in value (although you couldn't tell that from the debacle of 2008!), *the futures lead and are generally higher than the actual index itself.* Index futures expire quarterly (March, June, September and December) and are usually quoted (price, date, volume, open interest etc.) in reference to the next expiring futures contract The most active trading occurs in the near-month contract.

Fair Value- Fair value reflects the relationship between the futures contract (expected value of the index in the future) and the *present value* (or current *cash value*) of the index. It is relationship between the futures contract on a market index and the actual value of the index. If the futures are above fair value then traders are betting the market index will go higher, the opposite is true if futures are below fair value. When calculating fair value, investment banks and brokerages must also factor in the *borrowing costs* to own all the stocks in the index, as well as the *dividends* that are NOT received by those who own the futures contracts. For example, if the fair value is calculated at +5, the futures contract needs to be 5 points above the cash index's (S&P 500) close the previous day to be at its fair value relationship to cash. If it is, then the present value and future value are equal, and traders are not expecting any change in the market value of the index. However, if the futures are trading above the fair value of +5 before the market opens, stocks are likely to open higher. Fair value does not change during the course of a day, only day-to-day.

Hypothetical Example:

- The S&P 500 *Index* closes Monday at 1000 (4PM, EST)

- S&P *futures* closed at 1005 (9:15 AM)

- *Fair value* after factoring in borrowing costs and lost dividends, was calculated to be 1010, or + 5.

- On Tuesday morning when futures ended their overnight trading (9:15 AM, EST), the price was at 1015, or 5 points higher than their fair value relationship to cash value of the S&P 500 index. This indicates a higher market open. Had the futures ended their overnight trading at 1005, or 5 points lower than fair value, a lower opening would have been anticipated.

Program Trading:

When the spread is greater or lesser than fair value, institutional computerized programs kick in to buy or sell stocks. If the spread or premium of futures as it relates to cash (S&P 500 Index) is greater than fair value, the market will see a higher open. If the spread is lower than fair value, the market will open down. These programs are automatic and will quickly diminish the difference between the actual spread and fair value. This will create temporary volatility in the market, which will quickly calm down. Program trading is one of the reasons that *I do not like to trade early in the trading day*...there is simply too much potential volatility.

Arbitrage:

Fair value also has relevance during the trading day when both the S&P 500 index and the futures trade simultaneously. The two normally trade in a fair value relationship, but when there is a discrepancy, arbitrage traders jump at the opportunity to take advantage of the temporary difference. For example, if the futures are trading above the fair value to the S&P index price, a trader can sell the contract and then buy it back when it returns to the normal relationship. The trader profits in the difference between the sale and buy-back prices.

Conclusion:

Understanding the concept of fair value as it relates to S&P futures and the index itself should not influence stock or option selection. However, it does help us understand the driving forces behind a market open, and also assists us in differentiating *program trading* from *panic selling* and *buying sprees,* which are driven by business and/or market conditions. It will also give some meaning to that screen on CNBC we have been staring at in the morning for all these years.

Money Market Accounts and Money Market Funds- Where is Your Money Going

So you have a *money market account* and invest in a money market fund. You feel that your money is safe and you can access it quickly, but the interest rate is nothing to write home about. Unfortunately, this is about the extent of the knowledge many retail investors have about these money market instruments. As educated Blue Collar Investors, we need to explore this subject in greater detail.

The *money market* is a segment of the financial market where businesses, institutional investors, and the U.S. Government meet to buy and sell highly liquid (easy to buy and sell), short term debt securities. The money supply is controlled by the Federal Reserve Bank which buys and sells certain negotiable securities.

Retail, Blue Collar Investors can only participate in the money market *indirectly* by investing in a money market fund established by broker-dealers, or by saving in a pension fund that purchases money market instruments. This is because it takes huge sums of money to enter this market.

Money Market Savings Account:

A money market savings account is a bank liability. We deposit our cash in the bank and the bank owes us money. This money is not specifically aligned with any particular assets that the bank invests in, but rather, is simply an obligation owed by the bank. The risk, therefore, is with the bank (over and above any insurance that is applicable) and nothing else. However, much like checking accounts, money market savings accounts are insured by the FDIC. There is usually a limitation on the number of transactions that can be made in a money market savings account, in addition to a minimum balance that must be maintained. From the bank's perspective, our money is used to provide loans to other bank clients. The interest rate the bank charges for these loans is higher than the interest paid to us in our money market savings accounts, which is how the bank realizes a profit.

Money Market Fund:

A money market fund is a mutual fund in which investors acquire shares in the fund itself, not the underlying assets. These shares are maintained in $1 denominations. Based on the returns that the fund is earning, interest is paid in the form of additional $1 shares. If we write a check for $1000 to redeem fund equity, the fund simply sells 1000 shares. Money market funds provide investors with a safe place to invest easily accessible cash-equivalent assets characterized as a low-risk, low-return investment. For this reason, money market funds are required by law to diversify in low-risk securities such as US Treasury bills and commercial paper. Unlike a money market savings account at a bank, money market funds are not federally insured. Accordingly, when investing in a money market fund, the risk lies in the actual assets, not the bank or brokerage behind these funds. Money market funds hold 26% of mutual fund assets in the U.S. because of the low-risk, high liquid nature of this investment vehicle.

Assets in a Money Market Fund:

1- *Commercial Paper*- Unsecured, short-term debt (promissory notes) issued by corporations and banks. Commercial notes mature in 270 days or less, and are usually issued by highly regarded firms with outstanding credit ratings.

2- *Jumbo CDs*- Also called *negotiable certificates of deposit,* a jumbo CD is a certificate of deposit with a minimum denomination $100,000, though amounts of one million or more are not atypical. Money market managers are particularly fond of jumbo CDs.

3- *Banker's Acceptances*- A banker's acceptance is a promised future payment (time draft), written by a business and guaranteed by its bank. Essentially, a banker's acceptance constitutes the bank's obligation to pay the draft writer's bills from a specified creditor when the bills are due. In essence, the bank is lending money to the business to pay its creditors. Banker's acceptances are usually used in financing the import, export, transfer or storage of goods, and are traded in the secondary market at a discount from its face value. Banker's acceptances are considered low-risk investments that are similar to T-bills, and accordingly, are often used in money market funds.

4- *Repurchase Agreements (Repo)* - This is where the seller of a debt security (usually a Treasury security) agrees to buy the security back within a short time frame for a specified amount. The buyer makes a profit by setting the "sell-back" price higher than the original purchase price.

Conclusion:

The money market world is a relatively safe haven for our money which allows us easy access to our cash. In return for our money, money market savings accounts and funds offer us a slightly higher interest rate than a typical savings or checking account, but a much lower rate than that offered by higher risk investments (e.g. stocks and corporate bonds). We can put our funds in a money market savings account backed by a particular bank and insured by the FDIC, or into a money market fund which is backed by the actual assets purchased by the fund. The concept of asset allocation and diversification makes money market investment vehicles a viable option in our overall portfolio. Bear in mind, however, that placing too much money into such accounts/funds will unnecessarily expose us to the prospects of inflation (e.g. earn 2% interest, but the costs of goods increase by 3%), a decrease in purchasing power, and opportunity risk (money lost by not investing in other, higher-yielding investments).

Derivatives

All center fielders are baseball players, but not all baseball players are center fielders. In much the same way, stock options are derivatives, but not all derivatives are stock options. A derivative is a financial instrument whose value is "derived" from the underlying asset. It is a contract between two or more parties whose value is determined by fluctuations in the value of that asset. The most common of these underlying assets (upon which derivatives are based) are stocks, bonds, currencies, interest rates, commodities and market indexes.

Types of Derivatives:

Option Contracts- a contract that gives the owner the *right*, but not the obligation, to buy or sell a security or an index (basket of securities) at a certain price within a specified time frame.

Futures Contracts or Futures - A contract that *obligates* one to buy or sell a particular commodity or financial instrument at a pre-determined price in the future. This market is regulated by the *Commodity Futures Trading Commission*. Futures contracts may require the actual delivery of the underlying asset, while other future contracts are settled in cash. Futures can be used to hedge or speculate on the price movement of the underlying asset. For example, a farmer expecting a crop of 50,000 bushels of corn may opt to hedge his position by selling 10 futures contracts (5,000 bushels/contract) to "lock in" the current price.

Swap- A swap is a contract in which two parties agree to transfer risk through the exchange of periodic payment streams. For example, a fixed interest rate may be exchanged for a floating interest rate. In addition, maturities may be traded in a swap agreement, or stock and bond qualities can be exchanged based on new investment objectives. This market is UNREGULATED and is traded off-exchange in the over-the-counter (OTC) market.

Types of Derivative Traders:

1- *Hedgers-* These investors have a cash position in a commodity or an equity and protect themselves against an adverse price change by purchasing an offsetting position. An example is the "corn crop" example I gave above where a farmer expecting a crop of 50,000 bushels of corn may opt to hedge his position by selling 10 futures contracts (5,000 bushels/contract) to "lock in" the current price. Similarly, an owner of a stock who buys a put will give him the right to sell the stock at a certain price even if the market value is much lower.

2- *Speculators-* Speculators are investors who have no interest in the underlying commodity, but will accept the risk the hedger is reducing FOR A PRICE. They assume this higher risk level in order to profit from an anticipated price movement. Speculators also provide liquidity for hedgers. Speculators earn a profit when they offset futures contracts to their benefit. To do this, a speculator buys contracts then sells them back at a higher (contract) price than that at which they purchased them. Conversely, they sell contracts and buy them back at a lower (contract) price than they sold them. In either case, if successful, a profit is made.

Covered Call Writers- Both Hedgers and Speculators:

That's right. We are so special that we can be both a hedger and a speculator in the same investment. When we purchase an equity, we are speculating that the price of the stock will maintain or achieve a certain level so as to generate a profit. The risk is in the stock price falling to the point where we begin to lose money. For this reason, we have a complete set of exit strategies in place and ready to activate if required (see Chapter 10 for details on various exit strategies). We then hedge this speculative position by selling the call option, which creates downside protection. The protection for the position, in general, is the premium generated from the sale of the option. There is, however, another form of protection that can be used with the covered call writing strategy. Specifically, the time value of the option premium itself can be protected by selling *in-the-money* strikes. In these cases, the intrinsic value of the premium protects the time value and therefore our profits. This essentially serves as "insurance" which is *paid for by the option buyer.*

Conclusion:

All options are derivatives, but not all derivates are options. Derivative contracts are bought and sold by both hedgers and speculators. We, as covered call writers, are actually both hedgers and speculators, which is the reason covered call writing affords us the opportunity to generate outstanding returns with minimal risk.

Classification of Stock

Small cap stocks, defensive stocks, cyclicals, income stocks..... enough already, I'm getting a headache! These are terms bandied about on CNBC like a tennis ball at a Federer-Nadal final. We've all heard the terms, but do we know what they mean? Getting to know these phrases and their potential impact on our portfolios is the objective of this segment.

Stocks are often classified into broad categories that have similar investment characteristics. Some are based on industry affiliations, while others are based on size or other financial characteristics of the companies. Below is a list of the most important classifications that I feel is important to know and understand.

Market Capitalization:

This categorizes a stock according to the value of all the company's outstanding common shares, known as *market capitalization,* or "market cap." To calculate a company's market cap, multiply the number of outstanding common shares by its current price. For example, if BCI Corp. has 1 million shares of outstanding common stock priced at $30 per share, its market cap is $30 million. Here are the main categories for market capitalization:

- Ultra-Cap: More than $50 billion
- Large-Cap: More than $10 billion
- Mid-Cap Stocks: Between $1 billion and $10 billion
- Small-Cap Stocks: Less than $1 billion
- Micro-Cap Stocks: $250 million and less
- Nano-Cap: Less than $50 million

Large-cap stocks are *usually* blue chip companies (see below) that are major businesses and have a large segment of market share. Mid-cap companies are usually growth companies on their way to becoming large cap, and perhaps even blue chip companies. Small and micro-cap companies are usually growth companies with aggressive marketing plans, and are generally considered riskier, but potentially more lucrative investments than companies with a higher market capitalization.

Blue-Chips:

Blue chip companies are large-cap companies. They have a reputation for great management, a rich history of profits and dividends, and are traded on the NYSE and other major exchanges. Examples of blue-chip companies are American Express, Coke, and Disney.

Growth Stocks:

Growth stocks represent companies whose sales and earnings are growing faster than the economy or their individual sector. They tend to reinvest a majority of their earnings to allow for further expansion (R&D, or research and development) and therefore pay little to no dividends. Although considered riskier than other stocks, growth stocks offer greater potential for capital appreciation.

Income Stocks:

Income stocks pay greater than average dividends to their shareholders. These companies are usually stable, have gained a large market share, and can afford to heavily reward their shareholders via dividend payments. Historically, public utility companies have been considered income stocks.

Defensive Stocks:

These companies tend to be stable all year around (even in a recession) and provide important goods and services that are used in all economic times. Products and services typically provided by companies that are considered defensive stocks include food, drugs, cosmetics, and electric power and gas. These stocks will decline less in an economic downturn but also appreciate less when the market is strong. Examples would be Coca Cola and General Electric.

Cyclical Stocks:

Cyclical stocks are associated with prices that tend to rise and fall with fluctuations in the general economy. They produce products that consumers tend not to buy during difficult economic times. Examples of such products include steel, automobiles, and building materials. Cyclical stocks differ from blue-chip stocks in that they cut or eliminate dividends during an economic downturn.

Emerging Growth Stocks:

These companies are in the early stages of development. They usually are small or micro-cap companies offering new products or services. Emerging growth stocks are considered extremely volatile and risky.

Penny Stocks:

Penny stocks are low-priced, speculative stocks that sell for less than $5 per share. They do not trade on the major exchanges such as the NYSE or Nasdaq. Stay away!

American Depository Receipts (ADRs):

American Depository Receipts are receipts for shares of a stock of a foreign company which have been deposited in a U.S. bank. Its purpose is to facilitate the trading of foreign securities in the United States. Investors can purchase shares and receive dividends in U.S. dollars using these receipts, thereby eliminating the need to exchange currencies. American Depository Receipts allow U.S. investors to diversify their portfolios internationally without having to use foreign markets.

Conclusion:

All Blue Collar Investors are aware of the need to be educated. Knowing the category of a particular equity, the current status of the business cycle, and market conditions in general is critical to our success. Company information can be obtained directly from your brokerage account. Simply go to company profile and then look for the corresponding company information. Information on the health of the economy and the current business cycle can be obtained directly from the Conference Board's website:

http://www.conference-board.org/

Common Stock vs. Preferred Stock

We've all heard the terms common and preferred stock. Does the term "common" connote shares best suited for retail, Blue Collar Investors like us, while "preferred" indicates shares likely to be owned only by the Wall Street insiders? Not exactly. Let's clarify the difference between these two forms of stock.

Definitions:

Common Stock- Common stock is a security that represents ownership in a corporation. Owning common stock allows an investor to elect members of the Board of Directors and vote on corporate policy. Common stock is the first type of stock a corporation issues. In other words, not all corporations issue preferred stock.

Preferred Stock (also called "preferreds") - Preferred stock represents a class of ownership in a corporation that affords its owner a higher priority to claims on a company's assets than the priority afforded by common stock. Owners of preferred stock are usually entitled to dividend payouts *before* dividends are paid to common shareholders, (that's us), however such owners do NOT have standard voting rights. Additional differences exist in that preferred stock contains characteristics of both debt (fixed dividends) and equity (appreciation potential). More specifically, preferred shares are established by companies that already have common shares, and are intended for investors who are more interested in income than capital appreciation- the same type of investors who may otherwise purchase bonds. Despite these standard differences between preferred stock and common stock, it is important to note that *the structure of preferred stock is specific to each corporation.*

Advantages of Common Stock:

- Voting rights
- Outperform bonds and preferred shares in the long run
- Easy to manage without an expert
- Can be used for covered call writing
- Free information is easily accessible

Advantages of Preferred Stock:

- Preference over common shareholders in receiving dividends

- Preference over common shareholders with liquidation rights
- Dividend rights are often cumulative (if unpaid one year, it is made up at a later date)
- Most have a negotiated fixed dividend amount
- Many have a convertible feature, wherein they can be traded for common shares
- Good compromise between common stocks and bonds
- Most trade in round lots of 100 shares on the NYSE and NASDAQ, and thus are considered liquid. (Not as liquid as common stock, but liquid nonetheless)
- Tax advantages- preferred stock is currently taxed at 15% (as opposed to ordinary income), part of Bush tax reduction

Disadvantages of Preferred Stock:

- Minimal voting rights (only in unusual circumstances like a merger)
- Callability- most preferrreds can be called at a specified price after a certain date, which may leave us looking for a replacement investment in a declining interest rate environment
- Interest rate risk- the value of preferred stock will rise and fall with changes in interest rates, similar to the behavior of longer-term bonds
- Credit risk- if a company's fundamentals decline, an issuer may eliminate a preferred dividend before defaulting on debt

Practical Application:

It is relatively easy to access both fundamental and technical information when evaluating common shares. This is not the case with preferred shares. First of all, there is no official preferred stock rating system as there is with bonds. You need to ascertain if the company is financially healthy and where it stands with respect to cash. This will help determine your risk. We need to know that it has the cash to pay us those dividends. To ascertain this information, we look at the company's financial ratios, such as the *interest coverage ratio*. This will tell us how easily a company can pay interest on outstanding debt. A free site that will give some information related to this subject is:

www.quantumonline.com

In addition, preferred shares are generally associated with symbols that are tricky and data that is difficult to locate. Moreover, many brokers do not have specialized expertise with respect to investing in preferred shares. For most retail investors interested in investing in preferred shares locating a broker knowledgeable in this arena may be the safest route to take. Schwab (www.schwab.com) has a good reputation in this regard.

Conclusion:

One of the mission statements of Blue Collar Investing is to be (more than) well-informed before investing your hard-earned money. Whether you are writing covered calls, purchasing preferred shares, equities or bonds, you must know and understand the product and the associated risks. Covered call writing is my passion, however preferred shares do offer a hybrid investment between stocks and bonds that may be appropriate for some investors.

How to locate a list of preferred stock from the IBD website:

IBD- Get Preferred Stock List

1- Go to IBD Homepage (www.investors.com)

2- Look to "My Routine" Box on upper right

3- If "other IBD data" is not in this box, click on "modify"

4- Move "other IBD data" from "categories box" to "my routine" box

5- Click on "other IBD data"

6- Click on "futures options and other data"

7- Scroll down to list of preferred stock

8- Use the magnifier at the top toolbar to increase the size of the print (I use 400x)

Dark Pool Liquidity- Secrets of the Institutional Investors

What is the single most important factor in determining whether you should buy a particular stock? If you posed this question to a room full of investors, you would get a myriad of different responses:

- The fundamentals.
- The technicals.
- The uniqueness of the product or service.
- Research and development.
- The management team (and the list goes on…)

For me, there is only one answer, and it's so simple I'm reluctant to state it. But here it is anyway: *Are institutional investors buying this stock?* It is the institutional investors, not you and me, who move the price of an equity north or south. Such institutional investors include mutual funds, hedge funds, and money managers of banks, insurance companies and pension funds.

So how do we find out what these "big boys" are up to? One way would be to surreptitiously sneak into their board room meetings and listen in. However, this approach is illegal and may require the use of Woody Allen eyeglasses with the furry eyebrows and big noses. Another method is to check out the price charts of that security... technical analysis. If we see an uptrending moving average with confirming technical indicators, we know that these players are taking positions in this stock, and the momentum will be in our favor to join the party.

In order for us to feel confident in this approach (i.e. buying stock based on what the institutional investors are buying), there needs to be transparency and accuracy in the prices and volumes reported. This is not an issue with the major exchanges, however there is a hidden world of investing, called *dark pools*, that may be skewing the numbers and effecting our investment decisions.

What are dark pools? :

Dark pools is a slang term that refers to non-displayed liquidity sources that by definition do not publish quotes initially. Dark Pools primarily function to provide large institutional investors with a crossing system that allows them to trade blocks of shares without revealing themselves to the open market and exposing themselves to the attendant risks of front-running, shadowing and other forms of price disruption. The bulk of dark pool liquidity is represented by block trades (10,000 shares or more, not including penny stocks) facilitated away from the major exchanges. As indicated, "dark pools" are referred to as such because details of the trades are concealed from the public, clouding the transactions like murky water. Details of the trade are printed to the tape once the execution occurs. In essence, dark pools bring together buyers and sellers behind closed doors. Trades that are executed in dark pools are considered legal and necessary for the health of the market because of the liquidity provided , but do bring up concerns for average Blue Collar Investors should the percentage of dark pool trades rise.

Why institutional investors prefer dark pools:

Huge trades can be made without institutional investors tipping their hands as to the actions which they say, can affect prices. In other words, if an institutional investor wants to execute a large block of shares at a certain price, his quote would ordinarily be published on the major exchanges such as the NYSE and the NASDAQ. Other institutional investors who subscribe to these exchanges data feed would then be able to see the quote, and would enter their own quotes in the same stock to "go along for the ride," or in other words, in anticipation of the large price movement that will likely be associated with the large order. If however, the institutional investor places the large order in a dark pool, his or her quote is not displayed, which increases his chances of executing his entire block of shares at the desired price. In other words, by placing the order in a dark pool, the institutional investor decreases the chances that additional institutional interest will increase or decrease the price of a stock before his or her order is fully executed at the desired price.

Who runs the dark pools?

Dark pools are run by brokerage firms such as Goldman Sachs and Fidelity Capital Markets, as well as brokers and firms. There are currently over 40 dark pools. When the smoke clears, nearly 20% of Big Board stocks change hands in the dark! Because the New York Stock Exchange is losing market share to these dark pools, it is taking action. In a joint venture with BIDS Holdings(a dark pool owned by the major Wall Street firms), the NYSE is luring back these block trades - the large transactions this exchange once dominated by allowing hidden prices. In the past, floor brokers at the NYSE never fully displayed the real interest.

Who is watching out for us retail investors?

As of May, 2009 James Brigagliano, co-acting director of the SEC's Division of Trading and Markets, was apparently watching our backs. In a May 21, 2009 article published by *Traders Magazine,* Mr. Brigagliano stated that dark pools could impair price discovery by drawing valuable order flow away from publically quoting markets, and "could adversely affect the execution quality of those market participants who display their orders in the public markets." Mr. Brigagliano added that this could harm price discovery and exacerbate short-term volatility. Another concern noted by Brigagliano relates to the enhanced automation of market orders between dark pools which "could create the potential for significant private markets to develop that exclude public investors."

There is much the SEC does not know about the dark pool business. The regulatory agency has no numbers of its own on the size of the dark pools, and instead relies on industry reports (uh oh!). What does this mean for us?

In my view, dark pools are not yet a cause for concern for us retail investors, however the situation does bear monitoring. That dark pools garner approximately 20% of the trading volume does in fact seem to benefit the institutional investors, but to date, have not appeared to have a major impact on us as our executions have been better than ever. After the recent hits the SEC has taken (remember Bernie Madoff?), the agency appears to be all over this issue. The SECs director of trading and markets, Erik Sirri, has stated that if the volume flowing to dark pools were to become much larger (over 30% of the total according to analysts), regulatory intervention may be warranted.

All we ask in this David and Goliath world of Blue Collar Investors trading alongside Wall Street Insiders is a fair chance, a level playing field. I believe that such a playing field does exist. This is not to say, however, that we shouldn't closely monitor the world of dark pools to ensure this level playing field continues to exist.

The CBOE's Volatility Index (VIX)

Determining market tone before making any investment decisions is a theme consistently discussed throughout all my books and seminars. One of the primary tools that can be used to determine market tone is a volatility index. There are three variations of volatility indexes: the VIX, which tracks the S&P 500; the VXN, which tracks the Nasdaq 100; and the VXD, which tracks the Dow Jones Industrial Average. The VIX, the most commonly used index of the three, is also the most useful in this author's opinion, and accordingly will be the focus of this section.

The VIX is the ticker symbol for the Chicago Board Options Exchange (CBOE) Volatility Index, which is a measure of the implied or expected volatility of the S&P 500 options over the next 30 days. This implied volatility is reflected in the premiums paid for the options. The VIX is constructed using the implied volatilities of a wide range of S&P 500 index options. This volatility is meant to be forward looking and is calculated from both calls and puts. The VIX is a widely used measure of market risk, and is often referred to as the *investor fear gauge*.

The VIX is a useful indicator for short-term investors, including 1-month covered call writers. Generally speaking, as market volatility increases market pricing will diminish, and vice-versa. The VIX is said to have an inverse relationship with the S&P 500. If we see a declining VIX, or one that is remaining stable at a low level (below 30% implied volatility), along with an appreciating S&P 500, we have a favorable environment for selling covered call options. Figure 138 depicts the inverse relationship between the VIX and the S&P 500 over a 3- month time frame:

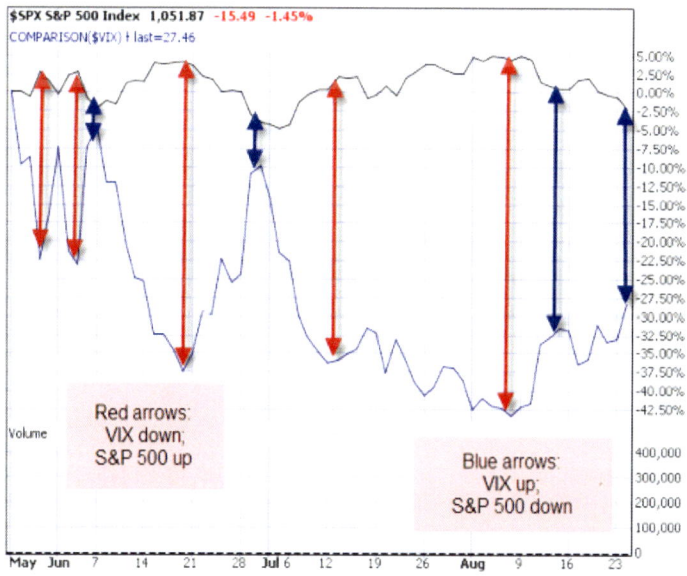

Figure 138- The VIX versus the S&P 500

The red arrows in Figure 138 highlight areas when the VIX was declining while the S&P 500 was simultaneously appreciating. The blue arrows demonstrate the exact opposite scenario. Although a clear inverse relationship between the VIX and S&P 500 (such as that depicted in Figure 138) will not be present 100% of the time, generally speaking we can obtain information from studying these indexes that will help guide us in our investment decisions, such as strike selection for example. The more bullish these charts appear, the more likely we are to sell out-of-the-money strikes. Like all other technical tools, the VIX should be used in conjunction with other fundamental, technical and common sense indicators.

After Hours Trading

It's 4 PM EST and the bell rings on the New York Stock Exchange marking the end of the trading day. As we watch CNBC, Bloomberg or Fox Business News we see the tickers till scrolling at the bottom of our TV screens! What's up with that? The New York Stock Exchange and the Nasdaq Stock Market—the highest volume market centers in the U.S. today—have traditionally been open for business from 9:30 a.m. to 4:00 p.m. EST. Although trading outside that window—or "after-hours" trading—has occurred for some time, it used to be limited mostly to high net worth investors and institutional investors.

But that changed by the end of the last century. Some smaller exchanges now offer extended hours. And, with the rise of Electronic Communications Networks, or ECNs, everyday Blue Collar Investors can gain access to the after-hours markets. Before you decide to trade after-hours, you need to educate yourself about the differences between regular and extended trading hours, especially the risks. While after-hours trading presents investing opportunities, there are also the following risks for those who want to participate:

- Inability to See or Act Upon Quotes. Some firms only allow investors to view quotes from the one trading system the firm uses for after-hours trading. Check with your broker to see whether your firm's system will permit you to access other quotes on other ECNs. But remember that just because you can get quotes on another ECN does not necessary mean you will be able to trade based on those quotes. You need to ask your firm if it will route your order for execution to the other ECN. If you are limited to the quotes within one system, you may not be able to complete a trade, even with a willing investor, at a different trading system.

- Lack of Liquidity. Liquidity refers to your ability to convert stock into cash. That ability depends on the existence of buyers and sellers and how easy it is to complete a trade. During regular trading hours, buyers and sellers of most stocks can trade readily with one another. During after-hours, there may be less trading volume for some stocks, making it more difficult to execute some of your trades. Some stocks may not trade at all during extended hours.

- Larger Quote Spreads. Less trading activity could also mean wider spreads between the bid and ask prices. As a result, you may find it more difficult to get your order executed or to get as favorable a price as you could have during regular market hours.

- Price Volatility. For stocks with limited trading activity, you may find greater price fluctuations than you would have seen during regular trading hours. News stories announced after-hours may have greater impacts on stock prices.

- Uncertain Prices. The prices of some stocks traded during the after-hours session may not reflect the prices of those stocks during regular hours, either at the end of the regular trading session or upon the opening of regular trading the next business day.

- Bias toward Limit Orders. Many electronic trading systems currently accept only limit orders, where you must enter a price at which you would like your order executed. A limit order ensures you will not pay more than the price you entered or sell for less. If the market moves away from your price, your order will not be executed. Check with your broker to see whether orders not executed during the after-hours trading session will be cancelled or whether they will be automatically entered when regular trading hours begin. Similarly, find out if an order you placed during regular hours will carry over to after-hours trading.

- Competition with Professional Traders. Many of the after-hours traders are professionals with large institutions, such as mutual funds, who may have access to more information than individual investors.

- Computer Delays. As with online trading, you may encounter during after-hours delays or failures in getting your order executed, including orders to cancel or change your trades. For some after-hours trades, your order will be routed from your brokerage firm to an electronic trading system. If a computer problem exists at your firm, this may prevent or delay your order from reaching the system. If you encounter significant delays, you should call your broker to determine the extent of the problem and what you can to get your order executed. [4]

How our trade orders are executed

Once we type our order from our computer into our online discount broker, there are a series of events that take place

[4] The information used in connection with this discussion on after-hours trading was extracted directly from the Securities Exchange Commission's website, located at http://www.sec.gov/investor/pubs/afterhours.htm.

Related Topics of Interest | 435

which lead to the successful execution of the trade. Here's how it works:

1- We place our trade order with our online discount broker.

2- The broker then utilizes an *electronic routing system* to send the order to a *market maker,* such as Citi, UBS and others.

3- The market maker pays our discount broker a fee for this order flow, generally about $0.01 or $0.10 for 100 shares.

4- The actual shares (assuming you placed a buy order) can come from one of several sources:

- *Internalization-* from the market makers own inventory
- The major exchanges like the NYSE and Nasdaq
- *Dark Pools*, such as Liquidnet (see discussion on dark pools earlier in this chapter).

How Market Makers Profit- The Math:

Let's say the market maker sells us a stock short at $30.10, and buys it a few seconds later for $30.09 for a profit of $.01 per share, or $1.00 for 100 shares. Since the market maker paid our online discount broker $0.10 for the order flow and garnered $1 in profit, that's a $0.90 profit for the transaction. It may seem like a mere bag of shells at first glance, but done millions of times per day, market making can become an extremely lucrative occupation.

"Pinning the Strike": Manipulation or Market Forces?

Definition and background

There is a tendency for stocks to close very close to a strike price when there is a large open interest on expiration Friday.

For example, if a stock is trading near its $50 strike and also has huge open interest, it will oftentimes get "pinned" at $50 on expiration Friday as traders unwind their positions. This is called "pinning the strike." This has everything to do with the *Max Pain Theory*, which states that the underlying security will tend to move towards the price where the greatest number of options contracts (in dollar value) will expire worthless. In other words, it is the point where option owners feel the maximum pain and option sellers capture the greatest reward.

Theories as to the cause of pinning

1- Conspiracy theory:

The conspiracy theory states that market makers use their immense firepower to manipulate share prices to close at the strike price, thus enabling them to capture the maximum profit as options expire worthless. In my view, it would take an immense conspiracy by the most powerful of institutional investors to accomplish this, which would also have to go undetected by the recently improved vision of the regulators. I give little or no credence to this point of view.

2- Dynamic hedging by institutional traders who are seeking delta-neutral trades:

Okay, we're going to need some review of definitions here, so brew up a mug of high-octane coffee…I'll wait for you…….

Take a sip, here we go!

- **DELTA-** Ratio amount that an option value will change for every $1 change in the underlying security. Call options have deltas between 0 and 1. Put options have deltas between 0 and (-) 1. For example, if a call or put option has a delta of .5, it will rise or fall $0.50 for every $1 change in the price of a stock. If a stock goes up $1, a call option will rise by $0.50 and a put option will fall by $0.50. As a call option nears expiration Friday it will approach a delta of 1.00 and a put option will approach a delta of (-) 1.00.

- **DELTA NEUTRAL**- This is a portfolio consisting of positive and negative delta positions which balance out to bring the net change to zero. Institutional traders use delta neutral positions to eliminate risk from their positions.

- **GAMMA**- This is the rate of change of delta with respect to a $1 change in the underlying security. It is a second generation delta, if you will. Long calls and long puts always have positive gammas, while short calls and short puts always have negative gammas. A positive gamma means that the delta of a long call will become more positive and move toward +1.00 when the stock prices increase, and become less positive and move toward 0.00 when the stock price declines. Similarly, a positive gamma also means that the delta of long puts will become more negative and move toward −1.00 when the stock price falls, and less negative and move toward 0.00 when the stock price rises. The reverse is true for a short gamma. For example, assume the BCI March 50 call has a delta of +.45, and the BCI March 50 put has a delta of -.55, with the price of BCI at $48.00. The gamma for both the BCI March 50 call and put is .07. If BCI moves up $1.00 to $49.00, the delta of the BCI March 50 call becomes +.52 (+.45 + ($1 x .07), and the delta of the BCI March 50 put becomes -.48 (-.55 + ($1 x .07). If BCI drops $1.00 to $47.00, the delta of the BCI March 50 call becomes +.38 (+.45 + (-$1 x .07), and the delta of the BCI March 50 put becomes -.62 (-.55 + (-$1 x .07).

- **HEDGING**- A type of transaction that limits investment risk with the use of derivatives, such as options or futures contracts. Hedging transactions involve the purchase of opposite positions in the market in order to ensure a certain amount of gain or loss on a trade. Portfolio managers and institutional investors utilize various hedging strategies to reduce portfolio risk and volatility,

438 | Complete Encyclopedia for Covered Call Writing

	A	B	C	D	E	F	G	H	I	J
1		CALL		PUT		TRADER	TRADER	ACTION TO HEDGE		
2		DELTA		DELTA		POSITION	POSITION			
3						CALL	PUT	CALL		PUT
4										
5	STOCK									
6	PRICE	UP		DOWN		LONGER	SHORTER	SELL SHARES		BUY SHARES
7	RISES									
8										
9										
10										
11										
12										
13	STOCK									
14	PRICE	DOWN		UP		SHORTER	LONGER	BUY SHARES		SELL SHARES
15	FALLS									
16										
17										
18										

Figure 139- Stock movement and delta- hedging chart

Influence of gamma

Pin pressure comes from "gamma traders" attempting to remain delta neutral. Since gamma (rate of change of delta for every $1 change in the stock price) increases as we get closer to expiration Friday, traders tend to buy and sell many more shares of stock to stay delta neutral and ensure minimal risk exposure.

Example

- BCI Corp. is trading at $50 per share

- The dealer (market maker) is long 100 x $50 calls, which have a delta of .50 and a gamma of .14. This means that the delta will change by .14 for every $1 change in share price.

- The dealer is also long 100 x $50 puts which has a delta of (-) .50 and a gamma of .14. Once again, the delta will change by .14 for every $1 change in share price.

- The dealer is currently delta neutral: (100 calls x .50 delta) + (100 puts x (-) .50) = 0. (Take another sip!)

- If the stock moves up $1, the new delta position will be 28 (100 calls x .64) + (100 puts x (-) 36) = 28 (call and put delta move up by .14)

- As a result of this $1 increase in share price, the dealer must sell 2800 shares of BCI Corp. to remain delta neutral

To roll or not to roll

If your stock is trading just under the strike price of the call we initially sold as 4 p.m. approaches on expiration Friday, and it meets the criteria for potential pinning, consider rolling the call position if your decision is to keep this stock for the next contract cycle.

Conclusion

The evidence suggests that pinning is a real phenomenon and unique to high open interest options on expiration Friday. Pinning is impacted by the normal hedging forces used by institutional traders to eliminate risk from their portfolios.

Using Covered Calls to Increase Dividend Yield

Innovative investors can develop ideas of implementing a strategy in unconventional ways. For example, we can invest in a money market or CD and perhaps not even beat the inflation rate. We can buy a quality bond and wait six months to receive our first (ho-hum) return. Covered call writers can invest with 1-month options and generate returns of 2-4% in normal market conditions while incurring some risk in the process (remember, the risk is in the stock, not in the sale of the option). Can we incorporate covered call writing and dividends to generate returns somewhere in between the two strategies? We are Blue Collar Investors, so of course we can! Let's buy a stock that we have confidence in and sell an option, which will decrease our cost basis thereby increasing our returns.

The covered call/dividend capture strategy

- Buy a high-dividend yield stock
- Sell a long term (LEAPS- an option with an expiration of 9 months or more) **deep in-the-money** call option to reduce cost basis
- Increase the dividend yield and create downside protection

Stock requirements

- Must be a candidate for a long-term holding
- Must have options
- Must have LEAPS
- Must provide a dividend yield that meets your goals

Procedure

1- Once we have located a stock that has met our requirements, we must look for the dividend and yield information. A good FREE site where this can be found is www.finance.yahoo.com. As shown in figure 140:

GlaxoSmithKline PLC Common Stoc (NYSE: GSK)			
REAL-TIME 38.07 ↓ 0.06 (0.16%) 10:28AM EST			
Last Trade:	37.96	Day's Range:	37.93 - 38.08
Trade Time:	10:14AM EST	52wk Range:	32.15 - 42.10
Change:	↓ 0.17 (0.45%)	Volume:	271,576
Prev Close:	38.13	Avg Vol (3m):	2,439,360
Open:	38.07	Market Cap:	96.61B
Bid:	37.95 x 600	P/E (ttm):	36.93
Ask:	37.96 x 1300	EPS (ttm):	1.03
1y Target Est	43.34	Div & Yield:	2.03 (5.30%)

Figure 140- Dividends and yields information

For GSK, the dividend is $2.03 per year, and the annual yield is 5.3% based on current market price of $38.07. Dividend yield information for stocks passing the BCI screens can be accessed from the premium report as shown in the yellow-highlighted area in figure 141:

Running List	Next ER Date	Industry Segment	Segment Rank	Beta	% Div. Yield	Comments
PASSED PREVIOUS WEEKS & PASSED CURRENT WEEK							
RL (2)	05/25/11	Apparel	A/A	1.21		
AVGO (2)	05/26/11	Chips	A/B	1.04	0.90	
SMTC (6)	05/26/11	Chips	A/B	1.05		
ULTA (6)	06/02/11	Retail	A/B	1.13		
NVLS (1)	07/12/11	Chips	A	1.27		
PLCM (3)	07/15/11	Computer	B/C	1.14		
CMG (44)	07/20/11	Retail	B/C	0.97		
TPX (7)	07/20/11	Consumer	A/A	1.39		
TSCO (4)	07/20/11	Retail	B/B	1.08	0.80	
UNH (2)	07/20/11	Medical	A/A	0.81	1.00	
CHKP (1)	07/21/11	Software	C	0.88		
NFLX (6)	07/21/11	Leisure	B/B	0.41		
XLNX (1)	07/21/11	Chips	A	1.05	2.10	
ATHN (1)	07/22/11	Software	A	1.22		
BCR (2)	07/22/11	Medical	A/A	0.63	0.70	
INFA (14)	07/22/11	Software	A/A	1.04		
RVBD (1)	07/22/11	Computer	B	1.51		
UTEK (5)	07/22/11	Chips	A/A	1.30		
DHX (4)	07/27/11	Internet	B/B	1.56		
ICON (2)	07/27/11	Apparel	B/B	1.39		
ILMN (4)	07/27/11	Medical	A/A	0.86		
BMC (1)	07/28/11	Software	A	1.03		
CERN (2)	07/28/11	Software	A/A	0.85		
NUS (1)	07/28/11	Consumer	A	1.22	1.40	
SRCL (7)	07/28/11	Machine	B/B	0.75		
TLEO (4)	07/28/11	Software	A/A	1.47		
VIV (1)	07/28/11	Telecom	C	1.03	7.80	
HS (9)	07/29/11	Medical	A/A	1.13		
LZ (1)	07/29/11	Chemical	A	1.17	1.10	
SHOO (3)	07/29/11	Apparel	B/B	1.35		
TLCR (4)	07/29/11	Medical	A/A	0.21		
ENDP (7)	07/30/11	Medical	A/A	0.81		
COH (2)	08/02/11	Apparel	A/A	1.31	1.00	

Figure 141 - Dividend yield and the Premium report

The column highlighted in yellow shows the dividend yield for a running list in a premium report.

2- Once we have decided on an equity, we need to access an option chain and check the premiums for long-term deep in-the-money calls as shown in figure 142:

Options   Get Optio

View By Expiration: Feb 11 | Mar 11 | May 11 | Aug 11 | **Jan 12** | Jan 13

Call Options   Expire at close Friday, January 20, 2012

Strike	Symbol	Last	Chg	Bid	Ask	Vol	Open Int
22.50	GSK120121C00022500	16.40	0.00	15.40	15.60	30	10
25.00	GSK120121C00025000	13.90	0.00	12.90	13.10	200	57
27.50	GSK120121C00027500	11.40	0.00	10.50	10.70	200	44
30.00	GSK120121C00030000	8.20	↓0.20	8.10	8.30	8	398
32.50	GSK120121C00032500	6.10	0.00	5.90	6.10	40	326
35.00	GSK120121C00035000	4.20	0.00	4.10	4.30	37	1,144
37.50	GSK120121C00037500	2.85	0.00	2.70	2.80	100	333
40.00	GSK120121C00040000	1.75	0.00	1.65	1.75	136	3,997
42.50	GSK120121C00042500	0.95	0.00	0.95	1.05	50	927
45.00	GSK120121C00045000	0.50	0.00	0.50	0.60	3	2,060
47.50	GSK120121C00047500	0.25	0.00	0.25	0.35	30	263
50.00	GSK120121C00050000	0.15	0.00	0.10	0.20	12	521
55.00	GSK120121C00055000	0.10	0.00	N/A	0.10	2	234
60.00	GSK120121C00060000	0.05	0.00	N/A	0.05	0	48

Figure 142- Options chain for deep in-the-money calls

As depicted in the options chain directly above, the January 2012 $25 call option is highlighted in green (this options chain was current as of February 2011). Accordingly, we can generate $12.90 per share, or $1290 per contract, by selling this option.

3- Calculations

Calculations before covered call writing:

$2.03/$38.07 = 5.3%

Calculations after covered call writing:

By generating $12.90 per share, we are reducing our cost basis to $25.17. Our new equation is:

$2.03/$25.17 = 8.07% (slightly lower if the option is exercised and we sell for $25).

Increase in returns:

8.07% - 5.3% = 2.77%

2.77%/ 5.3% = 52% increase

Advantages of this strategy

- Superior yields (+2.77% or 52%)
- Downside protection (from $38.07 to $25)
- Immediate cash flow + dividends
- You know maximum profit and breakeven
- Can implement exit strategies if needed
- Deep in-the-money strikes have high deltas because option value will decline dollar-for-dollar with the stock price decline
- Less time required to monitor positions
- Dividends can be increased, thereby increasing the yield even more

Disadvantages of this strategy

- No upside potential if stock price accelerates
- You can lose money if the stock drops more than the premium and dividends collected
- May be taxed at the unqualified rate. Check with your tax advisor
- Assignment risk because of deep in-the-money calls
- Must own securities through earnings reports
- Lower yields than selling 1-month options
- Dividends can be decreased or eliminated, thereby decreasing our yields

- If the time value of the option is less than the dividend, your option may be exercised prior to the ex-dividend date, which would require you to sell your underlying shares. In this scenario, you will not lose any money, however you will not generate any additional income from the position. The cash can then be used to enter a new position. Let's explore this possibility of early assignment in more detail:

Early Exercise of Calls for Dividends

When using this strategy we want to avoid early exercise of the option. When is it likely that the option holder will exercise the call option (we sold) early to capture a dividend? This will impact investors who have sold deep-in-the-money LEAPS on high dividend yield stocks to lower the cost basis and therefore increase yield. First let's recall the equation for the value of a call option:

$$\text{Call value} = \text{intrinsic value} + \text{time value}$$

This can be redefined as follows:

Call value = intrinsic value + interest rate value + volatility value − dividend value

Considerations just prior to the ex-dividend date (evaluating the possibility of early exercise):

Let's assume a stock is trading AT $50, and will go ex-dividend by $2 the next day. Assume further that there is a $40 call about to expire in 10 days that has a theoretical value of $10 and a delta of 1. Therefore, the stock and the option have similar characteristics. In this scenario, here are the three primary courses of action to consider just prior to the ex-dividend date:

1- *Hold the option and take no action:* Here, the stock will open

$2 lower because of the dividend deduction. The option will open at $8 since the delta is 1 and this is the new parity price. This approach will guarantee a loss of $2, clearly not a good choice for near-term options. Holders of LEAPS may opt for this choice since there is a long time frame until expiration.

2- *Exercise the option:* With this course of action, we buy the stock for $40, and lose $2 when the stock goes ex-dividend. However, we also receive the dividend because of our share ownership. This is clearly better than choice #1, as we break even rather than lose $2.

3- *Sell the option and buy the stock:* If the option is trading at parity (equal to the intrinsic value), this is the same as choice #2. If the option is trading for more than parity, let's say $10.25, we will generate an additional $0.25 per share, making this third choice the best one of the three.

Conditions for early exercise (rolling our option may avoid early exercise when these criteria are identified):

1- *The option must be trading at parity:* If the option is trading at more than parity, the option holder should sell the option and purchase the stock at its current market price. Most deep-in-the-money calls will be trading at parity.

2- *The option must have a delta close to 1*: This will ensure that the option and the stock have the same characteristics so that we are not losing out on any time value. In our example, if the call holder feels that there is a chance that the stock value can drop below $40 prior to expiration, he or she would prefer to hold the call, as the potential loss would be limited to the call premium. Holding a long stock on the other hand, can result in a much greater potential loss. If the option's delta is close to 1, there is almost no chance that the stock will drop below the strike price. Here is a breakdown of the parameters to consider:

- A delta of 1 will almost definitely be exercised

- A delta above .95 has a high probability of exercise

- A delta below .95 is unlikely to be exercised.

3- *Volatility considerations:* Options in low-volatility markets are exercised more frequently than those in high-volatility markets.

4- *Time to expiration considerations:* With all other factors being equal, the delta will rise as we approach the expiration date. This will increase the chance of early exercise. Those selling deep-in-the-money LEAPS to increase dividend yield may want to consider rolling the call option as the delta approaches .95.

Accessing delta information:

- Go to www.cboe.com

- Quotes and data

- Delayed quotes

- Enter ticker and get quote (right side of page)

- Select "options"

- Chain type- calls

- Chain type- all

- Expiration- enter LEAPS date

- Click on "view chain"

- Click on strike desired

- The next page will show delta stats

Strategy objective

Try to sell an option that will bring the cost basis down to as close to the strike price as possible. For example, if a stock trades at $38 and you can sell the $25 call for $13, we have an ideal scenario when using deep in-the-money LEAPS to increase dividend yield.

Conclusion

Selling deep in-the-money call options will enhance the dividend yield and provide downside protection.

Inverse Exchange Traded Funds and Covered Call Writing

In Chapter 11 we discussed exchange-traded funds and touched upon leveraged and inverse funds. Inverse ETFs use derivatives to bet against the direction of financial markets. These are known as short or bear ETFs and will make money if markets decline in value. They will lose money, however, if markets move against the bet. <u>Covered call writers who have a bearish market outlook may find these funds useful</u>.

Many sophisticated covered call writers can benefit from the use of inverse ETFs *in the short run when the market is bearish*. Over the long haul, shorting the market is NOT a sound strategy.

Advantages of Inverse ETFs over short selling:

- Retail investors can use these products to short the market without being required to achieve shorting privileges which usually will not be granted to retail investors
- There are no margin requirements as there are with traditional shorting
- The loss potential for shorting is unlimited (the underlying can appreciate exponentially) but limited to the initial

investment for Inverse ETFs

- Costs (interest) associated with short-selling are avoided
- Some funds include professional management which will assist less experienced investors

Disadvantages of Inverse ETFs over short selling:

- ETF share prices may not be exactly correlated to the underlying benchmark which may result is lower-than-anticipated returns
- As a general disadvantage we must re-tool our thinking to make decisions when to enter and exit our positions as we have been trained to look for positive market movers

Inverse ETFs (non-leveraged) that follow closely watched indexes (Figure 143 below):

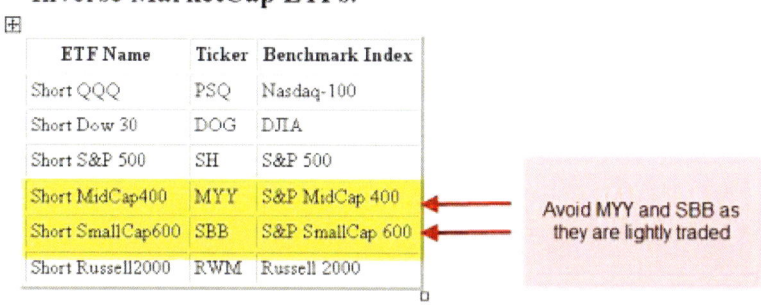

Figure 143- Inverse ETfs

Recent short and long-term performance of Inverse ETFs:

Since the market historically appreciates in value in the long run, this is a short-term strategy that must be monitored carefully. Let's first view a 1-month comparison chart of the four selected Inverse Funds compared to the S&P 500 as of 6-9-11:

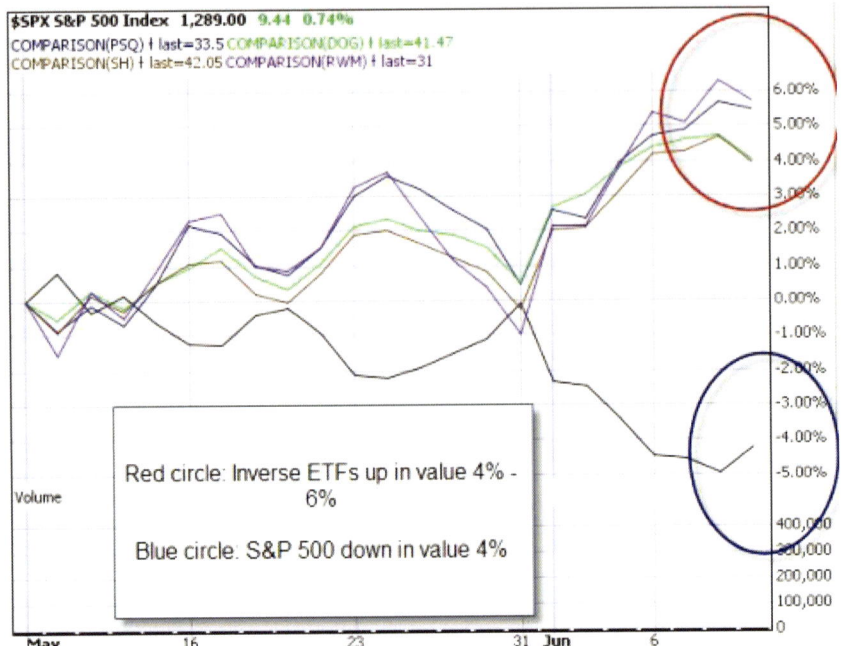

Figure 144: 1-month chart of Inverse ETFs vs. S&P 500

Now let's compare to a 1-year chart:

Related Topics of Interest | 451

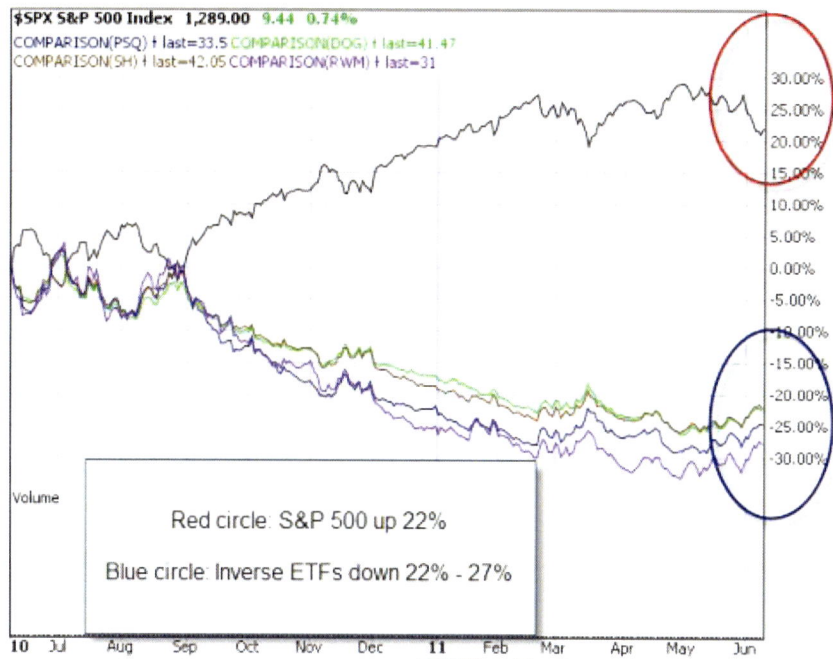

Figure 145: 1-year chart of Inverse ETFs vs. S&P 500

These two charts demonstrate how both beneficial and risky Inverse ETFs can be.

Options chain for Inverse ETF RWM:

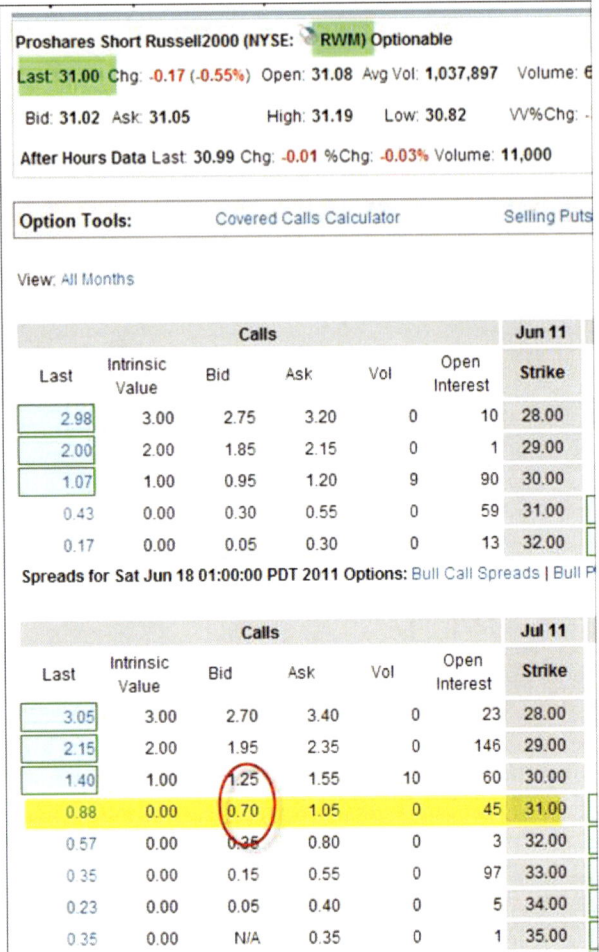

Figure 146: RWM options chain

The 5-week return for the at-the-money $31 call is $70/$3100 = 2.3%

Conclusion: The use of Inverse ETFs by experienced covered call writers in the short-term can be a way of enhancing returns in bearish market conditions.

Test your knowledge of key points

1- Using proceeds from one asset class within a portfolio to support or enhance another asset class within that same portfolio is called_____.

2- The _____ is the act of buying a security for its dividend, capturing the dividend, and then selling the stock to buy another dividend which is about to be paid.

3- To capture dividend yields utilizing covered call writing, you must purchase the stock BEFORE the _____ date.

4- _____ will generally devalue BOTH the price of the stock and the associated strike prices.

5- Rolling up from an in-the-money strike will result in an _____ capital gain until the position is closed.

6- _____ is a computerized trading practice offered by some stock exchanges, wherein high-speed technology allows certain traders to view orders fractions of a second before others in the marketplace.

7- Pump and dump scams tend to target companies with market capitalizations between _____ and _____. These companies are called _____.

8- _____ is an illegal trading practice wherein market manipulators buy and sell securities amongst themselves, creating artificial trading activity which is then reported on the ticker tape.

9- _____ are receipts for shares of the stock of a foreign company that has been deposited in a U.S. bank. Its purpose is to facilitate trading in foreign securities in the United States.

10- _____, also called _____, is a class of ownership in a corporation that entitles its owner to a higher claim on the assets and earnings than common stock. These securities contain characteristics of both debt (fixed dividends) and equity (appreciation potential).

11- _____ is a term that refers to non-displayed liquidity sources that by definition do not publish quotes initially.

12- The _____ is the ticker symbol for the Chicago Board Options Exchange (CBOE) Volatility Index, which is a measure of the _____ of S&P 500 options over the next 30 days.

13- The inability to see all quotes, the lack of liquidity, and larger quote spreads are a few of the risks involved in _____ on electronic communication networks (ECNs).

14- When market makers provide shares to us from their own inventory, this process is known as _____.

15- The tendency for stocks to close very close to the strike price of an option that has large open interest on or near expiration Friday is known as _____. This has everything to do with the _____, which states that the underlying security will tend to move towards the price where the greatest number of options contracts (in dollar value) will expire worthless.

16- To increase dividend yield on a stock utilizing covered call writing, we must buy a stock with _____ options and sell a _____ strike with a _____ expiration date.

Answers:

1- Commingling of asset classes

2- Dividend capture strategy

3- ex-dividend

4- Special one-time dividends (A change in strike price will not occur for regularly distributed dividends)

5- Unrealized capital gain

6- Flash trading

7- 50 million, 300 million, micro caps

8- Painting the tape

9- American depository receipts, or ADRs

10- Preferred stock, or "preferreds"

11- Dark pools

12- VIX, implied volatility

13- After-hours trading

14- Internalization

15- Pinning the strike, Max Pain Theory

16- LEAPS, deep in-the-money, long term

Appendix I

Master Figure List of Charts and Graphs

Figure #	Title	Chapter
1	Market condition	2
2	Mutual fund performanc	2
3	S&P 500- short term char	2
4	S&P 500- long term char	2
5	Option symbolog	2
6	Risk-reward profile of stock ownershi	2
7	Risk-reward profile of unmonitored call	2
8	Risk-reward profile of monitored call	2
9	Peg ratio information	3
9a	Location of MAR and OBV in Stock reports	3
10	Line chart	4
11	Candlestick line	4
12	Candlestick chart	4
13	OHLC bar	4
14	ANR- candlestick chart	4
15	ANR- bar chart	4
16	Simple vs. exponential moving averages	4
17	EMAs: short vs. long term	4
18	Support chart	4
19	Resistance chart	4
20	Uptrending price pattern	4
21	Uptrending moving average and support	4
22	Support and resistance	4
23	MACD- basic chart	4
24	MACD- positive divergence	4
25	MACD- bullish moving average crossover	4
26	MACD- positive centerline crossover	4
27	MACD vs. histogram	4
28	Stochastic oscillator	4
29	Stochastic oscillator- buy/sell signals	4
30	Volume confirmation chart	4

31	Volume divergence/trend reversal	4
32	Setting up a technical chart	4
33	Positive technicals	4
34	Mixed technicals	4
35	Weekly stock screen and watch list	4
36	Watch list of stocks	5
37	Watch list of options	5
38	Spreadsheet of options sold	5
39	Premium report/ stock screen	5
40	Premium report/running list	5
41	Efficient frontier	5
42	The option chain	6
43	Technical chart for PZZA	6
44	Strike selection for HITK	6
45	Ellman Calculator- single tab/ HITK	6
46	Ellman Calculator- single tab/ HITK - results	6
47	Ellman Calculator- Intro tab	6
48	Ellman Calculator- Single tab- info in	6
49	Ellman Calculator- Single tab- results	6
50	Ellman Calculator- Multiple tab	6
51	Ellman Calculator- What now tab- info in	6
52	Ellman Calculator- What now tab- results	6
53	PRGO gaps up	6
54	PRGO options value	6
55	PRGO options chain	6
56	Elite Calculator- Unwind tab- info in	6
57	Elite Calculator- Unwind tab- results	6
58	BUCY- technical chart	6
59	BUCY- options chain	6
60	BUCY- Ellman Calculator	6
61	Elite Calculator- Info tab	6
62	Elite Calculator-Entry tab D2	6
63	Elite Calculator- short-term profit	6
64	Elite Calculator- Entry tab D3- info in	6
65	Elite Calculator- Entry tab D3- results	6
66	Elite Calculator- Entry tab D4- info in	6
67	Elite Calculator- Entry tab D4- results	6
68	Theta- 1 month chart	7
69	Delta for 1-month options	7
70	Delta vs. strike price	7
71	NETL- price	7
72	NETL- options chain	7

73	NETL- Ellman Calculator- info in	7
74	NETL- Ellman Calculator- results	7
75	Expiration cycles	7
76	Open interest and volume	7
77	Mathematics of open interest	7
78	Non-standard options	7
79	RVBD- hold through ER	8
80	Banned stocks	8
81	Cash allocation	8
82	Stock purchase form	8
83	Trade execution activity	9
84	Call option trading form	9
85	Net debit combination form	9
86	Net credit combination form	9
87	Protective put- the collar	9
88	Time decay of options	10
89	Rolling down example	10
90	Hitting a double with BCSI	10
91	Convert dead money to cash profit	10
92	PRGO gaps up	10
93	PRGO- increase in option value	10
94	PRGO- option chain to unwind	10
95	Ellman Calculator- unwind PRGO	10
96	Ellman Calculator- unwind results	10
97	BUCY- technical chart	10
98	BUCY- options chain	10
99	BUCY- Ellman Calculator	10
100	BCSI gaps down	10
101	BCSI after gap down	10
102	BCSI options chain	10
103	BCSI vs. the S&P 500	10
104	Rolling out	10
105	Rolling out with LULU	10
106	LULU- earnings report date	10
107	LULU- buy-to-close options chain	10
108	LULU- sell-to-open options chain	10
109	LULU- Ellman Calculator- enter info	10
110	LULU- Ellman Calculator- results	10
111	Rolling out and up- O-T-M	10
112	Rolling out and up- I-T-M	10
113	Multiple exit strategies with NAV	10
114	Early assignment options chain	10

115	BXM vs. the S&P 500	11
116	Top performing ETFs vs. the S&P 500	11
117	Cash allocation for ETFs	11
118	XLY options chain	11
119	Multiple tab of the Ellman Calculator- ETFs	11
120	Premium Report for ETFs	11
121	FAS- leveraged ETF chart	11
122	FAZ- leveraged ETF chart	11
123	SHOO chart after stock split announcement	12
124	SHOO options chain	12
125	SHOO pre and post-split	12
126	Citi chart- reverse stock split?	12
127	INTC deep in-the-money calls	15
128	INTC out-of-the-money calls	15
129	Margin calculator	15
130	Compounding your money	18
131	S&P 500 and interest rates	19
132	Normal yield curve	19
133	Steep yield curve	19
134	Inverted yield curve	19
135	Flat yield curve	19
136	Yield curve in August of 2009	19
137	Commingling of asset classes	20
138	The VIX and the S&P 500	20
139	Stock movement and delta- hedging chart	20
140	Locate dividend yield information	20
141	Premium report- dividend yield information	20
142	Options chain for LEAPS	20
143	List of Inverse ETFs	20
144	Inverse ETFs vs S&P 500: 1-month chart	20
145	Inverse ETFs vs S&P 500: 1-year chart	20
146	Inverse ETF option chain example	20
147	Sample 1-month Profit & Loss Form	Appendix VI
148	Technical analysis chart and terms	Appendix X
149	Flow Chart I- Fundamental Analysis	Appendix XI
150	Flow Chart II- Technical Analysis	Appendix XII
151	Flow Chart III- Exit Strategies	Appendix XIII
152	Flow Chart IV- Expiration Fridays	Appendix XIV
153-156	Mean Analyst Rating (MAR)	Appendix XV
157-160	On Balance Volume (OBV)	Appendix XVI

Appendix II

My First Book, Cashing in on Covered Calls

Table of contents

Preface ix

Acknowledgements xv

THE BASICS OF SELLING COVERED CALL OPTIONS 1

    1 Why Sell Options? 3

    2 The Three Golden Rules 9

    3 Option Returns vs. the Market and Mutual Funds 17

    4 Definitions 23

    5 Components of an Option Contract 29

    6 What is Covered Call Writing? 37

        THE YTEM: HOW TO MAKE LOT$ OF $$$$ $$$$$ 41

    7 Creating a Watch List of the Greatest Optionable Stocks 43

    8 Technical Analysis 55

        Technical Analysis - Summary 81

    9 Calculating Option Returns 89

    10 Portfolio Management 101

11 Exit Strategies 115

12 Earnings Reports 135

13 Mathematics of Covered Calls 149

14 Diversification AND Dollar Cost Averaging 159

15 Other Factors Effecting Stock Performance 169

16 Additional Sources for Locating the Greatest Performing Stocks 179

17 Stock Splits 185

Conclusion 191

Appendix I Quick Start Form 197

Appendix II E-mail Alerts 201

Appendix III Stock Trading vs. Option Selling 267

Appendix IV Testimonials 269

Appendix V Forms 295

Appendix VI Commendation 301

Appendix VII Master Figure List of Charts & Graphs 303

Appendix VIII Resource Center 307

Glossary 313

Index 331

About the Author 345

Dear Reader 347

Appendix III

My Second Book, Exit Strategies for Covered Call Writing

Table of Contents

Preface ix
Acknowledgments xiii
Introduction 1

   1. The Basics of Covered Call Exit Strategies—Definitions 3
   2. Why Use Exit Strategies? 7
   3. The Mathematics of the 1-Month Contract Period 11
   4. Key Parameters to Consider Before Expiration Friday 15
   5. Key Parameters to Consider on or near Expiration Friday 27
   6. Exit Strategy Alternatives Prior to Expiration Friday 31
   7. Exit Strategy Alternatives on or near Expiration Friday 37
   8. Preparing Your Portfolio Manager Watch List 45
   9. Executing the Exit Strategy Trades 49
  10. Real Life Examples Prior to Expiration Friday 51
  11. Real Life Examples on or near Expiration Friday 85
  12. Using Multiple Exit Strategies in the Same Contract Period 105
  13. The Ellman System Options Calculator 115
  14. Concluding Remarks and Personal Observations 123

Appendix
   I. Master Figure List of Charts and Graphs 125
  II. My First Book, *Cashing in on Covered Calls* 129
 III. Articles Published in 2008 131
 IV. Resource Center 133
  V. Testimonials 137
 VI. Quick Start Form 141
 VII. Pre-Expiration Friday Flow Chart 143
 VIII. Expiration Friday Flow Chart 145

Glossary 147
About the Author 161
Index 163

Appendix IV
Resource Center*

Stock Research & Information - Free Web Sites:
1. The Blue Collar Investor: www.thebluecollarinvestor.com
2. http://finance.yahoo.com/
3. http://www.cnbc.com/
4. http://money.cnn.com/
5. http://www.fool.com/
6. http://www.marketwatch.com/
7. http://reuters.com/
8. http://www.finviz.com/

Stock Research & Information– Paid Sites:
1. http://marketsmith.investors.com/
2. http://www.investors.com/

Glossary/ Definitions - Free Web Sites:
1. http://stockcharts.com/school/doku.php?id=chart_school:glossary_a
2. http://www.zacks.com/help/glossary/index.php
3. http://www.cboe.com/LearnCenter/Glossary.aspx
4. http://www.investopedia.com/terms/o/optionchain.asp

Technical Analysis Charts
1. http://stockcharts.com/index.html
2. http://bigcharts.marketwatch.com/
3. www.freestockcharts.com

Earnings Reports Information:
1. http://biz.yahoo.com/research/earncal/today.html
2. http://www.earningswhispers.com/

Stock Split Information:
1. http://biz.yahoo.com/c/s.html
2. http://www.investmenthouse.com/

Stock Screens:
1. https://www.finviz.com/screener.ashx
2. http://screener.finance.yahoo.com/newscreener.html

Options Information:
http://www.cboe.com/
https://www.optionseducation.org/

Online Brokerage Web Sites (see chapter9):
1. www.usaa.com (military affiliation no longer required)
2. www.thinkorswim.com
4. https://www.schwab.com/
5. https://www.tdameritrade.com/

Financial Newspapers/Magazines:
1. Investors Business Daily: www.investors.com
2. Wall Street Journal: www.wsj.com/
3. Barrons Weekly: www.barrons.com
4. Forbes magazine: www.forbes.com

Bonds Online Account and Information:
1. www.treasurydirect.gov

Mutual Fund/Exchange-Traded Fund Information
1. www.vanguard.com
2. www.morningstar.com

Books/Suggested Reading
1. One Up On Wall Street, Peter Lynch
2. Common Sense on Mutual Funds, John C. Bogle
3. Jim Cramer's Real Money, James J. Cramer

4. Jim Cramer's Mad Money, James J. Cramer
5. The Road to Wealth, Suze Orman
6. Getting Started in Options, Michael C. Thomsett
7. New Insights on Covered Call Writing, Richard Lehman and Lawrence G. McMillan
8. Fundamentals of the Options Market, Michael S. Williams and Amy Hoffman
9. Cashing in on Covered Calls, Alan G Ellman (I really like this one the best!)
10. Exit Strategies for Covered Call Writing (This one too!)

* Some of the material contained in this book was accessed from many of these resources.

Appendix V

Quick Start Form

I. Buy Monday Edition of Investors Business Daily – Section B
• Circle all stocks with an "o" next to the price. These are optionable stocks.

USE STOCK WATCH LIST LOCATOR FORM FOR II, III, and IV*

II. Go to www.investors.com
  • Type in stock and hit "get quote".
  • Scroll down under chart to SmartSelect ratings
  • Accept only stocks with 6 green circles

III. Get MAR (www.finviz.com) and OBV (www.stockcharts.com) stats

IV. Go to **www.stockcharts.com**
  • Set up chart as per the technical analysis section in this book.
  • Accept only those equities with a favorable chart pattern.

V. Place all stocks remaining from screening process onto a watch list.

VI. Go to: **http://biz.yahoo.com/research/earncal/today.html or www.earningswhispers.com**

  • Access ER dates and avoid those companies reporting during the current contract period.

VII. Use **the Ellman Calculator (formerly called the**

ESOC) and the Elite Calculator to determine return on option (ROO), upside potential, and downside protection, *when ready to sell options.*

VIII. Select an appropriate number of stock/option combinations based on available cash. Make sure you are well diversified with at least 5 stocks in different industries.

IX. Fill out *Form to Take to Computer* before actually buying stock and selling options. This can be printed out from the Ellman Calculator.

X. Place all stocks purchased and options sold in your **portfolio manager.**

XI. Keep track of your monthly option profits in your option log.

XII. Be alert for possible **exit strategies**, especially if option value drops to 20% or 10% of original option premium sold.

Appendix VI

Sample 1-Month Profit-Loss Form

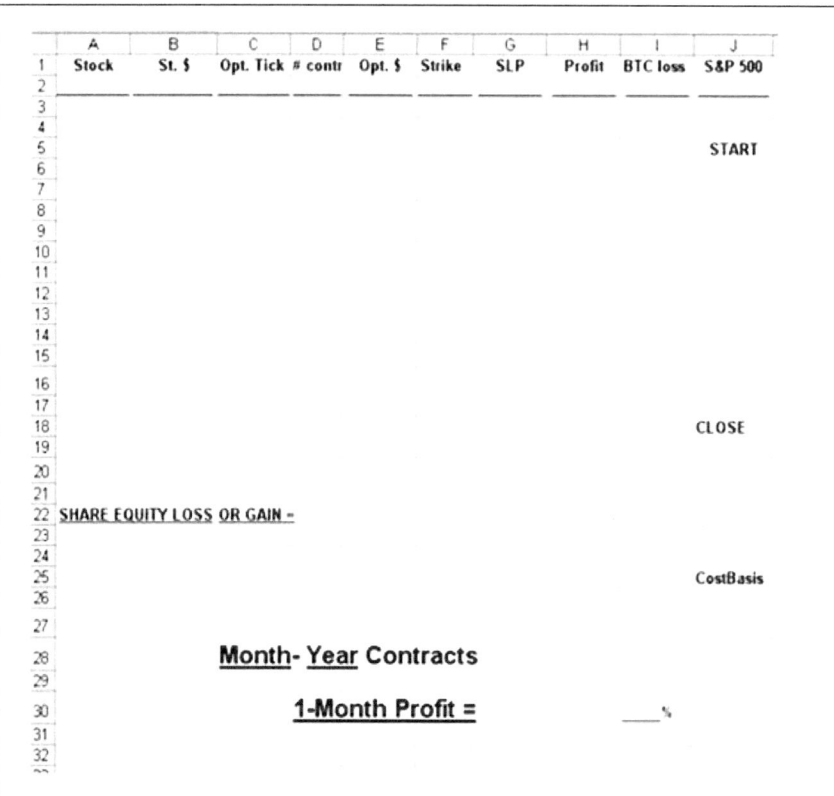

Figure 147

- A= stock name or ticker
- B= Stock share price
- C= Option ticker (month and date)
- D= # contracts to purchase
- E= Option premium per share
- F= Option strike price
- G= Breakeven, to some the stop-loss price
- H= Total cash profit (without intrinsic value of I-T-M options)

- I= Cost to buy back options, if applicable (exit strategies)
- J= Track and compare the S&P 500 over the same time frame

Appendix VII

Weekly Expirations

Securities with Weekly Options

Ticker Symbol	Name	Product Type
OEX	S&P 100 Index (American style)	Index
XEO	S&P 100 Index European-style	Index
DJX	Dow Jones Industrial Average	Index
SPX	S&P 500 Index	Index
NDX	NASDAQ 100 Index	Index
EEM	iShares MSCI Emerging Mkt Index	ETF
FAS	Direxion Daily Fin'l Bull 3X Shares	ETF
FAZ	Direxion Daily Fin'l Bear 3X Shares	ETF
GLD	ishares SPDR Gold Trust	ETF
GDX	Market Vectors Gold Miner ETF	ETF
IWM	iShares Russell 2000 Index Fund	ETF
QQQQ	Nasdaq-100 Index Tracking Stock	ETF
SPY	S&P 500 Depositary Receipts	ETF
USO	United States Oil Fund	ETF
XLF	Financial Select Sector SPDR	ETF
TLT	iShares Barclay's 20+ yr Treas. Bond	ETF
VXX	iPath S&P 500 VIX Short-Term FT	ETN
AAPL	Apple Corporation	Equity
AMZN	Amazon.com Inc	Equity
BAC	Bank of America Corp	Equity
BIDU	Baidu, Inc.	Equity
BP	British Petroleum	Equity
C	Citigroup	Equity
CSCO	Cisco Systems Inc.	Equity
F	Ford Motor Company	Equity
GE	General Electric Company	Equity
GOOG	Google Inc	Equity
GS	Goldman Sachs Group, Inc.	Equity
MSFT	Microsoft Corporation	Equity
NFLX	NetFlix Inc.	Equity

Appendix VIII
Quarterly Expirations

Quarterlys- List of Securrities with Quarterly Expirations

Quarterlys Products

Contract	Symbols	Type of Settlement	Specifications for Quarterlys
DIAMONDS Trust Series 1	DIA	Physical	Specifications
Energy Select SPDR	XLE	Physical	Specifications
iShares Russell 2000 Index Fund	IWM	Physical	Specifications
Mini-SPX	XSP	Cash-settlement	Specifications
Nasdaq-100 Index Tracking Stock	QQQQ	Physical	Specifications
S&P 100 - European-Style	XEO	Cash-settlement	Specifications
S&P 500	SPX	Cash-settlement	Specifications
S&P Depositary Receipts/SPDRs	SPY	Physical	Specifications
SPDR Gold Trust	GLD	Physical	Specifications

Appendix IX
Paper Trading and Monitoring Positions

Paper Trade or Track Covered Call Accounts for FREE

1- Go to www.optionseducation.org

2- Click "OIC Education" on upper right

3- Click on "Start Virtual Trading" on upper left

4- Sign up for FREE

5- Click on "Access Your VTS Account"

6- Agree to terms

7- Click on "Trade"

8- Click on Covered Calls

9- Enter your trades

10- If you buy a stock @ $30 and sell the call @$2, enter it as a **debit order** for $28 ($30 - $2)

Appendix X
Technical Analysis Chart and Terms

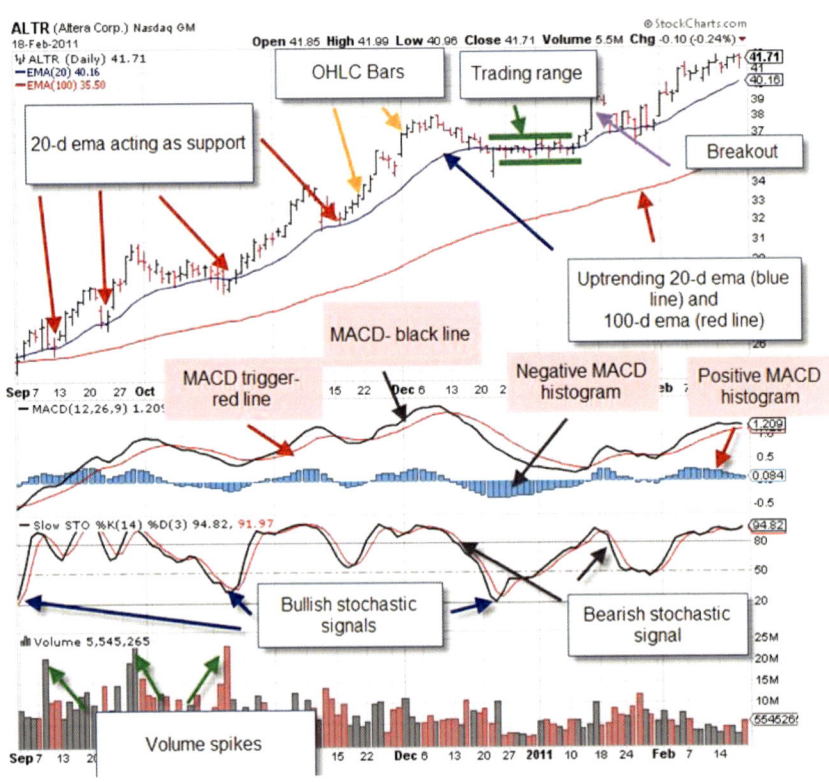

Figure 148

Appendix | 475

Appendix XI
Flow Chart I- Fundamental Analysis

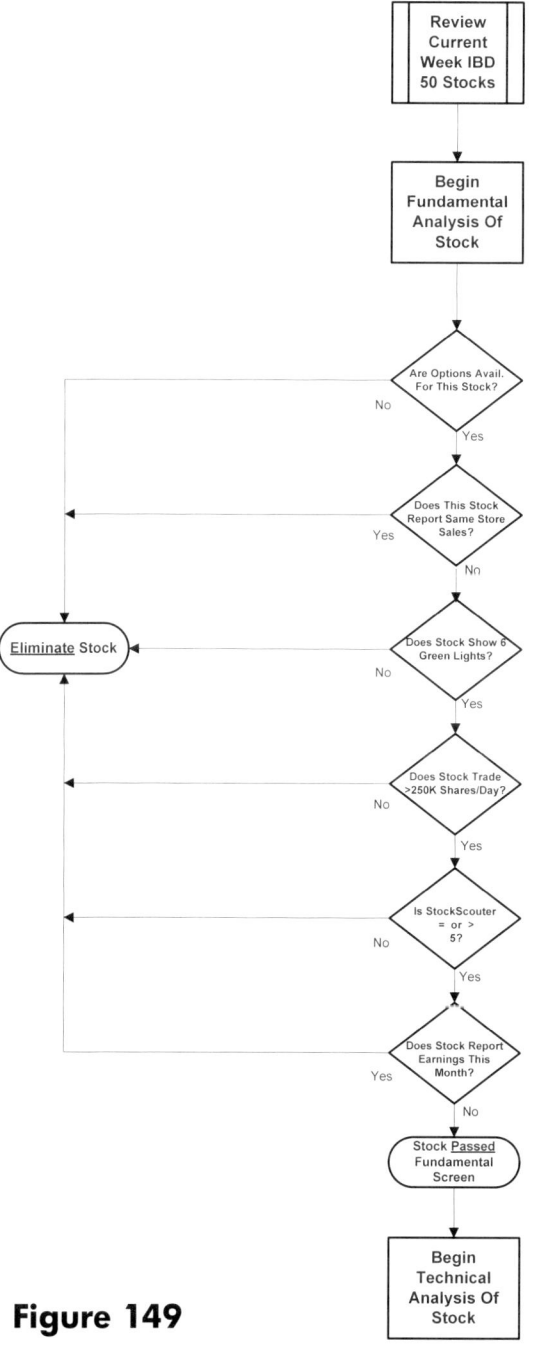

Figure 149

Appendix XII
Flow Chart II- Technical Analysis

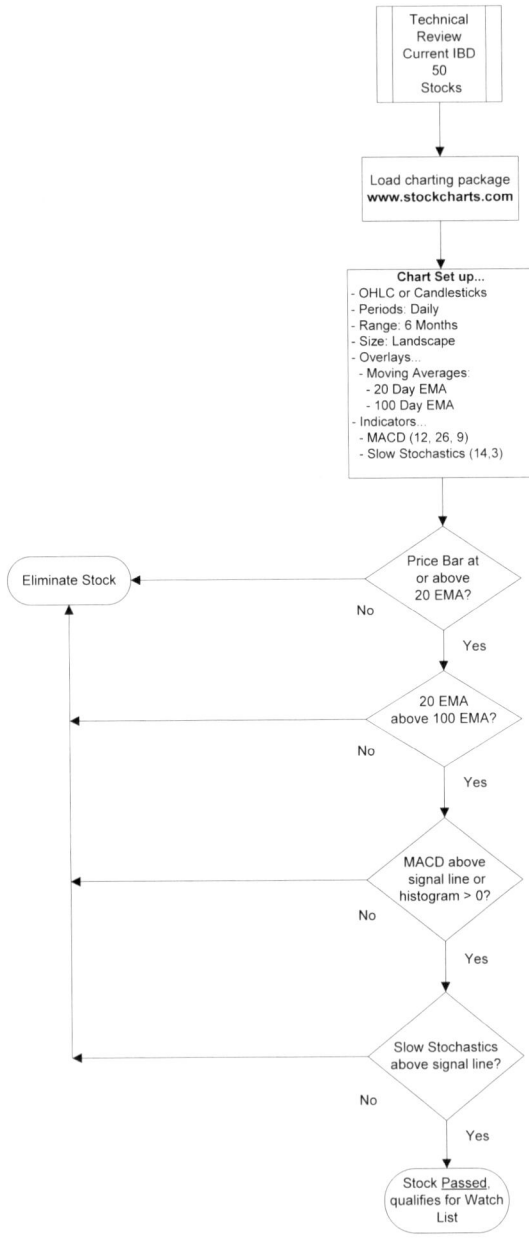

Figure 150

Appendix XIII
Flow Chart III
Pre-expiration Friday Exit Strategies

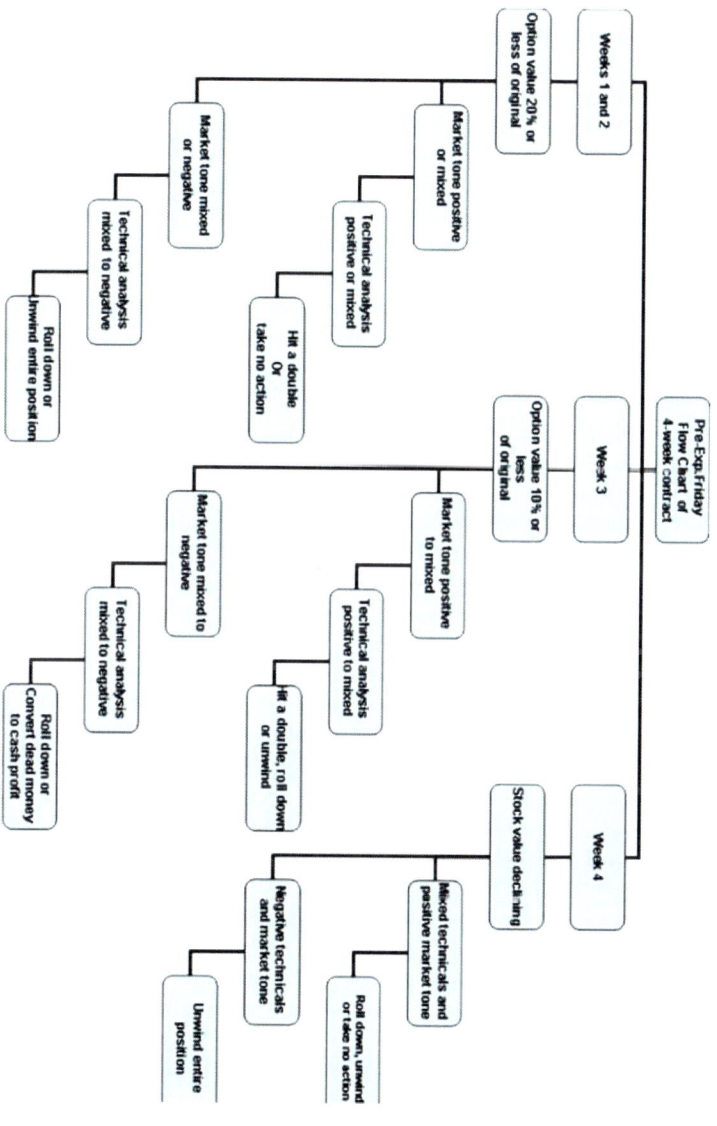

Figure 151

Appendix XIV

Flow Chart IV
Expiration Friday Exit Strategies

Figure 152

Appendix XV

Mean Analyst Rating (MAR)

The screening process for option-selling watchlists include fundamental analysis, technical analysis and common-sense screens. The BCI team is now adding a new screen the mean analyst rating (MAR) to replace the Scouter Rating we have been using for years. This will add an "institutional" component to our analysis.

What is MAR?

An investment analyst is a financial professional with expertise in evaluating financial and investment information, typically for making buy, sell and hold recommendations for securities. In order to reach an opinion and communicate the value and risk of a covered security, analysts research financial statements, listen in on conference-calls and talk to managers and the customers of a company, in an attempt to determine findings for a research report. Ultimately, the analyst decides whether the stock is a "buy," sell," or hold."

The Scale of Ratings

The analyst ratings scale is more involved than the traditional classifications of "buy, hold and sell." There are now various categories that include multiple terms for each of the ratings ("sell" is also known as "strong sell," "buy" can be labeled as "strong buy"), as well as a couple of new terms: underperform and outperform.

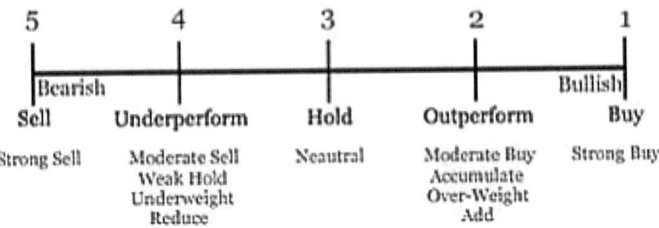

Figure 153 - Stock recommendation Range

Additionally, not every firm adheres to the same ratings terminology: an "outperform" for one firm may be a "buy" for another and a "sell" for one may be a "market perform" for another. Thus, when using ratings, it is advisable to use a consensus figure like mean analyst rating.

The basics

Let's review the traditional ratings of "sell," "underperform," "hold," "outperform" and "buy".

- Buy: Also known as strong buy and "on the recommended list." This is a recommendation to purchase a specific security.
- Sell: Also known as strong sell, it's a recommendation to sell a security
- Hold: A hold recommendation is expected to perform at the same pace as comparable companies or in-line with the market moving forward.
- Underperform: A recommendation that means a stock is expected to do slightly worse than the overall stock market return. Underperform can also be expressed as "moderate sell," "weak hold" and "underweight."

Outperform: Also known as "moderate buy," "accumulate" and "overweight." Outperform is an analyst recommendation meaning a stock is expected to do slightly better than the market return.

It is best to view these recommendations as a consensus stat with at least 3 analyst reviews. These consensus stats should then be used in conjunction with other fundamental, technical and common-sense parameters when making our investment decisions.

Sample free site with MAR stats: finviz.com

Figure 154 - Locating MAR from Finviz.com

Sample free site with MAR stats: finance.yahoo.com

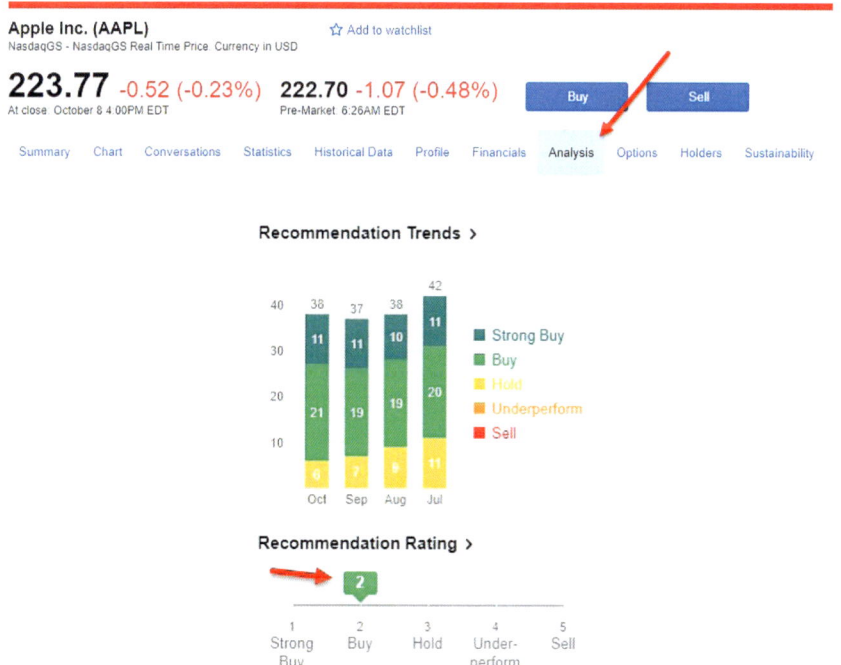

Figure 155 - Locating MAR from finance.yahoo.com

Location of MAR stats in our Premium Stock reports

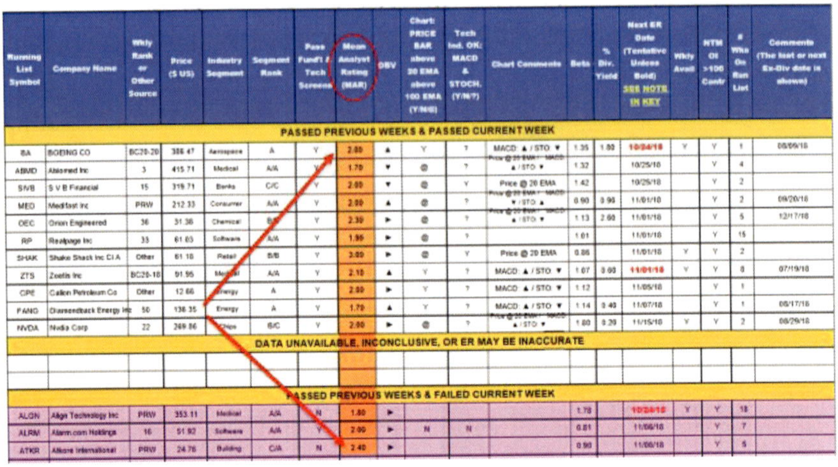

Running List Symbol	Company Name	Wkly Rank or Other Source	Price ($ US)	Industry Segment	Segment Rank	Pass Fund'l & Tech Screens	Mean Analyst Rating (MAR)	OBV	Chart: PRICE BAR above 20 EMA above 100 EMA (Y/N/@)	Tech Ind. OK: MACD & STOCH. (Y/N/?)	Chart Comments	Beta	% Div. Yield	Next ER Date (Tentative Unless Bold) SEE NOTE IN KEY	Wkly Avail	NTM OI >100 Contr	# Wks On Run List	Comments (The last or next Ex-Div date is shown)
PASSED PREVIOUS WEEKS & PASSED CURRENT WEEK																		
BA	BOEING CO	BC20-20	386.47	Aerospace	A	Y	2.00	▲	Y	?	MACD: ▲ / STO: ▼	1.35	1.80	**10/24/18**	Y	Y	1	08/09/18
ABMD	Abiomed Inc	3	415.71	Medical	A/A	Y	1.70	▼	@	?	Price @ 20 EMA / MACD ▲ / STO: ▼	1.32		10/25/18		Y	4	
SIVB	S V B Financial	15	319.71	Banks	C/C	Y	2.00	▼	@	Y	Price @ 20 EMA	1.42		10/25/18		Y	2	
MED	Medifast Inc	PRW	212.33	Consumer	A/A	Y	2.00	▲	@	?	Price @ 20 EMA / MACD ▼ / STO: ▲	0.90	3.90	11/01/18		Y	2	09/20/18
OEC	Orion Engineered	36	31.38	Chemical	B/B	Y	2.30	►	@	?	Price @ 20 EMA / MACD ▲ / STO: ▼	1.13	2.60	11/01/18		Y	5	12/17/18
RP	Realpage Inc	33	61.65	Software	A/A	Y	1.90	►	@	?		1.01		11/01/18		Y	15	
SHAK	Shake Shack Inc Cl A	Other	61.10	Retail	B/B	Y	3.00	►	@	Y	Price @ 20 EMA	0.86		11/01/18	Y	Y	2	
ZTS	Zoetis Inc	BC20-18	91.95	Medical	A/A	Y	2.10	▲	Y	?	MACD: ▲ / STO: ▼	1.07	0.60	**11/01/18**	Y	Y	8	07/19/18
CPE	Callon Petroleum Co	Other	12.66	Energy	A	Y	2.00	►	Y	?	MACD: ▲ / STO: ▼	1.12		11/05/18		Y	1	
FANG	Diamondback Energy Inc	50	138.35	Energy	A	Y	1.70	▲	Y	?	MACD: ▲ / STO: ▼	1.14	0.40	11/07/18		Y	1	08/17/18
NVDA	Nvidia Corp	22	269.86	Chips	B/C	Y	2.00	►	@	?	Price @ 20 EMA / MACD ▲ / STO: ▼	1.80	0.20	11/15/18	Y	Y	2	08/29/18
DATA UNAVAILABLE, INCONCLUSIVE, OR ER MAY BE INACCURATE																		
PASSED PREVIOUS WEEKS & FAILED CURRENT WEEK																		
ALGN	Align Technology Inc	PRW	353.11	Medical	A/A	N	1.80	►				1.78		**10/24/18**	Y	Y	18	
ALRM	Alarm.com Holdings	16	51.92	Software	A/A	Y	2.00	►	N	N		0.81		11/06/18		Y	7	
ATKR	Atkore International	PRW	24.78	Building	C/A	N	2.40	►				0.90		11/06/18		Y	5	

Figure 156 - MAR Stats in Premium Stock report

The BCI team will eliminate all stocks with MAR Ratings higher than "3" For those securities remaining, we will publish the precise stats to assist our members in making the best investment decisions possible.

Discussion

Analysts' recommendations are the culmination of analyzing equity research reports and should be used in conjunction with thorough investment methodologies to make investment decisions. Additionally, "buy, hold and sell" recommendation meanings are not as cut-and-dry as they first appear; a series of terms and differences in meanings exist behind the basic terminology.

Appendix XVI

On Balance Volume (OBV)

Introduction

On Balance Volume (OBV) measures buying and selling pressure as a cumulative indicator that adds volume on up days and subtracts volume on down days. OBV was developed by Joe Granville and introduced in his 1963 book, *"Granville's New Key to Stock Market Profits"*. It was one of the first indicators to measure positive and negative volume flow. Technical analysts can look for divergences between OBV and price to predict price movements or use OBV to confirm price trends.

OBV and the BCI Methodology

For years, the BCI methodology has stressed the significance of the institutional investors (the "big boys") in impacting stock performance. This explains why we require a minimum average stock trading volume and option open interest before entering our option-selling trades.

Volume is said to reflect the commitment on the part of traders. Because On-Balance Volume relates volume to price movements, many traders believe that it can offer great insights into the level of bullishness or bearishness that exists or is building among traders regarding a given stock or other asset.

By incorporating OBV, we are factoring in the trend of institutional interest or lack thereof in each security and adding another dimension to our stock screening process.

Calculation

The *On Balance Volume* (OBV) line is simply a running total of positive and negative volume. A period's volume is positive when the close is above the prior close. A period's volume is negative when the close is below the prior close. T

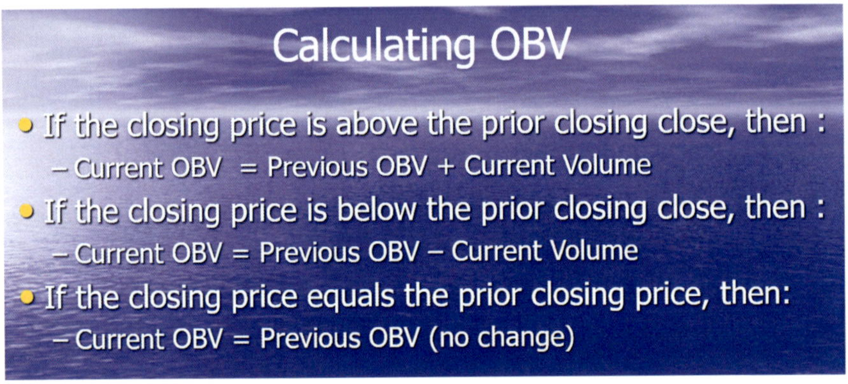

Calculating OBV

- If the closing price is above the prior closing close, then :
  - Current OBV = Previous OBV + Current Volume
- If the closing price is below the prior closing close, then :
  - Current OBV = Previous OBV – Current Volume
- If the closing price equals the prior closing price, then:
  - Current OBV = Previous OBV (no change)

Figure 157 - Calculating OBV

Interpretation

Granville theorized that volume precedes price. OBV rises when volume on up days outpaces volume on down days. OBV falls when volume on down days is stronger. A rising OBV reflects positive volume pressure that can lead to higher prices. Conversely, falling OBV reflects negative volume pressure that can foreshadow lower prices. Granville noted in his research that OBV would often move before price. Expect prices to move higher if OBV is rising while prices are either flat or moving down. Expect prices to move lower if OBV is falling while prices are either flat or moving up.

The absolute value of OBV is not important. Technical analysts should instead focus on the characteristics of the OBV line. First, define the trend for OBV. Second, determine if the current trend matches the trend for the underlying security. Third, look for potential support or resistance levels. Once broken, the trend for OBV will change and these breaks can be used to generate signals. Also, notice that OBV is based on closing prices. Therefore, closing prices should be considered when looking for divergences or support/resistance breaks. And finally, volume spikes can sometimes throw off the indicator by causing a sharp move that will require a settling period.

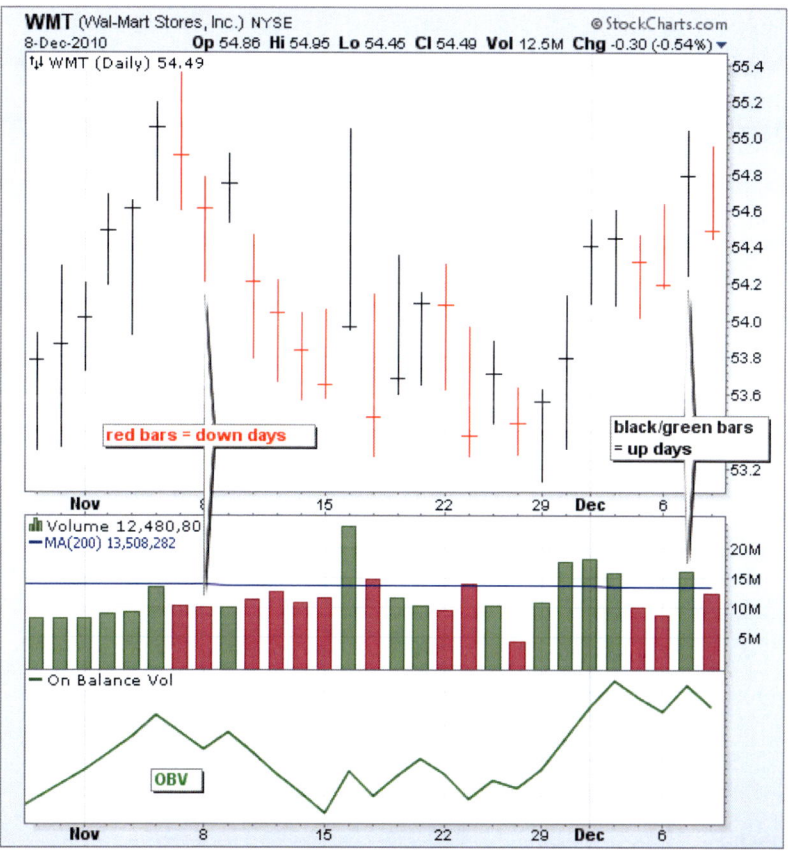

Figure 158 - OBV Interpretation

OBV Location in Premium Reports

Figure 159

Figure 160

Trend is identified with up, down or sideways arrows (▲, ▶, ▼).

Summary

- Cumulative indicator that adds volume on up days and subtracts volume on down days
- Look for divergences between OBV and price to predict price movements or use OBV to confirm price trends
- OBV rises when volume on up days outpaces volume on down days
- OBV falls when volume on down days is stronger
- A rising OBV reflects positive volume pressure that can lead to higher prices
- Falling OBV reflects negative volume pressure that can foreshadow lower prices
- Focus in on the OBV trend, not the actual number
- Look for bullish and bearish divergences with share price
- OBV can be used to confirm a price trend, upside breakout or downside break

Conclusions

On Balance Volume (OBV) is a simple indicator that uses volume and price to measure buying pressure and selling pressure. Buying pressure is evident when positive volume exceeds negative volume and the OBV line rises.

Selling pressure is present when negative volume exceeds positive volume and the OBV line falls. Technical analysts can use OBV to confirm the underlying trend or look for divergences that may foreshadow a price change. As with all indicators, it is important to use OBV in conjunction with other aspects of technical analysis. It is not a standalone indicator. OBV can be combined with basic *pattern analysis* or to confirm signals from *momentum oscillators*.

When we use OBV with the BCI methodology, we are looking at the trend of OBV, *not* the absolute value of the OBV. The relative direction (▲, ▶, ▼) of the indicator is what we are looking for. That is, we want to know if the institutions accumulating shares and supporting the stock (▲ & ▶) or are they exiting from the stock (▼) since they move the stock.

The OBV indicator can be found in most charting packages, including those that are free:

www.stockcharts.com
www.freestockcharts.com
www.barchart.com
www.tradingview.com

OBV is typically available in the charting packages provided by your broker as well.

For additional information, visit www.stockcharts.com and click on the "Chart School" tab (a free resource) on the command bar at the top of their home page.

***Some charts from www.stockcharts.com

Glossary

Accumulation: Buying of stock by institutional or professional investors over an extended period of time.

Acquisition: When one company purchases the majority interest in the acquired.

Actively Managed Mutual Funds: Shareholders, through a mutual fund manager, buy and sell stocks and bonds, within the fund, in an attempt to beat the market.

Advance-Decline Theory: Also called the Breadth of Market Theory, this theory states that the market direction can be determined by the number of stocks that have increased compared to those that have decreased in value. It is considered bullish if more shares are advancing than declining.

American Depository Receipt: A negotiable certificate issued by a U.S. bank representing a specified number of shares (or one share) in a foreign stock that is traded on a U.S. exchange. ADRs are denominated in U.S. dollars, with the underlying security held by a U.S. financial institution overseas. ADRs help to reduce administration and duty costs that would otherwise be levied on each transaction.

American Style Options: An option contract that may be exercised at any time between the date of purchase and the expiration date.

Arbitrage: The simultaneous purchase and sale of an asset in order to profit from a difference in the price. It is a trade that profits by exploiting price differences of identical or similar financial instruments, on different markets or in different forms.

Ask: The price a seller is willing to accept for a security. It includes both price and quantity willing to be sold.

Assignment: The receipt of an exercise notice by an option seller that obligates him to sell (in the case of a call) or purchase (in the case of a put) the underlying security at the specified strike price.

At-the-money: An option is at-the-money if the strike price of the option is equal to the market price of the underlying security.

Bar Chart: This price chart consists of session high and lows as well as the opening and closing prices. It is also referred to as the O-H-L-C bar.

Basis: Basis is often a moving target. Generally it is what you paid for a stock or option. There are adjustments which may be necessary to report the proper capital gain. These adjustments may include special dividends, stock splits and stock dividends, and some others.

Bearish: Pessimistic investor sentiment that a particular security or market is headed downward.

Beta: This is a measure of the volatility or systemic risk (market risk) of a security as compared to the market as a whole.

Bid: An offer made by an investor to buy an equity. It will include price and quantity.

BID/ASK SPREAD: The difference in price between the highest price that a buyer is willing to pay for the option and the lowest price a seller is willing to sell it.

Black-Scholes Option Pricing Model: A model used to calculate the value of an option, by factoring in stock price, strike price and expiration date, risk-free return, and the standard deviation of the stock's return.

Breakeven: The point at which gains equal losses

Bullish: Optimistic investor sentiment that a particular equity or market will rise.

Buy down price of stock: Using the intrinsic value of an in-the-money option premium to reduce the cost of the stock purchase.

Buy to close: A term used by many brokerages to represent the closing of a short position in option transactions.

Buy-write order: See net debit order

Calendar Spread: Simultaneously establishing long and short options positions on the same underlying stock with different expiration dates. For example, you buy the December, 2010 $20 call and sell the April, 2010 $20 call on the same equity.

Call: An option contract giving the owner the right (but not the obligation) to buy a specified amount of an underlying security at a specified price within a specified time.

Candlestick Chart: This chart is created by displaying the high, low, open and close for a security each day over a certain time frame.

Capital Asset: This is pretty much anything you own and use for personal, pleasure or investment purposes. The term includes such tangible assets as a boat, a coin collection, or a piece of real estate. It may also include intangible assets, such as a patent or copyright. The distinction between a capital asset and a non-capital asset is its use. Any capital asset becomes a non-capital asset if it is used in a trade or business, or is "for sale" to customers in a trade or business.

Capital Gain (Loss): A capital gain or loss is simply the difference between the proceeds of the sale and your cost basis of the asset sold. If you bought a stock for $25 and sold it for $30, you have a capital gain of $5. You can't have a capital gain or loss unless you have a sale of a capital asset. However, a sale of an asset does not necessarily mean you have a capital gain or loss. Why… because every capital gain requires two parts of the transaction, a sale AND an acquisition, or purchase.

Cash-secured put: When a brokerage company requires us to have the cash in our accounts to purchase the shares we are obligated to buy after selling a put option.

Collar (strategy): A protective options strategy that is implemented after a long position in a stock has experienced substantial gains. It is created by purchasing an out of the money put option while simultaneously writing an out of the money call option.

Consolidation: Sideways Pattern (consolidation) - the horizontal price movement of an equity where the forces of supply and demand are equal. The stock simply cannot establish an uptrend or a downtrend

Contract cycle: The period of time starting with the first trading day after expiration Friday through the end of the following expiration Friday (4 PM EST unless there is an exchange recognized holiday).

Convert Dead Money to Cash Profits: An exit strategy wherein an option is bought back and the underlying equity sold. The cash is then used to buy a better performing stock which is used to sell another covered call.

Correlation: This measures the degree to which investments are related.

Cost basis: The original value of an asset. It is used to determine the capital gain, which is equal to the difference between the asset's cost basis and the current market value. Also: the amount of your original investment.

Cost to carry: When money is borrowed from our broker in a margin account, interest is charged and needs to be calculated into our results.

Covered call writing: A strategy in which one sells call options while simultaneously owning the underlying security.

Currency carry trade: A strategy in which an investor sells a certain currency with a relatively low interest rate and uses the funds to purchase a different currency yielding a higher interest rate. A trader using this strategy attempts to capture the difference between the rates, which can often be substantial, depending on the amount of leverage the investor chooses to use.

Delta: This is the amount an option value will change for every $1 change in the price of a stock. The greater the chance of the strike ending up in-the-money, the higher the delta. Delta values for calls run from 0 to 1.

Derivative: A security whose price is dependent upon or derived from one or more underlying assets. The derivative itself is merely a contract between two or more parties. Its value is determined by fluctuations in the underlying asset. The most common underlying assets include stocks, bonds, commodities, currencies, interest rates and market indexes. Most derivatives are characterized by high leverage.

Diagonal Spread: A long and short options position with different expirations AND strikes. For example, you buy the December, 2010 $20 call and sell the April, 2010 $25 call.

Dilution: A reduction in earnings per share of common stock that occurs through the issuance of additional shares. This is avoided with stock splits by reducing the current market value of a stock by a similar ratio as was the number of shares increased.

Distribution: the selling of stock by large institutions over an extending period of time.

Diversification: A risk management technique that mixes a wide variety of investments within a portfolio. The rationale behind this technique contends that a portfolio of different kinds of investments will, on average, yield higher returns and pose a lower risk than any individual investment found within the portfolio.

Dollar cost averaging: The technique of buying a fixed dollar amount of a particular investment on a regular schedule, regardless of the share price. More shares are purchased when prices are low, and fewer shares are bought when prices are high.

Downside protection: The intrinsic value portion of an in-the-money call option premium divided by the original cost basis. It is the percentage of your investment that can be lost without affecting the option return on your investment. The formula is as follows:

$$\frac{\text{Intrinsic Value of option premium}}{\text{Original Cost of stock}} = \text{\% of downside protection}$$

Down trending Stock: A stock with a declining share price showing lower highs and lower lows.

The Dow Theory: This theory states that the market is in an upward trend if one of the averages (industrial or transportation) advances above a previous significant high and is accompanied by a similar advance in the other. A major trend is identified only when BOTH the Dow Industrial and Dow Transportation Averages reach a new high or a new low. Without this confirmation, the market will return to its previous trading pattern.

Earnings estimate: An analyst's estimate for a company's future quarterly or annual earnings.

Earnings guidance: Information that a company provides as an indication or estimate of their future earnings.

Earnings report: A quarterly filing made by public companies to report their performance. Included in these reports are items such as net income, earnings per share, earnings from continuing operations, and net sales. These reports follow the end of each quarter. Most companies file in January, April, July, and October.

Earnings surprise: When the earnings reported in a companies quarterly or annual report are above or below analysts' earnings estimates.

Efficient frontier: A line created from the risk-reward graph, comprised of optimal portfolios.

Elite Calculator: Expanded version of the basic Ellman Calculator (ESOC) which includes an unwind tab and a Schedule D.

Ellman Calculator: See ESOC.

ESOC: Ellman System Option Calculator which is an excel calculator used to compute option returns specifically for Alan Ellman's Cashing In On Covered Calls system.

ETFs: See exchange traded funds.

Exchange traded funds: A security that tracks an index, a commodity, or a basket of assets like an index fund, but trades like a stock on an exchange, thus experiencing price changes throughout the day as it is bought and sold. These securities provide the diversification of an index fund.

Exercise: When you exercise your stock option, you "trade in" your options for the actual stock.

European Style Option: An option contract that can only be exercised on the expiration date.

Execution (of a trade): The completion of a buy or sell stock order.

Exit strategy: A plan in which a trader intends to get out of an investment position made in the past. It is a way of cashing out or closing out a position.

Expected Return: Possible return on a portfolio in different market conditions (bullish, bearish and neutral) weighted by the likelihood that the return will occur.

Expense ratio: A measure of what it costs an investment company to operate a mutual fund. It is determined through an annual calculation, where a fund's operating expenses are divided by the average dollar value of its managed assets Operating expenses are taken out of a fund's assets and lower the return to a fund's investors. Some funds have a marketing cost referred to as a 12b-1 fee, which would also be included in operating expenses. It is interesting that a fund's trading activity - the buying and selling of stock - is NOT included in the calculation of expense ratio.

Expiration date: The last day (in the case of an American-style) or the only day (in the case of European-style) on which an option may be exercised. For stock option, this date is the third Friday of the expiration month. If Friday is a holiday, the last trading day is the preceding Thursday.

Exponential moving average or EMA: A type of moving average that is similar to a simple moving average, except that more weight is given to the most recent data. It reacts faster to recent price changes than does a simple moving average. The 12- and 26-day EMA's are the most popular short-term averages, and they are used to create indicators like the MACD.

First call: A company that gathers research notes and earnings estimates from brokerage analysts and forms a consensus estimate. The estimate is compared to the actual earnings reports, and then the difference between the two is the earnings surprise. The other major player in this estimate game is Zachs.

Fundamental analysis: A method of analyzing the prospects of a security by observing the accepted accounting measures such as earnings, sales, and assets and so on.

Gamma: The rate of change for delta with respect to the price of the underlying security. It is an estimate of how much the delta of an option changes when the price of the stock moves $1.

Gap: A gap is a break between prices on a chart that occurs when the price of a stock makes a sharp move up or down with no trading occurring in between.

Globalization: The tendency of investment funds and businesses to move beyond domestic and national markets to other markets around the globe, thereby increasing the interconnectedness of different markets. It has had the effect of increasing international trade and cultural exchange.

Greeks: A mathematical means of estimating the risk of stock options. Delta measures the change in the option price due to a change in the stock price, gamma measures the change in the option delta due to a change in the stock price, theta measures the change in the option price due to time passing, vega measures the change in the option price due to volatility changing, and rho measures the change in the option price due to a change in interest rates.

Historical volatility: This is the actual price fluctuation as observed over a period of time.

Hit a Double: An exit strategy wherein an option is bought back and then resold at a higher premium in the same contract period.

Hit a Triple: An exit strategy wherein an option is bought back and resold twice in the same contract period.

Horizontal Spread: A spread where both options have the same strike price as in the above example but different expiration dates. The terms calendar and horizontal spreads are interchangeable.

IBD 100: The Investor's Business Daily 100 is a computer-generated ranking of the leading companies trading in America. Rankings are based on a combination of each company's profit growth; IBD's Composite Rating, which includes key measures such as return on equity, sales growth and profit margins; and relative price strength in the past 12 months.

Implied Volatility: This is a forecast of the underlying stock's volatility as implied by the option's price in the marketplace.

Index fund: A type of mutual fund with a portfolio constructed to mirror, or track, the components of a market index such as the S&P 500 Index. An index mutual fund is said to provide broad market exposure, low operating expenses and low portfolio turnover. Indexing is a passive form of fund management that has been successful in out-performing most actively managed mutual funds.

Internal rate of return: IRR is a way to analyze an investment considering the time value of money. It basically calculates the interest rate which is the equivalent of the dollar amount your investment will return

In-the-money: A term describing any option that has intrinsic value. A call option is in-the-money if the underlying security is higher than the strike price of the call.

Intrinsic value: The value of an option if it were to expire immediately with the underlying stock at its current price; the amount by which the stock is in-the-money. For call options, this is the positive difference between the stock price and the strike price.

Inverse ETFs: These securities use derivatives to bet against the direction of financial markets. These are known as short or bear ETFs and will make money if markets decline in value. They will lose money, however, if markets move against the bet. Covered call writers who have a bearish market outlook may find these funds useful.

Investor Fear Gauge: See VIX.

Key economic indicator: Macroeconomic data that is used by investors to interpret current or future investment possibilities and judge the overall health of an economy. These are specific pieces of data released by the government and non-profit organizations.

These include:
The Consumer Price Index (CPI)
Gross Domestic Product (GDP)
Unemployment statistics
The price of crude oil

Laddering: This is an investment technique whereby investors purchase multiple financial products with different maturity dates. I have borrowed this term and used it to describe a covered call technique where different strike prices are used for the same equity.

Lagging indicator: A technical indicator that trails the price action of an underlying asset. It is used by traders to generate transaction signals or to confirm the strength of a given trend. Since these indicators lag the price of the asset, a significant move will generally occur before the indicator is able to provide a signal. It confirms long-term trends but does not predict them.

Large cap: An abbreviation for the term large market capitalization. Market capitalization is calculated by multiplying the number of a company's outstanding shares by its stock price per share. The expression large cap is used by the investment community as an indicator of a company's size. A large cap stock has a market-capitalization dollar value of over 10 billion.

LEAPS- Long-Term Equity Anticipation Securities. These are option contracts with expiration dates longer than one year. Only the more heavily traded stocks and ETFs have these types of options associated with them.

Legging in: A way of executing a covered call trade wherein we first buy the stock and, once owned, sell the corresponding call option.

Limit Order: An order placed by a brokerage to buy or sell a specified number of shares at a specific price or better. The length of time an order remains outstanding can also be specified.

Line Chart: This is a very basic chart created by connecting a series of closing prices of a particular security with a line.

Long (position): The buying of a security, such as a stock or options contract, with the expectation that the asset will rise in value.

MACD (Moving average convergence divergence): A trend-following momentum indicator that shows the relationship between two moving averages of prices. The MACD is calculated by subtracting the 26-day exponential moving average (EMA) from the 12-day EMA. A 9-day EMA of the MACD, called the signal line, is then plotted on top of the MACD, functioning as a trigger for buy and sell signals.

MACD Histogram: A common technical indicator that illustrates the difference between the MACD and the trigger line. This difference is then plotted on a chart in the form of a histogram to make it easy for a trader to determine a specific asset's momentum.

Margin account: This is a brokerage account where the client has the ability to borrow money from the broker to purchase securities. This loan is then collateralized by the cash and securities in that specific account.

Margin call: When the value of the securities in a margin account drop to a certain level, the investor will be required to put additional cash in the account or sell certain securities

Market capitalization: The total dollar market value of all of a company's outstanding shares. It is calculated by multiplying a company's shares outstanding by the current market price of one share. The investment community uses this figure to determine a company's size, as opposed to sales or total asset figures. Also referred to as market cap.

Market consensus: The average earnings estimates made by brokers and security analysts. Also known as earnings expectations.

Market Order: An order to buy or sell a stock at the current best available price.

Market Tone: The feeling of a market (general psychology) as demonstrated by the price activity of stocks. We use the VIX and S&P 500 chart patterns to help assess this sentiment.

Married put: When the protective put is purchased on the same day as the stock, it is referred to as a married put for tax purposes.

Mergers: A general term used to refer to the consolidation of companies. It is a combination of two companies to form a new company.

Modern portfolio theory: A portfolio optimization methodology that utilizes the mean variance of investment returns. It uses the standard deviation of all returns as a measure of risk.

Momentum indicator: Designed to track momentum in the price of a security to help identify the enthusiasm of buyers and sellers involved in the price trend development. Some indicators compare the closing price with some historical price so many periods before; others construct trend lines like the MACD. Others, like Stochastics, is a ratio using the high, low, and close values on various days.

Momentum Oscillator: A technical analysis tool that is banded between two extreme values and built with the results from a trend indicator for discovering short-term overbought or oversold conditions. As the value of the oscillator approaches the upper extreme value the asset is deemed to be overbought, and as it approaches the lower extreme it is deemed to be oversold. This oscillator is most advantageous when a stock price is in a trading range (sideways). An example is the stochastic oscillator

Money market securities: The securities market dealing in short-term debt and monetary instruments. These forms of debt mature in less than one year and are quite liquid. Treasury bills make up the bulk of the money market instruments. These securities are relatively risk-free.

Moving average: An indicator frequently used in technical analysis showing the average value of a securities price over a set period. Moving averages are generally used to measure momentum and define areas of possible support and resistance.

Multiple Tab of the ESOC: Compare returns, upside potential, and downside protection for many stocks, all on the same page.

Nasdaq 100 index: An index composed of the 100 largest, most actively traded U.S. companies listed on the Nasdaq stock exchange. This index includes companies from a broad range of industries with the exception of those that operate in the financial industry, such as banks and investment companies.

NAV (net asset value): A mutual fund's price per share or exchange-traded fund's (ETF) per-share value. In both cases, the per-share dollar amount of the fund is calculated by dividing the total value of all the securities in its portfolio, less any liabilities, by the number of fund shares outstanding.

Net debit order: This is where you buy the stock and sell the option at the exact same time, not for specific corresponding prices but for a limit net debit. Also called a buy-write.

Non Standard Options: These are options that don't have the standard terms of an options contract, namely 100 shares as the underlying asset.

Odd Lot Theory: This theory is based on the assumption that the small investor is always wrong. Since these investors usually buy and sell in odd-lot amounts (less than 100 shares) and have low risk-tolerance (the theory continues), they tend to buy high and sell low. A bullish signal is when odd-lot sell orders increase relative to odd-lot buy orders.

OHLC (bar) chart: Short for Open High, Low Close chart. This type of chart is used to spot trends and view stock movements, particularly on a short term basis.

Online Discount Broker: A stockbroker who carries out buy and sell orders online, at reduced commissions, but provides no investment advice.

Open interest: The open interest of an option contract is the number of outstanding options of that type which currently have not been closed out or exercised

Option: A contract that gives the owner the right, if exercised, to buy or sell a security or basket of securities (index) at a specific price within a specific time limit. Stock option contracts are generally for the right to buy or sell 100 shares of the underlying stock.

Option chain: A way of quoting option prices through a list of all the options for a given security. For each underlying security, the option chain tells investors the various strike prices, expiration dates, and whether they are calls or puts.

Options contract: Represents 100 shares in the underlying stock. Information included consists of the underlying security, type of option (call or put), expiration month, strike price and premium.

Option premium: The price at which the contract trades. It is the price paid by the buyer to the writer, or seller, of the option. In return the writer of the call option is obligated to deliver the underlying security to an option buyer if the call is exercised or buy the underlying security if the put is exercised. The writer keeps the premium whether or not the option is exercised.

Out-of-the-money: A call option is out-of-the-money if the strike price is greater than market value of the underlying security.

Over-the-counter option (OTC): An option traded off-exchange, as opposed to a listed stock option. The OTC option has a direct link between buyer and seller, has no secondary market, and has no standardization of strike prices and expiration dates. This securities market is not geographically centralized like the trading floor of the NYSE. Trading takes place through a telephone and computer network.

Overbought: A technical condition that occurs when prices are considered too high and susceptible to decline. Overbought conditions can be classified by analyzing the chart pattern or with indicators such as the Stochastic Oscillator. Generally, a security is considered overbought when the Stochastic Oscillator exceeds 80. Overbought is not the same as being bearish. It simply infers that the stock has risen too far too fast and might be due for a pullback.

Oversold: A technical condition that occurs when prices are considered too low and ripe for a surge. Oversold conditions can be classified by analyzing the chart pattern or with indicators such as the Stochastic Oscillator. Generally, a security is considered oversold if the Stochastic Oscillator is less than 20. Oversold is not the same as being bullish. It merely infers that the security has fallen too far too fast and may be due for a reaction rally.

Paper trade: A hypothetical trade that does not involve any monetary transactions. It is a risk-free way to learn the ins and outs of the market.

Passive management (of mutual funds): An investment strategy that mirrors a market index and does not attempt to beat the market.

PE Ratio: P/E Ratio or Price-Earnings Ratio is a valuation ratio that compares the price of a stock to it's per share earnings.

PEG Ratio: PEG = PE Ratio/Annual EPS Growth

PEGY Ratio: = PE Ratio/ Expected Earnings Growth + Dividend Yield

Pinning the strike: This is when puts and calls are near the money on expiration Friday. There is a tendency called pinning the strike for the stock to move to the strike price or slightly beyond.

Portfolio management: The art and science of making decisions about investment mix and policy, matching investments to objectives, asset allocation, and balancing risk versus performance. It requires organized lists of accurate information.

Portfolio overwriting: This is where a call option is sold on a stock already part of an existing portfolio. That option is selected in a manner such that the option is NOT expected to be exercised as every effort is made to retain the equity.

Premium report: The weekly stock screen and watch list published by the Blue Collar Investor Corp. This is a screen specific for candidates geared to writing 1-month covered calls.

Protective put: A put option purchased for a stock that is already owned by the owner of the option. A protective put defends against a decrease in the share price of the underlying security

Price bar: see OHLC.

Protective put: A put option purchased for a stock that is already owned by the owner of the option. A protective put defends against a decrease in the share price of the underlying security.

Put: An option contract that gives the holder the right, but not the obligation, to sell the underlying security at a specified price for a certain fixed period of time.

QQQ: This is the ticker symbol for the Nasdaq 100 Trust, which is an exchange traded fund (ETF) that trades on the Nasdaq. It offers broad exposure to the tech sector by tracking the Nasdaq 100 index, which consists of the 100 largest non-financial stocks on the Nasdaq. It is also known as the quadruple-Qs.

Resistance: The price level at which there is a large enough supply of a stock available to cause a halt in the upward trend and turn the trend down. Resistance levels indicate the price at which most investors feel that the prices will move lower.

Rho: Not considered a major Greek, measures the change in the option price due to a change in interest rates.

Glossary | 507

Risk-reward profile: A risk reward profile is a chart of the theoretical maximum profit or loss a particular investment can have in your portfolios.

Rolling down: Closing out options at one strike price and simultaneously opening another at a lower strike price.

Rolling out (forward): Closing out of an option contract at a near-term expiration date and opening a same strike option contract at a later date.

Rolling up: Close out options at a lower strike and open options at a higher strike.

ROO (return on option): The percent profit realized from the sale of a covered call option based on the cost basis of the underlying stock. If an in-the-money option was sold, the intrinsic value is deducted from the option premium before calculating the return.

Rule of 72: A rule stating that in order to find the number of years required to double your money at a given interest rate; you divide the compound return into 72. The result is the approximate number of years that it will take for your investment to double.

S&P 500 (Standard and Poor's 500): An index consisting of 500 stocks chosen for market size, liquidity, and industry grouping, among other factors. It is designed to be a leading indicator of U.S. equities and is meant to reflect the risk/return characteristics of the large-cap universe.

Sarbanes-Oxley Act of 2002 (SOX): An act passed by the U.S. Congress to protect investors from the possibility of fraudulent accounting activities by corporations. It includes the establishment of a Public Company Accounting Oversight Board where public companies must now be registered.

Securities and Exchange Commission (SEC): A government commission, created by Congress, established to regulate the securities markets and protect investors. It also monitors the corporate takeovers in the U.S. The SEC is composed of five commissions appointed by the U.S. President and approved by the Senate. The statutes administered by the SEC are designed to promote full public disclosure and to protect the investing public against fraudulent and manipulative practices in the securities markets. Generally, most issues of securities offered in interstate commerce, through the mail or on the internet, must be registered with the SEC.

Sell to open: A phrase used by many brokerages on the street to represent the opening of a short position in option transactions.

Short (or short position): The sale (also known as writing) of an options contract or a stock to open a position.

Short sale: Short sale is the sale of a stock not owned by the seller. It is borrowed from the broker and eventually must be replaced. The seller anticipates a decline in equity value and realizes a profit by covering (buying back) the short sale at a lower price in the future.

Show or Fill Rule: This regulation requires the market makers to show or publish any order that improves the current bid or ask prices unless it is filled.

Short Interest Theory: This theory states that a larger short interest is the predecessor of an increase in the price of a stock.

Sideways Pattern (consolidation): This is the horizontal price movement of an equity where the forces of supply and demand are equal. The stock simply cannot establish an uptrend or a downtrend.

Simple moving average (SMA): A moving average that gives equal weight to each day's price data.

Single Tab of the ESOC: Allows you to evaluate returns from different strikes for the same stock.

Standard Deviation: This is a statistical measurement that sheds light on historical volatility.

Stochastic Oscillator: A momentum indicator that measures the price of a security relative to the high/low range over a set period of time. The indicator oscillates between 0 and 100. Readings below 20 are considered oversold. Readings above 80 are considered overbought.

StockScouter Rating: MSN Money Central's rating of stocks from 1 to 10, with 10 being the best. It uses a system of advanced mathematics to determine a stock's expected risk and return.

Stock split: A change in the number of shares outstanding (in circulation). The number of shares is adjusted by the split ratio, e.g. 2 to 1. In this case, 1000 shares splits to 2000 shares but the opening price and current price are cut in half. The overall effect is to maintain the same cost and current value of an investment while increasing the number of shares and lowering the per share price. This makes it easier for small investors to own the stock in round lots.

Stop loss order: This is an order placed with your broker to sell a security when it reaches a certain price.

Stop Order: This is an order to buy or sell a security when its price surpasses a specific price called the stop price. At that point the stop order becomes a market order.

Stop Limit Order: This is a combination of a stop order and a limit order. Once activated, it becomes a limit order which means that it can only be executed at a specific price or better.

Street expectation: The average earnings estimates made by brokers and security analysts.

Strike price: The stated price per share for which the underlying security may be purchased (in the case of a call) or sold (in the case of a put) by the option holder upon exercise of the option contract.

Support: A price level at which there is sufficient demand for a stock to cause a halt in a downward trend and turn the trend up. Support levels indicate the price at which most investors feel that prices will move higher.

Technical analysis: The method of predicting future stock price movements based on observation of historical stock price movements.

Theoretical Value: The hypothetical value of an option as calculated by a mathematical model such as the Black-Scholes Option Pricing Model.

Theta: Theta is an estimate of how much the theoretical value of an option declines when there is a passage of one day while there is no change in the stock value or volatility. Theta is expressed as a negative number since the passage of time will decrease time value.

Time decay: A term used to describe how the theoretical value of an option erodes or reduces with the passage of time.

Time value: The portion of the option premium that is attributable to the amount of time remaining until the expiration of the option contract. Time value is whatever value the option has in addition to its intrinsic value.

Trading range: The spread between the high and low prices traded during a period of time.

Treasury note (one of the treasuries): A marketable, U.S. government debt security with a fixed interest rate and a maturity between one and ten years. T-notes can be bought either directly from the U.S. Government or through a bank.

Trend analysis: An aspect of technical analysis that tries to predict the future movement of a stock based on past data. It is based on the idea that what has happened in the past gives traders an idea of what will happen in the future. The concept is that moving with trends will lead to profits for the investor.

Trigger line / signal: Usually an exponential or simple moving average of a technical indicator which serves as a frame of reference for positive and negative divergences. For example, if the MACD indicator moves above its moving average, a bullish signal is produced.

Upside potential: Additional % of profit, as it relates to the underlying stock cost basis that can be realized if the stock price reaches the strike price at expiration. It applies to out-of-the-money strike prices.

Uptrending Stock: This is a stock increasing in price with higher highs and higher lows.

Vega: Vega is the only "Greek" not represented by a real Greek letter. It is the amount that the price of an option changes compared to a 1% change in volatility.

Velocity (of money): A term used to describe the rate at which money is exchanged from one transaction to another.

VIX- CBOE Volatility Index: Demonstrates the market's expectation of 30-day volatility. It measures market risk and is often referred to as the investor fear gauge.

Volatility: This is the fluctuation, not direction, of a stock price movement. It represents the deviation of day to day price changes. It measures the speed and magnitude at which the underlying equity's price changes.

Volume: The number of trades in a security over a period of time. On a chart, volume is usually represented as a histogram (vertical bars) below the price chart. The NYSE and Nasdaq measure volume differently. For every buyer, there is a seller: 100 shares bought = 100 shares sold. The NYSE would count this as 100 shares of volume. However, the Nasdaq would count each side of the trade and as 200 shares volume.

Volume surge: An increase in the daily trading volume of an equity equal to at least 1.5 times its normal trading volume.

Wash Sale: A wash sale loss is not deductible. A wash sale occurs when you sell a stock for a loss and, within 30 days before or after the trade, buy the same stock, or substantially the same stock. This means that if you sell a stock at $35 for a loss, and buy a $35 call option, you have a wash sale and cannot deduct the loss on the stock.

Watch list: A list of securities that are in consideration for investment buy/sell decisions.

What Now Tab of the ESOC: Calculates the returns for a package transaction where an option is bought back and another is sold.

Whisper number: The unofficial and unpublished earnings per share (EPS) forecasts that circulate among professionals on Wall Street. They were generally reserved for the favored (wealthy) clients of a brokerage.

Wilshire 5000 Total Stock Market Index: A market capitalization-weighted index composed of more than 6700 publicly traded companies. These companies must be headquarted in the U.S. and actively traded on an American stock exchange.

Yen carry trade: A strategy in which an investor sells the Japanese currency (yen) with a relatively low interest rate and uses the funds to purchase a different currency (dollar) yielding a higher interest rate. A trader using this strategy attempts to capture the difference between the rates-which can often be substantial, depending on the amount of leverage the investor chooses to use.

About the Author

Dr. Alan Ellman, author of best-selling Cashing in on Covered Calls and Exit Strategies for Covered call Writing has been devoting more and more of his time to teaching retail investors (Blue Collar Investors) the art and science of covered call writing. He is also a licensed general Dentist in the state of New York, a certified personal fitness trainer and a licensed Real Estate Salesperson. Dr. Ellman has also successfully completed his Series 65 certification as an Investment Advisor.

As a real estate investor, Alan owns both commercial and residential properties in Texas, Pennsylvania, New York and Florida. He has frequently been invited to speak about his successful investment properties in front of large groups of real estate investors.

In the past four years, Alan has been increasing the time he spends educating investors in the arena of stock options and specifically covered call options. He writes a weekly journal article that is published on his website and responds to email questions from all over the world. Alan has also been interviewed on financial radio programs and has hosted dozens of seminars on this investment strategy. His goal is for you to achieve financial independence through education, motivation and due-diligence. To learn how to best accomplish these goals and become CEO of your own money visit his web site at:

www.thebluecollarinvestor.com

Index

Advance-decline theory- 83, 489
After hours trading- 432-4324
All or none box- 220, 229
American depository receipts (ADRs)- 34, 204, 312, 423, 489
American style options- 249, 298, 489
Arbitrage- 300, 320, 389, 414, 489
Ask- 108, 220, 223, 225, 226, 227, 253, 489
Assignment- 249, 292, 297-301
At-the-money- 13, 103, 171, 254, 355, 490
Authorized participants- 319
Ax man- 204
Banker's acceptances- 417
Bar chart- 38, 41-45, 490, 503
Beta- 177-179, 490
Bid- 108-109, 226, 409, 490
Bid-ask spread- 194, 212, 222, 225-229, 241-242, 409, 411
Black-Scholes Model- 226, 490, 510
Blue-chips- 421
Book value- 25
Breakeven- 39, 91, 105-106, 112-113, 133, 336, 444, 469, 490
Buy stop order- 230
Buy Write Index (BXM)- 312-314
Buy-to-close- 91, 167, 208, 224, 250, 258, 297, 336, 406, 491
Buy-write order- 221-225, 491
Calendar spread- 351-352, 354, 491
Candlestick chart- 39-45, 491
CANSLIM- 34
Capital asset- 338-339, 491
Capital gain- 145, 151, 237, 250, 311, 336-340, 346, 398-399, 491-492

Capital loss- 337-338
Capitalization- 320, 326, 420-421, 499-501
Cash allocation- 212-214, 306, 315-316
Cash-secured puts- 367-370
CBOE (Chicago Board Options Exchange)- 180, 198, 391, 430-431, 511
Change- 108
Classification of stock- 420-423
Coincident indicators- 392-393
Collar strategy- 19, 235-238
Commercial paper- 417
Commingling of asset classes- 398-400
Common stock- 423-425
Company news- 380
Components of an options contract- 15-16
Compound your profit- 6, 373
Compounding- 225, 373-377
Conference Board- 391-394, 423
Consensus estimate- 204
Consolidation- 47, 49, 72, 482
Constructing a technical chart- 73-75
Constructing optimal portfolios- 97-98
Contract cycle- 88-89, 137, 173, 251-254, 266-267, 492
Convert dead money to cash profits- 250, 263-266, 492
Correlation- 96-97
Cost basis- 3, 103-104, 112, 130, 145, 207, 225, 235, 284, 293, 301, 338, 340, 342, 374, 440, 443, 492
Creation units- 319
Cyclical stock- 422
Dark pool- 427-430, 435
Debt/equity ratio- 24-25
Defensive stock- 420
Delta- 13-14, 120-121, 126, 159, 162-168, 254-256, 348, 355, 436, 437-439, 446-447, 493

Index | 517

Delta hedging- 437-439
Delta neutral- 436-438
Depository Trust Company (DTC)- 195
Derrivatives- 15, 181, 418-420, 437, 493
Diagonal spread- 352, 356, 493
Discounted cash flow (DCF)- 383
Diversification- 97, 212, 306, 310-311
Dividend capture strategy- 400-404, 440
Dividend declaration date- 401
Dividend yield- 25, 27-28, 439-448
Dividends- 7, 25, 27, 158, 300, 340, 355, 401-404, 441, 445
Dollar cost averaging- 306-313, 494
Dow theory- 83
Downside protection- 7,104-106, 111-113, 117, 125, 127, 129, 131-134, 144, 162, 206, 235, 237, 273, 283, 294, 494
Early exercise- 297-301, 445-447
Earnings guidance- 205, 485
Earnings per share growth- 24, 35
Earnings report- 54, 76, 81, 169-170, 204-210, 274, 281, 287, 390, 444
Efficient frontier-97-98
Elite calculator- 92, 136-152, 250, 269-270, 495
Ellman calculator- 127-136, 143, 173-176, 250, 272-273, 282-283, 289-291,
Emerging growth stock- 422
ESOC (see Ellman Calculator)
European style options- 298, 495-496
Exchange-traded funds- 92, 108, 156, 198, 321, 448
Ex-dividend date- 300, 401-404, 445
Exit strategy- Chapter 144, 161, 167, 207-209, 247-301, 496
Expected return- 96
Expiration cycles- 160, 172, 179-182
Expiration Friday- 133-134, 157, 160-162, 166, 199, 208, 235, 249, 251, 258, 265, 279, 282, 284, 286-289, 477

Exponential moving average (EMA)- 45-48, 62, 496
Fair value- 412-415
Federal Reserve (Fed)- 383, 385, 387, 415
Flash trading- 407-410
Forward PE- 26,
Free cash flow- 25, 383
Full stochastic oscillator- 69
Fundamental analysis- 23-35, 81, 474, 497
Future value- 373-374, 413
Futures- 321, 389, 412-415, 418-419
Gamma- 159-162, 437-438, 497
Gap down- 230, 274-279
Gap up- 274
Globalization- 382, 497
Greeks- 158-168
Growth stocks- 421-422
Hedger- 419-420
High man- 204
Historical volatility- 96, 157-158, 169-170, 497
Hit a double- 250-251, 261-263, 295-297, 497
Hit a triple- 251, 498
Hitting the bid- 227
Horizontal spread- 352, 498
IBD 50 Index- 30
IBD SmartSelect ratings- 29-31
Implied volatility- 120, 157, 164, 166-172, 223, 233, 347, 431, 498
Income stock- 422
Index fund- 110, 114, 309-311, 320, 390, 498
Index futures- 413
Inherited stock- 342
Interest coverage ratio- 426
Interest rates- 113, 157-158, 162, 360, 374-375, 382-388, 419, 425

Index | 519

Internal rate of return (IRR)- 374, 498
Internalization- 435
In-the-money- 13-14, 80, 91, 103-106, 111, 114-118, 137, 156-158, 162-164, 171, 235, 254-256, 266, 283-284, 287-294, 298-300, 347-348, 352-355, 440, 443, 498
Intrinsic value- 14, 91, 103-105, 112, 117, 123, 125, 133, 137, 139, 156, 160, 162, 166-168, 191, 262-263, 298-300, 445-446, 491, 494, 498
Inverse exchange-traded funds- 320-322, 398
Investors Business Daily- 29-30, 34, 465
Jumbo CDs- 417
Key economic indicators- 381, 391-394
Laddering of strikes- 114-115
Lagging indicator- 48, 56, 393-394, 499
Last- 108
Leading economic indicators- 390-391
LEAPS- 172-181, 336, 351-356, 440, 500
Legging-in- 218-225, 218-225
Leveraged exchange-traded funds- 321-322
Lifting the offer- 227
Limit order- 218, 220-221, 227-231, 241, 289
Line chart- 38-39, 53
Liquidity rebates- 408-409
Long position- 15, 193
Long-term capital gain- 151, 335, 346
MACD (Moving average convergence divergence)- 35, 49, 56-63, 71, 74, 77, 79, 265, 500
MACD Histogram- 45, 57, 62-64, 286, 500
Maintenance margin- 363-364
Margin account- 220, 359-365, 500-501
Margin calculator- 361-362
Margin call- 360, 364, 501
Marginable securities- 360, 364
Market capitalization- 410-411, 420-421, 498-499, 501

Market conditions- 5-6
Market consensus- 204, 492
Market order- 218, 227-230, 501
Market psychology- 169, 380-381
Market tone- 19, 76, 81, 113-114, 116, 133, 233, 237, 247, 256-261, 280, 282-283
Mean Analyst Rating- 29, 31-32, 479-482
Micro caps- 411, 455
Mid-contract unwind- 144, 258, 266-273
Minimum margin- 364
Modern portfolio theory- 95-98
Money market account- 415-416
Money market fund- 416-418
Moving average- 45-56, 77, 79, 113, 142, 233, 257, 280, 502
Mutual funds- 7, 23, 204
Naked put- 367-370
Net credit- 209, 223-225
Net debit- 221-223, 225, 503
Net profit margin- 24
Non-standard options- 195-198
Odd lot theory- 82-83
OHLC bar- 42-45
On Balance Volume- 29, 31-33, 483-488
One Point Strike Program- 182-190
One triggers other order (OTO)- 233
Online discount broker- 106, 229, 242-244, 250, 252, 295, 309, 503
Open a position- 222-223, 508
Open interest- 109-110, 191, 193-194, 197, 212, 300, 413, 435, 503
Operating margin- 24
Option chain- 102, 106-110, 129, 134, 139, 143, 174-175, 191, 278, 288, 316, 503

Index | 521

Option contract- 13-15, 104-105, 193, 196-197, 249-250, 329, 351, 418
Options Clearing Corp. (OCC)- 195, 298
Out-of-the-money- 14, 18, 53-54, 78, 103, 110-111, 116-118, 159, 163, 235, 253-256, 277, 292-293, 298, 317, 347, 354, 504
Owen Sargent- 127, 136, 152, 338, 342
Painting the tape- 412
Payment date- 402
PE ratio- 24, 26-27, 505
PEG ratio- 24-27, 505
Pegy ratio- 27-28, 505
Penny Pilot Program- 238-242
Penny stock- 325, 411, 423
Pinning the strike- 300, 435-439, 505
Playing the bid-ask spread- 139, 194, 224-229, 241-242
Portfolio management- 87-98
Portfolio overwriting- 345-347, 505
Practical risk-reward profile for covered calls- 19
Preferred stock (preferreds)- 423-427
Premium report- 75-81, 92-94, 318-319, 404, 442, 505
Pretax margin- 24, 30
Price-equity ratio- 25
Price-to-book ratio- 25
Program trading- 414-415
Protective puts- 235-238
Prudent man rule- 95
Pump and dump scam- 410-412
Put option- 13, 15, 106, 108, 235, 367-370, 436, 492, 506
Quadruple witching Friday- 389-391
Quarterly Expiration Options Contracts- 198, 472
Record date- 401-402
Redemption units- 319
Regression analysis- 177

Regulation T- 361, 363-364
Repurchase agreements (REPO)- 417
Resistance- 45-47, 50-52, 55-57, 506
Return on equity- 24, 30, 34
Reverse stock split- 329-332
Rho- 162, 506
Risk-reward profile- 17-20, 506
Risk-reward screen- 31
Rolling down- 249, 258-261, 297, 506
Rolling out- 78, 134-136, 248-250, 282-291, 405, 506
Rolling out and down- 249-250
Rolling out and up- 134-136, 248, 250, 291-293
Rolling up- 141, 249, 271, 507
ROO (return on option)- 103-106, 109-110, 133-136, 161, 163, 176, 236, 254, 255, 272-273, 284, 287, 293-294, 507
Rule of 72- 374-375, 507
Running list- 92-94, 179, 442
S&P 500- 10, 30, 116, 177-178, 198, 251, 257, 278, 318, 384, 391, 413-414, 431, 432, 450-451
S&P futures- 412-415
Sales growth- 24, 34
Same store monthly retail sales reports- 210
Schedule D- 92, 136, 144-152, 250, 339-341
Sell stop order- 230
Shadows- 40
Short interest theory- 82
Short position- 15, 82, 139, 149, 193, 250, 258, 269
Short sale- 82, 230, 339-340, 508
Short-term capital gain- 145, 150, 151, 250, 336-337
Show or fill rule- 220, 225, 227-229, 508
Simple moving average (SMA)- 46, 65, 68, 508
Slow stochastic oscillator- 68-69
Speculator- 419-420
Sponsorship- 25, 34

Standard deviation- 96-97, 170, 226, 508
Stochastic oscillator- 45-46, 65-69, 71, 75, 77, 79, 265, 286, 508
Stock split- 108, 195, 197, 509
Stop limit order- 230-231, 509
Stop loss order- 232-233, 509
Stop order- 232-233, 509
Strike price- 3, 12, 19, 53, 91, 107-114, 116-121, 129-133, 137, 148, 153-157, 161-162, 166, 182, 191, 195-196, 198, 208, 235-236, 249, 279, 283, 509
Strike price selection- 110-126, 191
Support- 45-47, 149-151, 153-156, 509
Swap- 419
Symbol- 15-16, 90, 108, 192, 195, 199
Systemic (market) risk- 177
Take no action- 265-266, 294
Technical analysis- 37-84, 113, 257, 280, 474, 476, 509
Technical nullification- 276-277
Theoretical risk-reward profile for covered calls- 17-18
Theta- 160-163, 510
Three golden rules- 9-12
Time value-14, 103-105, 112, 119, 125, 132-133, 137, 139, 144, 156-171, 251-258, 266-267, 273, 279, 285, 298-300, 373-374, 444-445, 510
Trailing PE- 26
Trailing stop- 231
Treasury notes- 375-377
Trendline- 47, 70
Triple witching Friday- 389-390
Unwind now- 136-144, 269
Upside potential- 117, 123, 125, 127, 129-136, 176, 293, 511
Vega- 162-163, 511
VIX- 257

Volatility- 9-10, 96, 98, 116, 118, 157-158, 161-164, 166-172 177-178, 205-206, 210, 257, 389-390, 433, 447, 497, 498, 511

Volume – 46, 54, 70-73, 75, 79, 108-109, 191-195, 197, 212, 229, 389, 433, 511

Volume surge- 73, 511

Wash sale- 341, 511

Weekly Expiration Options Contracts- 198-200

Weekly stock screen- 80-81, 92, 505

What now tab- 127-136, 139-140, 250, 282-283, 289-290, 512

Whisper number- 204-205, 512

Why sell options- 5-8

Yield curve- 385-389